British Social Attitudes

The 22nd
REPORT

Two terms of New Labour: the public's reaction

EDITORS
Alison Park
John Curtice
Katarina Thomson
Catherine Bromley
Miranda Phillips
Mark Johnson

SAGE Publications
London ● Thousand Oaks ● New Delhi

NatCen
National Centre *for* Social Research

SAGE Publications Ltd
1 Oliver's Yard, 55 City Road
London EC1Y 1SP

SAGE Publications Inc.
2455 Teller Road
Thousand Oaks, California 91320

SAGE Publications India Pvt Ltd
B-42, Panchsheel Enclave
Post Box 4109
New Delhi 110 017

British Library Cataloguing in Publication data

A catalogue record for this book is available from the British Library

ISSN 0267 6869
ISBN 0-7619-4279-3

Library of Congress Control Number available

Printed in Great Britain by The Cromwell Press Ltd, Trowbridge, Wiltshire

British Social Attitudes

Attitudes The 22nd
REPORT

The **National Centre for Social Research** (NatCen) is an independent, non-profit social research organisation. It has a large professional staff together with its own interviewing and coding resources. Some of NatCen's work – such as the survey reported in this book – is initiated by NatCen itself and grant-funded by research councils or charitable foundations. Other work is initiated by government departments or quasi-government organisations to provide information on aspects of social or economic policy. NatCen also works frequently with other institutes and academics. Founded in 1969 and now Britain's largest social research organisation, NatCen has a high reputation for the standard of its work in both qualitative and quantitative research. NatCen has a Survey Methods Unit and, with the Department of Sociology, University of Oxford, houses the Centre for Research into Elections and Social Trends (CREST).

The contributors

Arturo Alvarez-Rosete
Research Officer at the King's Fund

John Appleby
Chief Economist at the King's Fund

Alice Bell
Senior Researcher at the *National Centre for Social Research*

Catherine Bromley
Research Director at the *Scottish Centre for Social Research* and Co-Director of the *British Social Attitudes* survey series

Caroline Bryson
Research Director at the *National Centre for Social Research*

Sarah Butt
DPhil student in Politics, Nuffield College, University of Oxford

Georgina Christodoulou
Research Fellow in the Transport Studies Group, University of Westminster

John Curtice
Research Consultant at the *Scottish Centre for Social Research*, Deputy Director of CREST, and Professor of Politics at Strathclyde University

Geoffrey Evans
Official Fellow in Politics, Nuffield College, and Professor of the Sociology of Politics and Director of the Centre for Research Methods in the Social Sciences, University of Oxford

Ruth Hancock
Professor of Non-clinical Gerontology at the University of Essex

Alun Humphrey
Research Director at the *National Centre for Social Research*

Mark Johnson
Researcher at the *National Centre for Social Research* and Co-Director of the *British Social Attitudes* survey series

Peter Jones
Professor of Transport and Sustainable Development, Centre for Transport Studies, at UCL, London

Ann Mair
Computing Officer in the Social Statistics Laboratory at Strathclyde University

Alison Park
Research Director at the *National Centre for Social Research* and Co-Director of the *British Social Attitudes* survey series

Miranda Phillips
Senior Researcher at the *National Centre for Social Research* and Co-Director of the *British Social Attitudes* survey series

Tom Sefton
Research Fellow at the *Centre for Analysis of Social Exclusion* (CASE), an ESRC Research Centre at the London School of Economics

Katarina Thomson
Research Director at the *National Centre for Social Research* and Co-Director of the *British Social Attitudes* survey series

David Whibley
Senior Lecturer in Transport Policy, University of Westminster

Ted Wragg
Emeritus Professor of Education at Exeter University

Contents

6   Transport: are policymakers and the public on the same track?

7   Planning for retirement: realism or denial?

8   Leaders or followers? Parties and public opinion on the European Union

Geoffrey Evans and Sarah Butt   **197**

9   Are trade unionists left-wing any more?

John Curtice and Ann Mair   **221**

Appendix I: Technical details of the survey   **239**

List of tables and figures

Chapter 9

Appendix I

Introduction

This volume, like each of its annual predecessors, presents the results and interpretations of the latest *British Social Attitudes* survey – the 22nd in the series of reports on the studies designed and carried out by the *National Centre for Social Research* (NatCen).

Labour's first two terms

This year's Report focuses on exploring public attitudes towards some of the issues that have dominated the political arena since the New Labour government arrived in office in 1997. In particular, it asks how in tune the public are with key elements of recent government policy.

  In the 1997 election, two areas of government spending received particular attention, forming the basis of two of the Labour party's famous 'pledges': health and education. Chapter 5 considers the public's response to the significant changes in health policy that have taken place since then, while Chapter 4 examines the extent to which people share the government's enthusiasm for expanding opportunities to enable young people to enter higher education.

  Two chapters deal with issues which, despite being of relatively low prominence in 1997, have become increasingly important since then. In particular, concern about pensions policy has risen dramatically, with increasing attention being paid to current demographic trends which clearly point towards an ever-ageing Britain. Chapter 7 explores views about the state pension and considers what public attitudes and behaviour suggest for the possible future direction of pensions policy. Meanwhile, Chapter 2 considers employees' responses to the government attempts to promote 'family-friendly' ways of working that help people improve the ways in which they combine paid work with other aspects of their lives.

  Other chapters deal with issues which, although they might appear to be lower down the immediate political agenda, nonetheless remain important areas of social policy. For instance, Chapter 6 considers public attitudes and behaviour and the light they shed on transport policy, an area whose political importance has fluctuated considerably since 1997. It focuses on people's views about various transport problems and the measures proposed to tackle them, paying particular attention to those that relate to reducing car use. Chapter 3 examines whether the public is in tune with Labour's commitment to expanding owner-occupation, and what this might tell us about future levels of home ownership. It also examines the extent to which recent changes in the composition and nature of the social housing sector have occurred against a backdrop of popular support. Meanwhile, Chapter 8 considers the thorny issue of Europe. After all, in its 2005 election manifesto, the Labour Party expressed its pride in Britain's membership of the European Union, and pledged to hold a referendum on its new Constitutional Treaty (and to campaign whole-heartedly for a 'yes' vote). This chapter considers what impact the British public's long-standing suspicion of Europe might have on the government's pursuit of its European goals.

Prior to 1997, Labour Party manifestos had often contained grand statements about the redistribution of income from rich to poor. By contrast, New Labour has been reluctant to talk explicitly of 'redistribution', even though successive Budgets have consistently redistributed income in favour of lower income groups. Chapter 1 examines public attitudes towards redistribution and inequality, and teases out the constraints that appear to exist on people's willingness to support elements of redistribution within the welfare system.

The origins of the Labour Party lie within the trade union movement. So Chapter 9 offers a fitting conclusion to this Report. It examines the extent to which trade unionists, traditionally a fiercely left-wing and Labour-leaning group, remain distinctive in their attitudes and values. Over the last two decades, the composition of trade unions has changed dramatically, as has the proportion of the workforce who belong to them. What impact has this had on their members' attitudes and values? And to what extent do trade unions have a clear and certain role as part of Britain's 'left'?

Most of the tables in the Report are based on *British Social Attitudes* data from 2004 and earlier years. Conventions for reading the tables are set out in Appendix II of this Report.

Our thanks

This survey series has a widely acknowledged reputation as painting an authoritative and impartial picture of contemporary British values. Its reputation owes a great deal to its many generous funders. We are particularly grateful to our core funder – the Gatsby Charitable Foundation (one of the Sainsbury Family Charitable Trusts) – whose continuous support for the series from the start has given it security and independence. Other funders have made long-term commitments to the study and we are ever grateful to them as well. In 2004, these included the Departments for Education and Skills, Health, Transport, Trade and Industry, and Work and Pensions. Our thanks are also due to the Housing Corporation and the Hera Trust.

We are grateful to the Economic and Social Research Council (ESRC) which provided funding for the fascinating set of questions about attitudes to redistribution. The ESRC also supported NatCen's participation in the *International Social Survey Programme*, which now comprises over 40 nations, each of whom help to design and then field a set of equivalent questions every year on a rotating set of issues. The topic in 2004 was citizenship and these questions can be seen at the start of version A of the self-completion questionnaire in Appendix III. As always, the *British Social Attitudes* survey is developed in co-operation with its sister survey, *Scottish Social Attitudes*.

For those of you who want more information than is available in this Report, we draw your attention to a useful internet resource. Developed by the *Centre for Comparative European Survey Data* at the London Metropolitan University, this web site allows contents based or free text search of all *British Social Attitudes* questionnaires since 1983 and produces tables for the questions you are interested in. We would like to thank Professor Richard Topf for all his hard work in bringing this to fruition. This facility can be accessed at http://www.britsocat.com/. The full datasets also continue to be deposited at the UK Data Archive (http://www.data-archive.ac.uk/).

The *British Social Attitudes* series is a team effort. A research group designs, directs and reports on the study. They are supported by complementary teams who implement the sampling strategy and carry out data processing. They in turn depend on fieldwork controllers, area managers and field interviewers who are responsible for getting all the interviewing done, and on administrative staff to compile, organise and distribute the survey's extensive documentation. In this respect, particular thanks are due to Neil Barton and his colleagues in NatCen's administrative office in Brentwood. Other thanks are due to Sue Corbett and Sandra Beeson in our computing department who expertly translate our questions into a computer-assisted questionnaire. Meanwhile, the raw data have to be transformed into a workable SPSS system file – a task that has for many years been performed with great care and efficiency by Ann Mair at the Social Statistics Laboratory at the University of Strathclyde. Many thanks are also due to Lucy Robinson, Fabienne Pedroletti and Emily Lawrence at Sage, our publishers.

As always, we must praise above all the anonymous respondents across Britain who gave their time to take part in our 2004 survey. Like the 57,000 or so people who participated before them, they are the cornerstone of this enterprise. We hope that some of them will one day come across this volume and read about themselves with interest.

The Editors

1 Give and take: attitudes to redistribution

Tom Sefton[*]

Under New Labour, Ministerial statements about income inequality and redistribution have been ambivalent, even awkward at times. Perhaps most famous of all was Tony Blair's repeated refusal to answer a question posed to him during a *Newsnight* interview in 2001 regarding whether it was acceptable for the gap between rich and poor to widen. The 'R-word' appears virtually taboo, perhaps because it is seen to imply that the poor can only be helped at the expense of the rich.[1] This is a far cry from the 1983 Labour manifesto which promised a "fundamental and irreversible shift in the balance of power and wealth in favour of working people and their families" (Labour Party, 1983).

Nonetheless, successive Budgets have consistently redistributed income in favour of lower income groups (Sutherland *et al.*, 2003; Adam *et al.*, 2005). The net effect of fiscal reforms since 1997 has been to increase the incomes of the poorest two-tenths by over 10 per cent and to reduce that of the richest two-tenths by around four per cent. Reforms in the second term, whilst less generous on average, were more progressive than those in the first. These gains have helped to reduce poverty among those groups of most concern to government – pensioners and children. So, although income redistribution is not an explicit aim of the current government, many of the changes it has made to the tax and benefit system have been redistributive in their effect.

Experience to date highlights the challenge New Labour faces if it is to make further progress in reducing poverty and inequality.[2] All the resources that have been channelled to low income households – and these have been considerable – have just about been sufficient to reduce child poverty by a quarter since 1998/99, whilst overall poverty and inequality have fallen only marginally or not at all. To reduce poverty further would require substantially more redistribution to the poorest over and above what has already been done. To

---

[*] Tom Sefton is Research Fellow at the *Centre for Analysis of Social Exclusion* (CASE), an Economic and Social Research Council Research Centre at the London School of Economics.

reduce inequality would, in addition, almost certainly require something to be done to curb the growth in very high incomes; otherwise, any equalising changes in the bottom half of the income distribution are likely to be cancelled out by changes in the top half (Sefton, 2005).

Though levels of inequality are not at the forefront of people's minds when asked to consider the most important issues facing the government and the country, many of the issues that do concern people, and in some cases divide them, are intimately linked to their (re)distributive impact. Questions about the appropriate level of government spending and taxation, the structure of local taxation, the appropriate role of the state in meeting people's material needs in retirement, and tax rebates for people who opt out of public services, were hotly debated during the 2005 election campaign. All these issues have important implications for the distribution of income and wealth across British society.

Qualitative research suggests that many people do not see 'redistribution' as the intended outcome of the taxation and spending process – and certainly do not use that kind of language to describe it. However, there appear to be high levels of public support for redistribution as a *by-product* of spending and taxation (Hedges, 2005).[3] To examine these issues in detail, the 2004 *British Social Attitudes* survey included a set of questions about these issues. The chapter begins by examining what these questions tell us about overall attitudes towards inequality and redistribution. It then focuses upon how people's apparently muted support for income redistribution relates to their attitudes towards the welfare state and the taxes that pay for it (these being, after all, the principal instruments for redistribution). First, it attempts to tease out people's preferences for redistribution in more detail, examining the kinds of tax and spending policies favoured by the majority of our respondents. This allows us to assess how progressive people think the tax system ought to be, the extent to which they feel government spending should be concentrated on the poorest households, and whether (and how) opinion depends on the spending area in question. Next, it looks at some of the underlying attitudes that may account for individuals' support for, or opposition to, redistribution. This is essential if we are to understand how government might seek to lead or shape public opinion in this area. Are, for instance, people's attitudes to the welfare state driven largely by self-interest or do other factors (such as altruism and a belief that society as a whole benefits from the welfare state) matter more? What are the limits or constraints on people's willingness to support elements of redistribution within the welfare system?

Overall attitudes towards inequality and redistribution

As previous *British Social Attitudes* reports have noted, the majority of people think that there is too much inequality in incomes in Britain, though the extent of agreement depends on exactly how this question is phrased. The survey included three related questions concerned with this issue:

*Thinking of income levels generally in Britain today, would you say that the **gap** between those with high incomes and those with low incomes is too large, about right, or, too small?*

Respondents were also asked which of five answer options (running from "agree strongly" to "disagree strongly") best described their response to the following two statements:

Differences in income in Britain are too large

Ordinary working people do not get their fair share of the nation's wealth

When asked the first of these questions, nearly three-quarters (73 per cent) say they think the gap between those with high and low incomes is "too large". When asked whether they agree with the statement that "differences in income in Britain are too large", a very similar question, the proportion who agree falls to around two-thirds (63 per cent). And, when asked the third question, agreement drops further still, to just over a half (53 per cent). The lower level of support for the third statement is perhaps the easiest to explain: the language is very different from that used in the first two questions, and is suggestive of a more class-based explanation of inequality. This may be off-putting to some who would otherwise agree that there is too much income inequality.[4]

The difference in responses to the first two questions is harder to understand. One possible explanation is that, because the first question specifically refers to the gap between those on *high* and *low* incomes, people are more likely to be thinking about differences between the very rich and the very poor than they are when answering the second question (which could be referring to differences in incomes between the 'not-so-rich' and 'not-so-poor'). If some people are primarily concerned about the *extremes* of the income distribution, this could explain why they might respond differently to these two questions.

Either way, more striking still is the difference between people's responses to questions about the level of inequality and their responses to other questions about what, if anything, the government should do in response. These are all shown in Figure 1.1. The questions are as follows (as before, respondents were asked to choose between five answer options running from "agree strongly" to "disagree strongly"):

It is the responsibility of the government to reduce the differences in income between people with high incomes and those with low incomes

The government should spend more money on welfare benefits for the poor, even if it leads to higher taxes

Government should redistribute income from the better-off to those who are less well off

Whereas nearly three-quarters of people say the gap between those with high incomes and those with low incomes is too large, only 43 per cent think it is the government's responsibility to reduce income differences. And around a third are in favour of more redistributive spending on welfare benefits for the poor (36 per cent), or think the government should redistribute incomes from the better-off to those who are less well off (32 per cent). Only in the latter case, however, do a higher proportion of respondents disagree with the statement than agree with it.

Figure 1.1 Attitudes towards inequality and redistribution[5]

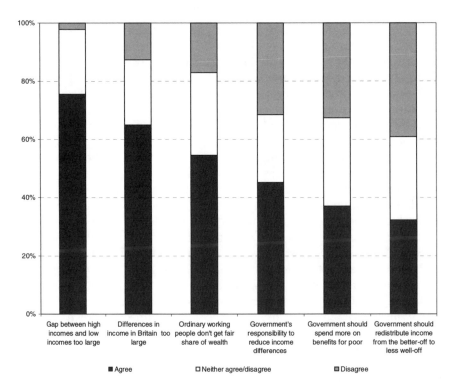

How should we interpret the fact that a third of people think that government should *explicitly* redistribute income, a far lower proportion than we might have expected given people's views about income inequality? Does this mean that support for redistribution is very much a minority pursuit? We should be wary of reaching such a conclusion, not least because there are two possible ways in which the question could be interpreted. On the one hand, it could be seen as inviting comment on the role of governments in general. On the other hand, however, it could be taken as a more relative question, one which will take account of people's views about the *current* performance of government in this area, and whether or not they think any further redistributive efforts are necessary. To examine this, we need to know what people think about current levels of redistribution. We asked:

> *Do you think government does too much or too little to redistribute income from the better off to those who are less well off, or have they got it about right?*

As Table 1.1 shows, nearly four in ten think that government is doing too little to redistribute income, while nearly three in ten think it has got it "about right". Only 13 per cent consider that government is doing too much on this front. It is notable that one in five people were unable to answer the question, most probably a reflection of people's uncertainty about the meaning or current scale of redistribution.

There is an interesting relationship between people's views about government's current performance on this issue, and their responses to our more general question about redistribution. This is shown in Table 1.1, which focuses upon three groups: those who agree that government *should* redistribute income (the first row of figures); those who disagree (the third row); and those who neither agree nor disagree with the statement (the second row). Two key facts emerge. Firstly, among those who think that government should redistribute income, most would favour *greater* redistribution than at present: seven in ten (70 per cent) think that government is currently doing "too little" to close the gap between rich and poor. Secondly, even among those who *disagree* with the general statement, a majority say that government is currently doing "about right" or "too little" to redistribute incomes and only a quarter (24 per cent) say they are doing "too much". This suggests that support for redistribution in principle is much higher than the 32 per cent who agree with the statement that government should redistribute income might suggest. As Table 1.1 shows, there is a substantial group who, despite not agreeing with this statement, still appear to support a degree of redistribution in practice – at or even above current levels.

Table 1.1 Views on the appropriate level of redistribution

Government should redistribute income		Too much	About right	Too little	Can't choose	Base
All	%	13	28	38	20	1737
Agree	%	7	15	70	8	532
Neither agree/disagree	%	6	30	37	27	512
Disagree	%	24	37	15	24	645

Explicit and implicit support for redistribution

So far we have seen that, although most people think there is too much income inequality, only a minority *explicitly* favour redistribution or, at least, greater redistribution than occurs at present. It is clear from other research, however, that many people have a very limited knowledge and understanding of the complex system by which tax is collected and spent, and its redistributive effects (Hedges, 2005). In particular, they do not generally associate the welfare state with redistribution, let alone see this as an important or primary aim of the system. It is possible, therefore, that people may support policies that are redistributive in practice, even though they may not be explicitly in favour of a policy of income redistribution. Support for these sorts of policies can thus be seen as *implicitly* favouring redistribution.

Government has two principal mechanisms for achieving redistribution: its spending on benefits and public services, and the taxes it needs to finance such spending. Depending on the design of the benefits system and the structure of the tax system, the government can significantly alter the overall redistributive impact of the welfare system. It can, for example, increase the role of means-tested benefits in order to target additional resources at the poorest households, or modify the tax system in ways that impact differentially on lower and higher income groups. We now turn to examine how Britain's apparently muted support for redistribution is reflected in people's attitudes towards these crucial elements of the welfare state.

A number of questions in the survey allow us to identify people's implicit support for redistribution, based upon their views about the appropriate structure of taxation and spending. We begin by considering people's responses to these questions about spending and taxation separately. To what extent, for instance, should government spending be targeted at those on low incomes who are most in need? How should the burden of taxation be distributed between households with lower and higher incomes. Should people who 'opt out' of public services be required to contribute less?

How progressive a benefits system do we want?

Like all welfare systems, the British welfare state contains a mixture of universal and targeted welfare provision. Most public services, including the National Health Service and state education, are provided universally, as are some of the major cash benefits, including the basic state pension (subject to having a complete contributions record), child benefit, and most disability-related benefits. The amounts may vary according to the composition of the household or the severity of a person's disability, but they are unrelated to people's incomes. In contrast, other cash benefits, including income support and housing benefit, are means-tested and only available to those with low incomes and limited assets. Tax credits for low earners and for pensioners are also income-related, but are linked to being in paid work (for those of working age) and extend higher up the income distribution than other means-tested benefits. Since coming into office, New Labour has shifted the balance of the system towards a greater reliance on means-tested or income-related benefits (principally due to the expansion of tax credits), although the share of expenditure on such benefits has not risen, because of falling unemployment and other changes over the same period. Around 30 per cent of total benefit expenditure in 2003–04 was means-tested, rising to 36 per cent if the value of tax credits is included.

The appropriate balance between means-tested and non-means-tested benefits is controversial. On the one hand, universal benefits generally command more political support, have higher take-up rates and are less likely to stigmatise recipients or unfairly exclude people in genuine need. On the other hand, targeted payments are a more efficient way of combating poverty, because a greater proportion of any expenditure goes towards helping low income households (although this may also create disincentives to work or save if benefits are withdrawn as income rises).

Attitudes towards income-related benefits vary substantially according to how the question is framed and the type of benefit in question. The first set of questions we consider is about how people's entitlement to different types of benefits should vary according to their earnings. People were asked the following question about disability benefits (and equivalent questions were asked about retirement benefits and child benefits):

Imagine two people who had to stop work due to a disability. One had been a high earner and the other had been a low earner. Which of the options on this card comes closest to your view about their entitlement to disability benefits?

The high earner should get more than the low earner because they have paid more in taxes
The high and low earner should get the same amount
The low earner should get more than the high earner because they are more likely to be in need
The high earner should not get anything because they can afford to provide for themselves

This scenario encourages people to weigh up the fact that high earners have contributed more in taxes against the greater need of low earners. As Table 1.2 shows, when faced with this scenario in relation to state pensions and disability benefits, a majority favour flat-rate benefits, and a substantial minority think that the low earner should get more. For child benefits, opinion is split evenly between these two options. Very few people, however, feel that high earners should not receive anything (that is, fully means-tested benefits).[6]

Table 1.2 Attitudes towards means-testing of benefits under different scenarios (i)

	State pension	Disability benefit	Child benefit
View about entitlement to state benefits	%	%	%
High earner should get more	12	10	4
Both should get same amount	56	55	42
Low earner should get more	27	30	44
Only low earner should get benefit	4	2	8
Base	*2146*	*2146*	*2146*

We turn now to examine what happens to people's views once it is made clear that there is a limited pot of money available to spend, our interest being particularly in how this affects support for means-testing. To assess this, we told respondents that "the government has a set amount of money to spend" on the benefit in question and asked what they thought was "the best way to spend that money". Two answer options were available, each spelling out a key argument related to means-testing. The example below shows the options relevant to child benefits:

> *Only families on low incomes should get child benefits, even if that means they have to fill in forms to prove it,*
> *Or, every family should get child benefits even if that means money goes to families who don't really need it?*

As Table 1.3 shows, this question results in a much higher level of support for fully means-tested benefits. In Table 1.2, only four per cent think that low earners alone should receive a state pension; now this applies to nearly four in ten (38 per cent). The corresponding figures for disability benefits are two per cent and 46 per cent, while support for means-tested child benefits goes up to 68 per cent (compared with eight per cent).

  Of course, means-testing need not be used only to decide whether someone should get a particular benefit or not. It could also be used to decide on the *level* of benefit that someone should receive. To assess support for this, we used the same preamble as described above (stressing the set amount of money that government has to spend on benefits) and offered two options:

> *Families on low incomes should get higher child benefits, even if that means they have to fill in forms to prove it,*
> *Or, every family should get the same amount of child benefits even if that means money goes to families who don't really need it?*

In this case, the balance of opinion swings decisively in favour of low earners getting more than others (although everyone gets something). Around two-thirds are in favour of higher pensions and higher disability benefits for those on low incomes and nearly three-quarters of respondents feel the same way about child benefits. These responses reveal broad support for the government's policy of 'progressive universalism', especially when resources are constrained.

Table 1.3 Attitudes towards means-testing of benefits under different scenarios (ii)

View on best way for government to spend a set amount of money on (different benefits)	State pension %	Disability benefit %	Child benefit %
Everyone should get benefit	59	51	29
Only those on low incomes should get benefit	38	46	68
Base	*1085*	*1085*	*1085*
	%	%	%
Everyone should get the same amount	37	28	24
Those on low incomes should get more	61	68	74
Base	*1061*	*1061*	*1061*

The highest levels of support for means-testing are found in relation to child benefits, which appear to be viewed slightly differently to other benefits. Certainly, qualitative work has found a strong perceived link between pension payments and contributions: people feel they have 'earned' their right to a state pension by making contributions throughout their working life, and so are reluctant to forego these benefits. Whilst it could be argued that parents have paid in to the system in the same way as pensioners have, the same research shows that this does not appear to be the way in which entitlement to child benefit is viewed. Consequently, there is a view that high-earning families should not receive child benefit because they don't need it (and perhaps because it was their choice to have children) (Hedges, 2005).

The volatility of responses to these questions suggests that people's opinions on this matter are in the balance. They can see both sides of the argument, and their answers change depending on whether one or other side of the argument is emphasised. There is, however, a surprising degree of consensus across different socio-economic groups in their responses to these questions. Lower socio-economic groups tend to be slightly more in favour of means-tested benefits, but in every case, the predominant view among the population as a whole is also the predominant view among different socio-economic groups.

How progressive a tax system do we want?

Perhaps not surprisingly, taxation has been an issue that New Labour has sought
to play down during its first two terms in office. Having decided that its
proposal to raise the higher rate of income tax was a decisive factor in it losing
the 1992 election, all subsequent Labour manifestos have explicitly ruled out
increases in either the basic or higher rates of income tax.

Changes in taxation since 1997, including the introduction of a new 10 per
cent tax band, have made the system somewhat more progressive, by reducing
the share of taxation paid by lower income groups relative to higher income
groups. But these changes have not gone very far in redressing the strongly
regressive impact of the changes in taxation that occurred over the preceding 18
years. Two changes stand out in particular – the large cut in higher rates of
income tax and the increase in Value Added Tax (which falls disproportionately
on the poorest). Various commentators on the left have argued, with varying
degrees of caution, that current taxation should be more progressive if the aim is
to reduce inequality (and not only to fund improved public services). This could
be obtained either by raising income tax rates for high earners and/or by
removing regressive elements within the current system (Hickson, 2002;
Diamond and Giddens, 2005).

To gauge people's views on how progressive the tax system should be, we
asked the following:

> *Suppose the government had to raise extra money from taxes to pay*
> *for spending on education, health, and social benefits. This card*
> *shows three different ways they could do this, and what this would*
> *mean for two different people, one earning £15,000 before tax and the*
> *other earning £30,000 before tax. Which option do you think the*
> *government should choose?*
>
> *Each person should pay the **same amount** of money in tax (say, £200*
> *a year extra)*
> *Each person should pay the **same share** of their earnings in tax (so*
> *the person earning £15,000 might pay £150 and the person earning*
> *£30,000 might pay £300)*
> *The person earning less should pay a **smaller share** of their earnings*
> *in tax, and the person earning more pay a **larger share** (so the*
> *person earning £15,000 might pay £100 and the person earning*
> *£30,000 might pay £400)*

The first of these options is *regressive,* in that a person with lower earnings
would pay a larger share of their income in tax. The second option is
proportional (or neutral), and the third option is *progressive.* As Table 1.4
shows, the vast majority of people think that those on the higher income should
pay either a larger share of their incomes in taxes or the same share. Only seven

per cent think those on the higher income should pay the same amount as those on low incomes (that is, a lower share of their income). So the balance of opinion appears to be that the tax system should be progressive or at the very least proportional.

As we might expect, support for progressive taxation is strongest among those on relatively low incomes, but it is also supported by a significant minority of respondents on very high incomes. Among those with annual household incomes of £50,000 or more, over a third say that people on higher incomes should pay a larger share of their incomes in tax than those on lower incomes, and over a half say that they should pay the same share.

This question is very specific in presenting the three options, including examples of the amounts a "low" earner (on £15,000) and "high" earner (on £30,000) might be expected to pay in each case, helping to clarify the financial implications of the choice that respondents are being asked to make (albeit hypothetically). And yet, even when the meaning is spelt out and it is clear that the question is not about higher tax rates only for the 'super-rich', nearly half of all respondents still say they would favour a progressive tax system. It is very likely that support for progressive taxation would be even greater if people had been asked about people on very high earnings in excess of £50,000 or £100,000.[7]

Table 1.4 Views on how progressive the tax system should be

		High earners should pay ...		
		... same *amount* as low earners	... same *share* as low earners	... larger *share* than low earners	*Base*
All	%	7	43	47	*2146*
Household income					
Low (below £15,000 per annum)	%	7	35	53	*716*
High (£50,000 or more per annum)	%	6	56	37	*244*

Views on opting out

One of the Conservative Party's proposals in their 2005 Election Manifesto was to offer a partial tax rebate to private patients who have an operation in an independent hospital rather than on the National Health Service. The rationale was as follows:

> Private patients have paid their taxes like everyone else. If they choose to go private and free up NHS space for other patients, they should not be punished, but helped (Conservative Party, 2005).

This approach potentially has significant implications for the distribution of income, in that many of the beneficiaries would be relatively well-off individuals currently paying the full cost of private health care.

How widespread is support for private education and health care, and to what extent do people feel that those who opt for these are being penalised by, in effect, 'paying twice' for services? To assess this, we asked "is it right or wrong that people with higher incomes can buy better education for their children than people with lower incomes?". We also asked the same question in relation to "better health care". As Table 1.5 shows, in both cases just under a half think that buying private provision is "definitely" or "somewhat right". The remainder are split fairly evenly between those who have mixed feelings and those who feel it is wrong. Perhaps most surprisingly, a significant minority of those who make use of private provision (namely, those who have private health insurance, who have a child at a fee-paying private school, or who themselves attended a private school) have mixed or negative feelings about whether it is right to do so; this applying to 40 per cent. The answers to these two questions are very highly correlated, with those who feel it is wrong to buy better education being almost universally disapproving of buying better health care and *vice versa*.

Table 1.5 Attitudes towards opting out of public services and tax rebates for those who do

	Education	Health care
Views on people with higher incomes buying better education for their children / better health care:	%	%
Definitely / somewhat right	48	47
Mixed feelings	25	27
Definitely / somewhat wrong	23	23
Base	*1737*	*1737*
View of taxation for those who choose not to use the state education system for their children / not to use the NHS:	%	%
Taxes should be reduced	21	21
Neither / it depends	2	2
Should pay same taxes as everyone else	77	77
Base	*2146*	*2146*

Given people's misgivings about opting out, it is not surprising that few favour tax rebates for those who do (the second question presented in Table 1.5). Only a fifth of respondents feel that people who choose not to use the state education system or the National Health Service should have their taxes reduced; over three-quarters think that they should pay the same in taxes as everyone else. This view is dominant among people from a range of different socio-economic groups. Most starkly, only a quarter of those who themselves use private welfare think they should pay reduced taxes, even though this would be of direct benefit to them. Some ideological differences are evident: around 30 per cent of Conservative supporters are in favour of tax rebates, compared with 15 per cent of Labour supporters. Again, these differences are smaller than might be expected.

Qualitative research offers various suggestions as to what might underpin these findings. Some feel that, because the decision to opt out is a personal one, those who do so should bear the extra cost. Others stress the impact on public services were government to lose the contributions of those who opt out, and feel that this situation could produce a two-tier service with those unable to afford private services receiving second-class treatment (Hedges, 2005). Our findings suggest that, for most people at any rate, these sorts of arguments outweigh the counter-argument that people should not be made to pay for services they do not use.

There is some evidence that fewer people now see purchasing education or health services as 'wrong' than did so in the past. When the first question shown in Table 1.5 was asked in 1999, just under four in ten thought it "definitely" or "somewhat wrong" that people with higher incomes could buy better health care or education (38 and 37 per cent respectively), compared with 23 per cent now. It is not clear what is driving this, as there has been no significant change in the use of private health or education over this period. One possibility is that people are influenced by the rhetoric of the two main political parties, which are promising greater choice (both within the public sector and across sectors) as well as seeking to blur the distinction between the public and private sectors (for example, by involving the private sector in the provision of public services). This development is important. As Hedges has argued, if people come to see public services like health and education as essentially being consumer goods, they are less likely to resist the idea of tax rebates for private purchasers, on the principle that consumers should not pay for what they do not receive (Hedges, 2005). Although there is no sign that this has happened yet, these changes could in turn reduce the scope for redistribution within the current system.

How much implicit support is there for redistribution?

What do these views about government spending and taxation tell us about people's preferences for redistribution? We turn now to consider the implications of our findings so far in relation to implicit support for redistribution. To do this, we need to examine people's views about taxation alongside their views about entitlement to benefits. This involves using two sets of questions. The first is the question about taxation considered in Table 1.4. This allows us to place people into one of three categories according to their views: regressive; proportional; or progressive. The second is the series of questions about entitlement considered in Table 1.2. These allow us to place people into one of three categories: those who tend to favour earnings-related benefits (that is, higher payments for those with higher prior earnings); flat-rate or universal benefits; or means-tested benefits (that is, higher payments for those with lower prior earnings).[8]

The results of this exercise are shown in Table 1.6. The most popular combination, chosen by just over a quarter of respondents (26 per cent), is proportional taxation combined with flat-rate or universal benefits. This is quite strongly redistributive, because someone on a low income will pay substantially less in tax but be entitled to the same amount in benefits as someone on a higher income. In addition, lower income groups are more likely to receive these benefits because they are more at risk of experiencing the adverse events that the social security system is designed to insure them against, such as unemployment or the onset of disability.

A further 62 per cent of respondents selected one of three even more strongly redistributive packages involving either progressive taxation and/or means-tested benefits. True, this may overstate people's preferences for redistribution somewhat, as it does not take into account spending on benefits in kind – public services like health and education – where people overwhelmingly support universal, as opposed to means-tested, services. On the other hand, as the preceding analysis showed, support for means-tested cash benefits is even greater when these questions are phrased differently.

Table 1.6 Views on appropriate distribution of spending and taxation (per cent of respondents)*

Views on distribution of benefits spending**	Views on appropriate structure of taxation		
	Regressive	Proportional	Progressive
Earnings-related	1	3	3
Flat-rate / universal	5	26	24
Means-tested	2	15	23

Base: 1964

* The light, medium and dark shaded boxes indicate packages of measures that are fairly, moderately and strongly redistributive, respectively.
** Based on responses to three questions about entitlement to different types of benefits (state pension, disability benefits and child benefits). People were asked how much they think high earners should receive in benefits relative to low earners.

Only one in nine (11 per cent) select a package that is *not* clearly redistributive. Of particular note is the fact that only six per cent select a combination of earnings-related benefits and either proportional or progressive taxation, which would be the closest to the tax and social security systems operating in many other western European countries.[9]

So, overall around nine in ten favour tax and spending policies whose overall impact is clearly redistributive. This includes most of those who, when asked directly, did *not* agree that government should redistribute incomes from the better-off to those who are less well off. It is also clear that the level of *implicit* support for redistribution is very high among all subgroups of the population. For instance, nearly nine in ten Conservative identifiers (87 per cent) and the same proportion of respondents with high incomes (£50,000 or more per annum) have views that place them in one of the shaded areas in Table 1.6, indicating implicit support for redistribution. This compares with 90 per cent of Labour identifiers and the same proportion of those with low incomes (below £15,000 per annum). Indeed, the only difference between these subgroups is in the *degree* of redistribution they would support. Conservative identifiers and high income respondents are more likely to favour the less strongly redistributive combination of proportional taxation and flat-rate benefits than are Labour identifiers and low income respondents.

This strongly supports Hedges' conclusion that there appear to be strong levels of support for redistribution as a *by-product* of spending and taxing in ways people want. He found a commonly held view that the welfare state should ensure that people have their basic needs met (whether or not they have enough money to pay), and that the amount that people should contribute should reflect what they can afford. This is redistributive in *effect*, but not necessarily redistributive in *intention* (Hedges, 2005)

The same research also provides some clues as to why levels of implicit and explicit support for redistribution differ so radically. It found that people are least comfortable with redistribution when they picture it as a direct transfer between particular individuals or groups. This might explain why only a minority of respondents agree that government should redistribute incomes from the better off to those who are less well off, which seems to imply a direct transfer between the two groups. People are more at ease with a model which portrays a central 'pot' into which everyone pays and draws out of according to their means and needs. By implication, the amounts put in and taken out will vary between individuals, so there will be a transfer of resources between them – but it is an *indirect* transfer. This is consistent with the much higher level of implicit support for redistribution, as reflected in the kinds of tax and spending policies favoured by the majority of respondents.

Perceptions of how progressive the welfare state actually is

Clearly, most people do not appear to think of the welfare state as an instrument for redistributing incomes from rich to poor. But to what extent do they recognise that it might have this effect in practice? To assess this we asked respondents three questions about who benefits most from, and bears the cost of, tax-funded public services:

*Thinking of people on low incomes, how much do you think they
benefit from overall government spending on health and education,
compared to people on high incomes?*

*Do you think that people with high incomes pay a **larger share** of their
income in various taxes than those with low incomes, the **same share**,
or a **smaller share**?*

*Imagine that people paid privately for things like schools and health
insurance, and taxes were lower as a result. In the long run, would a
system like this mean you and your household were financially better
off, or would you be worse off?*

Tax-financed spending on welfare services involves substantial redistribution
from higher to lower income groups, partly because higher income groups
contribute more in taxes, but also because lower income groups are more
intensive users of public services. Some of these effects even out over people's
lifetimes, but there remains a large net redistribution of resources from the
lifetime rich to the lifetime poor (Falkingham and Hills, 1995; Hills, 2004).

Perhaps not surprisingly, most people's understanding of the redistributive
effects of the welfare state is hazy, and in many cases inconsistent. Though
spending on the National Health Service and state education disproportionately
benefits the poorest households, this is certainly not the way in which these
services are usually viewed. In response to our first question, less than a third of
respondents (31 per cent) think that people on low incomes benefit more than
people on high incomes when it comes to public spending on health and
education – 41 per cent say they benefit about the same and 24 per cent say they
benefit less. As Table 1.7 shows, respondents from lower income groups tend to
think that higher income groups benefit more and *vice versa*.

The next question ascertains how progressive the tax system is seen to be.
Once indirect taxes, such as VAT, are taken into account, the overall tax
structure is in fact broadly neutral or even slightly regressive: across most of the
income range, people pay about the same share of their income in taxes
(between 33 and 36 per cent in 2002/03), but those at the very bottom pay a
slightly larger share (40 per cent) (Lakin, 2004). However, a majority believe
the current tax system is progressive. Nearly two-thirds of all respondents (and
over three-quarters of those with very high incomes) think that people with high
incomes pay a larger share of their income in taxes than those with low
incomes. This confirms exploratory qualitative research which found that, when
people are presented with information on the share of incomes paid in taxes by
different income groups, they were surprised to find that the poorest fifth of
households pay a higher proportion of their income in tax. The differences,
though not large, are contrary to what people expect; people tend to have an
income-related taxation model in their minds, whereas it is the impact of
spending taxes (such as VAT) that accounts for the slightly regressive pattern in
the overall incidence of taxation (Hedges, 2005). This suggests that a better
understanding of the taxation system might strengthen most people's view that

the system should be more progressive (or, at least, that the regressive elements in the current system should be removed). However, the debates during the 2005 election that surrounded the Liberal Democrat's proposals for a local income tax suggest that discussion about the fairness (or otherwise) of the current tax system as a whole can easily get drowned out by the specifics of who might lose out from any proposed changes.

Table 1.7 Views on how much different groups benefit from public services

Who benefits from government spending (low *versus* high incomes)?		Low incomes ...			
		...benefit more	... benefit the same	... benefit less	*Base*
All	%	31	41	24	*2146*
Household income					
Low (below £15,000 per annum)	%	23	38	33	*716*
High (£50,000 or more per annum)	%	41	44	14	*244*

Who pays higher share in taxes (high *versus* low incomes)?		High incomes pay ...			
		... smaller share	... same share	... larger share	*Base*
All	%	12	19	65	*2146*
Household income					
Low (below £15,000 per annum)	%	13	21	59	*716*
High (£50,000 or more per annum)	%	12	10	77	*244*

If paid for private provision and taxes were lower		Own household would be ...			
		... better off	... no difference	... worse off	*Base*
All	%	33	10	51	*2146*
Household income					
Low (below £15,000 per annum)	%	19	17	58	*716*
High (£50,000 or more per annum)	%	49	7	40	*244*

The final question in Table 1.7 encourages people to consider the broader financial implications of moving away from tax-financed public services to fully privatised services, and the impact that this would have on their own household's tax payments. Overall, a half of all respondents (51 per cent) think they and their household would be worse off in the long run under this scenario, and only a third think they would be better off. This is in spite of the strong perception that public services are often unsatisfactory and involve considerable waste and inefficiency. Even among high income households, 40 per cent feel they would be worse off under such a system, while a third of respondents in low income households think they would be better off or at least as well off as they are now.[10]

Although many people seem to be unaware of the strongly redistributive effects of the welfare state and the taxes that fund it, they generally accepted this as a fair outcome when presented with the evidence in focus group discussions on this topic; if anything, some people felt that higher income groups should be contributing more (Hedges, 2005).

What explains support for redistribution?

A better understanding of the factors that underpin individuals' attitudes towards the welfare state – and, in particular, the redistribution that is implicit within the system – is critical to thinking about how government might seek to lead or shape public opinion in this area. Whilst New Labour's policies have achieved a significant amount of redistribution in favour of low income households, it seems likely that it will need to shift the public mood in a more progressive direction if it is to make further progress towards its ambitious target of eliminating child poverty.

Attitudes to the welfare state

People's motives for supporting the welfare state are partly self-interested. Previous studies have shown that there is a clear tendency for individuals to be more sympathetic towards spending on the sorts of benefits that they might receive themselves. So, for example, single parents are significantly more likely to support higher spending on single parents, and disabled people are more likely to support higher spending on disabled people (Brook et al., 1998). People may also be willing to support others now so that they will receive support when they are in need.

Others have argued that neither support for the welfare state, nor opposition to it, can be adequately understood in terms of self-interest (Linos and West, 2003; Fong et al., 2004). There is, for example, substantial support for redistribution even among those on high incomes who are least likely to benefit from it (and substantial opposition among those on low incomes who stand to benefit most).[11] People also support redistributive policies at least in part for moral or altruistic reasons: because it is right to help others in need, and because one sympathises with their predicament. Some people also perceive societal or systematic benefits: living in a kinder society, for instance, or enjoying the economic and social benefits of a healthy, well-educated population. But there are conditions attached to most people's generosity. You may be willing, for example, to support others, but only if you think they have contributed what they reasonably can. And you may start to resent it if you feel you are paying a lot in and not benefiting at all.

To explore these issues, we included five new questions in this year's British Social Attitudes survey that seek to capture the relative importance of these different factors. Respondents were asked to agree or disagree (on a five-point scale) with the following statements:

> *It's only right that taxes paid by the majority help support those in need.*

> *If we want to live in a healthy, well-educated society we have to be willing to pay the taxes to fund it.*

> *The best reason for paying taxes now is that you never know when you might need benefits and services yourself.*

> *It's not fair that some people pay a lot of money in tax and hardly use the services their taxes pay for.*

> *It's not right that people benefit from services that they haven't helped to pay for.*

The responses to these questions suggest that people are motivated by a *combination* of altruism, self-interest, and a belief that the welfare state is in society's best interests. Most people believe that it is only right that taxes paid by the majority help those in need (69 per cent agree with this view); that the best reason for paying taxes is that you never know when you might need benefits or services yourself (74 per cent); and that if we want to live in a healthy, well-educated society, we have to be willing to pay the taxes to fund it (84 per cent). On the whole, people are more concerned about people benefiting from services they haven't contributed towards (48 per cent agree that this is not right, while only 26 per cent disagree) than they are about people paying too much and not using services (32 per cent agree this is not fair and 39 per cent disagree). The latter is consistent with our earlier discussion about the popularity (or lack thereof) of tax rebates for those who opt out of public services.

As Table 1.8 shows, there are some significant differences of view between different groups. Graduates and those on higher incomes are less likely than other groups to emphasise self-interest as a rationale for the welfare state, perhaps because they are themselves less dependent upon it. For instance, 62 per cent of graduates agree that the best reason for paying taxes is that you "never know" when you might need benefits and services, compared with 78 per cent of those with no qualifications. Instead, graduates and the better off are more likely than others to emphasise altruistic or societal reasons. They also show the least concern about people contributing to services they do not use, or using services to which they have not contributed. By contrast, less advantaged social groups (those with no qualifications or on low incomes) are more likely to express concern about this perceived unfairness. For example, nearly six in ten of those with no qualifications feel it is not right that some benefit from services they have not contributed towards, double the proportion found among graduates. This difference is perhaps surprising, as less advantaged groups, on average, will be paying less into the system than they are getting out of it.

Table 1.8 also shows the views of Labour and Conservative identifiers. They differ remarkably little in their views on whether it is right that taxes paid by a majority help a minority in need, and that a healthy and well-educated society requires taxation (views which attract very high levels of support from both groups). However, Conservative supporters are more likely than Labour supporters to think that it is wrong that some people benefit from services they haven't helped to pay for (56 and 38 per cent respectively) and that it is unfair that some people pay a lot more in taxes and hardly use services (40 and 21 per cent respectively).

These findings suggest that a mixture of motives – self-interest, altruism and societal benefit – helps to sustain support for the welfare state across all socio-economic groups, including those who stand to benefit least from it. However, younger groups, whilst still subscribing to these principles, seem to be less attached to them than older age groups, though it is not possible to tell whether this distinctiveness of view will remain with them as they get older.

Table 1.8 Attitudes influencing support for welfare state by subgroup

% who agree	Right that taxes help needy	Pay taxes for healthy society	Pay taxes as never know when need services	Wrong some pay more and don't use services	Wrong some use services haven't paid for	Base
All	69	84	74	32	48	*1737*
Age						
18–34	58	78	69	38	46	*384*
55+	76	87	80	31	54	*691*
Party						
Conservative	70	83	71	40	56	*474*
Labour	72	83	76	21	38	*543*
Education						
Degree	82	91	62	25	29	*312*
No quali-fications	68	78	78	36	58	*437*
Household income						
Low (below £15,000 p.a.)	67	79	78	36	48	*567*
High (£50,000 or more p.a.)	82	94	65	32	36	*205*

How do people's views on the issues explored in Table 1.8 relate to one another? Are there, for instance, some groups whose support for the welfare state is primarily based upon altruistic factors, and who pay little attention to self-interest or whether people have 'earned' help? To explore these issues further, we used people's responses to the questions shown in Table 1.8 to divide the population into different groups (or attitudinal clusters), each with a unique perspective on the welfare state. (For further details of this cluster analysis, see the appendix to this chapter.) In doing this, we also took account of people's responses to three other questions, each tapping key attitudes towards the welfare state and its beneficiaries:

> *If welfare benefits weren't so generous, people would learn to stand on their own two feet.*

> *Many people who get social security don't really deserve any help.*

> *Most people on the dole are fiddling in one way or another.*

Our analyses identified three key groups of interest. Their views are shown in Table 1.9. The first two groups both adhere to the basic principles of the British welfare state, but have different views concerning the basis for people's entitlement. The 'Samaritans' comprise around 30 per cent of the population. They believe that people are entitled because they are in need, and are inclined to be inclusive: people have a responsibility to help others in need, which does not depend on them having paid their 'dues' or being 'deserving' cases. Two-thirds of this group do not think it is wrong that people should benefit from services they haven't helped to pay for, contrary to the predominant view among the other two clusters (as shown in Table 1.9). Samaritans also have few concerns about people abusing the system (only four per cent agree that "most people on the dole are fiddling in one way or another") and they are much less likely to believe that benefit claimants do not really need or deserve support.

We call the second (and largest) group 'Club Members'. They comprise around 45 per cent of the population, and are committed to a system of social insurance, whereby taxes paid by the majority help to support those in need. The majority of this group appear to accept that this will entail an element of redistribution from those most able to pay more to those most in need. (Only a minority think it is unfair that some people pay a lot more in taxes and hardly use these services.) However, their support is conditional on the recipients having fulfilled their part of the bargain by contributing what they reasonably can and only drawing out what they reasonably need. Unlike the Samaritans, they are more likely to make a distinction between the 'deserving' and 'undeserving' poor. They are also much more likely to have concerns about fraud and about people taking advantage of the system. This membership model is more exclusive; entitlement is dependent on people's behaviour, as well as need. The welfare state is seen as a kind of club: if you don't abide by the rules, then you should not necessarily expect to enjoy the benefits of membership. The more anxious people are about fraud, abuse or unrestricted use of the club, the more inclined they are to interpret the rules strictly.

The third group, 'Robinson Crusoes', comprise around 25 per cent of the population. They are less wedded to the welfare state and much more resistant to the redistribution implicit within the current system. Unlike the other two groups, they feel (often strongly) that it is unfair that some people pay a lot more in taxes and hardly use the services they have helped to fund, and feel much more strongly that people should be paying their own way. Their motto is self-reliance: people should look after themselves more, rather than relying on the generosity of others. For instance, 93 per cent believe "if welfare benefits were lower, people would learn to stand on their own two feet". Those who are claiming unemployment benefits are generally seen to be fiddling the system.

Table 1.9 Samaritans, Club Members and Robinson Crusoes: different views of the welfare state

	Samaritans	Club Members	Robinson Crusoes
% of overall population	29	45	26
It's only right that taxes paid by majority help those in need	%	%	%
Agree	94	70	57
Neither agree / disagree	4	21	17
Disagree	2	9	26
It's not fair that some people pay a lot more in tax and hardly use the services	%	%	%
Agree	10	23	75
Neither agree / disagree	19	34	16
Disagree	71	43	9
It's not right that some people benefit from services they haven't helped to pay for	%	%	%
Agree	13	47	91
Neither agree / disagree	20	34	7
Disagree	67	19	2
If welfare benefits weren't so generous, people would learn to stand on their own two feet	%	%	%
Agree	4	49	93
Neither agree / disagree	26	42	4
Disagree	70	9	3
Most people on the dole are fiddling in one way or another	%	%	%
Agree	4	42	86
Neither agree / disagree	28	51	12
Disagree	68	8	2
Base	*444*	*669*	*380*

How well represented are these groups in different sections of British society? Club Members are the largest group, but all three are well represented among different income groups, classes, and supporters of the main political parties. Samaritans are most heavily represented among graduates (50 per cent), means-tested benefit recipients (45 per cent), Labour Party supporters (39 per cent), those with very high incomes (38 per cent), professional and managerial classes (37 per cent), and the middle-aged (33 per cent). By contrast, Robinson Crusoes are disproportionately found among those without educational qualifications (34 per cent) and Conservative supporters (33 per cent). The differences between those with degrees and those with fewer or no educational qualifications is particularly striking – only 11 per cent of degree-holders fall into the Robinson Crusoe cluster and only 19 per cent of those without educational qualifications are Samaritans. Lack of education may be a barrier to understanding how the welfare state operates and to appreciating the broader societal arguments for its existence. As a result, those without qualifications may place more weight on individualistic notions of self-reliance and self-sufficiency, although such views are by no means confined to this group.

  These attitudinal clusters are closely associated with (and may help to explain) people's explicit and implicit attitudes to redistribution. Table 1.10 shows each group's responses to some of the key questions about redistribution discussed earlier in this chapter. Not surprisingly, Samaritans appear to be the most enthusiastic supporters of the welfare state, and are also the most strongly in favour of greater redistribution: 41 per cent agree the government should redistribute incomes from the better-off to those who are less well off (while 29 per cent disagree). By contrast, only 24 per cent of Robinson Crusoes agree with this statement (while 53 per cent disagree). Samaritans are also more likely to support more government spending on welfare benefits for the poor than Robinson Crusoes (59 and 24 per cent respectively) and increased taxes and spending on health, education and social benefits (66 and 38 per cent respectively). The views of Club Members are more ambivalent: they are more likely to support redistributive policies than Robinson Crusoes and even more likely not to oppose them.

Table 1.10 Club Members and Robinson Crusoes: attitudes to redistribution

% agree government should ...	Samaritans	Club Members	Robinson Crusoes
... redistribute incomes from the better-off to those who are less well off	41	28	24
... spend more on welfare benefits for the poor	59	31	24
... increase taxes and spend more on health, education and social benefits	66	50	38
Base	*444*	*669*	*380*

So far we have found that support for redistribution varies considerably according to a person's views about the rationale for the welfare state and the conduct of its beneficiaries. However, when we combine people's views about taxation with their views about entitlement to benefits (as described earlier in relation to Table 1.6) we find that these differences are much less apparent. A larger proportion of Robinson Crusoes than of the other two groups are in favour of earnings-related benefits and regressive taxation, but even among this group the vast majority (84 per cent) favour tax and spending policies that are clearly redistributive.

Attitudes to inequality

We might also expect to find that people's views about redistribution are related to their feelings about the underlying causes of social inequality. To assess this, we asked respondents how much they agreed or disagreed with the statement "inequality continues to exist because it benefits the rich and powerful". Overall, nearly half (48 per cent) either "agree" or "strongly agree" with this view. As Table 1.11 shows, this group have distinctive views about redistribution as well. Four in ten of those who "agree" with this statement (and nearly six in ten of those who "strongly agree") think that the government should redistribute incomes from the better-off to those who are less well off, more than double the rate found among those who disagree with this explanation of inequality.

Table 1.11 Views on the underlying causes of inequality and attitudes to redistribution

% agree government should ...	Inequality continues to exist because it benefits the rich and powerful[*]			
	Strongly agree	Agree	Neither agree nor disagree	Disagree
... redistribute incomes from the better-off to those who are less well off	58	40	18	16
... spend more on welfare benefits for the poor	61	44	30	22
... increase taxes and spend more on health, education and social benefits	56	53	52	46
Base	197	631	420	298

[*] The number of respondents who strongly disagree with this statement is very small (40 out of 1737), so they were omitted from this analysis

However, while those with egalitarian views are much more likely than others to support redistribution and greater welfare spending on the poor, they are only marginally more likely to support increased spending on the welfare state as a whole (the final row in Table 1.11). In other words, they seem particularly to favour direct, and more strongly redistributive, transfers of income between high and low income groups, as opposed to in-kind and less overtly redistributive spending on public services.

Where do the boundaries of the welfare state lie?

As we have already seen, one view of the welfare state is as a kind of national 'club' into which people pay what they can and, having done so, are then entitled to seek help from it when they need to. Associated with this view is a feeling of resentment towards those who benefit without having contributed. So we conclude by exploring where the boundaries of this "club" should lie. We examined this by asking people whether there are *any* circumstances in which it would be right to limit a person's access to the services and benefits provided by the welfare state. We focused on three scenarios: "a person who can't find a job at the moment", "a person with an on-going illness that needs medical treatment", and "a 65 year old man who is not working". For each scenario, respondents were presented with a range of possible reasons as to why a person's access to the relevant services or benefits might be restricted – for example, that they "had recently come to Britain hoping to find work here", or "had lived in Britain all their life but not paid much in taxes because they were bringing up children". In each case, there was always the option of saying that "it would never be right" to limit access to these benefits or services.[12]

These questions allow us to examine how wide or narrow a view people have of the appropriate pool across which redistribution should occur. As Table 1.12 shows, one key issue relates to different types of immigrant. Here, people make a very clear distinction between recent economic migrants and other immigrants. A majority, for instance, feel that a person who has recently come to Britain to find work should *not* be entitled to receive unemployment benefits (59 per cent) or a state pension (57 per cent), whilst 41 per cent feel their access to free NHS treatment should also be restricted. Likewise, 43 per cent feel that people who come to Britain as visitors should not be entitled to free NHS treatment. On the other hand, fewer than 30 per cent of respondents think it is right to limit access to any of these benefits or services to political refugees or to immigrants who settled in Britain more than two years ago. What is perhaps surprising is the implication that people do not have to live in this country for very long before they are considered to be part of the 'welfare club'.

Another issue involves whether or not a person has paid much in taxes, either because they have been unemployed for long periods or have been caring for children. In these cases, only a small minority feel access should be restricted, especially where they had been looking after children. What appears to matter is not whether they have paid sufficient contributions, but whether they have done what they reasonably could in their particular circumstances. Thus, the one clear exception relates to cases where the person has not actively been looking for work. In these circumstances, nearly eight in ten feel it is right to limit entitlement to unemployment benefit. Similarly, in cases where someone might be held to be 'responsible' for their own ill health (due to a heavy smoking or drinking habit), there is a smaller, though still significant, proportion (25 per cent) who favour restricting access to free NHS treatment.

Table 1.12 also suggests that people are less inclined to limit people's access to free health care than to cash benefits. In no case is there a majority of respondents in favour of restricting free NHS treatment to any particular group, though only 26 per cent say it would never be right to limit access in any situation. The ranking of the different categories is very similar between the three areas. The only minor exception is that people seem more willing to restrict people's access to unemployment benefits on the grounds that they can afford to look after themselves (31 per cent) than they are to restrict their access to the state pension (18 per cent) or free health care (17 per cent).

Table 1.12 Views on limits of welfare state coverage

	Free NHS treatment	State pension	Unemploy- ment benefit
% who say it would *never* be right to limit access	26	21	4
% who say it would be right to limit a person's access in the following circumstances...			
... they were not actively looking for work	n/a	n/a	78
... they had come to Britain as visitors	43	n/a	n/a
... they recently came to Britain to find work	41	57	59
... their illness was due to a heavy smoking or drinking habit	24	n/a	n/a
... they were not born in Britain, but settled here more than two years ago	16	29	22
... they recently came to Britain because they were in danger at home	17	26	21
... they could afford to look after themselves	17	18	31
... they had not paid much in taxes because they had been unemployed for a long time	9	16	25
... they had not paid much in taxes because they were bringing up children	4	6	9
... some other reason	2	1	2

Base: 1737

n/a = not asked

These views about the boundaries of the welfare state seem to be widely shared across different sections of the population, including between people with different levels of income or political affiliations. The biggest divergence is between the different attitudinal clusters identified in the previous section. 'Samaritans', who are more inclusive, are the least inclined to restrict people's access to public services or state benefits. For example, 34 per cent of this group think that visitors to the UK should not have access to free NHS treatment, 28 per cent would restrict the entitlement of recent economic migrants, and only 11 per cent would feel this about people whose illness is due to a heavy smoking or drinking habit. For 'Robinson Crusoes', the corresponding figures are 55 per cent, 60 per cent and 36 per cent.

Conclusions

What is most striking about people's responses to questions about inequality and redistribution is that whilst nearly three-quarters of respondents say that the gap between those on high and low incomes is too large, less than a third agree that government should *redistribute* incomes from one group to the other. This chapter has examined how these views are reflected in people's attitudes towards the welfare state and the taxes that fund it – the principal means for achieving redistribution. When we combine people's views about these issues, nearly nine in ten favour tax and spending policies whose overall impact is clearly redistributive, including most of those who, when asked directly, are not explicitly in favour of redistribution. The most popular combination, applying to over a quarter of respondents, is proportional taxation with flat-rate or universal benefits, which is quite strongly redistributive. A further 62 per cent of respondents select options that are even more strongly redistributive, involving either progressive taxation and/or means-tested benefits. Consequently, there appears to be strong support for redistribution as a *by-product* of spending and taxing in the ways that people want, even though redistribution is not normally seen to be a primary objective of the system. Indeed, many people seem unaware of the likely redistributive effects of the current system.

Qualitative research has shown that there is general support for the principle of the welfare state as a system that supports people when they need help – whether or not they have enough money to pay – and that spreads the cost of doing so according to people's ability to pay. When the implications of such a system are brought out, most people accept its redistributive effects, although there is often resentment towards those who are seen to be abusing the system by not contributing what they reasonably can and drawing out more than they reasonably need. The analysis in this chapter suggests that this adequately describes the views of about half of the population (the 'Club Members'), but that there are two other important perspectives. The 'Samaritans', who comprise around 30 per cent of the population, are much more inclusive: people have a responsibility to others in need, which does not depend on them having paid their 'dues'. This group are the strongest supporters of the welfare state and the most likely to support overtly redistributive policies. The third group, the 'Robinson Crusoes', comprise around 25 per cent of the population and are much more resistant to the redistribution implicit within the current system, believing that people should look after themselves more, rather than relying on the generosity of others.

These findings have several implications for how we evaluate New Labour's policies in relation to poverty and inequality, though these conclusions are necessarily tentative. They suggest there is in fact a much stronger consensus in favour of redistributive policies than is apparent in people's responses to direct questions about redistribution. Even among those least sympathetic to the welfare state, there appears to be a high level of implicit support for redistribution. Accordingly, a 'progressive' government could have the courage of its convictions in pushing forward a more redistributive agenda, given the strong underlying support for redistributive tax and spending policies. However, redistribution should be seen as a beneficial by-product of implementing tax and spending policies that each conform to the majority's perceptions of what is fair, rather than as a goal in itself. There appears to be a large group of people who do not respond to the 'language' of redistribution, despite having broadly similar views on the appropriate structure of tax and spending policies to those who are more explicitly in favour of redistribution.

New Labour have been criticised by some commentators on the left for pursuing a policy of 'redistribution by stealth' and not being sufficiently open about its redistributive policies. Though it may need to pursue redistributive tax and spending policies even more vigorously than it has to date if it is to make further progress towards its target of eradicating child poverty, our analysis suggests that an *explicitly* redistributive agenda would attract the support of a significant minority but may put off many people who might otherwise support these kinds of policies.

In presenting the case for more redistributive policies, the government may also need to tackle people's misperceptions about the current system, particularly in relation to taxation. The balance of opinion is that the tax system should be progressive or at least proportional, but the majority of people think the current system is more progressive than it actually is; they believe that higher income groups already pay a larger share of their income in tax than lower income groups, when in fact they pay a slightly lower share. A better understanding of the system should help to strengthen support for removing the regressive elements within the current system.

The challenge for the government over the next term is how to build a consensus around a more progressive agenda. For those of a 'Samaritan' bent, this should not be too difficult; provided the beneficiaries are recognised as being in need, redistributive policies are likely to be supported by this group. At the same time, though, it is important that policies are designed that are also consistent with the value and belief systems of 'Club Members' who comprise the largest share of the population. This would mean, for example, avoiding redistributive policies that are seen to reward people regardless of their behaviour. This is a difficult balance to strike, though the analysis in this chapter gives some clues as to where most people would draw the boundaries – and these are not as narrow as might be expected. Whilst many people would want to limit the access of recent economic migrants to welfare benefits and free health care, for example, immigrants do not have to live here for very long before they are widely considered to be part of the 'welfare club'.

So far, New Labour has emphasised work as the best route out of poverty and pursued a policy of 'quiet' redistribution to more 'deserving' groups, in particular families with children and pensioners. Whilst this approach has succeeded in bringing about a significant reduction in poverty among selected groups, it has had relatively little impact on overall poverty or inequality. The danger is that by being so careful to take on board people's perceived concerns about the welfare system (for instance, fraud, disincentives to work, and asylum seekers), New Labour may have given more credibility to those concerns, especially among its own supporters, perhaps limiting the scope to pursue more strongly redistributive policies in future.

Notes

1. Tony Blair did talk about the need to continue to redistribute "power, wealth, and opportunity" in a speech he made in 2002 (on publication of the government's annual "Opportunity for All" report), but has otherwise avoided using the term.
2. The term poverty is used to refer to households with relatively low incomes (usually defined as below 60 per cent of the median household disposable income, adjusted for differences in household composition). The term inequality is used to refer to the *spread* of incomes, as measured, for example, by the ratio of incomes of households near the top and bottom of the income range.
3. This qualitative work, also funded by the Economic and Social Research Council (ESRC), preceded the 2004 *British Social Attitudes* survey. It was essential both in informing the design of the questions and in helping us interpret some of the survey results.
4. Moreover, the question about "ordinary working people" is directly preceded by a question about whether "big business benefits owners at the expense of workers", which would reinforce the interpretation of this statement as offering a very class-based view of inequality.
5. In Figure 1.1, the first column, which considers responses to the question "would you say that the gap between those with high incomes and low incomes is too large, about right, or too small", is plotted as follows: "too large" as agree; "too small" as disagree; "about right" as neither agree nor disagree.
6. A similar set of questions about entitlement to a state pension has been asked on previous surveys, and found greater support for flat-rate payments (chosen by 69 to 77 per cent of respondents in six surveys from 1993 to 2001). Unlike the questions being considered in this chapter, however, these earlier questions did not offer any reason as to *why* a high earner might be entitled to a higher pension than a lower

earner (or *vice versa*), making it difficult to compare them to the question being considered here.

7. When a similar question has been asked in previous years (most recently in 2001), a significantly higher proportion than here said that people with high incomes should pay a larger share of their income in taxes – between two-thirds and three-quarters of all respondents. This difference is likely to reflect the way in which the two questions are framed, rather than a change in attitudes. The earlier question asked about those on "high" and "low" incomes without specifying what this meant, an approach we avoided in the 2004 question (which referred to people earning £15,000 and £30,000 a year). Respondents who in previous years said that those on high incomes should pay a larger share of their incomes in tax may have had in mind higher tax rates only for very high earners. Across the relatively narrow income range quoted in this year's, some of these people may feel that proportional taxation would be more appropriate.

8. As individuals' responses to these questions frequently varied depending on the type of benefit, people were classified according to their most common response (that is, the one chosen for at least two out of three of the benefits). A small number of individuals responded differently in each case and were omitted from this part of the analysis.

9. Though the British system – and the one apparently favoured by most respondents – appears more redistributive, it has been argued that this may not hold in the longer term. According to the 'paradox of redistribution', a greater emphasis on targeting may, over time, undermine broad-based support for social security, because it largely benefits the poor (who are politically weak), and may thus lead to lower levels of welfare spending and ultimately to less, not more, redistribution (Korpi and Palme, 1998).

10. These findings are somewhat at odds with people's responses to the first two questions shown in Table 1.7. If, as most people believe, those on higher incomes are paying a larger share of their income in taxes (and, by implication, a much larger absolute amount in taxes) and if, as they also believe, everyone benefits about the same from spending on public services, the logical conclusion of this is a substantial redistribution from the richest to the poorest households.

11. Multivariate analysis confirms that individuals' socio-economic characteristics, including their income, age and employment status, explain very little of the variation in their attitudes to redistribution.

12. The precise wording and layout of these questions can be found in the self-completion questionnaire appended to this Report (questions 40 to 42, version A self-completion questionnaire).

References

Adam, S., Brewer, M. and Wakefield, M. (2005), *Tax and Benefit changes: Who wins and who loses?*, IFS Election Briefing 2005, London: Institute of Fiscal Studies

Brook, L., Preston, I. and Hall, J. (1998), 'What Drives Support for Higher Public Spending?', in Taylor-Gooby, P. (ed.), *Choice and Public Policy*, Basingstoke: Macmillan

Conservative Party (2005), available at:
http://www.conservatives.com/tile.do?def=policy.topic.page&tabID=4

Diamond, P. and Giddens, A. (2005), 'The new egalitarianism: economic inequality in the UK', in Giddens, A. and Diamond, P. (eds.), *The New Egalitarianism*, Cambridge: Polity Press

Falkingham, J. and Hills, J (eds.) (1995), *The Dynamic of Welfare: The Welfare State and the Life Cycle*, Hemel Hempstead: Harvester Wheatsheaf

Fong, C., Bowles, S. and Gintis, H. (2004), 'Reciprocity, Self-interest, and the Welfare State', in Gerard-Varet, L.-A., Kolm, S. and Mercier Ythier, J. (eds.), *Handbook on the Economics of Giving, Reciprocity and Altruism*, Amsterdam: Elsevier

Hedges, A. (2005), *Perceptions of Redistribution: Report on exploratory qualitative research*, CASEpaper 96, London: STICERD, London School of Economics

Hickson, K. (2002), *From Them That Hath: New Labour and the question of redistribution*, London: The Catalyst Forum

Hills, J. (2004), *Inequality and the State*, Oxford: Oxford University Press

Korpi, W. and Palme, J. (1998), 'The Paradox of Redistribution and Strategies of Equality: Welfare State Institutions, Inequality, and Poverty in the Western Countries', *American Sociological Review*, **63(5)**: 661–687

Lakin, C. (2004), The effect of taxes and benefits on household income, 2002–03', *Economic Trends*, **607** (June)

Labour Party (1983), available at:
http://www.labour-party.org.uk/manifestos/1983/1983-labour-manifesto.shtml

Linos, K. and West, M. (2003), 'Self-interest, Social Beliefs, and Attitudes to Redistribution, *European Sociological Review*, **19(4)**: 393–409

Sefton, T. (2005), 'Inequality and Redistribution under New Labour', in Hills, J. and Stewart, K. (eds.), *A More Equal Society? New Labour, poverty, inequality and exclusion*, Bristol: The Policy Press

Sutherland, H. , Sefton, T. and Piachaud, D. (2003), *Poverty in Britain: The impact of government policy since 1997*, York: York Publishing Services on behalf of the Joseph Rowntree Foundation

Acknowledgements

The *National Centre for Social Research* and the *Centre for the Analysis of Social Exclusion* (CASE), an ESRC Research Centre at the London School of Economics, are grateful to the Economic and Social Research Council for funding this special module of questions on attitudes to redistribution.

The author is grateful to John Hills for advice and guidance throughout this research project, to Alison Park and Miranda Phillips for their work in designing this module, and to Alan Hedges and the editors for helpful comments on an earlier draft of this chapter.

Appendix

Factors underpinning support for the welfare state

The methodology employed was non-hierarchical cluster analysis, using the "cluster kmeans" option within the Stata statistical software package. Three clusters were specified, because this produced stable and meaningful categories that distinguished a 'core' group with similar views to those identified in the exploratory qualitative research ('Club Members') and two groups with more 'extreme' views either in support of, or opposed to, the welfare state and the principles underlying the system ('Samaritans' and 'Robinson Crusoes', respectively).

  Eight questions were included in the cluster analysis. These include the five questions from Table 1.8 and three additional questions that are designed to capture other possible concerns about the welfare system (e.g. about benefit fraud). Responses to each of these statements were treated as ordinal variables on a scale of one to five (one for "strongly agree", two for "agree", three for "neither agree/disagree", four for "disagree", and five for "strongly disagree"):

- *It's only right that taxes paid by the majority help support those in need.*
- *If we want to live in a healthy, well-educated society we have to be willing to pay the taxes to fund it.*
- *The best reason for paying taxes now is that you never know when you might need benefits and services yourself.*
- *It's not fair that some people pay a lot of money in tax and hardly use the services their taxes pay for.*
- *It's not right that people benefit from services that they haven't helped to pay for.*
- *If welfare benefits weren't so generous, people would learn to stand on their own two feet.*
- *Many people who get social security don't really deserve any help.*
- *Most people on the dole are fiddling in one way or another.*

The resulting categories were found to be closely associated in ways we might anticipate with views on a whole range of other issues, including attitudes towards redistribution, the role of private welfare, and the circumstances in which it might be reasonable to limit someone's access to benefits or public services. The 'Samaritans', for example, are the most strongly in favour of redistributive policies, the most opposed to private education and health care, and the least likely to favour limiting access to free health care, the state pension and unemployment benefits.

2 Work-life balance – still a 'women's issue'?

*Alice Bell and Caroline Bryson**

Since 1997, the New Labour government has pursued a number of policies based on the principle that Britain's long-term social and economic interests will best be served by maximising the number of adults in paid employment. To this end, steps have been taken to make work more attractive by promoting ways of working that enable employees to combine paid work with other aspects of their lives more effectively. This trend accords with several European Union directives promoting choice for workers over working arrangements.

   On the face of it, this approach appears to be in line with public opinion. More than three-quarters of the employees who responded to the DTI's *Second Work-Life Balance Study* (Stevens *et al.*, 2004) felt that everyone should be able to balance their work and home lives in the way they want (78 per cent), while there was almost unanimous agreement that people work better when they are able to balance work with home and other aspects of their lives (95 per cent). However, employers do not necessarily agree, and employer groups (such as the Confederation of British Industry) and small business organisations have expressed concern about the impact that increased flexible working opportunities might have on competitiveness and economic performance (Dex and Scheibl, 2002). The government's former Work-Life Balance Campaign, launched in 2000, sought to raise awareness among employers of the advantages of allowing staff to work flexibly in ways that successfully reconcile the needs of both parties, and research evidence suggests that flexible working arrangements (such as part-time and term-time working, flexible hours, job shares and so on) can have benefits for business, in relation to turnover, motivation, commitment, employee relations, recruitment, absenteeism and productivity (Woodland *et al.*, 2003). So it seems that flexible working can be a good thing for employees and employers alike.

* Alice Bell is a Senior Researcher and Caroline Bryson is a Research Director, both at the *National Centre for Social Research.*

In addition, a debate has been burgeoning over recent years about the importance for families of allowing parents the flexibility to combine paid work with caring for children. Evidence has shown that working long hours, or being at work outside standard hours, can have a negative effect on family life, as parents have less time available to spend with their children or, in attempting to create time for children, miss out on time spent as a couple (La Valle *et al.*, 2002). Given the suggestion that the length, frequency and nature of parental interactions can have a significant impact on children's cognitive and behavioural development (Lefebvre and Merrigan, 1998; Zick *et al.*, 2001), this can be seen as a matter of particular urgency. And indeed, much of the legislation associated with New Labour's work-life balance agenda has focused specifically on families, including the right, introduced in 2003, for parents of children aged under six and disabled children under 18 to request flexible working from their employers.

To what extent has government policy in this respect moved beyond employers' – and even *employees'* – current attitudes? Are employers really making flexible work opportunities available equally to both sexes? Do both sexes want such opportunities? The DTI employees' survey showed that, while a significant number of parents were requesting flexible working, some employees had doubts over whether various flexible working options would be feasible in their type of job. Men were more likely than women to express such concerns, and the perceived feasibility of taking up certain options also varied by job type and organisation size. In addition, relatively high proportions of employees felt that adopting such arrangements might have a negative effect on their career prospects – men and managers were most likely to report such concerns (Stevens *et al.*, 2004). These findings give rise to the question of whether, in reality, it is mainly women – and particularly *mothers* – who want flexible working arrangements, as they struggle to cope with the 'triple burden' of work, home and childcare; or whether, in fact, men also welcome opportunities for flexible working, allowing them the chance to play a more active role at home. Put simply: does work-life balance matter as much to men?

This, in turn, raises a more fundamental question as to whether flexible working is really the 'answer' to helping employees achieve a good work-life balance, or whether other factors could be equally, if not more, important. After all, previous *British Social Attitudes* reports have shown that, while attitudes towards gender roles have continued to move steadily in favour of equality of the sexes at home and at work, a corresponding redistribution of family and household responsibilities – including childcare – has not been forthcoming (Crompton *et al.*, 2003). This suggests that a more complex kind of shift might be necessary if the crucial balance between employees' work and home lives is truly to be achieved.

This chapter uses data from the 2004 *British Social Attitudes* survey to explore these issues. We begin by examining the reported availability of a range of flexible working practices among British employees, and any changes in the extent and nature of what has been reported over the past 10 years.[1] We then consider the numbers and types of people who make use of flexible working options, as well as those who would like to do so if such opportunities were available to them.

In the second half of the chapter, we move on to look at the extent to which different types of employees achieve a good work-life balance, considering a range of factors related to time, stress, tiredness and people's capacity to fulfil home and work responsibilities. We explore whether and how flexible working options influence the levels of work-life balance employees achieve, as well as whether there is any relationship between flexible working arrangements, work-life balance and employees' overall satisfaction with their work and family lives.

Flexibility at work

In this section we explore issues around the availability and use of, and the demand for, flexible working arrangements. We begin by considering the various arrangements that might be considered as entailing 'flexible working'. We then assess how far working arrangements have changed in the past decade, focusing particularly on who has *access* to flexible working options, who *uses* them and who would *like* them.

What is 'flexible working'?

The *British Social Attitudes* survey collects information about a wide range of different working practices and arrangements that can be considered to come under the broad banner of 'flexible working'.[2] These fall into two key categories. The first comprises a variety of options best described as 'fixed', that is, practices that are agreed by employers and employees at a particular point in time and applied in a regular way on an ongoing basis thereafter. While employers display 'flexibility' *in offering* such options (and, very likely, in making the necessary arrangements to be able to offer such options), they are not necessarily required to behave flexibly in any significant way once the initial arrangement has been established, for example by reacting in a flexible manner to occasional and/or unforeseen events. The 'fixed' options we asked about were:

- *Part-time working, allowing you to work less than the full working day*[3]
- *Flexible hours, so that you can adjust your own daily working hours*
- *Job-sharing schemes, where part-timers share one full-time job*
- *Working from home at least some of the time*
- *Term-time contracts, allowing parents special time off during school holidays*

The survey also asked about a second set of options which, if available, can be seen as forming part of an employer's 'flexible ethos'. Having such an ethos is distinct from offering fixed flexible working options, as it does not require employers to be flexible about employees' permanent, ongoing working arrangements, but rather requires them to act flexibly when occasional unforeseen events occur. The 'flexible ethos' options we asked about were:

- *Time off, either paid or unpaid, to care for sick children*
- *Time off, either paid or unpaid, to care for people other than children*
- *Time off, either paid or unpaid, to care for children for reasons other than their sickness*

The distinction between being offered fixed flexible working options and working for an employer with a flexible ethos is intuitive, both because of the different types of flexibility required from employers, and because, by virtue of being either ongoing or occasional in nature, their impact on employees is likely to be different. This distinction is confirmed by factor analysis, which shows that the actual availability of such arrangements falls into two distinct 'dimensions' which correspond to our distinction between 'fixed' and 'flexible ethos' practices.

For each of the flexible working options described earlier, we asked employees "is this available to you at your workplace?". In responding, we asked them to choose between four options:

> **Not** *available – and I* **would not** *use it if it were*
> **Not** *available – but I* **would** *use it if it were*
> *Available – but I* **have not** *used it and am not likely to do so in the next year*
> *Available – and I* **have** *used it or am likely to do so in the next year*

These options allow us to assess levels of reported availability, actual use, unmet demand and overall demand (actual use plus unmet demand).[4] To help in analysis, we developed a scale for each of our two dimensions, based on a count of the number of options available to the employee. Thus, the 'fixed options' scale runs from zero (no options available) to five and the 'flexible ethos' scale from zero to three. Throughout the following sections, we report both on these scales and on the individual arrangements, as appropriate. Further details of the scales can be found in the appendix to this chapter.

The availability of flexible working

A similar set of questions – for fixed options at least – was asked in the 1994 *British Social Attitudes* survey, allowing us to assess the extent to which the reported availability of flexible working has changed over time. After all, since

1994 relevant new legislation has been introduced, and changes have taken place in attitudes towards gender roles and the appropriate balance between work and home life. Table 2.1 shows the current reported availability of flexible working options among employees and, where possible, responses to the same questions from 1994.

The most common fixed flexible work option reported is part-time working (shorter than the full day), available to just under two-thirds of people. Working from home and term-time work are the least common (each cited by 24 per cent). Since 1994, there have been significant increases in the reported levels of availability for all fixed flexible working options, although their rank order has not changed. The biggest percentage point increase has occurred among those options already most common in 1994 – part-time work and flexible hours. The latter, for instance, was reported by just over a third of employees in 1994, but is now available to a half. There have also been large proportional rises in the reported availability of the least common arrangements. The availability of term-time working arrangements has risen by two-thirds from 14 to 24 per cent, job sharing has risen by more than a half from 24 to 38 per cent, and the option of working from home has risen by a half from 16 to 24 per cent. Overall, the mean number of fixed flexible working options now reported is 1.99, up from 1.39 in 1994. And, while three in ten employees reported no such options being available at their workplaces in 1994, this now applies only to two in ten.

Table 2.1 Reported availability of flexible working, 1994 and 2004

% reporting available	1994	2004
Fixed flexible work		
Part-time work	49	64
Flexible hours	35	49
Job-sharing	24	38
Working from home	16	24
Term-time work	14	24
At least one of above available	68	82
Mean number available	1.39	1.99
Flexible ethos		
Time off for sick children	–	68
Time off to care for others	–	55
Time off for children for other reasons	–	53
At least one of above available	–	73
Mean number available	–	1.75
Base	*1447*	*1020*

Base: employees

In 2004, reported availability of the more *ad hoc* arrangements (denoting the 'flexible ethos' of the employer) is relatively high in comparison to some of the fixed arrangements. Over half of all employees say that their employer offers time off for each of the reasons given. However, it is notable that a relatively high proportion of employees do not know whether these arrangements are available (11 to 15 per cent say "don't know" to each of the ethos questions, compared with one to seven per cent for the fixed option questions). This suggests that employers tend to be less explicit about their policies on time off for occasional and unforeseen reasons, meaning that employees only find out about them if they have reason to make a request.

Similar increases were found among those *employers and employees* interviewed as part of the 2004 Workplace Employment Relations Survey (WERS) (Kersley *et al.*, 2005).[5]

These figures certainly provide evidence that more British employees have access to flexible working arrangements than they did a decade ago. But what types of employees are currently being offered flexible arrangements? Are they those who have been targeted in recent government reforms, namely parents of children under six?[6] And are they, as is traditionally expected, more often working mothers, or is flexible working now being offered to a wider range of employees? Tables 2.2a and 2.2b compare the available flexible working arrangements reported in 2004 by fathers, mothers and other male and female employees with comparable figures for 1994.[7]

There is clearly a connection between availability and gender here, with mothers in particular standing out from the other three groups. Women in general, and mothers in particular, are more likely than men to report the availability of both fixed options and employer ethos indicators: mothers report an average of 2.48 fixed options as being available, for example, compared with the 2.14 reported by female non-parents and 1.65 and 1.71 by fathers and male non-parents respectively (the differences between women and men, and between mothers and all other groups, are statistically significant). Average numbers of reported ethos indicators followed the same overall pattern. Although parenthood is related to the number of options reported as available to women, the same is not true among men; fathers and other men report very similar levels, usually lower than women.

These findings can be interpreted in a number of ways. They may indicate that women, and mothers in particular, have jobs in which flexible working is more feasible or more likely to be offered, or that they are specifically seeking out employers who take a flexible approach. Alternatively, perhaps employers with a greater proportion of female employees have become more flexible (more quickly). Certainly, WERS findings support this latter hypothesis, showing that, with one exception (homeworking), employees in workplaces where at least half the workforce were female were more likely than employees elsewhere to report that a number of flexible working practices were available to them (Kersley *et al.*, 2005). Nevertheless, it is important to keep an eye on the distinction between *awareness* (what we are measuring here) and actual availability: we might hypothesise, for example, that women have a more active interest in flexible work options, perhaps because, as other research has shown, they tend to bear the greater burden in terms of childcare and domestic responsibilities. Consequently, women might be more aware than men of the flexible working opportunities available to them.

Table 2.2a Reported availability of fixed flexible arrangements by gender and parenthood, 1994 and 2004

	Father		Mother		Male non-parent		Female non-parent	
% reporting available	**1994**	**2004**	**1994**	**2004**	**1994**	**2004**	**1994**	**2004**
Fixed flexible work								
Part-time work	28	46	80	81	30	52	63	75
Flexible hours	37	50	45	55	30	47	34	49
Job-sharing	15	26	32	55	15	27	33	44
Working from home	20	29	17	24	17	26	14	20
Term-time work	7	15	20	34	12	18	17	27
At least one of above available	58	71	88	96	53	74	78	87
Mean number available	1.07	1.65	1.94	2.48	1.04	1.71	1.60	2.14
Base	*242*	*145*	*286*	*215*	*461*	*327*	*332*	*458*

Base: employees

Table 2.2b Reported availability of flexible ethos arrangements by gender and parenthood

	Father	Mother	Male non-parent	Female non-parent
% reporting available				
Flexible ethos				
Time off for sick children	65	82	60	68
Time off to care for others	44	66	49	58
Time off for children, other reasons	49	67	48	51
At least one of above available	71	85	64	75
Mean number available	1.58	2.14	1.57	1.77
Base	*145*	*215*	*327*	*458*

Base: employees

There were substantial increases in reported availability of fixed flexible working options among all employees since 1994, irrespective of whether they were parents. The one exception to this relates to the availability of part-time working to mothers, which did not change. These changes have not affected the overall pattern, however, with women – and particularly mothers – consistently reporting higher levels of availability than men both now and in 1994.

However, the largest proportional increase in the availability of flexible working options took place among men without children, among whom the proportion reporting at least one fixed flexible work option as available rose by a half (20 percentage points). The second greatest increase, of about a fifth (13 percentage points), took place among fathers. So, in terms of reported availability at least, men may be starting to catch up with women.

Despite recent government policy, employees with children under six are no more likely than those with older children to say that flexible working options are available to them now than they were in 1994. Moreover, while there was an increase in the mean number of fixed flexible working options reported as available to employees between 1994 and 2004, the increase was no greater among parents with children under six than among parents of older children (the mean number of options increased from 1.55 to 2.12 and 1.49 to 2.12 respectively). This could suggest that the legal right for parents of young children to request flexible working, introduced in 2003, is not associated with the increases we have seen in the reported availability of flexible working options, although it is also possible that the legislation has played a role in encouraging employers to offer flexible working options more widely.

Earlier we speculated that women (and mothers in particular) might be more likely than men to have the sorts of jobs in which flexible working is common, accounting for some of the differences in the reported availability of flexible arrangements that we have observed. In order to understand the extent to which certain employee characteristics relate to the reported availability of flexible working arrangements, we undertook regression analysis. This allows us to assess separately the relationship between parenthood, gender and the reported availability of flexible working arrangements, taking into account differences in job type. Further details of this form of analysis can be found in Appendix I of this Report. We used the two scales (fixed flexibility and employer ethos) for this analysis.

Figure 2.1 summarises the findings from this multivariate analysis, showing the factors that emerged as being significantly associated with whether or not an employee reports the availability of flexible working arrangements. The full results can be found in the appendix to this chapter. The analysis shows that having a public sector job, and working as a manager or professional, are both significantly associated with having fixed flexible working arrangements (although neither is significantly associated with the employer having a more flexible ethos). So public sector workers, especially those in professional or managerial posts, are more likely than their colleagues in the private sector to be offered flexible working arrangements. Educational achievement, and the size of the establishment that the respondent works within are also associated with the availability of both types of flexible working arrangement. Those with a qualification at GCSE/O level or above are more likely to report availability of fixed flexible working arrangements than those with no qualifications. Intriguingly, there also appear to be regional differences, with employees in Scotland, and in the Midlands, being significantly *less* likely than those in the south of England to report the range of options we classify as relating to an employers' flexible ethos. Most importantly for our purposes, this analysis shows that, even when we control for these (and other) factors, women are more likely than men to be offered both fixed and more *ad hoc* flexibility in their work, regardless of the sector or level of their jobs. Although Tables 2.2a and 2.2b suggest that *mothers* are more likely than women without children to report the availability of flexible working options, these two groups did *not* differ significantly to one another in our regression. This is likely to reflect the fact that these groups differ in relation to some of the social and occupational characteristics included in the analysis; once these differences are taken into account, mothers and non-mothers do not report different experiences. All else being equal, therefore, it is being *female* (as opposed to being a mother) which makes employees particularly likely to report flexible working opportunities. Later, we will see whether this reflects employees' wishes or whether it could in fact signify unmet demand for flexible working among men.

Figure 2.1 Factors associated with reported availability of flexible working arrangements

Fixed flexibility options	Flexible ethos options
Gender and parenthood	Gender and parenthood
Highest educational qualification	Highest educational qualification
Manager/professional	Region
Size of establishment	Size of establishment
Sector	

So far we have seen that the reported availability of flexible working options has increased over the last decade, and that women have considerably greater access to these kinds of opportunity than men, independently of differences in job level and sector. We now turn to examine whether these same patterns emerge when we focus on the take up of flexible working options.

Take up of flexible working

Reported levels of availability of various flexible working arrangements provide a key measure of employees' ability to organise their working lives alongside their commitments at home. However, availability in itself may have little real effect on employees' lives if barriers exist which prevent them from making use of the arrangements available to them. So, in this section we focus on *take up* of flexible working options, looking at the extent to which usage is associated with gender and parenthood, as well as with the age of employees' children, and with the sector and level of their work.

Here, we focus on take up of what we have called fixed flexible working options, our interest being in those employees who have used such arrangements, or who think they will do so in the next year.[8] Table 2.3 shows the use of various flexible working options among employees, comparing 2004 with 1994. The first two columns present figures as a proportion of *all employees*. This allows us to identify changes in the overall proportions of employees who use flexible working arrangements. The third and fourth columns show the findings for each option *as a proportion of those employees who report it as available to them*. These figures help us to identify the extent to which any changes in the numbers of employees using flexible working arrangements can be explained simply by increases in the numbers for whom these arrangements are available. In other words, are we simply seeing a static proportion of employees taking up these arrangements if offered them, or are we also seeing an increase in take up rates?

Between 1994 and 2004, there was an increase in the proportions of employees using flexible working options. In 1994, 47 per cent of employees used at least one of the arrangements; by 2004 this proportion had increased by 10 percentage points to 57 per cent. The greatest percentage point rises were found for part-time work (working a shorter day), which rose from 22 per cent to 30 per cent, and in working flexible hours (27 to 33 per cent). Meanwhile, the proportion of employees job-sharing more than doubled in the 10-year period (from four per cent to nine per cent).[9] By contrast, the third and fourth columns of the table, which present use as a proportion of reported availability, show very little change (and, in relation to flexible hours, show a significant decline in the proportion taking up this option). The only flexible working option that showed a significant increase by this measure over the decade was job-sharing. This suggests that the increased levels of use among employees as a whole largely reflects the greater availability of flexible working, rather than increased take up by employees with access to flexible working arrangements.

Table 2.3 Use of fixed flexible working options, 1994 and 2004[10]

	All employees		Employees with option available	
% reporting use	1994	2004	1994	2004
Part-time work	22	30	44	47
Flexible hours	27	33	76	67
Job-sharing	4	9	15	24
Working from home	12	16	75	69
Term-time work	6	9	40	37
At least one of above used	47	57	n.a.	n.a.
Mean number used	0.7	0.97	n.a.	n.a.

Base for columns 1 and 2: employees
Base for columns 3 and 4: employees who report each option as available
n.a. = not applicable

Earlier we established that women, particularly mothers, are more likely to be offered flexible working arrangements than fathers or other male employees (although, as we saw, the difference between mothers and women without children disappears when we take account of some of the key social and occupational differences between these two groups of women). So we turn now to examine whether this same division is reflected in the types of employees who take up these options. Table 2.4 shows the differential use of flexible working options between men and women. It clearly illustrates that the key predictor of whether or not an employee makes use of flexible working provision is motherhood, as opposed to gender or parenthood. For instance, 83 per cent of mothers have used at least one flexible working option, compared with 57 per cent of female non-parents, and 47 per cent of fathers. This is supported by regression analysis (reported in the appendix to this chapter), which confirms that mothers are significantly more likely than other women, fathers and other men to use flexible working arrangements, even when a variety of job characteristics are taken into account. Once their gender and parenthood is taken into account, whether an employee works in the public or private sector is not significantly linked with their use of flexible working arrangements (even though such arrangements are more readily available to the former than the latter). However, managers and professionals are more likely than other employees to use such arrangements.

Table 2.4 Use of fixed flexible working options by gender and parenthood, 1994 and 2004

	Father		Mother		Male non-parent		Female non-parent	
% reporting use	1994	2004	1994	2004	1994	2004	1994	2004
Part-time work	6	9	54	61	4	16	29	36
Flexible hours	30	34	35	44	21	30	25	30
Job-sharing	*	2	8	17	*	5	6	11
Working from home	16	21	14	18	13	18	9	12
Term-time work	4	7	15	21	1	3	6	8
At least one of above used	43	47	72	83	31	45	51	57
Mean number used	0.56	0.74	1.27	1.61	0.40	0.71	0.75	0.97
Base	*242*	*145*	*286*	*215*	*461*	*327*	*458*	*332*

Base: employees

Table 2.4 also compares take up of flexible working between 1994 and 2004. Although the trend among all four groups is towards increased use, only mothers and male non-parents are now significantly more likely to have used at least one flexible working option than they were a decade previously (mothers increased by 11 percentage points, and men without children by 14). This differs somewhat from our earlier findings on reported availability of flexible work, which saw the biggest increases among men with and without children. There too, however, it was male non-parents who started from the lowest base and underwent the greatest increase. These two findings together suggest that the growing use and awareness of flexible working options among men are occurring not as a result of changes in parenting roles or the nature of fathering, but rather in response to a more general shift towards the diversification of working patterns for all employees, and – in this sense at least – greater equality between the sexes. The differences between fathers and men without children in terms of take up (but not in access or awareness) also suggests that there might be barriers which make it harder for fathers to make use of those flexible working options made available to them.

In line with our earlier findings on reported availability, employees with children under six are no more likely than other parents to make use of flexible working arrangements. And the increase in the mean number of fixed flexible work options used by parents of children aged under six between 1994 and 2004 was no greater than that which took place among parents of older children.

Demand for flexible working

It appears that significantly more employees are being offered flexible working arrangements than they were a decade ago. What we do not yet know, however, is how this relates to the level of *demand* for such arrangements. This means that we do not know whether employers are targeting the employees who really want to work flexibly or whether there remains unmet demand for flexible working arrangements among particular groups. In addition, while it is clear that women, particularly mothers, are still far more likely than men to be offered – and to take up – various types of flexible working arrangement, we do not know whether this gender balance truly reflects the types of employees who would *like* to be offered such opportunities. Assessing demand alongside use and availability is therefore crucial if we are to understand the links between flexible work, work-life balance and overall satisfaction with work and family life.

We can look at 'demand' for flexible working arrangements in two ways. Firstly, combining the proportions of employees taking up various forms of fixed flexible work with those who said they *would* take up such options if they were made available to them gives us a measure of *overall demand* for fixed flexible working options. Secondly, we can look at levels of 'unmet demand', that is, the proportion of employees who are not currently offered an arrangement, but say they would use it if it were available to them.

With regard to overall demand, there appears to have been little change over the past 10 years. While there has been a significant increase in the demand for part-time working (from 34 to 41 per cent), and a significant decrease in demand for flexible hours (from 70 to 65 per cent), neither was large, and no other changes were statistically significant. This suggests that the 'pool' of employees wanting flexible working arrangements has remained largely static. As usage has increased, the numbers of employees wanting arrangements that they cannot have has decreased in proportion. The data on *unmet* demand confirms this interpretation, showing a general decrease in unmet demand over the 10 years between 1994 and 2004. For instance, the proportion of employees reporting unmet demand for at least one fixed flexible working option decreased from 70 to 57 per cent over the period.

As we would expect from our knowledge of *who* is using flexible working arrangements, mothers tend to want more fixed flexible working options than other employees. This is illustrated in the top section of Table 2.5. For instance, two-thirds of mothers either have taken up, or would like to take up, the opportunity to work part-time, compared with a quarter of fathers. However, there is relatively little variation around flexible hours and working from home. Although mothers are the most likely to have, or want to have, the former (three-quarters), the same applies to over six in ten fathers and non-parents. And between 40 and 46 per cent of our four groups of interest either work from home for some of the time, or would like to be able to do so. Some elements of fixed flexible working are clearly of interest to non-parents as well as parents!

Table 2.5 also considers those working arrangements that indicate an employer's flexible ethos – their willingness to be flexible in particular circumstances. Once again, demand is highest among mothers, but is also notably higher among fathers than non-parents not only in terms of time off for children, but also in relation to other caring responsibilities.

Table 2.5 Overall demand for flexible working by gender and parenthood

% demand	Father	Mother	Male non-parent	Female non-parent
Fixed flexible working options				
Part-time work	25	66	29	44
Flexible hours	63	74	61	64
Job-sharing	9	36	20	29
Working from home	43	46	41	40
Term-time work	37	65	22	24
At least one of above wanted	78	95	79	84
Mean number wanted	1.78	2.87	1.73	2.00
Flexible ethos indicators				
Time off for sick children	41	57	16	15
Time off to care for others	35	38	19	22
Time off for children, other reasons	33	50	12	15
At least one of above wanted	49	70	26	31
Mean number wanted	1.09	1.45	0.47	0.53
Base	*145*	*215*	*327*	*332*

Base: employees

Regression analysis, taking into account employees' job characteristics, confirms that mothers' demand for fixed flexible working arrangements outstrips that of all other employees, including fathers. However, when looking at demand for the more *ad hoc* arrangements (the 'ethos' indicators), it is parents as a whole (rather than mothers or fathers) who express the highest demand.

Does this suggest a level of unmet demand among fathers for the ability to take time off at short notice to look after their children? Table 2.6 suggests that it does. While mothers are more likely than fathers to report unmet demand for term-time working and job-sharing, fathers are asking for part-time work and time off at short notice for caring reasons. One in seven fathers would like, but is not offered, the option of working part-time, compared with one in sixteen mothers. And one in five fathers would like, but says that their employer does not allow, staff time off to care for sick children, compared with one in ten mothers.

Table 2.6 Unmet demand for flexible working by gender and parenthood

% unmet demand	Father	Mother	Male non-parent	Female non-parent
Fixed flexible working options				
Part-time work	16	6	13	8
Flexible hours	30	30	32	34
Job-sharing	7	19	15	17
Working from home	22	28	23	28
Term-time work	30	44	19	16
At least one of above wanted	56	67	55	55
Mean number wanted	1.05	1.26	1.02	1.04
Flexible ethos indicators				
Time off for sick children	19	11	13	6
Time off to care for others	27	19	13	11
Time off for children, other reasons	21	18	10	10
At least one of above wanted	30	25	18	17
Mean number wanted	0.68	0.48	0.35	0.27
Base	*145*	*215*	*327*	*332*

Base: employees

Is flexible working still a women's issue?

The first half of this chapter has shown that there has been a general increase in the availability and use of flexible working by employees over the last decade, and, correspondingly, a steady decrease in the reported levels of unmet demand for such opportunities. It is clear that women, and especially mothers, are more likely than men to report that a range of flexible working options are available to them in their workplace, and – particularly if they have children – to make use of them. These differences by gender and motherhood persist even when we take account of men and women's varying employment characteristics. In this respect, therefore, it seems safe to say that flexible working continues to be primarily a women's issue.

However, as we have already suggested, the implications of these findings are not immediately clear. Could it be, for example, that employers are more active in providing or publicising opportunities for flexible working to female employees? Or could it be that women are more active in seeking out flexible employment (both when choosing an employer and/or within their workplaces), perhaps owing to the greater burdens they are bearing at home, in terms of childcare and other domestic responsibilities?

And what about men? Here the picture seems very mixed. While obviously starting from a lower base, men saw a comparatively greater rise than women in levels of reported availability of flexible working options in their workplaces over the 10 years from 1994 to 2004. However, it was men *without* children who showed the greatest increases, in terms of both reported availability and take up of flexible work over this period, suggesting that the changes were more to do with a growing acceptance of men undertaking flexible work among employers and employees, than to do with changes in fathers' parenting and domestic roles. The fact that, in 2004, there is still little difference between fathers and men without children in terms of reported availability and take up of flexible arrangements further supports this interpretation. Nevertheless, it should also be noted that fathers are particularly likely to express a desire for certain types of flexible working not currently available to them, including time off for caring reasons. Therefore, while our findings indicate that there is still a long way to go, they also appear to suggest that there is some interest among fathers in moving towards greater flexibility over the longer term.

Work-life balance: who's got it?

Concern about flexible working practices largely centres on the perceived links between opportunities to work flexibly and the scope that employees have to strike a good work-life balance. Thus, whilst it may be recognised that achieving a good work-life balance will often depend on a number of factors, having a level of flexibility in your working arrangements such that you can dovetail work with home responsibilities is perceived to be important. This raises obvious questions about the quality of employees' work-life balance in Britain today, and its connection – if any – with flexible work. This is explored in the second half of this chapter. We also consider whether government's interest in these issues is actually reflected in the views and priorities of British employees. What importance do employees – and different types of employees – really assign to a good work-life balance? How positive are they generally about their work and family lives, and do positive views have any relation to work-life balance and/or opportunities for flexible working?

We asked employees a series of eight questions, each tapping one of four key dimensions of work-life balance: time, stress, tiredness, and the capacity to fulfil home and work responsibilities. Four of the questions asked respondents to choose one option from a five-point scale (from "agree strongly" to "disagree strongly") for each of the following statements:

> *There are so many things to do at home, I often run out of time before*
> *I get them all done*
> *There are so many things to do at work, I often run out of time before*
> *I get them all done*
> *My life at home is rarely stressful*
> *My job is rarely stressful*

The second set of four questions asked respondents to indicate the rough frequency with which the following four incidences had occurred during the past three months:

> *I have come home from work too tired to do the chores which need to*
> *be done*
> *I have arrived at work too tired to function well because of the*
> *household work I had done*
> *It has been difficult for me to fulfil my family responsibilities because*
> *of the amount of time I spent on my job*
> *I have found it difficult to concentrate at work because of my family*
> *responsibilities*

Tables 2.7 and 2.8 show employees' responses to all eight questions. They suggest that substantial proportions of employees experience problems with balancing work and home life. They also indicate that – whilst many employees find their work stressful (58 per cent "disagree" or "disagree strongly" that it is rarely stressful) – the impact of poorer work-life balance more often manifests itself at home than at work. For example, they are more likely to say that they have difficulties finding time to do things at home than at work (66 per cent "agree strongly" or "agree" with the former compared to 52 per cent with the latter). They are also more likely to feel tired at home due to work than *vice versa*. Over half report coming home from work "too tired" to do everything they need to do several times a month or more, while only one in ten say that they have arrived at work "too tired to function well" because of family responsibilities with similar frequency. Employees are also more likely to have problems fulfilling family responsibilities because of work than they are to find it difficult to concentrate at work due to family responsibilities (27 per cent *versus* 12 per cent had felt this several times a month or more). While this could imply that work responsibilities are by their nature easier to fulfil, it seems more likely that it might reflect a lack of choice and control on the part of the employee, resulting in a situation where they are obliged to prioritise their duties at work over the needs and demands of the family.

Table 2.7 Time and stress at home and at work

% agree	
Time problems at home	66
Time problems at work	52
% disagree	
Home life rarely stressful	38
Job rarely stressful	58
Base	*877*

Base: employees[11]

Table 2.8 Tiredness and other problems at home and at work

% reporting occurrence several times a week or month	
Tiredness at home (due to job)	54
Tiredness at work (due to household work)	10
Problems fulfilling family responsibilities (due to work)	27
Difficult to concentrate at work (due to family responsibilities)	12
Base	*877*

Base: employees

We know from other work (e.g. Crompton *et al.*, 2003) that women – whether in paid work or not – still take a greater degree of responsibility for housework and child-rearing than men. We might therefore expect working women – and particularly working mothers – to experience the greatest difficulty in achieving a good work-life balance. However, when we examine the responses of parents and non-parents to our questions, a picture emerges which shows that there might be grounds for moving away from the traditional view of work-life balance as mainly a *maternal* matter, with some issues appearing to be more generally *parental,* and sometimes even *paternal.* For instance, while parents are no more likely than other employees to find their jobs stressful, they (and mothers in particular) *are* more likely to find their home lives stressful. Over a half of mothers (58 per cent) and 45 per cent of fathers "disagree" or "disagree strongly" with the statement "my life at home is rarely stressful", compared to 36 per cent of other women and 24 per cent of other men. In addition, while employees are generally more likely to report work-life balance problems as emerging at home than at work, parents are more likely than other employees to feel tired at work or to have problems fulfilling work responsibilities because of issues at home. For example, 15 per cent of fathers report that they have had difficulties concentrating at work due to family responsibilities on several occasions in the last month, compared with eight per cent of male non-parents; the comparable figures for mothers and female non-parents are 18 and 10 per cent respectively.

Mothers are more likely than other employees to experience difficulties finding time to do their household chores (39 per cent "agree strongly" with this statement, compared with 28 per cent of fathers, 22 per cent of male non-parents and 19 per cent of female non-parents). Fathers, in contrast, are the most likely of all the groups to say that there are several occasions a month or more when they find it difficult to fulfil their family responsibilities because of the time they spend on their job (44 per cent, compared with 22 to 29 per cent of the other groups). Both these findings reflect the unequal division of household labour (such as housework) between working parents. The fact that fathers are likely to identify problems with fulfilling family responsibilities but not with finding time for chores also suggests that their work-life balance concerns tend to be focused on child-rearing rather than other domestic responsibilities. There are no significant differences in work-life balance between parents who have children under six and those who have older children.

Work-life balance and flexible working

The fact that mothers appear to have the most difficulty in achieving a good work-life balance is particularly striking given that they are also most likely to make use of flexible working options. This throws doubt on whether the intuitive relationship between flexible working and work-life balance is actually borne out by the evidence. Our analysis would indicate that it is not; we found no clear patterns at all between, on the one hand, availability, take up of or demand for flexible work and, on the other, our work-life balance indicators. Employees who make use of flexible working options are no more or less likely than other groups to report difficulties with combining their lives at home and at work. Equally, those with work-life balance problems are no more or less likely than others to express a demand for flexible working options. However, while these findings suggest that work-life balance is not substantially enhanced by flexible working options, it is also important to recognise that the work-life balance of those employees who do make use of flexible working arrangements could have been even worse had they not been able to do so.

Does work-life balance matter?

So far, we have been concerned with the extent to which flexible work can bring about improvements in work-life balance. However, there is another, more fundamental, question that needs to be asked, namely: is work-life balance a good in itself? Is it something that employees in Britain hold up as an important goal to strive for when considering jobs and careers? And is it, ultimately, something the government ought definitely to promote?

We suggested earlier that, in thinking about their jobs and careers, employees might have a range of other competing concerns alongside work-life balance. These could include, on the one hand, earning money, having a fulfilling career and so on, and, on the other, dedicating oneself to raising a family, even if this gets in the way of a career. We also suggested that, in accordance with the traditional breadwinner family model, the views of men and women might differ markedly on these matters. We can shed some light on this issue by examining responses to the following question:

> *Now suppose you were thinking about a person's career in general and the choices that they have to make. Which **one** of these would you say is the **most** important for them to think about?*
>
> *Good pay*
> *A secure job*
> *Opportunities for promotion*
> *Interesting work*
> *A good work-life balance*
> *A chance to help other people*

Having made a first choice, each respondent was asked to choose the next most important item from the list.

A good work-life balance is clearly a key issue for many employees. A fifth (22 per cent) of employees choose it as the most important consideration from the list, with a further fifth (21 per cent) rating it as the next most important. However, job security and interesting work are mentioned by more employees as their top priority (33 and 25 per cent respectively). Intriguingly, men and women, and parents and non-parents, do not differ in their views on the importance of work-life balance, suggesting that it is not only women (or mothers) who think it matters. However, parents of children under six are more likely than parents of older children to say that good work-life balance is the most important issue when it comes to a person's choice of career (29 per cent and 20 per cent respectively).

Work-life balance considerations clearly matter a great deal to a significant proportion of employees. To explore this further we now examine the extent to which some are prepared to make sacrifices in terms of home and family life in order to prioritise work-related goals, such as making money or pursuing a fulfilling career. By answering the following question, employees had the chance to address the issue directly:

> *How much do you agree or disagree with the following statement? It is important to move up the ladder at work, even if this gets in the way of family life.*

The vast majority of British employees disagree with the statement that career progression should take priority over family life. Only one in ten (10 per cent) of employees agree with this statement (including just two per cent who "agree strongly"), while 68 per cent "disagree" or "disagree strongly". However, as we can see in Table 2.9, mothers are significantly less likely than all other employees to agree – just two per cent (although this still leaves open the question of whether they tend to desire a *balance*, rather than making the reverse prioritisation). This suggests that the higher demand among mothers for flexible working arrangements at least partly reflects differing priorities. Having younger or older children did not appear to be linked to employees' reactions to this statement.

Table 2.9 "It is important to move up the ladder at work, even if this gets in the way of family life", by gender and parenthood

	Father	Mother	Male non-parent	Female non-parent
	%	%	%	%
Agree	12	2	13	10
Neither agree/disagree	19	14	24	23
Disagree	68	83	62	66
Base	*116*	*174*	*269*	*275*

Base: employees

Flexible working and work-life balance: what makes the difference?

So it seems clear that employees do value work-life balance – but why? Does it ultimately make them happier or more satisfied? We might also ask the same question with regard to flexible working, particularly in view of the fact that we found no clear link between work-life balance and the availability and take up of flexible work. To assess this we turn now to focus upon employees' general levels of satisfaction or happiness, exploring any relationship between these, flexible working and work-life balance. This, in turn, should help us address the issue of whether the government has good grounds for pursuing its work-life balance agenda.

To assess satisfaction, we asked employees to rate – across a seven-point scale from "completely satisfied" to "completely dissatisfied" – how satisfied they were with their work and family lives:

> *All things considered, how satisfied are you with your (main) job?*

> *All things considered, how satisfied are you with your family life?*

Table 2.10 shows employees' responses to the two questions. Generally, they are more satisfied with their family lives than with their work lives. Getting on for two-thirds (62 per cent) of employees are "very" or "completely" satisfied with their family lives, compared to just over a third (36 per cent) saying this about their work lives. Although only a small minority express dissatisfaction with either their work or their family life, dissatisfaction with work is more common than dissatisfaction with life at home (12 and five per cent respectively).

Table 2.10 Employees' levels of overall satisfaction with job and family life

	Satisfaction with job	Satisfaction with family life
	%	%
Completely or very satisfied	36	62
Fairly satisfied	40	26
Neither satisfied nor dissatisfied	8	4
Fairly dissatisfied	8	3
Completely or very dissatisfied	4	1
Base	*877*	*877*

Base: employees

But, how far does satisfaction with people's work lives correlate with their views on family life? Debates about work-life balance assume a relationship between the two. Our analysis confirmed this, with strong correlations in our exploratory regression models between those employees who say that they are satisfied with both their work and their home lives.

In order to explore the extent to which flexible working and work-life balance affected employees' levels of satisfaction with their work and family lives, we ran a series of regression models (the full results of which are presented in the appendix to this chapter). These reveal that both work-life balance and the reported availability of flexible working arrangements do have some connection with employees' satisfaction with either their jobs or their family lives, or both.

Flexible working arrangements are clearly connected with employees' levels of job satisfaction. In particular, wanting and not having fixed flexible arrangements is associated with lower levels of job satisfaction, while employees whose employers have a more flexible ethos are more satisfied in their work than those whose employers have a less flexible ethos. Satisfaction with family life does not appear to be connected with having or wanting any kind of flexible working patterns, echoing the earlier findings that led us to query the intuitive connection between flexible work and work-life balance.

Having a stressful job was the only factor significantly associated with lower levels of satisfaction at work. Having an unstressful time at home and being free from family responsibilities that encroach into work life are associated with high levels of satisfaction with family life.

Once we take account of a person's job characteristics, their work-life balance and any flexible working arrangements, whether or not they are a parent is *not* associated with their satisfaction at work or at home. The contrast between this and our earlier findings on work-life balance (where we found that parents experience more problems than other employees), indicates that there is more to being satisfied with work and family life than just the balance that one manages to strike between them. We have seen that, in spite of the fact that employees are more likely to experience work-life balance problems at home than at work, they report higher levels of satisfaction with their family lives than with their work lives. This suggests that they tend to attribute any work-life balance problems to their working circumstances, rather than to the demands of the family. We have also seen that flexible work appears to be connected with greater job satisfaction, even when a wide range of other factors are taken into account. On the basis of these combined findings, we might draw the tentative conclusion that, in spite of appearing *not* to lead to greater work-life balance, flexible work is nevertheless a legitimate tool to use in the pursuit of greater overall employee satisfaction.

Conclusions

The findings reported in this chapter give some clear indications about the changing shape of flexible work and work-life balance in Britain over the last 10 years. The use of flexible working options has increased, and this appears to be largely the result of more widespread availability rather than an increase in overall demand. Women, and mothers in particular, are clearly more likely than men to be offered and to take up flexible working options. Nevertheless, there are signs that men are beginning to catch up. In some ways, the fact that fathers seem to be making slower progress than men without children may seem surprising, although it could suggest that fathers, perhaps particularly where they represent the main or sole breadwinner in a family, face greater obstacles in pursuing flexibility at work. Still, the evidence suggests that they are at least beginning to look for ways of overcoming these obstacles. The fact that fathers are especially likely to report difficulties associated with fulfilling family responsibilities due to time spent at work at least indicates that such circumstances are now acknowledged as problematic, although there are also signs that their concerns are focused more on child-rearing than on other aspects of domestic work.

For women, the problem is not so much about providing access to flexible work as about whether their higher levels of take up genuinely reflect their wishes. A *prima facie* look at our findings would indicate that they do: not only do women – and mothers in particular – report the highest levels of demand for flexible working options, but they are also least likely to express support for the idea of making family sacrifices in order to further their careers. But whether these findings are indicative of women's true feelings – or rather reflect the influences of a long-standing male breadwinner tradition – is at this stage still unknown. It may be that it is not yet time to let go and accept this dimension of gender difference as a simple matter of fact.

And finally, what of the New Labour approach? While it has not, of course, been possible to look at whether the expansion of flexible working is making progress towards the government's own targets – namely their hoped-for increases in employment rates – our data appear broadly to lend support to New Labour's approach from the *employee's* point-of-view. Given that parents report higher levels of work-life balance difficulty than non-parents, for example, the decision to focus the work-life balance agenda on the family seems to be a sensible one. Moreover, while there is no clear link between flexible work and work-life balance, the connection between access to flexible working arrangements and increased job satisfaction indicates that extending flexible work opportunities to more employees is nevertheless a valid goal to pursue, particularly – of course – if, in pursuing it, the gender gap can be narrowed.

Notes

1. This chapter, like the DTI survey, focuses on the experiences and attitudes of employees and so does not cover those who are not in paid work.
2. The battery of arrangements we asked about also included maternity and paternity leave entitlement. However, given our focus upon the ongoing use of flexible working arrangements, as well as our interest in those arrangements suitable for parents of children of all ages, and for non-parents, these more specific arrangements are not included in our chapter.
3. The battery did not include 'part-time, working fewer days per week'.
4. These questions shed light on *perceived* availability, that is, employees' awareness of what is available to them in their workplaces, rather than being a reliable measure of the current state of play in British workplaces. As certain groups of employees may be more aware than others of the available options, reliable data on actual availability is most likely to come from employers (see, for example, Kersley *et al.*, 2005). It should also be noted that there may be some scope for varying interpretations of the phrase "available to you". While some respondents might take this to mean 'available to you personally', others might take it to mean 'available to people in general at your workplace'.
5. We should bear in mind that WERS includes establishments only with 10 or more employees.
6. Government reforms have also targeted parents of disabled children, but as it is not possible to examine this group in our data we focus here on parents of children under six.
7. 'Fathers' and 'mothers' are defined as respondents with a biological, adopted or stepchild aged under 18 living in the household with them.

8. Two of the answer options available to respondents in 2004 were not offered in 1994. In 2004, respondents who had certain flexible working options available to them could choose between "available but I **have not** used it and am not likely to do so in the next year" or "available and I **have** used it or am likely to in the next year". By contrast, in 1994, respondents were only able to choose between "available but I **do not** use it" or "available and I **do** use it". Though the broadening of these answer options to cover the forthcoming year does not affect reported rates of *availability*, it may cause a slight increase in reported levels of *take up* of flexible work.

9. These increases are substantially greater than those we would expect to have occurred as a result of the differences in question wording between the two surveys. The fact that other research (e.g. Kersley *et al.*, 2005) has shown an increase in take up of flexible work would also support this finding.

10. The bases for Table 2.3 are as follows:

	All employees		Employees with option available	
	1994	2004	1994	2004
Base all employees	1447	1020	–	–
Base part-time work	–	–	717	663
Base flexible hours	–	–	534	521
Base job-sharing	–	–	364	401
Base working from home	–	–	257	259
Base term-time work	–	–	219	246

Base for columns 1 and 2: employees
Base for columns 3 and 4: employees who report each option as available

11. In Tables 2.7, 2.8 and 2.10 a slightly different definition of 'employees' is used (this comes from the respondent's answer to a question in the self-completion questionnaire).

References

Crompton, R., Brockmann, M. and Wiggins, R. D. (2003), 'A woman's place … Employment and family life for men and women', in Park, A., Curtice, J., Thomson, K., Jarvis, L. and Bromley, C. (eds.), *British Social Attitudes: the 20th Report*, London: Sage

Dex, S. and Scheibl, F. (2002), *SMEs and flexible working arrangements*, Bristol: Policy Press/Joseph Rowntree Foundation

Kersley, B., Alpin, C., Forth, J., Bryson, A., Bewley, H., Dix, G. and Oxenbridge, S. (2005), *Inside the Workplace: First Findings from the 2004 Workplace Employment Relations Survey*, London: DTI

La Valle, I., Arthur, S., Millward, C., Scott, J. and Claydon, M. (2002), *Happy Families? Atypical work and its influence on family life*, Bristol: Policy Press/Joseph Rowntree Foundation

Lefebvre, P. and Merrigan, P. (1998), 'Work Schedules, Job Characteristics, Parenting Practices and Children's Outcomes', *Cahiers de Recherche CREFE/CREFE Working Papers,* **77**, Montreal: CREFE, University of Quebec

Stevens, J., Brown, J. and Lee, C. (2004), *The Second Work-Life Balance Study: Results from the Employees' Survey*, DTI Employment Relations Research Series No. 27, London: DTI

Woodland, S., Simmonds, N., Thornby, M., Fitzgerald, R. and McGee, A. (2003), *The Second Work-Life Balance Study: Results from the Employers' Survey*, DTI Employment Relations Research Series No. 22, London: DTI

Zick, C.D., Bryant, K.W. and Osterbacka, E. (2001), 'Mother's Employment, Parental Involvement, and the Implications for Intermediate Child Outcomes', *Social Sciences Research*, **30**: 25–49

Acknowledgements

The *National Centre for Social Research* is grateful to the Department for Trade and Industry for their financial support which enabled us to ask the questions reported in this chapter. The authors would also like to thank Alex Bryson, who provided advice and support with the regression analysis for this chapter.

Appendix

Flexible working scales

This chapter reports on three 'flexible working' scales. Two relate to the availability of different flexible working arrangements (one refers to 'fixed options' and the other to the employers 'flexible ethos'). The Cronbach's alpha (unstandardised items) for these scales is 0.6187 and 0.8671 respectively.

The third scale used reports actual use of fixed flexible working options. The Cronbach's alpha (unstandardised items) for this scale is 0.5975.

Regression analysis

The following tables show the results of the ordered probits models described in this chapter. The heading of each column defines the dependent variable, that is, the characteristic which the model seeks to predict, and the remainder of the column reports the coefficients and the absolute values of the t statistics (in brackets) for each variable significant at a five per cent level. It also shows variables included which were not significant.

The method used compares each characteristic against a comparison category (which is defined in brackets). So, for instance, fathers in the first set of models reported below are compared to mothers. A negative coefficient means that the characteristic is associated with the dependent variable being *less* likely to occur than it is for the comparison category; a positive coefficient means it is more likely to occur.

Regression models: Availability, use and unmet demand

Characteristics (comparison group in brackets)	Available		Use	Overall demand	
	Fixed options	Flexible ethos	Fixed options	Ethos options	Fixed options
Gender and parenthood (mum)					
Dad	-0.612	-0.551	-0.952	-0.126	-0.871
	(4.91)**	(4.26)**	(7.23)**	(0.88)	(6.72)**
Male non-father	-0.505	-0.426	-0.957	-0.786	-0.695
	(4.63)**	(3.40)**	(8.39)**	(5.77)**	(5.57)**
Female non-mother	-0.130	-0.219	-0.595	-0.729	-0.453
	(1.25)	(1.81)	(5.33)**	(5.53)**	(3.76)**
Lone parent (not)	ns	ns	ns	ns	ns
Children under 6 (not)	ns	ns	ns	ns	ns
Union member (not)	ns	ns	-0.329	0.262	-0.237
			(3.46)**	(2.38)*	(2.54)*
Highest educational qualification (none)					
Degree	0.554	0.173	0.354	-0.252	0.357
	(3.90)**	(1.19)	(2.31)*	(1.57)	(2.37)*
Higher education	0.137	0.165	-0.037	-0.286	-0.003
	(0.87)	(1.00)	(0.23)	(1.63)	(0.01)
A level	0.438	0.392	0.389	-0.327	0.285
	(3.38)**	(2.73)**	(2.71)**	(2.12)*	(2.16)*
GCSE/O level	0.353	0.213	0.106	-0.050	0.168
	(2.87)**	(1.57)	(0.76)	(0.37)	(1.34)
CSE	0.137	0.086	-0.014	0.053	-0.047
	(0.90)	(0.51)	(0.08)	(0.31)	(0.31)
Other quals	0.519	0.061	-0.093	-0.547	-0.149
	(1.93)	(0.19)	(0.37)	(1.53)	(0.35)
Region (South)					
Scotland	ns	-0.454	-0.298	ns	0.074
		(3.24)**	(2.35)*		(0.59)
North	ns	-0.184	-0.072	ns	0.102
		(1.79)	(0.71)		(1.05)
Midlands	ns	-0.259	-0.088	ns	0.029
		(2.28)*	(0.78)		(0.28)
Wales	ns	-0.363	-0.639	ns	-0.467
		(1.65)	(3.45)**		(2.31)*
London	ns	-0.213	-0.145	ns	0.006
		(1.32)	(1.06)		(0.04)
Manager/professional (not)	0.464	ns	0.260	ns	ns
	(5.50)**		(2.82)**		

table continued on next page

Continuation of Regression models: Availability, use and unmet demand

	Available		Use	Overall demand	
	Fixed options	Flexible ethos	Fixed options	Ethos options	Fixed options
Size of establishment (25–99 employees)					
Under 10	0.077 (0.68)	-0.021 (0.16)	ns	ns	ns
10–24	0.019 (0.17)	0.219 (1.61)	ns	ns	ns
100–499	0.096 (1.00)	0.055 (0.50)	ns	ns	ns
500+	0.265 (2.29)*	0.183 (1.46)	ns	ns	ns
Recognised union (not)	ns	ns	ns	ns	0.207 (2.09)*
Sector (public)					
Private sector	-0.293 (3.17)**	ns	ns	ns	ns
Other sector	-0.074 (0.41)	ns	ns	ns	ns
Overall demand for flexible ethos scale (high score = high demand)					0.239 (6.85)**
Overall demand for fixed flexibility scale (high score = high demand)				0.222 (6.74)**	
Base	1019	1019	1019	1019	1019

* = significant at 5% level
** = significant at 1% level
ns = variable not statistically significant at 5% level

Regression models: Satisfaction

	Satisfaction with work	Satisfaction with home
Characteristics (comparison group in brackets)		
Gender and parenthood *(mum)*		
Dad	-0.158 (1.11)	ns
Male non-father	-0.384 (2.64)**	ns
Female non-mother	-0.051 (0.36)	ns
Lone parent *(not)*	ns	-0.416 (2.10)*
Children under 6 *(not)*	ns	ns
Union member *(not)*	-0.223 (2.02)*	ns
Highest educational qualification *(none)*		
Degree	ns	ns
Higher education	ns	ns
A level	ns	ns
GCSE/O level	ns	ns
CSE	ns	ns
Other quals	ns	ns
Region *(South)*		
Scotland	ns	ns
North	ns	ns
Midlands	ns	ns
Wales	ns	ns
London	ns	ns
Manager/professional *(not)*	0.236 (2.31)*	-0.242 (2.49)*
Size of establishment *(25–99 employees)*		
Under 10	0.255 (1.90)	ns
10–24	0.245 (1.66)	ns
1004–99	0.142 (1.23)	ns
500+	-0.031 (0.22)	ns
Recognised union *(not)*	ns	ns
Sector *(public)*		
Private sector	ns	-0.026 (0.25)
Other sector	ns	-0.501 (2.08)*

table continued on next page

Continuation of Regression models: Satisfaction

	Satisfaction with work	Satisfaction with home
Use of fixed flexibility scale *(high score = more use)*	ns	ns
Flexible ethos availability scale *(high score = more use)*	0.098	ns
Unmet demand for flexible ethos scale *(high score = more demand)*	ns	ns
Unmet demand for fixed flexibility scale *(high score = more demand)*	-0.095 (2.50)*	ns
Being tired at work because of home *(high score = tired less often)*	ns	ns
Work life is hard *(high score = hard less often)*	ns	0.294 (3.74)**
Being tired at home because of work *(high score = tired less often)*	ns	ns
Home life is hard *(high score = tired less often)*	ns	ns
Run out of time at home *(disagree)*	ns	ns
Run out of time at work *(disagree)*	ns	ns
Rarely stress at home *(disagree)*	ns	0.558 (5.96)**
Rarely stress at work *(disagree)*	0.257 (2.23)*	ns
Base	*779*	*776*

* = significant at 5% level
** = significant at 1% level
ns = variable not statistically significant at 5% level

3 Home sweet home

*Alun Humphrey and Catherine Bromley**

The 20th century saw a fundamental shift in the way in which people in Britain occupy their homes. At the beginning of that century, the majority rented accommodation from a private landlord; by its end, around 70 per cent of households owned their own home. Between the 1950s and 1980s, this growth in home-ownership was fuelled by rising living standards, more widely available mortgage finance and a favourable tax regime (Williams, 2003). More recently, its continued rise has been encouraged by specific government policies. The most notable of these was the Conservative government's introduction of the 'right to buy' in 1980, whereby council tenants were given the opportunity to buy their homes, often at heavily discounted rates. Many did, resulting in both an increase in home-ownership and a decline in the number of available council properties.

The Labour government elected in 1997 has maintained this commitment to expanding owner-occupation, and estimates suggest that one million more households now own their home than did so at the time of Labour's election victory in 1997. Further, the government has pledged to create an additional one million homeowners, the equivalent to an overall increase in home-ownership from 70 per cent to 75 per cent. The Chancellor of the Exchequer, Gordon Brown, underlined this commitment to widening access to home-ownership by stating:

> ... this Britain of ambition and aspiration is a Britain where more and more people must and will have the chance to own their own homes (HM Treasury, 2005).

However, recent years have seen accelerated growth in house prices and a shortage of supply in areas such as London and the South East. There has been

* Alun Humphrey is a Research Director at the *National Centre for Social Research*. Catherine Bromley is a Research Director at the *Scottish Centre for Social Research*, part of NatCen, and is Co-Director of the *British Social Attitudes* survey series.

considerable debate about the impact this is having on those who wish to buy, particularly focused on the difficulty first-time buyers and those on lower incomes have in buying property. There has also been growing concern about the problems faced by public sector workers, such as nurses, teachers, fire-fighters and police, when trying to buy property in parts of the country with particularly expensive housing markets. Attention has focused particularly on the impact that housing markets can have on public sector recruitment and retention – for example, areas characterised by acute teacher shortages also appear to have particularly high house prices (Weaver, 2004).

Concerns such as these prompted the government to commission a review of housing supply, conducted by Kate Barker. Building on recommendations made by Barker (2004), the government's recent five-year strategy for housing outlined plans to increase the level of new house building significantly (ODPM, 2005a). In addition, it set out a number of initiatives aimed at helping social housing tenants buy property, including plans to allow them to buy a share in their local authority or housing association home. To address the specific problems faced by public sector workers in London, the South East and the East of England, the Key Worker Living programme was launched in 2004.[1] The types of assistance available to a range of 'key workers' include subsided loans and rents and shared ownership.

To what extent is it realistic to expect levels of home-ownership, the tenure of seven in ten households at the moment, to rise further still? Some have highlighted the need for a more flexible and adaptable housing system, and argue that the policy framework should be neutral, rather than setting targets for any particular tenure type such as owner-occupation or social renting (Williams, 2003). Others note that, following the recession of the early 1990s, confidence in home-ownership fell sharply, perhaps affecting people's willingness to make the considerable commitment entailed by home-ownership (Murie, 1997). So we begin this chapter by considering whether the government's desire to expand home-ownership has the support of the public as a whole. In particular, does it reflect the aspirations of those who do *not* currently own their home (for instance, the social housing tenants targeted by the sorts of initiatives we outlined earlier)? We then assess what our findings tell us about the likelihood of continued increases in owner-occupation in the future.

Alongside the increase in owner-occupation, the composition and nature of the social housing sector (which largely comprises housing association and council or local authority accommodation) has changed significantly in recent years. Again, government policy has been a key factor in bringing about these changes. Firstly, the advent of 'right to buy' has resulted in a shrinkage in the overall size of the sector. Secondly, within the sector itself, a large number of council properties have been transferred into the hands of housing associations. We consider the implications of these changes in the second half of this chapter, focusing particularly on whether or not they are occurring against a background of popular support. We also consider whether people have distinct views of housing associations compared with councils and, if they do, whether they are viewed in a more positive or negative light.

Throughout the chapter we will pay particular attention to the views of four different tenure groups. In addition to owner-occupiers we will focus on three groups of tenants: those in private rented accommodation; those living in local authority properties; and those who rent from housing associations. Of course, the characteristics of these four groups are very different. In some respects they fall into two distinct categories. The first category comprises owner-occupiers and private renters, both of whom are much more likely to be in paid work than those in social housing. They also tend to have higher household incomes, although owners are better off than private renters. What distinguishes private renters from owner-occupiers is their comparative youth, with more than half aged under 35. The second category comprises those in social housing. Indeed, the profiles of council and housing association tenants are now quite similar (Kemp, 2000) and contrast sharply with those in other tenures. These groups are much less likely than others to be in paid employment. Rather, they are more likely to be retired (a quarter), looking after the home or family (a fifth) or be permanently sick or disabled (one in six). As might be expected, they are much less well off financially than owner-occupiers and private renters, with around two-thirds in households receiving less than £15,000 per year. Social renters are also disproportionately more likely to be female (71 per cent of housing association tenants and 60 per cent of council tenants were women).

A home of one's own ...

We begin by considering people's aspirations as regards their ideal type of housing. We asked:

> *Leaving aside any plans you might have for the future, which of these,*
> *if any, is the type of housing you would most want to live in?*

As the final column in Table 3.1 shows, over four in five people would choose to live in owner-occupied accommodation, demonstrating that home-ownership remains the goal of a clear majority. However, attitudes do vary significantly according to the type of tenure a person currently has. Among those in social housing (whether council or housing association), the desire for owner-occupation, though still high, is half the rate found among those who currently own their own homes.

The proportion in each group whose preference is to remain in their current tenure is shown in bold in the table. As can be seen, support for each type of tenancy tends to be greatest among those already in that tenure. Council tenants are the most likely to advocate renting from a council or local authority, and housing association tenants the most likely to opt for renting from a housing association. The exception to this is found among private renters, very few of whom would opt for this form of tenancy ideally. Rather, nearly three-quarters of private renters see owner-occupation as their preferred tenure. Earlier we saw that private renters and owners have very similar socio-demographic characteristics, excepting that private renters tend to be younger. It is likely therefore that, for many of this group, private renting is an interim undertaking until their circumstances allow them to buy a property of their own. The question of how tenancy preferences differ by current tenure is important, and we shall return to it later in this chapter.

There is only very limited support for shared ownership, the type of tenure the government plans to make more widely available to social housing tenants (three per cent of council tenants and one per cent of housing association tenants opted for this). This relatively low level of support might reflect the fact that the attraction of such a tenure might be as a stepping stone to full ownership (rather than as an end in itself).

Table 3.1 Type of housing would most like to live in by current tenure

	Owner-occupiers	Council tenants	HA[+] tenants	Private renters	All
	%	%	%	%	%
Owner occupier/buying	**90**	46	45	72	82
Rent from council/local authority	2	**39**	14	7	7
Rent from housing association	1	4	**33**	5	3
Rent from private landlord	1	1	1	**8**	2
Shared ownership	1	3	1	1	1
Live with friends/relatives	2	1	1	3	2
Sheltered accommodation	2	4	3	3	2
Base	*2303*	*352*	*210*	*297*	*3199*

+ Housing association

Changing attitudes to home-ownership

Home-ownership clearly remains the most popular form of tenure for large proportions of the population. But how have attitudes to this changed over time? And to what extent do events within the housing market dent or boost people's confidence in owner-occupation? To understand how views about home-ownership have changed, the *British Social Attitudes* survey series has routinely asked the following question:

> *Suppose a newly-married young couple, both with steady jobs, asked your advice about whether to buy or rent a home. If they had the choice, what would you advise them to do?*

To buy a home as soon as possible
To wait a bit, then try to buy a home
Not to plan to buy a home at all

Table 3.2 shows that just over seven in ten would now advocate buying a home "as soon as possible", a similar proportion to that found in 1986 when we first asked the question. However, between these two dates, support has fluctuated considerably.

Table 3.2 Advice to a newly-married couple about housing

	1986	1989	1990	1991	1996	1997	1998	1999	2004
	%	%	%	%	%	%	%	%	%
Buy as soon as possible	74	78	70	60	54	61	61	65	71
Wait a bit	20	17	24	31	35	30	30	29	24
Not buy	1	1	1	2	3	2	1	2	1
Can't choose	4	3	5	5	7	6	7	3	3
Base	*1416*	*1297*	*1233*	*1224*	*3085*	*1080*	*2531*	*2450*	*2609*

The fluctuation shown in Table 3.2 corresponds very clearly with the fortunes of the housing market. This is illustrated in Figure 3.1, which shows both the annual change in UK house prices (indicated by the black line, which is plotted against the left-hand axis) and the proportion of people choosing the "buy a home as soon as possible" option in those years in which we included the question on our surveys (the single points, which are plotted against the right-hand axis). For example, by 1989, the height of the house price boom, support for home-ownership stood at 78 per cent, only to fall markedly during the recession of the early 1990s and the associated fall in property prices. During this period, increasing numbers of households were unable to meet their mortgage payments, many became trapped in 'negative equity' (whereby their outstanding borrowing exceeded the value of the property), and home repossessions rose. Not surprisingly, then, attitudes toward home-ownership cooled markedly, such that by 1996 the figure advocating immediate home-ownership stood at only 54 per cent. During the late 1990s, the housing market recovered and house prices recorded double-digit growth once again; by 1997, the proportion advocating buying as soon as possible had recovered to 61 per cent. In *The 16th Report* we speculated that if property prices continued to rise, we should see a further increase in support for home-ownership (Ford and Burrows, 1999). Evidence suggests that this is indeed the case, at least to some extent. The strong growth in house prices did continue and now just over seven in ten say they would advise a young couple to buy as soon as possible.

Figure 3.1 Annual change in UK house prices, and attitudes to home-ownership, 1985–2004

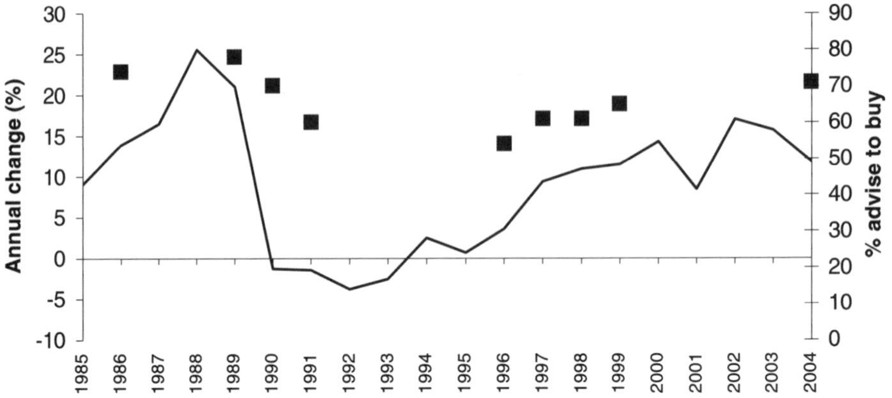

Figures are for 'mix-adjusted prices'
Source: ODPM (2005b)

The attitudes of non-owners

Public confidence in home-ownership clearly remains at a high level. But to what extent is there sufficient public support to warrant plans to increase it further still? Earlier we saw that significant proportions of non-owners would, ideally, like to own their own home (Table 3.1), suggesting that there is a gap between the proportion who own their own home and the proportion who aspire to this. However, although this gap has narrowed over time, constraints around affordability and a number of other factors might make the gap harder to close as it gets narrower (Smith, 2005). So we turn now to consider in more detail the views of those who are *not* currently home owners. After all, if the prevalence of ownership is to increase overall, a proportion of this group will need to buy.

 Table 3.3 examines the responses of different tenure groups to our question about a fictional young couple and whether or not they should buy a home. This shows a strong relationship between a person's views and their current tenure. Most notably, non-owners are markedly more cautious than owners; 46 per cent of council tenants, 38 per cent of housing association tenants and 49 per cent of private renters would advise a couple to buy as soon as possible, compared with 78 per cent of owners. Although renters are less emphatic in their views about ownership when compared with owners, they are not necessarily averse to buying altogether. More than two-fifths in each group of renters say the young couple should "wait a bit before buying", while only a relatively small proportion would advise them not to buy at all. It is also notable that around one in ten of those renting from a council or housing association was not able to express a view on the issue.

Table 3.3 Advice to a newly-married couple about housing, by current tenure

	Owner-occupiers	Council tenants	HA[+] tenants	Private renters	All
	%	%	%	%	%
Buy as soon as possible	78	46	38	49	71
Wait a bit	18	41	46	43	24
Not buy	*	2	3	3	1
Can't choose	2	9	11	4	3
Base	1934	257	161	232	2609

+ Housing association

Table 3.4 shows how different tenure groups have responded to this question over time. Among owner-occupiers and those renting from a council, results have fluctuated in much the same way as they have among the population as a whole, with the proportion advocating home-ownership increasing from 1996 onwards. However, those in housing association accommodation have followed a different pattern; among this group, enthusiasm for home-ownership is largely the same now as it was in 1996.

Table 3.4 Advice to a newly-married couple about housing, by current tenure over time

	Owner-occupiers				Council tenants				HA[+] tenants		
	'89	'96	'99	'04	'89	'96	'99	'04	'96	'99	'04
	%	%	%	%	%	%	%	%	%	%	%
Buy as soon as possible	88	62	72	78	50	30	38	46	33	36	38
Wait a bit	10	30	23	18	36	50	45	41	47	53	46
Not buy	1	2	1	*	3	5	5	2	6	4	3
Can't choose	1	5	2	2	10	13	9	9	14	7	11
Base	936	2121	1763	1934	272	565	364	257	111	136	161

+ Housing association

We turn now to consider the factors that might underpin attitudes toward home-ownership. To assess this, we asked people to choose what they saw as the main advantage of owning a home from the list of options shown in Table 3.5 (the options are presented here in order of their popularity, rather than the order in which they were presented in the survey). As the table shows, a third identified "good investment" as being the main advantage of home-ownership. So, despite the slump in property prices in the early 1990s, there remains a clear expectation that house price inflation will continue in the future. The second and third most popular reasons, each chosen by just over a fifth, concerned long-term security and the fact that owners have the freedom to do what they want with their homes. It is notable that different tenure groups have very similar views on the attractions of home-ownership, with the exception of housing association tenants whose responses were more varied. In particular, they are significantly less likely than owner-occupiers to see the main advantage of home-ownership as being its investment opportunities.

Table 3.5 Advantages of home-ownership, by current tenure

	Owner-occupiers	Council tenants	HA[+] tenants	Private renters	All
	%	%	%	%	%
Good investment	34	29	22	33	32
More secure in long-term than renting	23	17	22	28	22
Gives you freedom to do what you want with it	21	22	19	22	21
Less expensive than rent	13	14	17	11	13
Something to leave to your family	9	13	15	5	9
Base	2303	352	210	297	3199

+ Housing association

Future levels of home-ownership

We conclude this section by considering what light our findings shed on future levels of ownership. We begin by focusing on people's anticipated behaviour, and then examine whether the views of young people, relative to older groups, provide any indication of future trends.

So far we have focused on people's general aspirations, either by asking what advice they would give to others, or by specifically asking them about their own ideal. In practice, of course, people face a number of constraints on their behaviour, most notably their financial circumstances. Given this, we also asked respondents whether they themselves planned to move over the next two years and, if this was likely, what sort of tenure they would move into. This allows us to shed some light on future levels of home-ownership.

The results are shown in Table 3.6. Overall, a quarter of people think it likely that they will move in the next two years, rising to six in ten of those in the private rented sector. Among the other three groups in which we are interested, between one in five and one in four think it likely they will move over this time. When it comes to the tenure into which people plan to move, a familiar pattern emerges, with people's plans being strongly related to their current tenure. Among non-owners, private renters (which was the most likely tenant group to cite owner-occupation as their ideal tenancy preference), are the most likely to be planning to move into owner-occupation, nearly half saying this. This also applied to around a quarter of tenants in council or housing association accommodation. Only a small proportion in each of these two groups of social renter (two per cent and five per cent respectively) plan to enter into shared ownership.

If we assume that people's expectations are accurate, it is possible to make a very rough prediction as to if, and how, the size of the owner-occupied sector will change in the next two years. Of course, in reality, intentions do not always match behaviour – especially when looking at a period as long as two years. Additionally, over the next two years, some households will die out and other, newly formed ones, will take their place (whose intentions we do not know). Putting these caveats aside, however, such an analysis would suggest that there will be little change in the size of the owner-occupied sector. That is, the number of renters who plan to buy does not vastly exceed the number of owners who plan to move into rented accommodation. This lends support to the theory that it will be increasingly difficult to narrow the 'home-ownership gap' (Smith, 2005). It also appears to resonate with other evidence which suggests that there is some scepticism about the continued ease of getting onto the property ladder, with most thinking that future generations will find it more difficult to own their own homes (ODPM, 2004).

Table 3.6 Likelihood of moving in next two years and planned tenure, by current tenure

	Owner-occupiers	Council tenants	HA[+] tenants	Private renters	All
% likely to move in next two years	22	19	26	59	25
Base	*2303*	*352*	*210*	*297*	*3199*
Planned tenure of new accommodation	%	%	%	%	%
Owner-occupier (buying)	76	27	24	47	63
Rent – council/local authority	1	38	22	10	7
Rent – housing association	1	17	33	7	5
Rent – private landlord	12	8	13	21	14
Shared ownership	1	2	5	2	2
Live with friends/relatives	4	3	0	7	4
Sheltered accommodation	1	3	3	1	1
*Base**	*468*	*71*	*53*	*161*	*763*

+ Housing association
* Based on all those who plan to move in the next two years

When considering likely future rates of owner-occupation it is also important to consider the views of young people. After all, tenure is strongly related to age, with younger people being far less likely to own their accommodation than older groups, for obvious reasons. Consequently, this group contains a greater 'pool' of potential owners, making it important to examine their views and whether they have changed over time. If we do find that the views of younger people increasingly diverge from those held by older groups, this may have important consequences for what may happen in the future.

To consider this further, we return once again to our question about the best advice that could be given to a newly-married young couple. As Table 3.7 shows, responses do indeed vary markedly by age, with those in the youngest age group being much less likely to recommend buying as soon as possible, only 44 per cent doing so, compared with 71 per cent overall. There is a sharp increase in the proportion holding this view between the ages of 18–24 and 25–34, but support continues to increase with age, peaking at 84 per cent among those aged 55–59.

Table 3.7 Advice to a newly-married couple about housing, by age

	18–24	25–34	35–44	45–54	55–59	60–64	65+	Total
	%	%	%	%	%	%	%	%
Buy as soon as possible	44	70	72	77	84	79	70	71
Wait a bit	46	26	24	18	12	18	23	24
Not buy	1	1	1	1	1	1	1	1
Can't choose	9	2	2	3	2	2	3	3
Base	181	419	514	461	242	194	595	2609

Of course, the fact that an age gap exists does not necessarily tell us anything about how societal views might change in the future. After all, young people's views on this matter are likely to be fairly fluid, and subject to change as they get older, rather than being fixed from an early age. Such developments reflect the impact of changing financial circumstances and increasing familial responsibilities (Ford and Burrows, 1999). In order to explore this issue further, Table 3.8 shows the responses of different age groups to this question, and how this has changed over time. It confirms that there is a strong relationship between enthusiasm for owner-occupation and age, with older groups consistently being keener on home-ownership than younger ones. However, it is also important to consider whether the 'gap' between young people's views and those of the general population has remained constant, or whether it is changing over time. To do this, the table compares the views of three groups: 18–24 year olds, 25–34 year olds and those aged 35 and above. In 1986, when the question was first asked, the 'gap' between the proportion of those aged 18–24 who advocated home-ownership and the equivalent proportion among those aged 35 and over stood at 18 percentage points, a gap which remained fairly consistent until 1999. Now, however, the gap stands at 31 points. This illustrates the fact that, while the proportion of those aged 25 and older who advocate home-ownership increased significantly between 1999 and 2004, no similar increase occurred among 18–24 year olds. It is also notable that, while the 25–34 age group had very similar views to their older counterparts during the 1980s, the gap between their views and those held by older groups also widened somewhat in the late 1990s (although it has since shrunk). This suggests that the recent recovery in positive attitudes towards home-ownership has not been as strong among the young. A number of potential explanations have been put forward to account for this, including the residual effect of the last house price recession, worsening affordability, increased debt, the improved mobility associated with renting, and the delayed onset of marriage and childbearing (Smith, 2005). This will be important to monitor over future years as, were this cohort to retain its less enthusiastic attitude toward home-ownership as it ages, it would have important implications for policy makers eager to raise levels of home-ownership throughout society as a whole.

Table 3.8 Young people's attitudes to ownership, 1986–2004

% newly-married couple should buy as soon as can	1986	1989	1990	1991	1996	1997	1998	1999	2004
18–24	59	64	50	49	38	43	43	47	44
25–34	76	79	72	58	51	60	55	59	70
35+	77	80	73	63	57	65	65	69	75
Difference: 18–24 & 35+	**-18**	**-15**	**-23**	**-14**	**-20**	**-21**	**-22**	**-22**	**-31**
Difference: 25–34 & 35+	**-1**	**-1**	**-1**	**-5**	**-6**	**-4**	**-10**	**-10**	**-5**
Base 18–24	*184*	*144*	*154*	*141*	*238*	*81*	*186*	*165*	*181*
Base 25–34	*266*	*248*	*246*	*239*	*637*	*233*	*520*	*448*	*419*
Base 35+	*966*	*899*	*827*	*839*	*2202*	*766*	*1818*	*1835*	*2006*

Our findings so far show that confidence in owner-occupation has largely recovered since the housing market crash of the mid-1990s, and is now nearly as high as it was in the mid-1980s. Clearly, owner-occupation remains the preferred tenure for the majority of people. Although this view is less common among non-owners, they nonetheless include a sizeable group which has aspirations of home-ownership. Overall, therefore, public attitudes appear to be broadly in sympathy with current government attempts to widen access to this form of tenure further still. However, it is clear that some barriers exist to a further expansion in the overall levels of home-ownership in Britain. Certainly, people's expectations of their own behaviour suggest that we should not expect to see much change over the next few years.

Social housing

So far we have focused on owner-occupation. Although this accounts for the majority of households in Britain, it is not appropriate for everyone at all stages of their lives, for a variety of reasons. We therefore now turn to consider the social housing sector, an area which has undergone substantial change in the past two decades. Firstly, the size of the sector has shrunk, a consequence of an increase in the size of the owner-occupied sector over the past two decades. In 1981, social housing accounted for 31 per cent of dwellings in Great Britain. By 2003, this had fallen to just 20 per cent (Wilcox, 2004). A key element in this change was the introduction of the 'right to buy' in the 1980s. Secondly, the make-up of the sector itself has changed. The Conservative government's 1988 Housing Act allowed for the transfer of local authority housing to housing associations, known as large-scale voluntary transfer. This theme has been continued by the current Labour government. In its 2000 Housing Green Paper, it underlined its belief in the benefits of stock transfer and outlined proposals to support continued transfer, provided this was backed by the tenants (DETR and DSS 2000). As a result, while in the 1980s almost all social sector housing was accounted for by local authorities, by 2003 housing associations had increased their share to around a third of social housing properties.

Housing associations are likely to continue increasing their share of the social sector, making it relevant to consider people's views about this form of landlord. Prior to any particular stock transfer taking place, tenants are balloted on whether they are in agreement, and the outcome of such ballots tends to be supportive (Pawson, 2004). However, these ballots occur at a single point in time, and among the specific group of tenants affected, meaning we know little about the general public's views about different types of social landlord and their housing stock. This is the area to which we now turn.

Attitudes towards landlords

Respondents were asked to give their views of three different types of landlords: councils, housing associations and private landlords. For each type of landlord, we asked:

> From what you know or have heard, how good or bad do you think they are at...
> ... providing a good standard of repairs and maintenance in their homes?
> ... charging reasonable rents?
> ... allowing tenants to stay in their homes as long as they want to?
> ... providing housing in good neighbourhoods?

With respect to repairs and maintenance, housing associations are generally viewed in a better light than are councils. As the left-hand side of Table 3.9

shows, over a third think housing associations are often or nearly always good in this respect, compared with just over a quarter who say this in relation to councils. Conversely, one in ten feel that councils are often or always bad, double the rate found for housing associations. But the least impressive view relates to private landlords, with only 16 per cent saying they are often or always good at providing a good standard of repairs and maintenance, and a quarter that they are often bad or nearly always bad.

What is also clear is that despite – or possibly because of – the relatively quick growth in the size of the sector, general awareness of the merits or otherwise of housing associations has not quite reached the levels of the other two types of landlord. Nearly a quarter of respondents were unable to choose an answer for housing associations, compared with 14 per cent for councils and 16 per cent for private landlords. In order to account for this in our analysis, we developed a mean score based only on those who were able to choose an answer. This is calculated by attributing respondents who said "nearly always good" a score of five, those who said "often good" a score of four and so on until those who said "nearly always bad" are assigned a score of one. The higher the mean score for any group of respondents, the more favourable that group's views generally are. This enables an easier comparison of the different types of landlord, and confirms the story told above. Thus, with respect to repairs and maintenance service, private landlords are viewed the *least* favourably with a mean score of 2.9, with housing associations the highest at 3.5. As part of the justification for encouraging stock transfer in the 2000 Housing Green Paper was to attract private investment so as to improve the quality of social housing, our findings suggest that current government policy does resonate with public opinion, in the sense that the public clearly sees housing associations as offering a better service than council landlords.

Table 3.9 Views on "providing a good standard of repairs and maintenance"

	All			Among own tenants		
	Council	HA[+]	Private landlords	Council	HA[+]	Private landlords
	%	%	%	%	%	%
Nearly always or often good	27	37	16	51	60	34
Sometimes good, sometimes bad	45	32	41	32	23	40
Often or nearly always bad	11	5	25	12	14	19
Can't choose	14	24	16	2	1	7
Base	2609	2609	2609	257	161	232
Mean score	3.2	3.5	2.9	3.6	3.7	3.2
Base (mean)	2184	1943	2115	244	155	218

+ Housing association

The right-hand side of Table 3.9 shows responses to the question from different tenant groups. This confirms our earlier reading, with housing association tenants being the most likely to say that their landlord provides a good standard of repairs and maintenance, six in ten doing so. Again, it is notable that a relatively low proportion of private renters, around a third, feel their type of landlord offers a good service.

Table 3.10 focuses on the extent to which different landlords are seen to charge reasonable rents. Figures from the Survey of English Housing show that private sector rents are on average much higher than social sector rents and that, within the social sector, housing association rents are slightly higher than those for councils (Robinson *et al.*, 2004). Our findings show that the difference between private sector and social sector rents is certainly recognised by the public; around two-fifths rate both housing associations and councils as either "nearly always good" or "often good", compared with only one in ten of private landlords. Overall, around a third think private landlords are "often bad" or "nearly always bad", compared with less than a tenth for social landlords. Even among private sector tenants, the image of private landlords is little better, a finding confirmed when we focus on the mean scores relevant to each landlord. However, we did not find any significant difference between perceptions of housing association and council rents, perhaps reflecting a lack of sufficient knowledge about the rents charged by these two landlords.

Table 3.10 Views on "charging reasonable rents"

	Overall			Among own tenants		
	Council	HA[+]	Private landlords	Council	HA[+]	Private landlords
	%	%	%	%	%	%
Nearly always or often good	42	38	10	56	55	19
Sometimes good, sometimes bad	30	27	38	20	20	41
Often or nearly always bad	9	7	34	14	19	32
Can't choose	17	25	16	6	4	6
Base	2609	2609	2609	257	161	232
Mean score	3.5	3.5	2.7	3.7	3.5	2.8
Base (mean)	2095	1901	2093	231	149	218

+ Housing association

In general, councils are seen as offering better security of tenure than housing associations. When asked about how good each type of landlord is at allowing tenants to stay in their homes as long as they want, the mean score for councils was 3.8, higher than the 3.6 for housing associations (Table 3.11). The majority of private sector tenants have assured shorthold contracts which usually run for a fixed period of time. It is unsurprising, therefore, that private landlords are viewed much less favourably in this respect.

Table 3.11 Views on "allowing tenants to stay in their homes as long as they want to"

	Overall			Among own tenants		
	Council	HA[+]	Private landlords	Council	HA[+]	Private landlords
	%	%	%	%	%	%
Nearly always or often good	50	39	13	73	70	29
Sometimes good, sometimes bad	23	26	39	14	16	38
Often or nearly always bad	4	3	26	3	6	23
Can't choose	20	29	20	7	5	9
Base	2609	2609	2609	257	161	232
Mean score	3.8	3.6	2.8	4.2	4.0	3.1
Base (mean)	2014	1782	2001	230	147	212

+ Housing association

Of course, a key aspect of people's housing is not just the accommodation itself, but the area in which it is situated. In this respect, housing associations are viewed the most favourably and councils least favourably. Nearly a quarter think that councils are "often" or "nearly always bad" at providing housing in good neighbourhoods, compared with around a tenth for housing associations. The mean scores are 2.9 and 3.3 respectively. Private landlords fare better on this issue, with a mean score somewhere in between, of 3.1.

These findings suggest that housing associations are viewed more positively than local authorities as landlords, although they are also the least well known of the three types of landlords we asked about. Although local authorities fare better on the issue of security of tenure, housing associations are viewed more favourably when it comes to repairs and maintenance, and providing homes in good neighbourhoods. This supports other evidence which suggests that housing association tenants tend to be more satisfied than council tenants with their landlords (Robinson et al., 2004).

Table 3.12 Views on "providing housing in good neighbourhoods"

	Overall			Among own tenants		
	Council	HA[+]	Private landlords	Council	HA[+]	Private landlords
	%	%	%	%	%	%
Nearly always or often good	19	27	23	41	46	42
Sometimes good, sometimes bad	39	36	42	33	34	39
Often or nearly always bad	23	10	13	18	15	8
Can't choose	17	24	19	5	3	10
Base	2609	2609	2609	257	161	232
Mean score	2.9	3.3	3.1	3.4	3.5	3.5
Base (mean)	2101	1901	2015	236	151	210

+ Housing association

The advantages and disadvantages of housing associations

Thus far we have compared housing association with councils and private landlords on a number of specific issues. We turn now to consider how housing associations are viewed more generally. To assess this, we asked respondents to pick out three good and three bad points about being a housing association tenant, from the lists of options shown in the next two tables.

Table 3.13 Good points about housing associations

% mentioning:	
Fair rent	41
Good repairs and maintenance services	30
Cheaper than buying	26
Homes are kept in a good state of repair	18
Good quality housing	17
Housing associations provide decent homes	14
Good landlords	14
Being able to choose where to live	11
Better than being a council tenant	10
Access to other housing association services	7
Access to tenants' associations	5
More choice over what happens to the property	5
Access to support services	5
Housing associations provide modern homes	5
Friendly neighbours	4
Don't know	19
Base	3199

Table 3.13 shows the most frequently mentioned positive response about housing associations to be fair rents, chosen by two in five people. The general state of repair of their homes was also frequently mentioned; four of the top six aspects mentioned relate to the quality of their housing or state of repair. One in ten chose an option that explicitly pits housing associations against council accommodation, the view being that an advantage of renting from the former is that it is "better than being a council tenant". A fifth were unable to identify any positive features of housing associations, no doubt reflecting the fact that many people know very little about this form of landlord.

By contrast, perceptions of the bad points about being a housing association tenant tended to relate to more general disadvantages of the tenure itself rather than to particular aspects within the control of that particular type of landlord. Given the general preference for ownership highlighted earlier in the chapter, it is perhaps unsurprising that two of the top three bad points identified revolved around the fact that housing association tenants, by definition, do not own their home and therefore miss out on the associated benefits that ownership might bring. Such a disadvantage would, of course, apply equally to other forms of rented accommodation. A second theme relates to the local environment in which housing association homes are situated. Nearly a third (31 per cent) mentioned antisocial neighbours and a sixth mentioned the location of homes. A third theme relates to choice, firstly in terms of what happens to the property and secondly in terms of the type of house.

Table 3.14 Bad points about housing associations

% mentioning:	
Don't own the property	34
Antisocial neighbours	31
Can't invest in the housing market	26
Little choice over what happens to the property	25
Little choice over the type of house tenants can live in	18
The location of their homes	17
Rents are too high	11
Poor repairs and maintenance service	7
Bad landlords	6
Having to deal with tenants' associations	5
Poor quality housing	4
Homes are kept in a poor state of repair	3
Homes are of a poor standard	3
Other	1
None of these	3
Don't know	23
Base	*3199*

Preferred landlords

How do these views about the strengths and weaknesses of different landlords transfer into general preferences for types of tenancy? If housing associations are generally viewed as being better landlords, we might expect this to result in a general preference for this type of rented tenure, at least over councils. In order to see if this was the case we asked people who their preferred landlord would be, were they to rent.

Overall, preferences were mixed, with similar proportions opting for each type of landlord (Table 3.15). In fact, a higher proportion opted for local authority accommodation than opted for housing associations (32 per cent compared with 27 per cent), despite the slightly better reputation that housing associations have. As we might expect, the results are heavily influenced by current tenure, with the majority of tenants indicating a preference for a landlord of their current type (the emboldened figures indicate the proportion in each tenure type who said that this was their preferred landlord). This effect is most marked among council tenants, over four-fifths of whom would prefer to stay as they are. Only eight per cent would prefer to rent from a housing association. By contrast, those in housing association properties are less loyal, with 70 per cent saying they would prefer to stay as they are and 23 per cent preferring to rent from a council. Given the likely continued flow of council properties into housing associations, this is particularly interesting and echoes findings from earlier in the *British Social Attitudes* survey series (Kemp, 2000). The least loyal of all were private renters, just over half of whom would opt to stay with their current type of landlord. One in five would opt for local authority housing, and a further 13 per cent a housing association property. There was no clear pattern among the largest group of all, owner-occupiers, who were equally split between the three landlords in question.

Table 3.15 Preferred landlord by current tenure

	Owner-occupiers	Council tenants	HA[+] tenants	Private renters	All
	%	%	%	%	%
Council/local authority	29	**82**	23	19	32
Housing association	29	8	**70**	13	27
Private landlord	33	6	3	**56**	31
Some other landlord	2	*	2	4	2
Base	2303	352	210	297	3199

+ Housing association

These findings would appear to fly in the face of current policy, which encourages the flow of local authority tenants into housing associations. They also seem inconsistent with our earlier findings that showed housing associations to be viewed slightly more favourably than councils on a range of issues. An obvious question then becomes: why is it that housing association tenants are less 'loyal' to their current tenure than council tenants? One possible answer is provided by comparing the responses of groups with different tenancy preferences to our questions about the good and bad points about being a housing association tenant. This shows that housing association tenants who would prefer to rent from the council were more likely to identify "little choice over what happens to the property" and "rents are too high" as bad points than those who would rather remain housing association tenants (43 per cent compared with 15 per cent, and 42 per cent compared with 19 per cent respectively). This suggests that unhappiness with the stock transfer process itself and higher levels of rents may have influenced the views of these particular tenants.

A second possible explanation is that feelings of 'better the devil you know…' may be greater among council tenants than among their counterparts in housing association accommodation. Given that a significant element of the increase in the size of the housing association sector has been due to the transfer of stock from local authority control to housing associations, it is likely that a greater proportion of housing association tenants are ex-council tenants than the other way around. Data from the Survey of English Housing would seem to support this assertion. Of households who had recently moved into housing association properties, 21 per cent had previously rented from a local authority. However, of those recently moving into council properties, only six per cent had previously rented from a housing association (Robinson *et al.*, 2004). So, if a lower proportion of council tenants have experience of housing association landlords than *vice versa*, then we might expect the former to show more loyalty toward their current landlord than the latter.

A third explanation is provided by the relative age profiles of the two different types of social tenant. Housing association tenants include a slightly higher proportion of younger people, and younger groups are more likely to express a preference for a different type of tenure other than their own.

As to why overall preferences are slightly skewed toward councils, the most obvious explanation is a simple lack of awareness of the merits of housing associations. As we found earlier, people were less able to indicate how good or bad they thought housing associations were on a range of different aspects than they were to do the same either for councils or private landlords. Research by the National Housing Federation confirms that among the general population, knowledge about council housing is greater than about housing association properties (Greensitt, 2001). People are probably less likely to say they would prefer to rent from a type of landlord they know very little about. Indeed, if we exclude those who were unable to say how good they felt housing associations or councils were on any of the issues covered in Tables 3.9 to 3.12, we find that tenancy preferences converge at 30 per cent and 31 per cent for housing associations and councils respectively.

Of course, in reality, people do not necessarily have a free choice as to which type of landlord they would like to rent from. In order to explore perceptions of housing associations in more detail, we asked those who did *not* currently rent from a housing association the extent to which they agreed with the statement "I would like to live in a housing association property if I could get it". The results are shown in Table 3.16. The majority (57 per cent) disagreed with the statement, indicating that they would not be willing to take up a housing association tenancy. This does not necessarily imply a dislike of housing associations in particular; rather, it reflects the overwhelming preference that people have for home-ownership. Indeed, as Table 3.16 shows, nearly two thirds of current owner-occupiers would not like to live in a housing association property. However, attitudes are more favourable among renters; around a third of both private renters and council tenants agreed that they would like to live in housing association accommodation. Slightly over a third in each group disagreed.

Table 3.16 "I would like to live in a housing association property if I could get it" by current tenure

	Owner-occupiers	Council tenants	Private renters	All
	%	%	%	%
Agree	12	33	34	17
Neither	21	25	23	21
Disagree	63	37	35	57
*Base**	*2303*	*352*	*297*	*2989*

* Based on all those not currently renting from a housing association

In view of the likely increase in size of the housing association sector, and the growing role it is playing as a provider of housing for key workers, we also asked people for whom they thought this type of housing should be provided:

Who do you think Housing Association homes should mainly be for?

People on very low incomes
People on very low incomes and people like nurses or teachers if local property is very expensive
Anyone, regardless of their income

On balance, more people think that housing associations should provide homes for people on low incomes and key workers (39 per cent), than think it should be solely restricted to people on low incomes (26 per cent), or open to all (28 per cent). However, there is a marked contrast in views between owners and private renters on the one hand, and those in the social rented sector on the other. The latter take a more inclusive view; nearly half (48 per cent) of housing association tenants and 39 per cent of those renting from a local authority feel that housing association homes should be for anyone, irrespective of their income. This is interesting, given that these are the two same groups which are most likely to be *negatively* affected by the increased competition for properties which such a policy would entail, and perhaps can be seen to reflect a desire for social housing to occupy more socially mixed environments.

Table 3.17 Who housing association homes should mainly be for, by current tenure

	Owner-occupiers	Council tenants	HA[+] tenants	Private renters	All
	%	%	%	%	%
Low incomes	25	32	24	27	26
Low incomes and nurses/teachers	43	22	26	39	39
Anyone regardless of income	26	39	48	24	28
Base	*2303*	*352*	*210*	*297*	*3199*

+ Housing association

Conclusions

It is clear that Britain's confidence in home-ownership is returning. Following the recession and slump in house prices that occurred in the late 1980s and early 1990s, there was a distinct cooling of attitudes towards owner-occupation. However, confidence has returned almost to levels comparable with those found in the mid-1980s and owner-occupation remains very much the type of tenure to which the vast majority of people aspire. This clearly lends support to the current government's policy of seeking to widen further access to home-ownership. However, we also find evidence to suggest that it will become increasingly hard to push levels of home-ownership higher still, and it appears unlikely that there will be large increases in the proportion of homeowners in the next few years. There are also the first signs of a widening in the traditional gap between the levels of enthusiasm for home-ownership shown by young people and their older counterparts, a gap that will be important to monitor over the next decade.

It is more probable that the most significant changes in the tenure profile will occur in the continued decline in the proportion of local authority tenants at the expense of those renting from housing associations. Here, again, our findings would seem to indicate some support for this policy. Housing associations do seem to be viewed in a more favourable light than local authorities (and indeed private landlords) in respect of their repairs and maintenance service and the provision of housing in good neighbourhoods. Although, overall, this does not seem to have transferred into a general preference for housing associations over councils as landlords as yet, this may take more time to build as knowledge and experience of housing associations continues to grow.

Notes

1. See http://www.housingcorp.gov.uk/resources/keyworkerliving.htm for full details of this programme.

References

Barker, K. (2004), *Review of Housing Supply, Delivering stability: securing our future housing needs, Final report – recommendations*, Norwich: HMSO

Department of the Environment, Transport and the Regions and Department for Social Security (2000), *Quality and Choice: A decent home for all,* London: DETR

Ford, J. and Burrows, R. (1999), 'To buy or not to buy? A home of one's own', in Jowell, R., Curtice, J., Park, A. and Thomson, K. (eds.), *British Social Attitudes: the 16th Report – Who shares New Labour values?*, Aldershot: Ashgate

Greensitt, G. (2001), 'Fact-finding mission', *Housingtoday,* 20 September: 18–19

HM Treasury (2005), Press release 1 April 2005, www.hm-treasury.gov.uk/newsroom_and_speeches/press/2005/press_35_05.cfm

Kemp, P. (2000), 'Images of council housing', in Jowell, R., Curtice, J., Park, A., Thomson, K., Jarvis, L., Bromley, C. and Stratford, N. (eds.), *British Social Attitudes: the 17th Report – Focusing on Diversity*, London: Sage

Murie, A. (1997), 'The Housing Divide', in Jowell, R., Curtice, J., Park, A., Brook, L., Thomson, K. and Bryson, C. (eds.), *British Social Attitudes: the 14th Report – The end of Conservative values?*, Aldershot: Ashgate

Office of the Deputy Prime Minister (2004), *Survey of English Housing – New results: April–December 2003*, London: ODPM

Office of the Deputy Prime Minister (2005a), *Sustainable Communities: Homes for All,* Norwich: The Stationery Office

Office of the Deputy Prime Minister (2005b), Live tables Table 502, www.odpm.gov.uk

Pawson, H. (2004), 'Reviewing stock transfer', in Wilcox, S., *UK Housing Review 2004/2005*, Coventry: Chartered Institute of Housing, and London: Council of Mortgage Lenders

Robinson, C., Humphrey, A., Kafka, E., Oliver, R. and Bose, S. (2004), *Housing in England 2002/3*, Norwich: The Stationery Office

Smith, J. (2005), 'Attitudes to home-ownership and moving in 2004', *Housing Finance,* April, London: Council of Mortgage Lenders

Weaver, M. (2004), 'Key worker housing: the issue explained', SocietyGuardian.co.uk, 25 May, http://society.guardian.co.uk/keyworkers/story/0,1266,547935,00.html

Wilcox, S. (2004), *UK Housing Review 2004/2005*, Coventry: Chartered Institute of Housing, and London: Council of Mortgage Lenders

Williams, P. (2003), 'Owning up – where is home-ownership going?', in Wilcox, S., *UK Housing Review 2003/2004*, Coventry: Chartered Institute of Housing and London: Council of Mortgage Lenders

Acknowledgements

The *National Centre for Social Research* is grateful to the Housing Corporation for funding the module of questions on which this chapter is based. Responsibility for the analysis of this data, and the views expressed within the chapter, lie solely with the authors.

4 Higher education: a class act

*Ted Wragg and Mark Johnson**

Class inequality in education has been a concern of policymakers, educationalists, sociologists and other commentators for many years. Research has consistently shown that people from middle-class backgrounds do, on average, considerably better, and stay in education longer, than their contemporaries from working-class backgrounds (Piatt, 2003). The differentials have persisted stubbornly over several decades, despite the dramatic expansion of educational provision during the second half of the 20th century (Heath and Clifford, 1990).

Given the critical role education plays in determining people's future opportunities as well as their class location in the social order, this has the effect of limiting the prosperity and status mobility of significant sectors within British society. Education could have the power to change the pattern of advantage, but it can also reinforce the existing distribution of both advantage and disadvantage.

A number of different theoretical perspectives have been developed to explain this situation. These can be divided into two general approaches, depending on whether learners are seen as being largely at the mercy of external forces, or more in control of their own destiny: are they pushed or pulled? Both positions start with the notion that people make decisions during their educational careers about whether or not to continue to study (Gambetta, 1987), but differ in their view of how these decisions are made.

The first approach emphasises factors that 'push' people in certain directions and over which they actually appear to have little control, such as the economic situation and cultural environment into which they are born – in other words, structural and normative factors. Such 'culturalist' arguments are put forward by Bourdieu (1977) and Willis (1977).

* Ted Wragg is Emeritus Professor of Education at Exeter University. Mark Johnson is a Researcher at the *National Centre for Social Research* and Co-Director of the *British Social Attitudes* survey series.

The second approach emphasises factors that 'pull' people in certain directions, where they then make purposive, rational decisions, so as best to meet their intentions for the future. An example of this approach is rational choice theory, which sees individuals as seeking to maximise their own utility by choosing between various courses of action on the basis of an assessment of their costs, benefits and probability of success. If the costs and benefits of education are perceived differently by different social groups, class inequalities may still result (Breen and Goldthorpe, 1997).

Both approaches have appeal and limitations. For example, culturalist perspectives that stress the apparent incompatibility between working-class culture and school culture, do not explain why increasing proportions of working-class children are, in fact, staying on longer in education. Similarly, rational choice theory may exaggerate the extent to which people in their daily lives actually make a cool calculation about the value of different courses of action.

The whole debate has achieved a new importance through the Labour government's avowed emphasis on 'Education, education, education'. It has been the aim of the Labour government, since its 2001 election victory, to raise the proportion of young people going to university to 50 per cent by 2010. In this it has had some success – for the academic year 2003–04 the proportion stood at 43 per cent, a record high (Department for Education and Skills, 2005). Such a figure helps illustrate the huge increase in numbers entering higher education over a relatively short period of time – 40 years ago the figure was nearer seven per cent (Halsey, 1992).

At the same time, the Labour government has also put social inequalities in education on the agenda, by exerting considerable pressure on universities to widen access to their courses. Each individual institution has been given targets in terms of percentages of students to be recruited from less affluent backgrounds, or 'poor postcodes' as it was often known. A former university vice-chancellor was appointed in October 2004 to act as 'access regulator'. The policy soon became controversial, especially when some heads of independent schools, accusing Bristol University of being biased against their pupils, threatened to tell their pupils to boycott the university. Attempts to shift the balance of power through education almost invariably spark conflict between interested parties.

Over the decades grant and loan schemes have been used at various times, as financial incentives to help the less well off stay on beyond the minimum school leaving age, or to go on to further and higher education. Most recently, an Education Maintenance Allowance worth £30 a week was introduced for older secondary pupils. At the same time, university top-up fees of up to £3,000 per annum are being introduced from 2006, but alongside these will be the reintroduction of grants and bursaries for less affluent students.

The effects of educational inequality can be traced in the *British Social Attitudes* sample. Table 4.1 shows the proportion of respondents who have a degree, broken down by age and class. The first point to note is that ten times as many professionals have a degree as routine manual workers[1] (39 per cent compared with just four per cent). This is not a direct measure of class inequalities in the access to education: people with degrees will, of course, be more likely to go into professional occupations than into routine manual ones, whatever their class of origin. However, it does illustrate the stark differences of the past educational experience of people from different classes.

Clearly, there has been some narrowing of this gap in more recent years, as can be seen when looking at the individual age groups. Interpretation of the youngest (18–24) age group is problematic as some of these respondents may still be in the process of gaining their degrees (and also because class, as based on their current or last job, may still be fluid). Looking instead at the more settled 25 to 34 age group, we see that half of professionals have a degree, compared with eight per cent of routine manual workers. Although the class difference is much smaller than for the 65+ age group (where a quarter of professionals but less than half a per cent of routine manual workers have a degree), this still means that six times as many professionals have degrees as routine manual workers among people educated, roughly speaking, in the 1980s and 1990s.

Table 4.1 Proportion who are graduates, by age and social class

% who are graduates	Professionals		Routine manual		All	
Age group		Base		Base		Base
18–24	46	40	12	104	16	243
25–34	51	216	8	128	28	524
35–44	41	255	2	169	20	641
45–54	39	218	4	129	19	553
55–64	30	167	2	155	16	503
65+	24	180	*	251	7	729
All	39	1079	4	936	18	3199

Given the enduring importance of social class as a basis for attitudes in British society, charted many times in *The British Social Attitudes Reports* (see, for example, Park and Surridge, 2003), it is not unreasonable to suppose there will be class differences in people's attitudes towards education, especially higher education, where the differences between social classes in terms of access and success are most pronounced. We also know from previous *British Social Attitudes* surveys that there is a perceived class bias in higher education – in 2002, 43 per cent of respondents thought that a young person from a well-off background was more likely to be offered a university place than a young person with similar A levels from a less well-off background (Wragg and Jarvis, 2003).

This chapter will focus specifically, therefore, on the issue of social class and higher education. There are three strands to the analysis. We first discuss attitudes towards the relative merits of academic and vocational qualifications. Is it the case, for instance, that people from working-class backgrounds see less value in academic qualifications than those from middle-class backgrounds? We then look at views on the opportunities that are open for entering higher education – how do the different social classes vary in their views about increasing or reducing opportunities for higher education? Finally, we analyse opinions on the funding of higher education, in particular, student tuition fees. How does their appeal vary by class, and are they likely to exert a positive or negative effect on the aspirations of people from class backgrounds traditionally under-represented at university?

Vocational or academic?

We saw earlier that the 'culturalist' theory posits that young people are pushed into educational choices by their economic situation and cultural environment. In particular, there is a stereotypical view of the working classes as being uninterested in higher education and not encouraging their children to pursue this path. If this is the case we ought to find signs of a difference in perceptions between the classes about the merits of academic qualifications, and how they compare with vocational qualifications. This divide has been subject to a lot of scrutiny over recent years. Public debate has covered such matters as whether school education should be focused more on future employment or be 'liberal' and detached from jobs; whether so-called 'academic' courses are in some way superior to vocational courses; and the extent to which both our society and our education system are influenced by bias against practical skills.

In 2003 and 2004, a committee, chaired by Sir Mike Tomlinson, conducted a thorough review of the whole of post-16 education. Its conclusion that there should be four levels of diploma, covering both academic and vocational courses, proved controversial just before the 2005 general election, leading to both the Labour and Conservative parties asserting that they would not want to see the end of the traditional examination system for 16 to 19 year olds. The Labour government produced its own proposals for vocational awards in a 2005 White Paper.

The 2004 *British Social Attitudes* survey addresses some of these issues. An opening general question, about the relative merits of practical skills *versus* academic results, produces some most interesting, and perhaps surprising, responses:

> *In the long-run, which do you think gives people more opportunities and choice in life ...*
> *... having good practical skills and training,*
> *or, having good academic results?*

Given the traditional accusation that we are, as a nation, biased against practical skills, one might have expected a strong endorsement of the second half of the question. Yet the opposite is the case. By far the largest category, just under half (47 per cent), take the first view, that good practical skills and training give people more opportunities in life, compared to a distinctly lower 22 per cent thinking good academic results do. Even though it was not explicitly offered to respondents as an option, 30 per cent opted for a mixture of the two.

How do these views compare to views in previous years? There are good grounds for expecting attitudes to have altered over time, reflecting changes in emphasis in the education debate. As Table 4.2 shows, there have been some interesting shifts. The proportion of people in 2004 opting for practical skills and training is significantly higher than in 2002, but actually no higher than in 1993. As for the proportion choosing academic results, in 2004 this was lower than for any previous year.

This is a most intriguing finding. Perhaps media coverage about the dearth of plumbers and other skilled workmen has highlighted to people the value of pursuing such a career, not least in terms of newspaper stories claiming that plumbers in London could earn £1,000 a week. Meanwhile, the increasing numbers of people proceeding to university, may mean that there is less public faith in the 'graduate premium' (the amount graduates can earn above the average school leaver). Of course, the distinction that the question employs is not explicit about vocational *qualifications*. Practical skills and training may often come within a job which would only be possible *after* getting academic qualifications.

Table 4.2 More opportunities in life – practical skills or academic results, 1993–2004

	1993	1995	2002	2004
	%	%	%	%
Practical skills and training	44	43	38	47
Academic results	30	32	31	22
(Mixture)	25	25	30	30
Base	*1493*	*1253*	*3435*	*3199*

But the question we want to address is to what extent are there class differences on this matter. Is it the case that the working-class respondents are more likely to be supportive of vocational qualifications, or the 'university of life', than the academic route, and how do they compare to the middle classes in this respect? If working-class people see fewer benefits accruing from a purely academic education, then universities will face an uphill struggle trying to recruit more students from less affluent backgrounds.

As Table 4.3 illustrates, there are some class differences in attitudes to practical skills and training. More than half of those in the routine manual class chose practical skills and training, compared to only 40 per cent of professionals, though there was surprisingly little difference in the views about academic qualifications.

Table 4.3 More opportunities in life – practical skills or academic results, by social class

	Professionals	Routine manual	All
	%	%	%
Practical skills and training	40	52	47
Academic results	24	22	22
(Mixture)	35	26	30
Base	1079	936	3110

To make the direct contrast between vocational and academic qualifications we use another question. Respondents were also asked:

> Suppose you were advising a 16 year old about their future.
> Would you say they should ...
> ... stay on in full-time education to get their A-levels (or A2-levels),[2]
> or, study full-time to get vocational, rather than academic
>   qualifications,
> or, leave school and get training through a job?

Can we detect a trend similar to that found above with fewer people now favouring the academic route? Table 4.4 shows this is indeed so. Back in 1995, 53 per cent said they would advise academic qualifications, as did 51 per cent in 2002, but by 2004 this had dropped to 42 per cent.

Table 4.4 Advice to a 16 year old, 1995, 2002, 2004

	1995	2002	2004
	%	%	%
A levels	53	51	42
Vocational qualifications	12	11	13
Training through a job	12	10	12
(Depends on person)	22	29	32
Base	1227	3435	3199

As Table 4.5 shows, there were, again, class differences. But they were somewhat different from what we might have expected. Rather than the working class being less likely to emphasise academic qualifications than the middle class, the reverse is the case. Nearly half of those in the routine manual class would have advised the 16 year old to stay and get academic qualifications, compared to only 38 per cent of professionals. It seems to represent a faith – largely from the outside since few members of this group have A-levels or above – in the power of qualifications *per se*.

Significant numbers of all groups wanted to stress that it depended on the person, and it is notable that professionals were more likely to take this more guarded view than routine manual workers.

Table 4.5 Advice to a 16 year old, by social class

	Professionals	Routine manual	All
	%	%	%
A levels	38	48	42
Vocational qualifications	13	12	14
Training through a job	7	13	12
(Depends on person)	42	25	32
Base	*1079*	*936*	*3110*

In terms of party allegiance, Labour supporters were more likely (46 per cent) to say "academic", Conservative supporters less likely (39 per cent), though these distributions are partly affected by social class themselves. This perhaps also represents an endorsement of the views of one's party, since the Conservative Party nationally has been less in favour than Labour of expanding higher education.

We can push the issue slightly further because those who either said "academic qualifications" or that "it depends on the person" were then asked how they would advise a 16 year old who had actually *failed* their school exams. As Table 4.6 shows, the class differences persist, and indeed widen compared to our other question. Fewer people in all classes would advise this young person to stay on in education by retaking their exams, and the proportion of professionals choosing vocational qualifications almost doubled. As a result of this, the difference between the professional and routine manual classes widens. On our previous question this difference was 10 percentage points, on this question it is 15 percentage points. Again this appears contrary to the common assertion that working-class children who fail in education are likely to be advised by their families to quit their studies and get a job.

Table 4.6 Advice to a 16 year old who had *failed* school exams, by social class

	Professionals	Routine manual	All
	%	%	%
A levels	27	42	33
Vocational qualifications	25	17	22
Training through a job	14	21	17
(Depends on person)	34	20	27
Base	*859*	*691*	*2310*

Does the advice people would give depend on whether or not they have children themselves? There might be differences between what people advocate for others and what they tell their own children. This is, in fact, the case to some extent: those with children were slightly more likely than those without to advise a 16 year old to stay on and pursue academic qualifications (46 per cent compared with 41 per cent), while those without children were more likely to advise the vocational route (14 per cent compared with 11 per cent), but the differences are not substantial.

Could it simply be, however, that these differences are not explained by social class at all, but are determined by factors associated with class, like education, for example. Is it the case that people with lower educational qualifications have realised, through experience, how essential academic results are? Multivariate analysis of the responses confirms that even whilst controlling for level of education, and a number of other factors, social class is still a strong predictor for encouraging a 16 year old to study academic qualifications, whether they had failed their school exams or not. True, education level reached was also important in its own right. Counter-intuitively – but in line with the results reported above – those with no qualifications were more likely than average to say they would advise a 16 year old to pursue academic qualifications.[3]

We can therefore challenge two common stereotypes, one being that the British do not value practical skills compared with academic ones, and the other that working-class people are less likely than professionals to believe in the value of their children staying on in education.

More opportunities for entering higher education?

If people have become less likely over the years to emphasise academic qualifications and also less likely to advise a 16 year old to stay on to do academic qualifications, we may expect that views on opportunities for entering higher education will also have moved in a negative direction, with fewer people wanting the increased opportunities on offer.

We have already commented on the great expansion that has taken place in higher education. But, as Rootes and Heath (1995) argue, many of the pressures for expansion that existed previously are not present to the same extent nowadays. The post-war 'baby boom' generation meant that there were simply a greater number of people to educate, so in order just to keep the proportion of people going to university constant there needed to be expansion in the 1960s. The situation is made turbulent by dramatically fluctuating annual birth rates, which go up and down in cycles, like a roller coaster, every peak followed by a trough. Similarly, higher educational qualifications came to be regarded as necessary for 'salariat' careers. It could further be argued, now that so many people have degrees, that a situation of over-supply is emerging. In this situation, it may actually be to greater benefit for the individual not to go on to higher education but to leave school earlier and get a head start in the labour market – the so-called 'fallacy of consumption' (Gambetta, 1987). Perhaps in this atmosphere there is no public appetite for any further expansion of higher education.

Increase or reduce opportunities?

We therefore ask whether the government's aim to get 50 per cent of young people into university is supported in general, or have views on expansion of higher education become more negative over time? To do this, we employ two measures from the *British Social Attitudes* survey. The first is a general question about opportunities, and the second looks at ideas about the actual numbers entering higher education.

The first question we put to respondents was as follows:

> *Do you feel that opportunities for young people in Britain to go on to* **higher education** *– to a university or college – should be increased or reduced, or are they at about the right level now?*
> *IF INCREASED OR REDUCED: a lot or a little?*

What we find in Table 4.7 is that, in 2004, the public was less supportive of increasing opportunities than at any time since the question was first asked in 1983. A mere 14 per cent want opportunities to be increased "a lot". In contrast 16 per cent want opportunities to be reduced. It is only since 2003 that more than 10 per cent have favoured a reduction – a doubling since 1999. Before 2004, the proportion who wanted higher education to be increased a lot outnumbered those who wanted it to be reduced by an average of 20 percentage points. In 2004, attitudes had reversed so that those wanting a reduction outnumbered those wanting a big expansion by two percentage points. Note in particular that there has been a 16 percentage point decrease among those wanting increased opportunities, in just one year since 2003. Clearly it is too early to know whether this change in views will be sustained in the future.

Table 4.7 Increase or reduce opportunities for young people to go to higher education, 1983–2004

Opportunities for HE should be ...	1983	1990	1995	1999	2003	2004
	%	%	%	%	%	%
... increased a lot	22	32	28	25	25	14
... increased a little	22	19	19	19	25	20
Are about right	49	43	47	47	37	47
... reduced a little	4	1	3	4	8	12
... reduced a lot	1	1	1	1	2	3
Base	1761	1400	1227	1052	1056	3199

To some extent one would expect this sort of trend irrespective of other factors when the numbers in higher education are going up. Back in 1983 only about one in seven went to university, so there was plenty of scope for expansion. Today with nearer half going to university, there is far less headroom for increased participation.

A key factor is likely to be the extent to which people expect their own children to benefit from university. If we find that there are differing expectations between the classes, then differing views on expansion may make more sense. However, if this is the case, then any policy trying to reduce the class inequalities faces an uphill battle because of the central role of parental attitudes and expectations in encouraging the ambition and abilities of their children. That parental attitudes count strongly in education has been found regularly in research from the Plowden Report in 1967 to the present (Elliott *et al.*, 2001).

As Table 4.8 shows, there are very clear, perhaps predictable, class differences. Of those who have children, 84 per cent of professionals think it is likely their children will go to university, compared with 65 per cent of routine manual workers. These differences become even more pronounced when we look at the proportions saying "very likely" – more than double the proportion among professionals (45 per cent) than routine manual workers (20 per cent) thought it very likely that their children would go to university.

Despite the differences, the very fact that nearly two-thirds of routine manual workers expect their children to go to university, it could be argued, is evidence of the success of policies encouraging all groups in society to aspire to higher education. Given the proportion of graduates in routine manual jobs shown in Table 4.1, the aspirations of the working classes for their children may well be over-optimistic (although many of the working-class respondents presumably hope that their children will go on to have professional jobs as well as a degree). Perhaps working-class respondents are less able to predict their children's educational chances than professionals, since they have less first-hand experience of the education system beyond minimum school leaving age. If so, they could end up being disappointed unless the government succeeds in its policy to increase working-class access to higher education.

Table 4.8 Likelihood of own child going to university, by social class

	Professionals	Routine manual	All
	%	%	%
Very / Fairly likely	84	65	75
Not very / Not at all likely	14	32	23
Base	*225*	*193*	*645*

Base: Respondents with own child aged 5–16 in the household

What class differences would we expect for views on expansion of higher education? On the one hand, we might expect the working class to want increased opportunities for higher education so that they and their children have a greater chance of entry and subsequent upward mobility. On the other hand, if they perceive a university education as a middle-class preserve, we would expect them to resent the public subsidy of higher education and hence to oppose increased opportunities.

Similarly, we might posit two competing hypotheses for middle-class views. On the one hand, they might not want to lose their advantage over the working class in higher education and we would then expect them to oppose expanding opportunities (Goldthorpe, 1982). On the other hand, they may want everyone to have the same sorts of experience and opportunities they themselves enjoyed during their educational career, and we would then expect them to think that opportunities should be increased.

Reports in the *British Social Attitudes* series have previously considered the related issue of whether support for an expansion of higher education depended on people's own educational qualifications. *The 12th Report* found that those who were themselves graduates were far more supportive of further expansion than those without degrees, but the authors predicted that this might well change as the educated chose to "pull up the ladder of advancement behind them" (Rootes and Heath, 1995: 185). Indeed, *The 19th Report* found that such a change had taken place and that graduates were no longer any more in favour of an expansion in higher education than others (Wragg and Thomson, 2002).

Given these findings and the link in Britain between social class and educational attainment, Table 4.9 perhaps comes as no surprise. A mere 28 per cent of professionals want opportunities increased, compared to 45 per cent of routine manual workers. Nearly a quarter of those professionals actually want opportunities reduced, whereas fewer than one in ten of routine manual workers felt that way.

Table 4.9 Increase or reduce opportunities for young people to go to higher education, by social class

	Professionals	Routine manual	All
	%	%	%
Increased	28	45	35
About right	48	46	48
Reduced	24	9	17
Base	*1062*	*904*	*3033*

Do these large differences persist once other potentially relevant characteristics are taken into account, however? In short, they do: professionals are still much less likely to support increasing opportunities than are routine manual workers. Additionally, there is an age effect, with the younger groups more likely to support increasing opportunities. Those with lower incomes want more opportunities, as do those with a child in the household who is likely to go to university. People without children are less likely to want to increase opportunities, as are men. Interestingly, people's own level of education did not influence views, over and above the effect of social class.

So, to return to our hypothesis outlined earlier, we find support for the view that professionals are "pulling up the ladder of advancement behind [themselves]". As for the working class, there is little evidence of a resentment of higher education as a middle-class preserve, and rather an appetite for having a bite at the cherry themselves. This fits well with our earlier findings that working-class respondents are more likely to recommend to a young person to stay on in education than professionals are, and that a majority of working-class respondents expect their children to go on to university (which has clearly not happened in the past).

Knowledge of numbers

We mentioned earlier that working-class respondents may be less knowledgeable about the higher education system and that this may colour their responses. 'Opportunities' can mean different things to different groups. Luckily, we are actually in a position to explore the extent to which their knowledge of the actual numbers who go to university affects their judgement.

To assess public knowledge about current opportunities we asked:

*Of every 100 young people leaving school in Britain today, about how many do you think **will** go to university?*

As mentioned previously, the actual figure is currently about 43 per cent. The mean estimate by respondents was 38 per cent, five per cent below the true figure. As Table 4.10 shows, there is a clear link between perceptions of the current situation and attitudes towards future expansion: those who want *increased* opportunities gave a lower mean estimate of current participation rates than those wanting *reduced* opportunities.

Table 4.10 Mean estimates of number of young people out of 100 who go to university, by views on opportunities for higher education

	Mean estimate	Base
Opportunities for HE should be...		
... increased a lot	32	457
... increased a little	36	610
Are about right	39	1425
... reduced a little	43	354
... reduced a lot	44	109
All	38	3011

We might have predicted that the middle class would be better at estimating the number of young people going to university than the working class because of their greater experience within the system, but this need not necessarily be true. The middle class may be knowledgeable about the number of people they know who *do* go, whereas the working class may be knowledgeable about the number of people they know who do *not* go, so these two counteracting forces may balance themselves out. In fact, the mean estimate for the number of young people out of a hundred going on to higher education was 39 among professionals and 38 among routine manual workers, which is not statistically significantly different.

However, we must be wary about these average scores. There was a lot of variation around the mean and we cannot in any case expect members of the general public to know the exact figure (which changes from year to year). In order to give a better measure of knowledge we created a group whose estimates were within five percentage points either side of the true figure (i.e. between 38 and 48). Comparing the proportions of the different classes in this group allows us to assess their relative levels of knowledge. On this measure, we found that a slightly larger group among the professionals (20 per cent) got the figure about right than among routine manual workers (16 per cent). Although the difference is statistically significant, it is not of a magnitude to suggest that we can attribute the cause of the class differences in views on expanding higher education to this factor.

Not just numbers?

Along with the question asking how many people respondents think actually *do* go to university, we asked respondents how many (out of every 100) they think *should* go. The average figure given was 48 per cent, i.e. close to the Labour government's target, but again with wide fluctuations around the mean.

Using the two questions about the proportion that 'do go' and the proportion that 'should go' to university, we have created three categories – respondents who believe that fewer should go than now, that about the right number go now and that more should go. Table 4.11 shows, as is to be expected, the very strong relationship between this measure and the earlier question about expanding or reducing opportunities for higher education. Interestingly, though, almost half (45 per cent) of those who thought that opportunities for higher education were about right, actually thought that more young people should go to university than at present.

Table 4.11 Views on number of people who should go to university, compared with views on current opportunities for going to higher education

School leavers going to university:	Opportunities for higher education should be ...			
	Increased	About right	Reduced	All
	%	%	%	%
Fewer should go	6	19	78	24
The right number go	11	36	11	23
More should go	83	45	11	53
Base	*1067*	*1425*	*463*	*2955*

When social classes were compared, there were similar marked differences to those reported above. Twice as many professionals (32 per cent) as routine manual workers (16 per cent) wanted fewer young people to go to university than actually go at present.

More funding?

Nonetheless, a large proportion of people still want opportunities for entering higher education to be maintained or increased, and a majority also want more people to go to university. This would undoubtedly cost more money. How does the public think these aspirations should be funded?

When asked, in general, about priorities for extra government spending, 26 per cent opt for education, compared with, for example, 52 per cent who choose health. When asked specifically what should be the priority for extra spending on education, only a small minority (14 per cent) opt for "students at colleges or universities". This is higher than the figure for 2000, which was nine per cent, but no higher than any of the intervening years. School age pupils are seen as more deserving of extra cash. Thus there seems to be no great appetite for pouring extra public money into higher education. Where then, do people propose that any extra funding should come from? The government's answer to that question has been through student tuition fees, but does the public accept this as a solution?

Tuition fees

Since 1998 students have had to pay yearly tuition fees of around £1,000 up-front before their course started. From 2006 there will be top-up fees of up to £3,000 in England, though this will not apply to Welsh students attending Welsh universities, and the Scottish Parliament has introduced a limited option so it can protect Scottish students, since it opposes top-up fees in principle. This policy has led to protests and a fierce public and political debate that has persisted. Those against tuition fees have argued that their introduction will continue, and perhaps enhance, the existing class inequalities in university attendance. Others suggest that since the poorest students are not required to pay them, it will have the reverse effect, with those at the less affluent end of the middle class being the most put off by them.

In this section we look at their overall level of support, paying particular attention to the way the social classes do or do not differ in their views. For example, are the working class more, or less, in favour of tuition fees than the middle class? We might expect them to be more in favour if they do not expect to benefit from higher education and therefore do not want to be subsidising through their taxes, the middle classes who are more likely to benefit. But equally we might expect working-class respondents to be against top-up fees because they would like their children to go to university and fear that they will not be able to afford to pay for it. Similarly, the middle classes may see university education as a right that people should not have to pay for – 'I benefited from free education, others should, too' – and therefore oppose tuition fees. Or maybe they do not object to the idea of tuition fees, seeing it as unfair that those who will not themselves directly benefit should pay for higher education in taxes. Perhaps they may even see tuition fees as a way of retaining their own dominance of higher education by making it too expensive for those working-class families that do not qualify for the grants and bursaries.

All, some or no students?

To assess support for tuition fees we asked our respondents the following question:

*I'm now going to ask you what you think about university or college
students or their families paying towards the costs of their tuition,
either while they are studying or after they have finished. Which of the
views on this card comes closest to what you think about that?*

All *students or their families should pay towards the costs of their
tuition*

Some *students or their families should pay towards the costs of their
tuition, depending on their circumstances*

No *students or their families should pay towards the costs of their
tuition*

Perhaps contrary to expectations, given the public debate and student protests
against tuition fees, less than a quarter of the public think *no* students should
pay tuition fees. The most popular view, held by two-thirds of the public, is that
some students should pay depending on their circumstances. Interestingly, that
is quite close to the proposals for 2006, when grants will be reintroduced for
less well-off students and universities will also offer bursaries for them.

How do attitudes to financing vary across the social classes? As Table 4.12
shows, there is not a great deal of difference. Routine manual workers were
indeed significantly less likely than professionals to think *all* students should
pay tuition fees, nine per cent compared with 13 per cent, but the difference is
hardly startling. Essentially, the two classes hold pretty much the same views.

Table 4.12 Views on tuition fees, by social class

Who should pay tuition fees	Professionals	Routine manual	All
	%	%	%
All students	13	9	11
Some students	64	65	66
No students	23	24	23
Base	*1079*	*936*	*3110*

Perhaps there are other factors bound up with people's class location also
influencing their views? Views on tuition fees may be pushed and pulled in
opposite directions, so that class actually may have more effect than the above
table suggests. Indeed, in further analysis, we found that those who have higher
education qualifications were less likely than average to support tuition fees,
possibly reflecting the feeling that if they had benefited from a free education,

as many did, so others should too (including their own children). In contrast, those who have no qualifications were more likely to support tuition fees.

When?

A related question, and one that has been prominent in political debates, is *when* fees should be paid. On their introduction, fees were paid up-front each year before students began their course. More recently, the government has moved towards the idea of graduates paying them back after their course is over, once they have started working in a job and reached a certain level of income. Clearly there are pros and cons of each approach. The idea of having to pay a lump sum of £1,000-plus each year is bound to be a deterrent to some people, and perhaps disproportionately the lower classes, who tend to have less disposable income. If that is the case then education as means to social mobility faces a problem. Equally, many people worry that that idea of deferred payment encourages a 'buy now pay later' mentality that may well have far-reaching consequences. In March 2005 the Department for Education and Skills announced that the average student debt on graduating, in future, was likely to be £15,000.

To find out which repayment option the public supported, we asked those people who had expressed support for tuition fees at the question reported above the following:

> *And when should students or their families start paying towards the costs of their tuition ...*
>
> *... while they are studying,*
> *or, after they have finished studying and have got a job?*

Of those people asked the question there was a fairly even split in preferences. Forty per cent felt that students should pay while they were studying and 48 per cent thought it should not be until after they have finished studying and got a job.

How did the different social classes feel about this? If it is true that the working class are more put off by up-front fees, then we would expect that they would prefer the payment to fall due after students have finished studying (assuming they expect or want their children to go). We may also expect that a sizeable portion of the middle classes would prefer payment whilst students are studying, largely because they could probably afford to pay for their children and therefore not saddle them with debts.

In the event, there were actually no significant differences between the classes on this. Instead, it is age, income, having or not having a child and the likelihood of it going to university, and sex of respondent that were more important factors. Thus concerns about up-front tuition fees *disproportionately* putting off people from working-class backgrounds seem unfounded.

Variable or not?

Having discussed 'whether' and 'when', the next area to consider is the 'what' and 'where'. Should different subjects and different institutions charge different fees? This is a relatively new proposal because for the first few years of their life tuition fees were uniform across all institutions and subjects. For the moment top-up fees are capped at a maximum of £3,000, but many believe that, eventually, varying fees by institution, or indeed by subject, will create a two-tier system, with elite universities charging more, and therefore disproportionately putting off those from poorer backgrounds, who are likely to be more wary of paying large sums of money. Others argue that someone going to a university that offers them poorer tuition, or a less stimulating environment, should not have to pay as much as people elsewhere.

On subject differences, there are vastly different costs associated with different courses. For instance, a science course on average costs much more per student than a humanities subject, because of laboratory and equipment factors. Is it not justified, some argue, for the fees people pay to reflect this? Others argue, however, that there are already too few people doing the scientific and technical subjects, and charging more for them will only discourage more people.

In short, the debate opens up the issue of whether higher education should or should not be opened up to market forces. But what do the public think and can we detect support for either side of the debate? The responses show that the public seems to hold a fairly strong conviction that institutions should *not* be allowed to charge different fees – with about two-thirds (65 per cent) expressing that view.

It is not clear what we would expect to see in terms of social class factors here. On the one hand, if the working class does not expect to benefit from university, then it presumably makes little to difference to them. However, given that analysis of people's responses above show a sizeable proportion seem to hope that their children will indeed attend university, then the opportunity to have a cheaper option may appeal, as it might to middle-class members. At the same time there is no reason to assume that those in the working class who do wish to go to university would not want to go to the better universities.

As Table 4.13 shows, there are, in fact, some class differences on this. When considering how different universities should charge fees, professionals were more likely than routine manual workers to believe they should be different, 35 per cent compared to 29 per cent.

As for charging by *subject*, there is more support for differential fees than between institutions – 43 per cent overall favouring them. On this question it is even harder to predict how the classes will vary as there is no reason to suppose either would do better or worse from such a situation. Professionals are again more likely to believe in different fees, 46 per cent compared to 35 per cent. Indeed the difference between the classes is wider on this measure than for institutions – 11 percentage points compared to six.

Table 4.13 Views on fees for institutions and subjects, by social class

	Professionals	Routine manual	All
Institutions' fees should be ...	%	%	%
...the same	62	68	65
...different	35	29	32
Subject fees should be ...	%	%	%
...the same	52	61	54
...different	46	35	43
Base	*1079*	*936*	*3110*

Conclusions

Social class factors do appear to play a part in forming people's attitudes to higher education. In some cases the effect is small, but in others it is more noteworthy. One of the most striking findings concerns attitudes to academic and vocational education. There is a common belief that the British are especially biased against practical skills in general, and vocational education in particular, but, in fact, all social groups placed "practical skills and training" much higher than "academic results" in terms of offering opportunities in life. Particularly important, is the forceful endorsement by working-class people of the need for academic qualifications, stronger even than that expressed by middle-class respondents. Even in the case of children who fail their exams, the support among working-class people for continued study is firm – putting a lie to the view that working-class parents do not want their children to carry on in education.

The perceived need for substantially increased access to higher education has clearly declined as the number of places actually available has increased, but many people express an ambivalence. On the one hand, while there is more of a feeling now that we may be reaching saturation point, few would actually support a reduction. Working-class people are more likely to support an increase in higher education opportunities than are professionals. This suggests that professionals may not wish to have their position challenged by a continuously increasing influx of more graduates. Conversely, the working class appear to be well aware of the potential of individual advancement through education and are keen that higher education should be widely available, even if this has in the past mainly benefited the middle class. It would therefore appear that those theories which try to explain the lower levels of working-class participation in higher education in terms of a working-class culture which lacks support for academic education are wrong nowadays (although they may, of course, have been right in the past). Indeed, two-thirds of routine manual parents expect their children to go on to university. Although this is lower than the proportion of professionals with such expectations, it is an extraordinarily high figure given the historically low levels of working-class students going on to higher education. If the current government policies do not deliver a substantial increase, this could well lay the basis for significant discontent in the future.

If it is not cultural factors that are at work, then we have to look elsewhere for explanations for the continuing social inequalities in access to higher education. Clearly, other structural factors, such as the quality of school education provided in different neighbourhoods are likely to be important, but are beyond the scope of this chapter. However, economic considerations is one area that we have dealt with. Are the working classes put off higher education by the costs? On the face of it, it would appear not: the public of all social classes accepts the idea of some tuition fees being paid by students themselves. However, very few want *everyone* to have to pay, and this may, of course, mean that working-class respondents think that wealthier families should pay, and not themselves.

Variable fees are not a popular notion. Most people do not want different institutions to charge different fees. There is slightly more sympathy (though still from a minority) for subject differentials. Professionals are slightly more in favour of both sorts of variable fees than are routine manual respondents, suggesting that there may be some worry among the latter group that they will be priced out of the best institutions and courses.

The two most striking features of this analysis are probably (1) the strong support for vocational education, much greater than is often believed, and (2) the greater support than commonly imagined by working-class parents for gaining academic qualifications, even after exam failure, and the strong aspiration that their own children will get into university, despite the many obstacles they may face.

Notes

1. The measure of social class we use in this chapter is the National Statistics Socio-Economic Classification (NS-SEC). In its compressed form, there are five categories – 'Professional and Managerial occupations', 'Intermediate occupations', 'Small employers and own account workers', 'Lower supervisory and technical occupations' and 'Semi-routine and routine occupations'. For simplicity, in much of this chapter we refer only to the first and last of these, calling them respectively 'professionals' and 'routine manual workers' (or simply 'working class' for short). Not only do these two groups represent the extremes of the class spectrum, but they are also the two largest groups, accounting for around 62 per cent of the population.
2. In Scotland, the wording was 'Highers (or Higher Stills)'.
3. The multivariate analysis done for this chapter is not reported in detail here, but is available from the authors on request.

References

Bourdieu, P. (1977), 'Cultural reproduction and social reproduction', in Karabel, J. and Halsey, A. H., *Power and Ideology in Education*, New York: Oxford University Press

Breen, R. and Goldthorpe, J. (1997), 'Explaining educational differentials: towards a formal rational action theory', *Rationality and Society*, **9**: 275–305

Department for Education and Skills (2005), *Participation Rates in Higher Education for Academic Years 1999/2000–2003/2004 (Provisional)*, http://www.dfes.gov.uk/rsgateway/DB/SFR/s000572/index.shtml

Elliott, J., Hufton, N., Illushin and Willis, W. (2001), "The kids are doing all right': differences in parental satisfaction, expectation and attribution in St. Petersburg, Sunderland and Kentucky', *Cambridge Journal of Education*, **31(2)**: 179–204

Gambetta, D. (1987), *Were they pushed or did they jump?: Individual decision mechanisms in education*, London: Cambridge University Press

Goldthorpe, J. (1982), 'On the service class, its formation and future', in Giddens, A. and Mackenzie, G. (eds.), *Social Class and the Division of Labour*, Cambridge: Cambridge University Press

Halsey, A.H. (1992), *Decline of Donnish Dominion: the British Academic Professions in the Twentieth Century*, Oxford: Clarendon Press

Heath, A.F. and Clifford, P. (1990), 'Class Inequalities in Education in the Twentieth Century', *Journal of the Royal Statistical Society Series A*, **153**: 1–16

Park, A. and Surridge, P. (2003), 'Charting change in British values', in Park, A., Curtice, J., Thomson, K., Jarvis, L. and Bromley, C. (eds.), *British Social Attitudes: the 20th Report – Continuity and change over two decades*, London: Sage

Piatt, W. (ed.) (2003), 'Social Mobility', *New Economy,* **10(4)**, London: Institute for Public Policy Research

Plowden Report (Central Advisory Council for Education) (1967), *Children and their Primary Schools*, London: HMSO

Rootes, C. and Heath, A.F. (1995), 'Differences of degree: attitudes towards universities', in Jowell, R., Curtice, J., Park, A., Brook, L. and Ahrendt, D. (eds.), *British Social Attitudes: the 12th Report*

Willis, P. (1977), *Learning to Labour*, Aldershot: Gower

Wragg, E.C. and Jarvis, L. (2003), 'Pass or fail? Perceptions of education' in Park, A., Curtice, J., Thomson, K., Jarvis, L. and Bromley, C. (eds.), *British Social Attitudes: the 20th Report – Continuity and change over two decades*, London: Sage

Wragg, E.C. and Thomson, K. (2002), 'Education, education, education' in Park, A., Curtice, J., Thomson, K., Jarvis, L. and Bromley, C. (eds.), *British Social Attitudes: the 19th Report*, London: Sage

Acknowledgements

The *National Centre for Social Research* is grateful to the Department for Education and Skills for their financial support which enabled us to ask the questions reported in this chapter, although the views expressed are those of the authors alone.

5 Public responses to NHS reform

John Appleby and Arturo Alvarez-Rosete[*]

Now into its third term, and eight years since it came to power, it would be fair to say that New Labour have been on a significant health policy journey. Under its slogan "We will save the NHS", New Labour's 1997 manifesto pledged to remove 100,000 patients from waiting lists, abolish the internal market (but retain the separation between purchasers and providers), do away with GP fundholding, and set targets for increasing the quality of health care. It also promised unquantified, but real, increases in NHS funding (to be spent, as all governments promise, on direct patient care not bureaucracy) (Labour Party, 1997). While the manifesto was long on criticisms of past Conservative health policy – particularly the internal market[1] – it was somewhat short on practical alternatives.

The incoming Labour government inherited the lowest satisfaction ratings with the NHS ever recorded by the *British Social Attitudes* survey. In 1996, net satisfaction (satisfaction minus dissatisfaction) with the overall running of the NHS stood at minus 14 points, with half the survey sample being very or quite dissatisfied. Things, as was said hopefully at the time, could only get better.

However, over the first few years of the 1997 administration, some things did not get better. In particular, the iconic waiting list target looked increasingly difficult to meet as inpatient waiting lists in England rose from around 1.1 million in 1997 to nearly 1.3 million in 1999. Waiting times, too, also rose. By 1999, the number of outpatients waiting over 13 weeks had risen by around 30 per cent and the number waiting over 15 months or over 12 months for inpatient admission had more than doubled. Paradoxically, net satisfaction with the overall running of the NHS hit an all time high of plus 13 percentage points in 1999 – a remarkable turnaround in three years.

But while the public may have paid more attention to the rhetoric than what was actually happening to some of the NHS's key performance indicators,

---

[*] John Appleby is Chief Economist at the King's Fund. Arturo Alvarez-Rosete is a Research Officer at the King's Fund.

ministers were only too aware of the shortcomings. While fulfilling the letter of their 1997 manifesto pledge to increase NHS funding in real terms, the increases in the early years of the parliament had been relatively small – around two to three per cent. The message from the NHS was that it could not achieve the targets it had been set without substantially higher investment to boost capacity. The turn of the century was also a turning point for the NHS. Decisions were made to increase NHS funding substantially. At the same time, '*The NHS Plan*' was published, in essence stating that now the NHS had more money it would be expected to change – to 'modernise' – to meet tough new targets (Department of Health, 2000).

The NHS Plan was significant in setting a new policy course for the NHS – in England, at least. Another 1997 manifesto pledge had, by 1999, lead to the creation of a Welsh Assembly and a Scottish Parliament with powers to run and organise their respective health care systems. While, amongst other things, *the NHS Plan* highlighted the destination of New Labour's health policy journey – laying out the rudiments of a reactivated internal market in England, with greater patient choice and new financial incentives for hospitals – Wales and Scotland were not so keen on such an economic model. Policy in these countries developed accordingly. More recently, however, and following a relative lack of improvement in performance, policy towards the NHS in Wales, and to an extent in Scotland, suggest some moves towards the English strategy.

The government's policy towards the NHS has been nothing if not pragmatic: what works is what counts. In hindsight, there have been three phases in policy. Stevens describes these as: support for providers, hierarchical challenge and localist challenge (Stevens, 2004). Put more simply, these phases can be described as:

- First, increasing resources (money, labour and facilities) and capacity generally (including access by the NHS to the independent health care sector).
- Secondly, engaging in tough and very direct management to improve performance through target setting coupled with rewards and sanctions.
- Thirdly, an attempt to devolve decision making through the introduction of more 'automatic' performance enhancing mechanisms. For example, patients' and primary care trusts' choices of hospital are supposed to send signals in the market to providers to stimulate improvements in performance, while hospital reimbursement will be directly linked to the work they carry out.

In hindsight, these phases appear reasonably coherent. At the time, policy development was somewhat more haphazard.

While there have been significant measurable improvements in targeted objectives, such as reduced waiting times, a key issue for any government is how its policies and, more particularly, the outcomes of policies are perceived by the public. This chapter will use *British Social Attitudes* data from the last seven years to look in turn at each of the three phases of New Labour's health policy strategy, ending by looking at overall measures of satisfaction, to establish whether the public appreciate Labour's changes to the NHS.

Investing in the NHS: more money

A key political decision for New Labour in late 1999/early 2000 was to increase substantially investment in the NHS. In 2000, the Prime Minister personally pledged to increase total (public and private) health care spending in the UK with an eventual goal of matching the average of the UK's European Union neighbours – from around seven per cent of GDP to over nine per cent. This decision recognised long-running complaints of a history of underfunding in the NHS relative to the demands being placed upon it.

Priorities for tax and spend

Previous *British Social Attitudes* surveys have consistently shown that when people are asked which area of government spending should have priority for extra spending, health is always given top priority. Every year since 1984 over 70 per cent have picked it as their first or second priority (see Figure 5.1).

Figure 5.1 Health: first or second priority for extra government spending

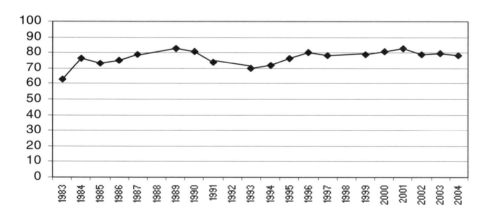

When New Labour first came to power, NHS spending across the UK was around £43 billion. In 2005/6 spending will have more than doubled in cash terms. Even allowing for NHS-specific inflation, it will have increased by more than 50 per cent. This represents the equivalent of around an additional two-and-a-half percentage points of GDP between 2000 and 2007. Moreover, the commitment is planned to be long term. Given these resources flowing into the

NHS, it is hardly surprising that Figure 5.1 shows that public demand for *extra* expenditure has tailed off after 2001 – although support for health as a priority spending area remains very high.

This finding is to some extent mirrored in the responses to another long-running *British Social Attitudes* question concerning taxation and spending:

> *Suppose the government had to choose between the three options on this card. Which do you think it should choose?*
>
> *Reduce taxes and spend **less** on health, education and social benefits*
>
> *Keep taxes and spending on these services at the **same** level as now*
>
> *Increase taxes and spend **more** on health, education and social benefits*

As Figure 5.2 shows, support for increased taxation and spending is lower now than at any time since 1987. Again, this is likely to be related to the fact that spending on health care (and, indeed, education and other services) has been increasing substantially over the last few years, going some way to satisfying previous demands. Nevertheless, there is no great appetite for *reduced* taxes and spending, rather for keeping them at current levels.

Figure 5.2 Taxation *versus* social spending

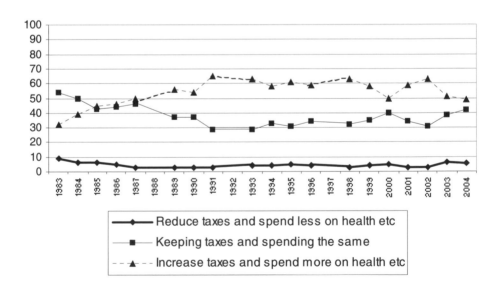

The government's long-term commitment to increased spending on the NHS was confirmed by a review published in 2002 of total health care spending across the UK up to 2022/23 by Sir Derek Wanless (commissioned by the Chancellor, Gordon Brown) (Wanless, 2002). This built on the political decision to commit more resources to the NHS in the short term by suggesting that, by 2022, spending should reach between 10.5 and 12.5 per cent of GDP.

Whether future governments will commit to the increases suggested by Wanless remains to be seen. The 2006 spending review (set to announce spending plans beyond 2007/8) has been postponed until 2007. Heavy hints from health ministers that the NHS has had its fair share from the public purse and should in future expect a scaling back in current spending increases, suggest a more parsimonious future.

The Wanless review also affirmed a commitment to a tax-funded NHS (at least in terms of the cost-effectiveness of such a funding source) and also, by implication and otherwise, to the NHS as a universal service. In this respect Wanless reaffirms what the *British Social Attitudes* survey has for many years revealed to be the public view. Since 1983, respondents have been asked:

> *It has been suggested that the National Health Service should be available only to those with lower incomes. This would mean that contributions and taxes could be lower and most people would then take out medical insurance or pay for health care. Do you support or oppose this idea?*

As shown in Figure 5.3, around three-quarters of those asked have consistently opposed such a system. Indeed, the 2004 survey records an increase in opposition to one of its highest levels since the mid-1990s.

Figure 5.3 Proportion opposed to the NHS being only for the poor, with a consequent reduction in taxation

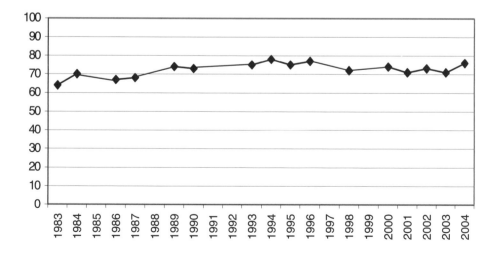

Spending the money: improving infrastructure

The government's largess did not come without strings, however. As mentioned above, *The NHS Plan*, published in 2000, set out long-term strategies and targets for modernising the NHS, using the additional resources allocated by government. A whole section of *The NHS Plan* was devoted to plans for investing in health care facilities and infrastructure. The shopping list was extensive: 7,000 more beds, 100 new hospitals by 2010, modernisation of over 3,000 GP premises, and the promise of cleaner wards and hospitals. By 2010, the plan was to ensure that 40 per cent of the value of the NHS estate was less than 15 years old.

Of course, building hospitals takes time, but, even so, we can begin to ask whether the increases in capital expenditure has registered with the public. The answer seems to be, not yet. Figure 5.4 shows trends in the proportion of the public saying that they are "very" or "quite" satisfied with various aspects of the NHS in their area that might be affected by a programme of capital expenditure. While there has been some increase in satisfaction with waiting areas in outpatient and accident and emergency (A&E) departments, satisfaction with waiting areas in GP surgeries (although higher) remains static. In contrast, satisfaction with the general condition of hospitals has fallen, to reach its lowest point for 15 years, with only a third now saying that they are satisfied. This may, of course, be linked to the media coverage of MRSA in hospital wards.

Figure 5.4 Proportion who are very or quite satisfied with the condition of hospitals, and waiting areas

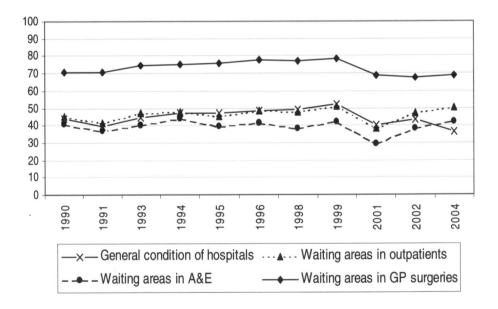

Getting tough: targets for waiting times

If there is one aspect of the patient experience that the British NHS is known for, it is the need to wait. Even at its inception in 1948, the NHS immediately took on a waiting list of around half a million patients. Since then, numbers have risen and the waiting time for patients to see a specialist as an outpatient, or to be admitted to hospital, has increased. For both the public and patients, waiting has consistently been seen as a (if not *the*) problem with the NHS.

Over the last 30 years there have been numerous attempts to reduce both the total numbers of people waiting and waiting times. Some have been successful, at least for a time, others have failed. None have really got to grips with the reasons why waiting lists exist or have fully understood that tackling waiting times is not a one-off, isolated activity of little consequence to the rest of the health system (Harrison and Appleby, 2005).

When Labour came to power in 1997 it pledged to reduce the number of people waiting for hospital treatment. Three years later, with the publication of *The NHS Plan* (Department of Health, 2000), it committed the NHS to a sustained assault on waiting times and launched a wide range of policies to achieve this. *The NHS Plan* heralded a hitherto much more interventionist approach by government. Along with extra funding, the NHS needed to reform, to modernise. In its first few years in office from 1997, the waiting list problem had worsened – lists and waiting times were longer than those inherited from the previous Conservative administration. A key strategy was a 'get tough' policy with the NHS. Challenging targets (and even more challenging sanctions) to reduce waiting times were set – first for inpatients and outpatients, and later for other areas such as cancer and accident and emergency treatment.

The use of targets (though contentious for some in the NHS), the increased capacity arising from increased funding, and a number of other initiatives such as waiting times 'hit squads' to help trusts in particular difficulties, all backed up with a consistent political will to crack the problem, produced results. Maximum waiting times in England have fallen dramatically over the last few years (the rest of the UK is another story), to the extent that the latest waiting times target – that no one should wait more than 18 weeks from GP referral to admission to hospital – while not without risks of failure, certainly looks more attainable now than even a few years ago.

Have the public noticed the reduced waiting times?

But do the public recognise these successes? And given the inevitability of at least some waiting, what do they see as a reasonable period to wait?

Respondents to the *British Social Attitudes* survey were asked to say whether the following aspects of the NHS in their area were in need of a lot of improvement, in need of some improvement, satisfactory or very good:

> *Hospital waiting lists for non-emergency operations*
> *Waiting time before getting appointments with hospital consultants*

Time spent waiting in accident and emergency departments before being seen by a doctor

Figure 5.5 shows that dissatisfaction with inpatient and outpatient waiting times reached a low in 1995, but then rose up to 2000/2002, with around eight out of ten of those surveyed stating that waiting times in these areas need some or a lot of improvement. A similar pattern was evident for waiting times in accident and emergency departments. But the government can draw some encouragement from the 2004 results. Figure 5.5 shows reductions in the proportion of respondents stating that improvements are needed in waiting times for all three services. For A&E, this is the first reduction in a decade, and for inpatient waits, the lowest expression of dissatisfaction recorded since 1989.

Figure 5.5 Proportion thinking inpatient, outpatient or accident and emergency waiting times needed a lot or some improvement

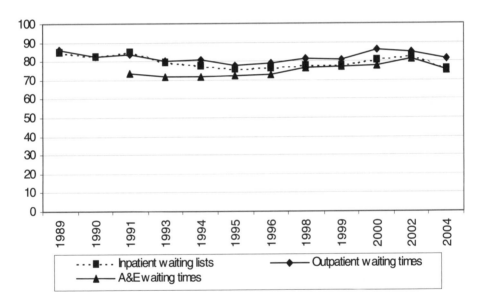

Further evidence for the optimism about outpatient waiting can be gained from another question that asks:

> *Now suppose you had a back problem and your GP referred you to a hospital out-patients' department. From what you know or have heard, please say whether you think you would get an appointment within three months.*

Forty six per cent of those surveyed (up 10 points since 2001) now think that they would "definitely" or "probably" receive an outpatient appointment within three months.

It would appear, then, that the successful efforts to reduce waiting times have begun to be noticed by the public just recently. This coincides quite closely with steady reductions (in England) since 2000 in the numbers of outpatients waiting over 13 weeks (see Figure 5.6) and the virtual elimination of inpatient waits of over 15 months by 2002, and of waits of over 12 months by 2003 (see Figure 5.7).

Figure 5.6 Outpatient waiting: of those not seen, numbers still waiting over 13 weeks

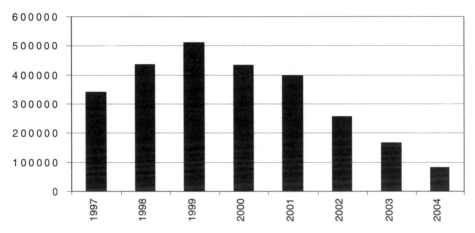

Source: King's Fund (2005)

Figure 5.7 Inpatient waiting: numbers waiting over 15 and over 12 months for admission to hospital

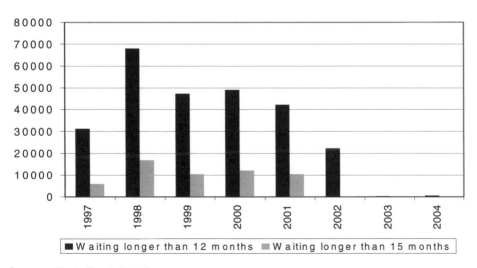

Source: King's Fund (2005)

However, the picture is not altogether rosy. It should be noted that although the *trend* in dissatisfaction with waiting lists may be downwards, the *absolute levels* are still very high. As shown in Figure 5.5, over three-quarters of those surveyed still felt improvement was needed. Moreover, a majority still think they would not get an appointment for a back problem within three months – this despite the fact that of the 2 million or so patients seen in English outpatient departments in the second quarter of 2004, around 83 per cent waited less than three months.[2]

What is a reasonable wait?

Part of the explanation for the continuing high levels of dissatisfaction with waiting times may lie with the public's opinion of what constitutes a 'reasonable' wait. To explore this, the 2004 survey set out a number of scenarios involving different conditions and then asked how long it would be reasonable to wait to see a GP, wait to attend hospital as an outpatient or wait in an accident and emergency department.

Table 5.1 Reasonable wait to see a GP

Patient condition		Days						Mean	Median
		<1	1	2	7	14	30		
Mild back problem	%	6	12	19	42	13	6	8.0	5
Chest infection	%	38	39	16	7	n/a	n/a	1.3	1

Base: 3199

Table 5.2 Reasonable wait for an appointment at hospital outpatients' department

Patient condition		Weeks			Months			Days	
		<1	1	2	1	2	3	Mean	Median
Mild back problem	%	9	12	19	30	15	11	35.7	28
Severe back problem	%	37	29	18	11	2	1	10.8	7

Base: 3199

Table 5.3 Reasonable wait in Accident and Emergency department

Patient condition		Hours					Mean	Median
		0	1	2	3	4		
Broken wrist	%	5	47	33	7	5	1.8	1

Base: 3199

Tables 5.1 to 5.3 show the distribution of responses. These results are of course based on hypothetical scenarios, but lend some support to the argument that the public's expectations of a reasonable wait outstrip actual performance. For example, it would seem that regardless of the severity of a back pain problem, a majority of those surveyed would want an outpatient appointment within four weeks. However, the current median wait for an outpatient appointment in England is nearly seven weeks.

No national data exist on the distribution of actual waiting times for a GP appointment. On waiting in accident and emergency the current target in England is four hours which is now reported as almost always met. Some 97 per cent of respondents indicated that a reasonable wait for a broken wrist should be four hours or less. However, since a large majority actually believed the acceptable waiting time is two hours or less, the government's target may not be sufficiently tough to satisfy people. Expectations for a reasonable wait to see a GP for someone with a chest infection seem to be broadly in line with the current target that no one should wait more than 48 hours to see a GP. Interestingly, for a mild back problem, around six in ten would be willing to wait longer than the current target to see a GP.

Letting go: devolution and plurality

While the period between 2000 and 2004 saw benefits from the new extra health resources and tough management regime, principally in large reductions in waiting times and the achievement of other targets set by government, there were also costs. Complaints about micro management by ministers, the distortion in clinical priorities arising from tactics to meet stringent targets, and some evidence of managerial manipulation of performance data, became more common. In part this lead to greater emphasis on 'earned autonomy' – that is, less central interference earned by meeting targets. *The NHS Plan* had already flagged this as the next stage in the development of the performance system. In particular, the creation of Foundation Trusts embodied this devolutionary shift.

From 2004, the NHS in England entered a new phase – greater devolution, with encouragement for independent providers to meet NHS demands, and a new system for reimbursing hospitals for their work,[3] but also increased monitoring and regulation and the start of experiments in patient choice. Despite this search for more 'automatic' or devolved mechanisms for levering up NHS performance, the system still retains some tough targets – notably the goal of reducing maximum waiting times from GP referral to hospital admission to 18 weeks. But what do the public feel about the idea of choice in the NHS?

Patient choice

Over the last five years patient choice has emerged as an important policy in England and is starting to emerge as a tactic to reduce waiting times in Wales and Scotland. And indeed, the origins of patient choice lie in the government's key priority to reduce maximum waiting times. Experiments such as the London Patients Choice Project and the National Coronary Heart Disease Choice Scheme[4] focused on providing elective patients already on waiting lists with the choice of quicker treatment – mainly in NHS hospitals, but also in the independent sector and paid for by the NHS. Since these trials, choice of quicker treatment has been rolled out in England and similar initiatives are starting in other parts of the UK. From December 2005, all patients in England needing an outpatient appointment are to be offered a choice of around four hospitals.

In order to explore the public's attitudes to choice, for the first time the *British Social Attitudes* survey asked a series of questions concerning different aspects of choice: whether there *should* be choice of the hospital to go to for inpatient care, the time of outpatient appointments and the treatment given. In addition, the survey asked to what extent the NHS *actually* offered choice in these areas.

As Table 5.4 shows, not only do a majority state that there should be "a great deal" or "quite a lot" of choice in all these areas, but very few feel that the NHS currently provides such choices. Clearly, the NHS does not appear to be meeting the public's expectations on choice. It is interesting to note, however, that a significant minority in all areas stated that only "a little" or no choice at all was needed.

Table 5.4 Proportion thinking there should be, and actually is, patient choice of hospital, outpatient appointment time and treatment

	Patients should have a great deal or quite a lot of choice	Patients actually have a great deal or quite a lot of choice
Which hospital to go to	63	9
Outpatient appointment time	53	14
Kind of treatment	65	17

Base: 3199

Are some groups more pro-choice than others? For example, is the concern with choice a middle-class preserve? Recent comments by Culture Secretary Tessa Jowell, who has stated that she viewed choice as a mechanism by which the middle classes could be re-engaged with public services,[5] suggest that the government may think this is the case.

It is therefore worth looking in more detail at which groups in society are more concerned with choice. Table 5.5 shows the proportion of people in various groups who think that patients should have "a great deal" or "quite a lot" of choice of hospital. Interesting differences are immediately apparent. For example, women are considerably more enthusiastic about choice than men. And those with recent experience of being an inpatient are also more enthusiastic than those without such contact with the NHS.

The results also provide some perhaps counter-intuitive observations. Given the Conservative Party's advocacy of choice in health services, we might have expected a difference on party lines, but there is none. Nor is the idea that choice is a middle-class concern borne out. Those classified as working in professional and managerial occupations are actually *less* pro-choice than those in semi-routine and routine manual occupations. Similarly, those on low incomes tend to be more enthusiastic about choice than those on high incomes – perhaps because those on high incomes see themselves as having the choice to go private if the NHS does not deliver what they want. And those with lower educational qualifications are more supportive of choice than those with higher education qualifications.

Table 5.5 Characteristics of those supporting patient choice of hospital

		% saying people should have a great deal or quite a lot of say over which hospital to go to if they need treatment	*Base*
All		63	*3199*
Sex	Men	56	*1391*
	Women	69	*1808*
Party identification	Conservative identifiers	63	*831*
	Labour identifiers	64	*1038*
	Lib Dem identifiers	64	*404*
	No party identification	59	*508*
Social class	Managerial & professional	59	*1079*
	Intermediate occupations	64	*367*
	Self-employed	64	*268*
	Lower superv. & technical	62	*460*
	Semi-routine and routine	67	*936*
Household income	<£10,000	70	*689*
	£10,000–£32,000	65	*1291*
	£32,001–£50,000	57	*466*
	>£50,000	59	*363*
Country	England	62	*2684*
	Wales	73	*331*
	Scotland	62	*184*
NHS contact	Recent inpatient	65	*1120*
	Not recent inpatient	60	*1328*
Age	18–34	57	*767*
	35–54	62	*1194*
	55–64	69	*503*
	65+	68	*729*
Highest educational qualification	Higher education	56	*872*
	A level	59	*475*
	GSCE/O level	67	*929*
	None	69	*854*

Older age groups (those aged over 55) tend to be more pro-choice than younger age groups. The most pro-choice group are people in Wales, with nearly three-quarters stating that NHS patients should have "a great deal" or "quite a lot" of choice of hospital.

However, some of the groups in Table 5.5 overlap and we need to use multivariate analysis to identify the effect of each factor when the others are taken into account. This analysis is reported in more detail in the appendix to this chapter. In summary, it confirms that women, people with recent experience as inpatients and older people are keener than their counterparts on choice. The multivariate analysis also confirms that party identification is not a significant factor. Although social class and income no longer have an independent effect, the related factor of educational qualification does: those with higher educational qualifications are *less* interested in choice, which is obviously in line with the findings for class and income in Table 5.5.

Table 5.5 also showed that the Welsh were more pro-choice than the English. One possibility is that in England, where patient choice of hospital is already an important element of government health policy – much more so than in Wales – and choice has figured strongly in ministerial rhetoric about the modernisation of the NHS, there is less demand for further changes. However, we need to be cautious about this conclusion as the finding is not replicated in the multivariate analysis. Hence the different views held in Wales may be more to do with the age and social structure of the Welsh population than the separate health policies adopted in Wales.

The use of the independent sector

Another aspect of choice is the thorny issue of the role of the independent or private sector in health care. Since 1997, New Labour has moved considerably in its attitudes to the use of the independent sector to treat NHS patients. From Frank Dobson's and, in his earlier tenure as Secretary of State for Health, Alan Milburn's position of 'over my dead body' on the use of the independent sector, policy changed. *The NHS Plan* announced in 2000 that a 'concordat' between the NHS and the independent sector would be drawn up (Department of Health, 2000). There was a recognition that the increases in capacity needed to achieve NHS waiting times targets could not be delivered quickly, and that use of the independent sector would be one solution to this short-term difficulty.

Use by the NHS of the independent sector is not new, of course. Ever since 1948 the NHS has paid for NHS patients to be treated in private hospitals on an *ad hoc* basis. What is different now is the suggestion of a more deliberate move to greater plurality in the supply of secondary care, with NHS hospitals competing for business with other NHS hospitals and the independent sector. This is seen both in the introduction of formal offers of choice for inpatient elective care, and now for patients requiring a specialist outpatient consultation, as well as in the view that NHS hospitals could benefit from being exposed to a limited form of competition. Indeed, as part of the expansion of choice to GP referral to outpatients, all patients in England are to be offered a choice of hospitals from December 2005 which, as far as possible, should include at least one independent sector provider (Department of Health, 2004).

While government attitudes to the independent sector have changed rather radically, how do the public view the private health sector? Although we do not have a direct measure of this in *British Social Attitudes*, it is worth referring to a question which looks at the public/private split in general. As Table 5.6 shows, people believe the private sector is better than the government at running services cost-effectively and providing a good quality service. However, the government is best at making sure services go to the people who need them most. As far as we can tell from this question, the greater use of the independent sector by the NHS is likely to be acceptable so long as the allocation decisions remain in the public sector.

Table 5.6 Government or private companies best at service provision

Who is best at:		Govern- ment	Private company
Running services cost-effectively	%	39	55
Providing a good quality service	%	41	51
Making sure services go to people who need them most	%	73	21
Base: 2146			

The bottom line: improved satisfaction?

Having looked at public attitudes to various aspects of government health policy, we turn now to the question of whether the changes have delivered greater satisfaction with the NHS. For many years, an important element of the *British Social Attitudes* survey has been the questions it poses about satisfaction, not just with the NHS overall, but with specific services. And satisfaction provides a key barometer of the public's opinion on government health policy. Table 5.7 shows the trends in satisfaction with the NHS overall and with specific aspects of the service since 1996 along with a measure of net satisfaction (satisfied minus dissatisfied).

Given earlier discussions, it is perhaps not surprising that net satisfaction ratings for the various parts, as well as the NHS as a whole, follow a general pattern of rising satisfaction in the early years of the Labour government, some disillusionment setting in around 2000/2001, and then a revival since about 2003 when the extra spending really started to make a difference. This is typified by the score for the NHS which started out on an all time low of minus 14 in 1996 (i.e. those who were dissatisfied outnumbered those who were satisfied by 14 percentage points). From there, net satisfaction rose to plus 13 in 1999, despite, as we have seen, few obvious improvements being delivered in this period. Public opinion then caught up with events and net satisfaction fell to minus 1 in 2002, during a period when more money was being spent but the benefits were perhaps not yet apparent. Finally, as the extra resources began to make themselves felt, satisfaction rose to plus 7 by 2004.

There are some differences between the services. Satisfaction with inpatient services has fallen recently, perhaps as a result of the MRSA scare. On the other hand, satisfaction with GP services, albeit higher than the rest of the NHS, have not yet recovered from the fall in 2001. And the picture for dental services is quite different to the rest of the NHS. The large dip in satisfaction with dental services in 2004 is almost certainly a reflection of the well-publicised increase in difficulty in many parts of the country in being able to access dentists carrying out NHS work.

Table 5.7 Satisfaction with the NHS overall and specific services, 1996–2004

	1996	1998	1999	2000	2001	2002	2003	2004
NHS overall	%	%	%	%	%	%	%	%
Satisfied	36	42	46	42	39	40	44	44
Dissatisfied	50	36	33	39	41	41	37	37
Net satisfaction	-14	+6	+13	+3	-2	-1	+6	+7
GPs	%	%	%	%	%	%	%	%
Satisfied	77	75	76	76	71	72	72	72
Dissatisfied	13	14	14	15	17	18	17	17
Net satisfaction	+64	+61	+62	+61	+54	+54	+56	+54
Dentists	%	%	%	%	%	%	%	%
Satisfied	52	53	53	62	53	54	52	42
Dissatisfied	25	23	24	19	24	22	26	38
Net satisfaction	+27	+30	+29	+43	+29	+32	+27	+4
Inpatients	%	%	%	%	%	%	%	%
Satisfied	53	54	58	59	51	51	52	48
Dissatisfied	22	17	17	21	24	23	21	24
Net satisfaction	+31	+37	+41	+38	+27	+28	+31	+24
Outpatients	%	%	%	%	%	%	%	%
Satisfied	52	52	56	58	51	52	54	54
Dissatisfied	25	22	21	24	27	26	24	23
Net satisfaction	+27	+30	+35	+34	+24	+26	+30	+32
A&E departments	%	%	%	%	%	%	%	%
Satisfied	n/a	n/a	53	51	43	43	45	47
Dissatisfied	n/a	n/a	24	29	32	32	32	31
Net satisfaction	n/a	n/a	+29	+22	+11	+11	+13	+16
Base	*3620*	*3146*	*3143*	*3426*	*2188*	*2287*	*2293*	*3199*

n/a = not asked

While satisfaction scores are of interest in themselves, an important question is why satisfaction rates have changed over time, and, what factors could explain or are driving current rates of satisfaction. In order to explore possible reasons for changes in satisfaction and the underlying drivers for current rates of satisfaction, we therefore examine satisfaction in relation to various other factors.

Satisfaction and recent contact with the NHS

Previous survey reports have noted the difference in satisfaction ratings between those members of the public who have had recent contact with the NHS and those with no recent contact (Mulligan and Appleby, 2001; Appleby and Alvarez-Rosete, 2003). Fortunately for the NHS, the former tend to be more satisfied than the latter. And, as Table 5.8 shows, this is still true in the 2004 survey, with those with recent experience of general practice and inpatients and outpatients, for example, being more satisfied (42 per cent) than those with no recent NHS contact (37 per cent). Interestingly, those with a lot of recent contact with the NHS also tend to be a bit more dissatisfied than others, suggesting a possible polarisation of views among frequent users.

Table 5.8 Satisfaction with NHS by experience of NHS

	Recent contact with NHS			
	None	GP only	GP and either inpatient or outpatient	GP, inpatient and outpatient
	%	%	%	%
Satisfied	37	44	45	42
Neither	26	23	20	19
Dissatisfied	33	34	34	39
Net satisfaction	4	10	11	3
Base	89	502	844	964

Satisfaction and views of waiting times

Given the central importance of waiting lists and waiting times – not just to government policy, but to patients and the media – it might be expected that satisfaction with the NHS would be a function of the public's opinion about waiting lists.

However, at the aggregate level, there is little or no significant association in trends between the public's view that inpatient waiting lists need improvement and dissatisfaction with inpatient services overall. A similar lack of association was found for the need to improve outpatient waiting times and overall dissatisfaction. And there was no association with the need to improve waiting times with overall dissatisfaction with the NHS as a whole. Somewhat oddly, the only substantial relationship[6] was a *negative* association between the view that inpatient waiting lists were satisfactory or very good and satisfaction with inpatient services in general.

However, at the individual respondent level, there is definitely a link between views of waiting times and satisfaction. As seen in Table 5.9, those who were "very" or "quite" satisfied with outpatient services in general were much more optimistic that they would get an outpatient appointment within three months for a back problem than those who reported being "very" or "quite" dissatisfied (56 per cent compared with 29 per cent). But the fact that 42 per cent of those who were generally satisfied with outpatient services *also* stated that they did not think they would receive an appointment within three months,[7] suggests that perceptions of waiting times is only a partial explanation for the level of outpatient services satisfaction revealed by the 2004 survey.

Table 5.9 Views on likelihood of receiving an outpatient appointment within three months for treatment of a back problem, by satisfaction with outpatient services in general

	Satisfaction with outpatient services	
Expectation of receiving an outpatient appointment for a back problem within 3 months	Satisfied	Dissatisfied
	%	%
Probably/definitely would	56	29
Probably/definitely would not	42	70
Base: 3068		

Finally, there is some, albeit mixed, evidence from the 2004 survey that waiting times – in this case, views of what constituted a reasonable wait under different patient scenarios for A&E, outpatients and general practice – were associated with significant differences in levels of satisfaction. For example, those who expressed *dissatisfaction* with accident and emergency services in general would like shorter waits in A&E for the treatment of a broken wrist than those who were generally satisfied: 54 per cent of the very dissatisfied, compared with 44 per cent of the very satisfied, suggested that a maximum wait of one hour would be reasonable. It is worth noting that virtually the whole sample would want to be seen within the government's current maximum A&E waiting time target of four hours.

Satisfaction and variations in health policy and performance

Another way of examining the effect of the government's health policy is to look at the 'natural experiment' created by the different policies being implemented in England, Scotland and Wales.[8] Since the first elections to the Scottish Parliament and the Welsh Assembly in 1999, there have been significant differences in the performance of the NHS in the different parts of the UK, particularly with respect to waiting times (Alvarez-Rosete *et al.*, 2005). Could changes in satisfaction rates for these countries reveal a pattern linked to such divergence?

Table 5.10 shows net satisfaction with the NHS overall since 2001 for England, Scotland and Wales. Net satisfaction for England shows a steady increase since 2001, while in Wales there has been a decline, with more people now stating they were dissatisfied than satisfied. For Scotland, the trend is rather unclear, with an extreme peak in net satisfaction in 2003. The diametrically opposed trends in England and Wales are certainly interesting. It might be tentatively concluded that these results suggest support for the policy approach taken in England over the last few years.

Table 5.10 Net satisfaction (satisfied minus dissatisfied) with the NHS overall in Scotland, Wales and England

Net satisfaction with the NHS		2001	2002	2003	2004
England		-3	-1	+5	+8
Scotland		+4	+2	+26	+5
Wales		+5	+2	-8	-7
Base	*England:*	*1837*	*1924*	*1917*	*2684*
	Scotland:	*212*	*229*	*238*	*331*
	Wales:	*139*	*134*	*138*	*184*

However, this is a very broad brush analysis which fails to pinpoint specific factors underlying the trends in net satisfaction. Nor does it disentangle the fact that satisfaction is a relative concept, and a function not just of individuals' perceptions of the state of the NHS (or of government policies), but also of their prior expectations. Interpreting any change in satisfaction therefore requires some knowledge of expectations, too. As noted earlier, the 2004 survey asked a set of questions which probed the public's opinions about one aspect of their expectations: whether or not choice of hospital, outpatient appointment time and treatment was important to them and, further, whether the NHS provided choice in these areas. Using the results from these questions, it is possible to ascertain the importance of expectations in explaining overall satisfaction with the NHS, along with other factors – such as party affiliation, age and so on. To do so requires us to use multivariate analysis, which allows us to assess the importance of each factor while taking the others into account.

The appendix to this chapter reports the details of the logistic regression analysis. In summary, six factors were found to be statistically significantly linked to overall satisfaction with the NHS. These were: party identification, household income, country, age, views about the need for improvement in various areas of the NHS and expectations of choice over treatment. Labour identifiers were more satisfied with the NHS, as were those aged over 65 and people in Scotland. Conversely, those with a household income above £50,000 per year were less satisfied than average, as were people aged under 35, and those indicating that various areas of the NHS needed improvement (for example, GP appointment systems, outpatient waiting times and waiting times in accident and emergency).

When it came to expectations about choice, only one factor – choice of treatment – proved significant: those who felt that there was already sufficient choice over treatment options were more satisfied with the NHS. Thus, in the scheme of things, although views on greater choice are not without a role, they are only part of the explanation of why people are satisfied or dissatisfied with the NHS. Factors such as age, social standing, party identification and the health policies of your particular part of Britain are as much in evidence.

Conclusions

The results from the 2004 *British Social Attitudes* survey reveal, as ever, a mixed picture about the public's attitudes towards the NHS, as well as some surprising views about some current policies – particularly concerning patient choice.

The government has clearly caught the public mood by focusing on the NHS. Even after all the recent massive investment in the NHS, the public still see health care as the most important priority for extra government spending. Support for a universal health service, available to all, also continues to be strong. However, a fall in the number who want increases in taxes perhaps indicates that the increases in NHS spending are beginning to satisfy the desire for more investment, which is reflected in improved public satisfaction with the NHS since about 2003 when the extra spending really started to make a difference.

This is coupled with a growing public recognition that various objectives are being met: there has been a reduction in the numbers saying that improvements are needed in inpatient, outpatient and A&E care. However, the reduction is perhaps not as big as we might have expected given actual improvements in these areas. The explanation for this may lie in the public's expectations being higher even than the government's targets. This appears to be particularly the case for outpatient appointment waiting times. When asked what would be a reasonable wait for an appointment for a back problem, the median given by respondents was about a week for a severe condition and about a month for a mild condition. This does not compare favourably with the current median waiting time of seven weeks for an outpatient appointment.

Views about patient choice provide interesting reading. This policy is currently being rolled out in England as part of a strategy to drive down waiting times even further. Around two thirds of the public want choice of hospital, outpatient appointment time and treatment, and few think the NHS currently offers this, leaving a big gap in expectations of what the NHS should be offering. But the issue may not be as big a deal as it is sometimes made out to be – a third of the public seem not to be bothered about having these choices.

Perhaps a surprising result from the survey was the characteristics of people who were most enthusiastic about choice. It is sometimes thought that this is a middle-class issue, but those who were most keen on choice were those on low incomes, low or no educational qualifications and the elderly. Conversely, the relatively well-off, the young and managerial/professional classes were less pro-choice. This may of course in part reflect a lack of interest in choice among groups who use the NHS less than average, or who can afford to pay for an alternative. Indeed, those without recent experience of inpatient care, for example, were much less pro-choice than those with recent experience. Of course, as NHS patients start to experience the reality of the choice initiatives (such as choice of hospital at the time of GP referral, going live in England at the end of 2005) these views may change.

A key aspect of the *British Social Attitudes* survey is the near continuous collection since 1983 of views about satisfaction – with the NHS overall, and with various parts of the service. Although there have been some improvements in satisfaction since a low point in 2001, the changes appear relatively small compared with the rise in funding and actual improvements in waiting times. A pessimistic view might be that expectations are shifting ahead of improvements in actual performance, with the NHS having to run to keep up. A more optimistic view is that the public has yet to notice all the improvements and that satisfaction will rise after a few years.

These results also raise the question of what the NHS and government have to do to improve the public's satisfaction. Results from a multivariate analysis of satisfaction with the NHS overall suggest that improving patient choice may have little impact on satisfaction generally. On the other hand, improving GP appointment systems, the time GPs give patients in their consultations and the waiting times in accident and emergency departments as well as reducing waiting times for an outpatient appointment may well have a significant impact on overall satisfaction with the NHS. While significant efforts are being made to tackle waiting times (reinforced by the 18-week GP referral to hospital admission target to be achieved by 2008), there needs to be more attention paid to policy in primary care – particularly policy that directly affects patients' experience of the service.

Notes

1. "There can be no return to top-down management, but Labour will end the Conservatives' internal market in healthcare. The planning and provision of care are necessary and distinct functions, and will remain so. But under the Tories, the administrative costs of purchasing care have undermined provision and the market system has distorted clinical priorities. Labour will cut costs by removing the bureaucratic processes of the internal market." (Labour Party 1997)
2. For orthopaedics, the speciality to which a back problem may well be referred, the equivalent figure was 71 per cent.
3. See the Department of Health website:
   http://www.dh.gov.uk/PolicyAndGuidance/fs/en, link 'Payment by results'.
4. See the Department of Health website:
   http://www.dh.gov.uk/PolicyAndGuidance/fs/en, link 'Health and Social Care Topics> Coronary Heart Disease'.
5. *Public Finance*, 27 May 2005.
6. This showed an association of $R^2 = 0.43$. It should be noted that these aggregate associations are limited by the relative small number of observations, there being only 12 years when both sets of questions have been asked.
7. And conversely, that 30 per cent of those stating they were dissatisfied with outpatient services also thought they would receive an appointment within three months.
8. For example, the English NHS has pursued policies on patient choice and a tough management regime on waiting times targets, whereas in Scotland the focus has been to create professionally led clinical networks, and Wales has promoted partnerships with authorities and communities at the local level (Greer, 2004).

References

Alvarez-Rosete, A., Bevan, G., Mays, N. and Dixon, J., (2005), 'Diverging policy across the UK NHS: what is the impact?', *British Medical Journal*, forthcoming

Appleby, J. and Alvarez-Rosete, A. (2003), 'The NHS: Keeping up with public expectations?', in Park, A., Curtice, J., Thomson, K., Jarvis, L., Bromley, C. (eds.), *British Social Attitudes: the 20th Report – Continuity and change over two decades*, London: Sage

Department of Health (2000), *The NHS Plan: a plan for investment, a plan for reform*, White Paper, Cm 4818-I, London: The Stationery Office

Department of Health (2004), *"Choose and Book"– Patient's Choice of Hospital and Booked Appointment*, London: Department of Health, Gateway reference 5467

Greer, S.L. (2004), *Four Way Bet: How devolution has led to four different models for the NHS*, London: The Constitution Unit, UCL

Harrison, A. and Appleby, J. (2005), *The war on waiting for hospital treatment: What has Labour achieved and what challenges remain?*, London: King's Fund

Labour Party (1997), *New Labour: because Britain deserves better*, London: Labour Party

Mulligan, J. A. and Appleby, J. (2001), 'The NHS and Labour's battle for public opinion', in Park, A., Curtice, J., Thomson, K., Jarvis, L. and Bromley, C. (eds.), *British Social Attitudes: the 18th Report – Public policies, Social ties*, London: Sage

Stevens, S. (2004), 'Reform strategies for the English NHS', *Health Affairs*, **23(3)**: 37–44

Wanless, D. (2002), *Securing our Future Health: Taking a long-term view*, *Final Report*, London: HM Treasury

Acknowledgements

The *National Centre for Social Research* is grateful to the Department of Health for their financial support which enabled us to ask the questions reported in this chapter, although the views expressed are those of the authors alone.

Appendix

Multivariate analysis

Two logistic regressions were carried out. The first analysed various factors – age, sex, occupational class, etc. – to assess the propensity to agree with the statement that NHS patients should have a great deal or a lot of choice of hospital. In a similar way, the second model examined answers to the question on overall satisfaction with the NHS.

Model 1: 'NHS patients should have a choice of hospital'

Forward stepwise variable inclusion in the regression produced four significant factors, age, educational qualification, sex and recent experience of the NHS.
The interpretation of the statistical measure 'Exp(B)' is as follows:
Exp(B) > 1: More likely than the average to say that patients should have a great deal or quite a lot of say over which hospital they go to
Exp(B) < 1: Less likely than the average to say that patients should have a great deal or quite a lot of say over which hospital they go to

Significant variables	Exp(B)	
Sex		
Male	0.79	**
Female	1.27	**
Age		
18–34	0.70	**
35–54	0.97	
55–64	1.26	**
65+	1.18	
Recent experience of inpatient care?		
Yes	1.03	
No	0.79	**
Educational qualification		
Higher education	0.77	**
A level	0.89	
O level/CSE	1.22	**
None	1.20	*
Constant	1.91	

* = significant difference from the average at the 5% level
** = significant difference from the average at the 1% level

Model 2: Overall satisfaction with the NHS

Forward stepwise variable inclusion in the regression produced six significant factors: party identification, household income, country, age, area of NHS in need of improvement and whether or not expectations of choice of treatment were met or not. The statistical measure 'Exp(B)' should be interpreted as in model 1, but related to very or quite satisfied with the NHS overall.

Significant variables	Exp(B)	
Party identification		
Conservative	1.15	
Labour	1.43	**
Lib Dem	1.03	
Other party	0.51	**
No party	1.16	
Household income		
<10K	1.10	
10–32K	1.01	
32–50K	1.18	
>50K	0.76	**
Country		
England	0.93	
Scotland	1.45	*
Wales	0.74	
Age		
18–34	0.80	**
35–54	1.07	
55–64	0.89	
65+	1.31	*
Area of NHS in need of improvement		
GP appointment system need improvement	0.81	**
Time GP gives patient needs improvement	0.74	**
Waiting time before app'ment with consultant needs improving	0.77	**
Waiting time in A&E needs improvement	0.77	**
Time waiting for ambulance needs improvement	0.85	**
Expectations of choice over treatment		
Not enough choice over treatment	0.84	
Right amount of choice	1.27	*
Constant	1.14	

* = significant difference from the average at the 5% level
** = significant difference from the average at the 1% level

6 Transport: are policymakers and the public on the same track?

Peter Jones, Georgina Christodoulou and David Whibley*

Since the Labour government came to power in 1997, transport policy has fluctuated considerably in national importance. At its peak, it has been a very high political priority – on some occasions attracting the personal interest of the Prime Minister; at other times it has seemed to be of only secondary importance. Over this period there have been a number of Secretaries of State for Transport which has made it difficult to maintain momentum and stability, at least in certain aspects of national transport policy.

In its early years in office the Labour government seemed to offer the British public a new, more comprehensive and refreshing approach to transport policy, based around notions of sustainability. By developing a more integrated transport network, it would encourage alternatives to private car use and give more priority to environmental issues. It proposed to give more prominence to bus, rail and light rail systems, and to encourage more cycling and walking in urban areas by reallocating road-space in towns and cities. And the government promised that, over time, it would invest more in transport than its predecessor.

These policy aims were given further authority by the Deputy Prime Minister's remark that he had set himself the goal of reducing car vehicle trips on the UK road network by five per cent within a five-year period. This would be achieved through a combination of switching car travel to alternative modes, land-use development control, and demand management measures, such as urban road-user charging schemes.

Things got off to a promising start, with the establishment of an integrated Department of the Environment, Transport and the Regions (DETR) in July 1997, and the publication of a Consultation Document on Integrated Transport Policy (Department of the Environment, Transport and the Regions, 1997). The

* Peter Jones is Professor of Transport and Sustainable Development, Centre for Transport Studies, at UCL, London. Georgina Christodoulou is Research Fellow in the Transport Studies Group, University of Westminster. David Whibley is Senior Lecturer in Transport Policy, University of Westminster.

policy was given additional impetus the following year by the publication of the first transport White Paper in over 20 years, promoting an integrated, sustainable transport system (Department of the Environment, Transport and the Regions, 1998a) and a Review of the Roads Network (Department of the Environment, Transport and the Regions, 1998b) which severely scaled down the inherited road building programme.

The moratorium on new road construction for two years was claimed to be part of a more sustainable transport policy, but in reality the need for cuts in transport expenditure was probably the key determinant of this decision. For its first two years in office, Labour was committed to sticking to the Conservative's projected expenditure plans, which had been to reduce transport expenditure substantially. Therefore, there was no increase in resources available in the short term to implement these integrated policies. The absence of transport legislation in the period 1998–2000 was an early indicator of the relatively low priority given by the government as a whole to introducing enabling measures to facilitate the implementation of these new transport policies.

The predominant trends since 2000 have in many respects moved away from an integrated transport/land-use policy, based on sustainability principles, at least at the national level.[1] Transport gradually became less integrated within government, until it became a separate department and, starting with the Ten Year Transport Plan published in July 2000, increasing priority has been given to economic policy objectives (congestion reduction, growth in GDP) over broader sustainability objectives (Department of the Environment, Transport and the Regions, 2000a). Some road building is back on the agenda, and the fuel duty protests in autumn 2000 put a cap on further increases in fuel duty. Indeed, the Chancellor actually reduced the fuel excise duty in 2000/2001, under pressure from the road transport lobby, and has subsequently scrapped the fuel duty escalator. The multi-modal corridor study reports recommended that motorway widening schemes should only be constructed if demand management measures, in the form of road-user charging or tolled motorway schemes, were instigated simultaneously (Kellogg Brown and Root, 2002). But, in most cases, widening schemes have been approved without the accompanying charging measures.

Meanwhile, very large – and unanticipated – sums of taxpayers' money have gone into the national rail network since 1998. Currently, Network Rail requires public investment and taxpayer support at more than twice the level of financial support available to British Rail pre-privatisation (Department for Transport, 2004a: Table 1.14). This is taking a major proportion of the additional funding made available to transport. The benefits are now beginning to become apparent to rail travellers but, despite this large investment, there is little spare capacity to accommodate future growth on many key links. There is even talk of the need to 'congestion price' people off the rail network.

One important area where the original ambitions of the 1997 Labour government have largely been followed through, is with respect to local transport provision. Local authorities have sought to improve alternatives to the car, taking into account both social and environmental sustainability objectives, as well as economic factors. One of the major achievements has been the reduction in the numbers of people killed and seriously injured on our roads each year (Department for Transport, 2004a: Table 8.2). The first five-year Local Transport Plans have been successfully implemented and funding has been substantially increased (Atkins, 2005) – although lack of control over the bus industry has limited the improvements that some authorities have been able to offer.

However, even here, the government has changed its views concerning some key policy initiatives. Initially, urban road-user charging schemes were supported in the White Paper, and expected to be a key factor in Local Transport Plans, to restrain traffic growth and generate additional revenue for local authority transport budgets. However, the government had cooled its support for such measures by the time the Mayor of London was planning to implement the Central London Congestion Charging scheme. Instead, the policy focus is switching to national road-user charging, with an initial emphasis on lorry charging (subsequently replaced by proposals for a longer term scheme covering most categories of road vehicle).

Support for light rail transport schemes (LRT) in urban areas has also oscillated over the past seven years. Initially in the White Paper (Department of the Environment, Transport and the Regions, 1998a), the government gave lukewarm support for LRT schemes, favouring bus improvements as the key public transport mode in urban areas. However, by the time of the Ten Year Plan, it had been persuaded that the benefits of the LRT schemes were substantial. Their ability to persuade car users to switch modes and the wider regeneration benefits were key factors. Less than two years later, however, LRT schemes were once more under pressure, owing to the failure of several schemes to achieve passenger forecasts and the rising capital costs of new schemes.

Thus, while much has been achieved, many of the early ambitions for modal switch have been abandoned or scaled down, and the primary transport policy emphasis has shifted from environmental to economic policy objectives. National targets to increase rail passengers, rail freight, bus use and cycling have all now been quietly dropped, and previous plans for up to 25 LRT schemes have been substantially scaled back. At a time when the government states internationally its continued commitment to the Kyoto protocol and CO_2 reduction targets, recent figures indicate that transport CO_2 emissions are continuing to rise (Department for Transport, 2004a: Table 3.7). Yet this issue does not feature as one of the top transport policy objectives.

So, where does this leave the British public in 2004? Have they been left uncertain and confused by the changes in policy emphasis over the years, or are they and the government in agreement over the issues to be addressed and how they might be achieved? In this chapter, we explore public attitudes to various transport problems and the measures proposed to tackle them, especially those in relation to reducing car use. We focus on data from the 2004 *British Social*

Attitudes survey but, where similar questions have been asked in past years, we briefly explore trends in public attitudes over time.

Priority given to transport expenditure

Table 6.1 shows the relatively low proportions of respondents who would give first or second priority to transport, were additional government expenditure available. This contrasts with around half the public naming additional health expenditure as their first priority. Nevertheless, the figures shown in Table 6.1 typically rank extra transport spending in third place, behind health and education and ahead of other areas like housing and law and order. Note the consistent levels of support for transport since 1999, and the greater support for any extra spending to go on public transport rather than on roads; as we shall see, this is consistent with other views expressed by the public.

Table 6.1 Transport as a priority for extra government spending, 1997–2004

	1997	1999	2000	2001	2002	2003	2004
1st priority	%	%	%	%	%	%	%
Public transport	2	4	4	4	5	4	4
Roads	1	3	2	2	2	2	2
All transport	3	7	6	6	7	6	6
1st or 2nd priority	%	%	%	%	%	%	%
Public transport	6	10	10	11	13	13	11
Roads	3	7	6	5	6	6	6
All transport	9	17	16	16	19	19	17
Base	*1355*	*3143*	*3426*	*3287*	*3435*	*4432*	*3199*

The drivers behind transport policy

The government has recently published a set of shared transport priorities, which provide the context for deciding on transport investment and management, by both central and local government (Department for Transport, 2004b). Top of the list is the alleviation of traffic congestion, both on motorways/inter-urban roads, and in urban areas. The other priorities cover improved accessibility for disadvantaged social groups, safer roads, and better air quality.

The *British Social Attitudes* survey does not explore attitudes towards all of these problems, but there is a sequence of questions dealing with some of the key issues:

*Now thinking about traffic and transport problems, how serious a problem **for you** is ...*

... congestion on motorways?

... traffic congestion in towns and cities?

... exhaust fumes from traffic in towns and cities?

As seen in Table 6.2, only 29 per cent of respondents in 2004 regard motorway congestion as a "very serious" or a "serious" problem, affecting them personally, with a higher proportion (36 per cent) viewing it as "not a problem at all". As would be expected, respondents who drive are significantly more likely to view congestion as a problem, but still only a third of drivers do so. Motorway congestion does not appear to be a top transport priority for most people.

Table 6.2 How serious a problem is motorway congestion?

		A very serious problem	A serious problem	Not a very serious problem	Not a problem at all	*Base*
All	%	9	20	34	36	*1053*
Drivers	%	11	22	40	28	*715*
Non-drivers	%	7	15	22	56	*338*

Table 6.3 shows that respondents' views appear to be much more in line with the government's priorities when it comes to traffic-related problems in urban areas. In 2004, over half rated traffic congestion in towns and cities as being a "very serious" or a "serious" problem for them personally, and only 17 per cent regard it as not being a problem at all. A slightly higher proportion of respondents (58 per cent) regard exhaust fumes from traffic as being a "very serious" or "serious" problem, and only 15 per cent rate this as not being a problem at all. This is in line with other surveys (Jones, 2003; Lex, 1996), that also give much higher priority to urban than inter-urban traffic problems, and rate air quality concerns slightly above those of traffic congestion – particularly when it comes to accepting the need to take restrictive action to address the problem.

Table 6.3 also explores the differences in responses between drivers and non-drivers. Drivers are slightly more likely to see town traffic congestion as a problem, but the difference between drivers and non-drivers is less than for motorway congestion, perhaps because buses also get stuck in urban congestion. On traffic exhaust fumes, there is no real difference between the groups – pedestrians and public transport passengers are, of course, also affected by pollution.

Table 6.3 How serious are traffic-related problems in towns and cities?

		A very serious problem	A serious problem	Not a very serious problem	Not a problem at all	Base
Traffic congestion						
All	%	18	36	30	17	1053
Drivers	%	18	38	33	11	715
Non-drivers	%	17	32	21	30	338
Traffic exhaust fumes						
All	%	20	38	27	15	1053
Drivers	%	19	38	31	12	715
Non-drivers	%	24	37	17	22	338

Have these levels of concern changed over time? With regard to motorway congestion, the answer is no, as seen in Table 6.4. While there have been fluctuations in levels of concern since 1997 (in particular, an increase in 1999 and 2000), there is no clear trend of rising concern to mirror the current higher political priority given to tackling motorway congestion.

In contrast, for both urban traffic congestion and traffic fumes, levels of concern have actually *fallen* significantly over time, in the latter case possibly because of the widespread adoption of new technologies like catalytic converters. In both cases there has been a sharp drop since 2000 in the proportions viewing these as "very serious" or "serious" problems. Again, this seems to be at odds with the recent government prioritisation of transport objectives, at a national level – although it is important to stress that we are looking here at the severity of problems faced by individuals, not directly at the perceptions that they might hold of the national significance of these issues.

Table 6.4 Proportion thinking traffic problems are serious, 1997–2004

% saying very serious or serious problem	1997	1998	1999	2000	2001	2002	2004
Motorway congestion	32	32	36	35	31	31	29
Congestion in towns	70	67	71	73	52	57	53
Exhaust fumes	77	72	75	74	n/a	60	58
Base	1355	1075	1031	1133	1099	1148	1053

n/a = not asked

Car use: freedom *versus* restraint

At the heart of government transport policy for many years has been an underlying tension between the competing ideologies of facilitating the freedoms associated with using a car and seeking to limit car use to reduce congestion and pollution. The former requires additional road capacity. The latter requires the discouragement of car use either through improving alternative modes (public transport, walking and cycling), or through direct restraints on car use. The public position has been tracked through several questions in the *British Social Attitudes* survey over a number of years.

Extreme support for unfettered car use is tested by asking for agreement or disagreement with the proposition that "people should be allowed to use their cars as much as they like, even if it causes damage to the environment". As seen in Table 6.5, views have remained broadly stable, with around 20 per cent support and 40 to 50 per cent opposition to this statement. There are no significant differences between drivers and non-drivers. This suggests a widespread acceptance of the case for some limits on car use, where there is a strong environmental imperative. What we do not know is whether responses would be the same if 'severe congestion' were substituted for 'damage to the environment'.

Table 6.5 Views on allowing unlimited car use, even if it damages the environment, 1997–2004

People should be allowed to use their cars as much as they like, even if it causes damage to the environment	1997 %	2000 %	2002 %	2003 %	2004 %
Agree	15	20	20	22	17
Disagree	49	42	48	41	49
Base	*1080*	*972*	*989*	*972*	*872*

One way to support unlimited car use and meet the government objective of reducing motorway congestion would be to build more motorways. As Table 6.6 shows, levels of support and opposition towards this proposition have fluctuated widely from year to year, with support ranging from 26 per cent in 1998 to 46 per cent in 2003. In the early years of the Labour government, there was a clear net opposition to such a policy, but in the last few years views have been much more volatile, perhaps reflecting varying media coverage. The 2001 and 2003 surveys show net support for new motorway building, but the balance swings back into net opposition by 2004.

One of the main arguments against major road building in general – aside from any environmental and financial concerns – has been the view that 'you can't build your way out of congestion' because 'new roads generate traffic'. While Table 6.6 shows that more people agree than disagree with the proposition that "building more roads just encourages more traffic", the gap has been narrowing considerably, from 20 to 30 per cent net agreement in the late nineties, down to an average of 10 per cent in the last two years.

Table 6.6 Views on building more motorways, and whether road expansion increases traffic, 1997–2004

	1997	1998	2000	2001	2003	2004
The government should build more motorways to reduce traffic congestion	%	%	%	%	%	%
Agree	30	26	33	38	46	32
Disagree	42	45	36	34	29	38
Building more roads just encourages more traffic	%	%	%	%	%	%
Agree	49	55	43	47	46	41
Disagree	27	24	33	29	32	34
Base	*1080*	*877*	*972*	*912*	*972*	*872*

Another way of approaching this general issue is to ask respondents:

> *How important do you think it is to **cut down on the number of cars** on Britain's roads?*

As shown in Table 6.7, in most years since 1997, some 70–75 per cent of respondents have regarded reducing the number of cars as "very" or "fairly important". However, there has been a slight downward drift in recent years, so that net support has narrowed from 60 per cent to 50 per cent.

Table 6.7 Attitudes to cutting the number of cars on Britains roads, 1997–2004

How important to cut the number of cars on Britain's roads?	1997	1998	1999	2000	2001	2002	2003	2004
	%	%	%	%	%	%	%	%
Very important / fairly important	75	79	74	75	73	74	70	72
Not very important / not at all important	16	16	18	18	20	18	22	21
Base	*1080*	*877*	*813*	*972*	*912*	*989*	*972*	*872*

Interestingly, looking at the 2004 data, car drivers and non-drivers seem to hold very similar views. On the other hand, there are some differences according to whether or not respondents regard congestion as a serious problem that affects them personally, but the differences are not as large as might perhaps have been expected. Around three-quarters (78 per cent) of respondents who regard congestion in towns and cities as a "very serious" or "serious" problem, also feel that it is "very" or "fairly important" to cut the numbers of cars on Britain's roads. This is compared to two-thirds (65 per cent) of those who view urban congestion as "not a serious problem" or "not a problem at all". The comparable figures according to whether people view motorway congestion as a problem or not, are broadly similar at 79 per cent and 69 per cent, respectively.

Were the aspiration to cut the number of cars on Britain's roads to be achieved, it might be done either through improving alternatives to the car – the 'carrots' – or through increasing car costs – the 'stick' policies. The responses to these options, in the form of improving public transport and raising taxes on car use "for the sake of the environment", are shown in Table 6.8. Support for improving public transport is very high and has been drifting upwards over time. (Although it should be noted that the question does not spell out the possible costs to taxpayers.) Similar findings have been noted before in *British Social Attitudes Reports* (most recently in Exley and Christie, 2003) and replicated in countless opinion surveys over the last decade.

On these 'carrot' policies, the views of drivers and non-drivers are indistinguishable. Conversely, the 'stick' policies are not popular. Support for raising car taxes has always been low and resistance has consistently hardened over the period of the Labour government, from a net opposition of 33 per cent in 1997 to 58 per cent in 2004. Perhaps surprisingly, car drivers and non-drivers share similar views here too.

Table 6.8 Attitudes to 'carrot' and 'stick' policies to reduce car use, 1997–2004

	1997	1998	1999	2000	2001	2002	2003	2004
How important to improve public transport	%	%	%	%	%	%	%	%
Very important/ fairly important	93	93	94	94	94	95	96	96
Not very important/ not at all important	4	3	4	4	3	3	2	2
For the sake of the environment car users should pay higher taxes	%	%	%	%	%	%	%	%
Agree	20	19	11	14	15	15	15	12
Disagree	53	59	69	67	66	70	71	70
Base	*1080*	*877*	*813*	*972*	*912*	*989*	*972*	*872*

What this suggests is that there is continuing concern about the levels of traffic on Britain's roads, and a general desire to see reductions in car use. Support for public transport improvements to provide attractive alternatives to car use remains extremely high. But on the roads side, support for motorway building is much lower (although it is growing) and support for raising car taxes is low and falling. We could speculate on a large number of reasons for this trend, including perceived increases in the costs of motoring in recent years (although in real terms the cost of motoring has not in fact increased). But one factor is likely to have been government-induced, namely a shift in policy emphasis from the environment and sustainability as the primary concern, to a greater focus on achieving congestion reduction and economic development – where a stronger case for road building can be made.

Support for particular policy instruments

So, the public supports reducing car use, but which specific policy options do they favour or oppose? Questions in the *British Social Attitudes* survey have particularly probed public reaction to policy instruments that restrain car use or otherwise control or encourage reductions in car use, through pricing, regulatory or physical controls. In this section we assess support for each of them in turn.

Pricing controls

Pricing as a means of controlling traffic congestion has been a recurring theme under the last eight years of Labour administrations – though with intervening periods when it has been largely 'off limits'. The introduction in February 2003 of congestion charging in London (and a small-scale scheme in Durham some months before) has begun to bring home to a hitherto largely sceptical public the effectiveness of pricing as a means of reducing congestion (Transport for London, 2005). Both the government and bodies such as the Confederation of British Industry have started to prepare people for the possible introduction of inter-urban charging to limit traffic congestion and 'lock in' the benefits of new road capacity. What effect has all this had on public opinion?

Table 6.9 shows the degree of public support in 2004 for five pricing-related restraint polices, described in the question as "things that might be done to reduce congestion". The least popular option is "gradually doubling the cost of petrol over the next ten years", with only six per cent supporting this policy and 79 per cent against. As we found with car taxes, car drivers and non-drivers are equally opposed. While the fuel price protests and the rising costs of fuel have undoubtedly contributed to this strong rejection, this approach to traffic restraint never achieves more than 10 to 20 per cent support in British public opinion surveys.

Table 6.9 Comparison of drivers' and non-drivers' attitudes to various pricing options

	All	Drivers	Non-drivers
Double cost of petrol in 10 years	%	%	%
In favour	6	5	6
Against	79	83	71
£2 to enter town at peak times	%	%	%
In favour	28	30	23
Against	50	49	51
£1 per 50 miles on motorway	%	%	%
In favour	23	25	17
Against	57	56	61
Increase parking costs in town	%	%	%
In favour	16	16	15
Against	64	66	60
Tax employer parking spaces	%	%	%
In favour	18	16	22
Against	58	62	51
Base	*872*	*594*	*278*

"Charging £1 for every 50 miles motorists travel on motorways" is less heavily rejected, with 23 per cent in favour and 57 per cent against. Interestingly, car drivers are significantly *more* in favour of this option than non-drivers. But the government clearly still has a long way to go in gaining majority support for this kind of initiative – particularly since the low level of charge proposed in this question is unlikely to be high enough to achieve its stated objective of significant motorway congestion reduction.

There is slightly more support for urban congestion charging, probably because of the London experience and the previously noted much higher levels of concern about congestion in urban areas than on motorways. Even so, it could hardly be described as popular. Faced with the proposition of "charging all motorists £2 each time they enter or drive through a city or town outside London at peak times", only 28 per cent voiced support against an opposition of 50 per cent. This is in line with other findings over several years. However, what is more surprising is that we find higher support among car drivers (30 per cent) than non-drivers (23 per cent), so perhaps the London experience is starting to demonstrate to drivers the effectiveness of charging for congestion reduction.

The conventional form of pricing-based control in urban areas is through parking charges. Although this is widespread, it does not necessarily make it a popular solution to reducing traffic congestion. Only 16 per cent lent their support to the idea of "increasing parking costs in town and city centres", compared with 64 per cent against. Here the differences between drivers and non-drivers are not statistically significant. It is probable that most people feel that parking charges are already very high.

Although recent debates about controlling urban traffic congestion through pricing have focused on congestion charging, the legislation in England and Wales (although not Scotland) also allows for the introduction of a Workplace Parking Levy (Department of the Environment, Transport and the Regions, 2000b). When presented with this option, described as "taxing employers for each car parking space they provide to their employees", respondents reacted in a similar way to their views about higher parking charges, with only 18 per cent support and 58 per cent opposition. Again, drivers and non-drivers share similar views.

Clearly, pricing is not a popular solution to tackling traffic congestion, with none of the five options gaining more than 28 per cent support (and a minimum of 22 per cent net opposition). One reason is almost certainly that people do not like paying higher charges. Another reason is probably that, notwithstanding the London experience, the majority of people in Britain do not think that pricing effectively tackles the problems of traffic congestion. Nevertheless, the higher support among drivers than non-drivers both for motorway charging and urban congestion charging does suggest that the links between direct road-user charging and congestion reduction are beginning to be understood.

Regulation: priority for buses, pedestrians and cyclists

A second approach to discouraging car use and making the alternative modes more attractive in urban areas is to give the latter more of the available road capacity. This has been partially addressed through two questions in the *British Social Attitudes* survey. Respondents are asked to indicate how strongly they agree or disagree with the following statements:

> *Buses should be given more priority in towns and cities, even if this makes things more difficult for car drivers*

> *Cyclists and pedestrians should be given more priority in towns and cities even if this makes things more difficult for other road users*

Table 6.10 shows that overall responses to both questions are remarkably similar, with around 59 per cent agreement and only 20 per cent disagreement – a complete contrast to the views expressed about pricing, even though in the question no reason is given for adopting such a policy. In the case of bus priority, non-drivers are significantly more supportive than drivers, but even the latter show majority support.

Table 6.10 Attitudes towards prioritising buses, cyclists and pedestrians over other road uses in towns and cities

	All	Drivers	Non-drivers
Give buses more priority	%	%	%
Agree	58	56	65
Disagree	21	24	15
Give cyclists and pedestrians more priority	%	%	%
Agree	60	58	61
Disagree	19	21	4
Base	*872*	*594*	*278*

Support for both of these policies has been tracked intermittently since 1999 (see Table 6.11). In both cases, net support was a little greater in the earlier years of the Labour government, particularly in the case of walking and cycling. Again, this might in part reflect the switch in national government emphasis towards congestion reduction and away from environmental policy objectives, or the increasing adoption of such measures already by local authorities in urban areas across the country. Still, it appears that reallocating road capacity is a more popular policy option among the public than road pricing.

Table 6.11 Attitudes towards prioritising buses, cyclists and pedestrians, 1999–2004

	1999	2000	2002	2004
Give buses given more priority	%	%	%	%
Agree	64	62	62	58
Disagree	17	18	19	21
Give cyclists and pedestrians more priority	%	%	%	%
Agree	66	68	60	60
Disagree	14	14	18	19
Base	*813*	*972*	*989*	*872*

Residential areas – including physical controls

The third policy instrument for restraining car use that the *British Social Attitudes* survey asks about relates specifically to residential areas, and involves measures to reduce the dominance of motor vehicles. The question was as follows, with respondents asked whether they would be in favour or not in favour of each:

> *Here are some things that could be done about traffic in residential streets that are not main roads:*
>
> *Closing residential streets to through traffic*
>
> *Having speed limits of 20 miles per hour in residential streets*
>
> *Making cars stop for people to cross residential streets even if they are not at a pedestrian crossing*
>
> *Having speed bumps to slow down traffic in residential areas*

Note that there was no indication in the question as to *why* these measures might be introduced, although it is probable that most people would associate them with policies to reduce traffic volumes and road accidents.

As shown in the next table, closing residential streets to through traffic was supported by around half the respondents, with only 27 per cent against. Car drivers were slightly less enthusiastic than non-drivers, but the differences are not statistically significant. The other physical measure, speed bumps, also received overall net support, with 46 per cent in favour and 37 per cent opposed. This time, however, non-drivers were significantly more supportive than drivers, with drivers being roughly equally split between support and opposition.

Table 6.12 Attitudes to various traffic calming controls

	All	Drivers	Non-drivers
Closing residential streets to traffic	%	%	%
In favour	49	50	47
Against	27	28	25
20 mph speed limits in residential areas	%	%	%
In favour	74	72	79
Against	13	15	8
Cars to stop for pedestrians	%	%	%
In favour	28	25	37
Against	45	51	30
Speed bumps to slow traffic	%	%	%
In favour	46	43	53
Against	37	41	28
Base	*872*	*594*	*278*

The most popular measure by far is having speed limits of 20 miles per hour in residential streets. This policy is being increasingly adopted by local authorities as a means of reducing traffic accidents, and nationally enjoys strong support, with 74 per cent in favour and only 13 per cent opposed. Again, non-drivers are the more enthusiastic; here differences are statistically – but perhaps not politically – significant.

The least popular of the four suggestions has only recently been discussed in policy circles, namely "making cars stop for people to cross residential streets, even if they are not at a pedestrian crossing". Only 28 per cent are in favour and 45 per cent against. This result also is the most polarised of the four, with many more non-drivers in favour than drivers.

These questions have previously been asked in the 2000 and 2001 *British Social Attitudes* surveys. Public support for road closures has remained virtually unchanged, fluctuating around half in favour and a quarter against. Meanwhile support for 20 mph speed limits has declined very slightly from 79 to 74 per cent, with opposition hardening from nine to 13 per cent, giving a downward drift in net support (the difference between those in favour and those against) of around 10 percentage points. Nevertheless, there is still overwhelming support.

Conversely, support for speed bumps has dropped sharply since 2000 and 2001, when support stood at 60 and 63 per cent respectively, so that this option no longer has majority support. Net support slumped from 36 per cent to only nine per cent. This probably reflects the bad press that speed bumps have received in recent years, with reports of damage to vehicles, delays to emergency services and localised increases in noise and air pollution.

Speed cameras

One of the most controversial measures for regulating car traffic in recent years has been the introduction of speed cameras, both within and between urban areas. Traffic engineers claim that they are there to reduce speeds and save lives, while many in the media and elsewhere argue that they are just another revenue-raising device. In response to media pressure, all speed cameras now have to be clearly identifiable from a distance. What do our sample think about these issues? Respondents were offered two propositions: "speed cameras save lives", and "speed cameras are mostly there to make money".

As seen in Table 6.13, on balance, a majority agree that speed cameras are mainly there to make money, while just under half of respondents support the notion that they save lives. Of course, these are not necessarily contradictory propositions.

As might be expected, car drivers are significantly more likely to agree that speed cameras are primarily there mainly to make money than non-drivers, and less likely to support the notion that they save lives. This suggests that proponents of speed cameras are losing the argument with the general public, particularly among car drivers.

Table 6.13 Attitudes to speed cameras

	All	Drivers	Non-drivers
Speed cameras save lives	%	%	%
Agree	47	44	55
Disagree	30	35	19
Speed cameras mostly make money	%	%	%
Agree	58	63	46
Disagree	22	19	29
Base	*872*	*594*	*278*

Effectiveness of particular policy instruments

We have seen what the public think about a number of policy instruments to cut car use *in theory*. But how viable are such instruments, and how likely is it that they will make any difference? The *British Social Attitudes* survey has investigated how effective different policy instruments might be in two respects. One sequence of questions looks at what scope there might be for increasing the use of more sustainable modes under current conditions (for example, through running awareness or marketing campaigns). In another set of questions, drivers are asked for their likely responses to the introduction of particular policies for car restraint.

Scope for reducing car use

Respondents were asked to show whether they agreed or disagreed with the following statements:

> *Many of the short journeys I now make by car I could just as easily...*
> *... walk*
> *... go by bus*
> *... cycle, if I had a bike*

As seen in Table 6.14, there appears to be most scope for switching short car trips to cycle, closely followed by walking – in both cases around two-fifths of people agree they could easily switch away from the car. Just under a third say they could easily switch from car to bus. However, in all three cases, more people disagree than agree that they could switch many of their short trips by car to other modes.[2]

  Table 6.14 is based only on those who ever travel by car, but this group, of course, includes some people who do not themselves drive but sometimes travel by car as a passenger. How do the views of drivers and these non-drivers compare? Looking at the scope for substituting walking trips for short car trips, the responses of the two groups are very similar, but they react differently with regard to the two other options. Non-drivers are twice as likely as drivers to see the bus as a possible substitute for short car trips. In the case of cycling, it is drivers who are more likely to do so than non-drivers.

Table 6.14 Attitudes to using alternative modes to the car for short journeys

	All	Drivers	Non-drivers
Could walk	%	%	%
Agree	38	38	40
Disagree	49	51	39
Could use bus	%	%	%
Agree	31	25	49
Disagree	58	66	31
Could cycle	%	%	%
Agree	41	42	35
Disagree	45	44	41
Base	*872*	*594*	*278*

Base: respondents who ever travel by car

These questions have been asked on a number of occasions since 1997. The proportion indicating that they could switch some short car trips to bus has remained broadly stable, at about one-third. There has been a slight drop in the proportion who said they could just as easily walk (from 45 per cent in 2000 to 38 per cent in 2004) and an increase in the proportion disagreeing (from 38 per cent in 2000 to 49 per cent in 2004). Until 2000, the proportion who said they could easily switch from the car to walking for short journeys used to outnumber those disagreeing, but now the picture has reversed. The situation regarding cycling is very similar. This is a disappointing outcome, given the efforts that most local authorities have put into improving cycling facilities and bus services, in particular, over the past few years.

Nevertheless, these figures suggest that there is considerable scope for reducing the number of short car trips among certain target groups. These trips contribute disproportionately to air pollution because engines are cold, and in local areas they may contribute significantly to congestion (in conjunction with the school run). Cutting local car use would also contribute to other government efforts, for example, to reduce heart disease and improve public health.

Responses to increased costs of driving

We found earlier that people were generally not very supportive of pricing solutions to reduce congestion, but would such measures be effective? Respondents who drive were asked:

*I am going to read out some of the things that might get people to **cut down** on the number of car journeys they take. For each one, please tell me what effect, if any, this might have on how much **you yourself** use the car to get about:*

... gradually doubling the cost of petrol over the next ten years?

... charging all motorists around £2 each time they enter or drive through a city or town centre outside London at peak times?

... charging £1 for every 50 miles motorists travel on motorways?

... making parking penalties much more severe?

Respondents were asked whether each of these measures would make them use the car less or give up using it altogether or whether, on the contrary, it would make them use the car more,[3] or perhaps make no difference. They were, of course, also asked separately whether they were in favour or against each of these measures (see Table 6.9).

From Table 6.15 we can see that the instrument most likely to lead to a drop in car use is doubling the cost of petrol, where 62 per cent of drivers thought it would make them use the car less and only 37 per cent thought it would make no difference. Unfortunately, as we know from Table 6.9 – and the experience of the fuel duty protests – this measure is also likely to be very unpopular, with 83 per cent of drivers opposing it.

The next most effective measure is likely to be town centre congestion charges where 58 per cent of drivers thought it would make them use the car less. Although also unpopular, at least some drivers seem to agree that this would reduce congestion. As we saw earlier, support from car drivers is actually higher than among non-drivers.

Table 6.15 Anticipated changes in car use, if various restraint measures were implemented

		Might give up using car	Quite a bit less	A little less	No difference
Double petrol prices over 10 years	%	8	23	31	37
£2 town centre peak entry charge	%	5	22	31	42
£1 per 50 miles to use motorways	%	4	13	22	60
Much more severe parking penalties	%	4	15	22	58

Base: 699

Base: drivers

Motorway charging and more severe parking penalties are expected to influence substantially fewer drivers, with around 60 per cent claiming that it would make no difference to them. This is probably partly due to the relatively small proportions of daily trips that involve motorway driving or paying for parking. Note that twice as many respondents said that they might give up using their car in response to a doubling of petrol prices (eight per cent) than in the case of the other three instruments.

These questions, other than urban peak pricing, have been included on an annual basis since 1997, but the data shows no discernible trend in the patterns of response.

Given the recent interest in urban congestion charging, drivers were asked further questions about the impact that imposing a £2 charge for driving into town centres at peak periods might have on their behaviour, if coupled with different types of improvement to local public transport services:

> *Now suppose that ... two things ... were done **at the same time**. What effect, if any, might this have to how much you yourself use the car?*
>
> *Charging motorists £2 for entering town centres outside London at peak times **but at the same time** greatly improving the **reliability** of local public transport?*
>
> *And what about charging motorists £2 for entering town centres outside London at peak times **but at the same time** greatly improving the **frequency** of local public transport?*
>
> *And what about charging motorists £2 for entering town centres outside London at peak times **but at the same time halving the fares** for local public transport?*

The results are shown in Table 6.16. (The responses to the stand-alone imposition of a £2 charge have been included as a comparison.)

Table 6.16 Effect of urban charging, coupled with public transport improvements, on car use

		Might give up using car	Quite a bit less	A little less	No difference
£2 town centre peak charge only	%	5	22	31	42
Plus, greatly improved reliability of public transport	%	7	31	31	30
Plus, greatly improved frequency of public transport	%	7	32	30	31
Plus, halving public transport fares	%	11	34	21	33

Base: 699

The results are quite complex. Improved local public transport reliability and frequency result in the highest proportion of drivers saying that they will cut down on car use compared to the base case (69 per cent in each case *versus* 58 per cent). But the halving of public transport fares causes the largest increase in the number of respondents saying that they might give up using their car. In all cases, coupling the 'stick' measure of town centre charging with a 'carrot' measure of better public transport is more effective than the 'stick' measure alone, but the difference is perhaps not as large as might have been expected.

Air transport

Air transport is the fastest growing form of transport among the British population, due on the one hand to EU transport deregulation and the huge growth in services offered by low cost carriers, and to rising disposable incomes on the other (Department for Transport, 2003). Nevertheless, it has remained largely separate from the general transport debate.

While there is a general recognition in government and elsewhere that car use needs to be curbed, in some places and at some times (for both congestion and environmental reasons), this philosophy has not been carried through to the treatment of air transport. Indeed, the previous Conservative government's implicit policy for road transport, characterised as 'predict and provide', well describes the current Labour government's policy approach to air transport. The publication of the Aviation White Paper in December 2003 placed the emphasis on providing new airport capacity, with no serious discussion of the need to restrain air travel demand (Department for Transport, 2003).

This expansion is opposed by many environmental and public organisations who claim that this is hard to reconcile with any sustainable approach to aviation policy. Given the government's commitment to the Kyoto protocol and achieving its CO_2 emission target reduction, the continued growth in air travel is of increasing concern. Although air transport's current contribution to CO_2 emissions is relatively low, it is forecast to grow rapidly in the next 20 years (Department for Transport, 2003).

So, where do the public stand? Are they in favour of unlimited expansion in air services, or would they support some form of restriction, in recognition of the environmental and other problems caused by air transport? The *British Social Attitudes* survey asked respondents to agree or disagree with the following three statements:

> *People should be able to travel by plane as much as they like*
>
> *People should be able to travel by plane as much as they like, even if new terminals or runways are needed to meet the demand*
>
> *People should be able to travel by plane as much as they like, even if this harms the environment*

In response to the first statement that "people should be able to travel by plane as much as they like", over three-quarters of respondents agree and only five per cent disagree – apparently resounding support for current government policy.

But, as seen in Table 6.17, once the caveats are introduced, support drops off considerably. When the need for additional runways and terminals is mentioned, agreement drops by 34 percentage points. When harming the environment is mentioned, agreement drops further to only 15 per cent. Note, however, that a third of respondents hold no clear view – displaying a degree of confusion and lack of knowledge among the population.

In addition, respondents were asked to agree or disagree with this statement:

> *The price of a plane ticket should reflect the environmental damage that flying causes, even if this makes air travel much more expensive*

As we can also see in Table 6.17, views on this 'stick' measure to reduce air travel are very divided: around a third of respondents agree, another third disagree, while the remaining third neither agree nor disagree or have no view. As was the case with car travel, it is quite possible that pricing *per se* may not be the most acceptable way of curbing demand.

Table 6.17 Attitudes to constraining demand for air travel

People should be able to travel by plane ...		Agree	Neither	Disagree
... as much as they like	%	77	14	5
... as much as they like, even if new runways / terminals are needed	%	43	28	23
... as much as they like even if it harms environment	%	15	34	46
Ticket prices should reflect environmental damage	%	36	25	34

Base: 872

Again, as with the earlier analysis of car drivers, some views are very dependent on personal travel behaviour, while others are not. Table 6.18 shows how levels of agreement with the four statements vary according to the number of air trips that the respondent made in the last year.

Unsurprisingly, people who travel by plane are more in favour of allowing air travel than those who do not travel by plane. In particular, the proportion of frequent air travellers who would allow unlimited air travel even if this means new runways and terminals is almost twice that among non-air travellers. However, the impact of the caveat about environmental impacts is very strong across all groups. Support for the proposition that air travel should remain unrestrained, even if it harms the environment, remains very low even among frequent air travellers – less than a fifth agreed while almost half (49 per cent) disagreed.

As would be expected, those who fly are less likely to support including environmental costs in air ticket prices than those who do not fly. Among the fliers, those who disagree outnumber those who agree with price rises. Among non-fliers, on the contrary, those who agree with price rises outnumber those who disagree. Nevertheless, the differences between the two groups are not as great as might have been expected.

Table 6.18 Attitudes to restraining air travel, by the number of air trips made per year

	Number of air trips in past year		
Percent who agree that people should be able to travel by plane ...	None	1 or 2	3+
.. as much as they like	69	83	86
...as much as they like, even if new runways / terminals are needed	34	45	60
... as much as they like even if it harms environment	12	17	18
Per cent who agree that ticket prices should reflect environmental damage	42	30	32
Base	*530*	*310*	*213*

This suggests that the government focus on meeting demand and providing increased capacity seems to be a popular policy – particularly among the growing ranks of air travellers – *provided that* increased air travel poses no major environmental problems. Many would argue, however, that it *does*, and that such risks are underplayed in government documents. The evidence from this survey suggests that, were the government to emphasise the environmental damage arising from air travel, then support for the unrestrained growth of air transport might largely disappear. However, as with car travel, simply relying on pricing to restrain demand might not be the most popular policy response.

Conclusions

At the start of this chapter, we posed the question as to whether the government and the public are in agreement on the transport issues to be addressed and the means of doing so. The questions included in the 2004 *British Social Attitudes* survey only provide a partial coverage of the broad spectrum of transport policy, and – of course – policy is driven by more than short-term public opinion, but there are some interesting messages that can be derived from the findings discussed here.

 First, that people are generally more concerned about traffic problems in urban areas than on our motorways, and that air quality is just as important an issue to them as traffic congestion. Most recent government pronouncements have emphasised the benefits in terms of congestion reduction of their policies, but this is simply not the only – or necessarily the most effective – basis for gaining public support for restrictive transport policy measures.

Second, in line with findings from other British surveys, people are much more supportive of improvements to public transport than major road building, as a solution to transport problems. We see this in terms of the roughly double support for any extra government expenditure to go to public transport rather than roads (Table 6.1), and the astonishingly high support, at 96 per cent, for improving public transport (compared to 32 per cent support for more motorway building). This is despite the extra investment that has already been put into public transport in recent years. There is a great deal of scepticism among professionals and politicians as to why the public supports public transport improvements – in particular, that it will encourage *other* people to get out of their cars – but this is still a significant finding, that should not be readily dismissed.

A third consistent message from this survey is that, while most people would like to see fewer cars on Britain's roads, pricing is not a very popular means of achieving this. Only six per cent of respondents support a doubling of petrol prices over 10 years (although it is reported to be the most effective instrument for reducing car use). The least unpopular of the five pricing measures presented to respondents (£2 peak period charge to enter towns and cities), achieved less than a third support and half the respondents were opposed. In contrast, regulatory approaches, involving shifting the balance in mode use by reallocating road space in towns and cities to buses or to those on foot and cycling, achieved around 60 per cent support and only 20 per cent opposition. Again, other surveys have come to broadly similar conclusions.

One area where this survey breaks new ground, is in its finding that support for motorway tolling and urban congestion charging, although low, is *higher* among car drivers than non-drivers. This would indicate that the government is beginning to convince drivers that pricing can be an effective weapon in controlling traffic levels and hence congestion.

When we look specifically at residential areas, we find very high levels of support for another regulatory measure, namely 20 mph speed limits in residential areas, both among drivers and non-drivers. However, the survey charts a sudden drop in support for using speed bumps, between 2001 and 2004, probably associated with increasingly adverse media coverage. In this case, drivers are less supportive of the measure than non-drivers.

Another area where media messages and public views seem to be in accord – though there is much debate as to which is cause and which is effect – is in relation to speed cameras. In 2004, we find that more people agree with the statement that "speed cameras are mostly there to make money" than with the proposition that "speed cameras save lives". This is an area where professionals and politicians will need to work hard to turn around public views, if cameras are to continue to play a major role in the effort to reduce death and serious injury on our roads.

One section of the questionnaire explored what scope there is for people to cut back on car use, either voluntarily, or through direct restraint measures. One target area is the short distance car trip, and here survey findings are encouraging, with 30 to 40 per cent agreeing that they could switch some trips to more sustainable transport modes. This looks a promising focus for the several 'Smart Travel' initiatives that the government is currently supporting (Department for Transport, 2004c).

And, although unpopular, the survey suggests that some of the pricing measures would be quite effective. Around 60 per cent of drivers reported that they would cut down on car use, if petrol prices double over 10 years, or if there were a peak period £2 charge to enter town centres. In the latter case, simultaneously improving public transport services adds around a 10 percentage point increase to those saying that they would reduce car use. These results probably overstate the likely effect, but are nevertheless indicative of a significant sensitivity among car drivers to price increases. However, the government faces a major challenge in making these measures, which appear to be very effective in achieving traffic reduction objectives, acceptable to the general public.

Finally, the survey has uncovered new findings concerning public attitudes to air travel, which show how strongly public attitudes are sensitive to the way in which the issues are presented. When simply asked if people should be free to travel by air as much as they like, nearly four-fifths of respondents support this general proposition, suggesting – superficially – that the government has correctly gauged the mood of the electorate.

However, support drops off sharply when some of the consequences of unlimited air travel are put to respondents. Fewer than half support unrestricted traffic growth when this requires the building of new terminals and runways, and this drops to only 15 per cent with the caveat "even if this harms the environment". What is particularly important is that, while support for the first two statements increases significantly the more a person flies, concern about environmental impacts does *not* reduce significantly with increased levels of flying.

Most public and policy debate about air traffic growth has been in the context of catering for demand and avoiding congested conditions. Were environmental issues to be brought much more to the fore by government, both in terms of local air quality and noise, and issues relating to global warming, it is probable that the policy pressures and outcomes would be very different. As we have suggested at various places in this chapter, the same might also be true – though to a more limited extent – in debates about road traffic, where the recent framing of the debate in terms of congestion reduction and economic advantage, rather than environmental damage, is likely to be influencing attitudes to road investment *versus* traffic restraint.

Notes

1. However, it should be noted that, since April 2005, the Department for Transport has accepted shared responsibility for reducing greenhouse gas emissions in line with the Kyoto agreement.
2. Responses are most evenly divided in the case of cycling. Note, however, that this question adds the rider "… if I had a bike", so it is more hypothetical than the others (e.g. there is no equivalent rider "if there was a bus service nearby").
3. Only one per cent or less of respondents thought that any of these measures would make them use the car more.

References

Atkins (2005), *Long term process and impact evaluation of Local Transport Plan policy (Interim report)*, London: Department for Transport

Department of the Environment, Transport and the Regions (1997), *Developing an Integrated Transport Policy: An invitation to contribute*, London: Department of the Environment, Transport and the Regions

Department of the Environment, Transport and the Regions (1998a), *A New Deal for Transport: Better for Everyone,* Cm 3950, London: The Stationery Office

Department of the Environment, Transport and the Regions (1998b), *A New Deal for Trunk Roads in England,* London: HMSO

Department of the Environment, Transport and the Regions (2000a), *Transport 2010; The 10 Year Plan,* London: Department of the Environment, Transport and the Regions

Department of the Environment, Transport and the Regions (2000b), *Transport Bill,* Part III: Chapter II, Section 182, London: The Stationery Office

Department for Transport (2003), *The Future of Air Transport*, Cm 6046, London: The Stationery Office

Department for Transport (2004a), *Transport statistics Great Britain 2004, 30th ed., 2004*, London: The Stationery Office

Department for Transport (2004b), *Full Guidance on Local Transport Plans: Second Edition*, London: Department for Transport

Department for Transport (2004c), *Making Smarter Choices Work*, London: Department for Transport

Exley, S. and Christie, I. (2003), 'Stuck in our cars? Mapping transport preferences', in Park, A., Curtice, J., Thomson, K., Jarvis, L. and Bromley, C (eds.), *British Social Attitudes: the 20th Report – Continuity and change over two decades*, London: Sage

Jones, P (2003), 'Acceptability of road user charging: meeting the challenge', in Schade, J. and Schlag, B (eds.), *Acceptability of transport pricing strategies*, Oxford: Elsevier

Kellogg Brown and Root (2002), *Orbit: transport solutions around London*, London: Kellogg Brown & Root (KBR)

Lex (1996), *Lex report on motoring: Listening to all road users*, London: Lex Service

Transport for London (2005), *Central London Congestion Charging, Impacts monitoring, Third Annual Report*, London: Transport for London

Acknowledgements

The *National Centre for Social Research* is grateful to the Department for Transport for their financial support which enabled us to ask the questions reported in this chapter, although the views expressed are those of the authors alone.

7 Planning for retirement: realism or denial?

Miranda Phillips and Ruth Hancock*

Pensions are high on the policy agenda in Labour's third term, and some would argue this comes not a moment too soon. The government set up the Pensions Commission in 2002. Their First Report (2004) raised the profile and intensity of the debate around pensions, and, at the time of writing, their final report is imminent. Commentators on all sides – from the shadow Pensions Minister to the TUC and the Association of British Insurers (ABI) – have voiced concerns about the direction of pensions policy in Britain. At the same time media coverage has heated up in recent months, with frequent references to the "impending pensions crisis"[1] or similarly dire warnings of the apparently disastrous situation ahead.

The concern stems from the difficulties encountered in ensuring adequate living standards for retired people: around one in five pensioners is currently living in poverty (defined as below 60 per cent of median income) (DWP, 2005a). Criticism of the level of the state pension is long-standing, particularly the policy of uprating it by price rather than by earnings inflation. Matters came to a head in April 2000 when this policy led to a mere, and now infamous, 75 pence increase in the level of the basic state pension. Some groups do not receive even the full amount of the basic state pension. In particular, many women do not have a full National Insurance contribution record, and therefore are far less likely to be entitled to a full basic state pension than men. Indeed, Alan Johnson, the last Work and Pensions Secretary, recently referred to the "national scandal" of women's pensions.[2]

Meanwhile, Britain is experiencing striking demographic trends which have serious implications for the future. The Pensions Commission has predicted that increasing life expectancy combined with low birth rates will produce, between now and 2050, a "near doubling" in the percentage of the population aged 65

* Miranda Phillips is a Senior Researcher at the *National Centre for Social Research* and is Co-Director of the *British Social Attitudes* survey series. Ruth Hancock is Professor of Non-clinical Gerontology at the University of Essex.

years and over (Pensions Commission, 2004:1). That trend has created fears of a 'gap' in pension provision (be that in terms of state benefits, personal savings or company schemes).

So what have New Labour been doing in terms of pensions policy? Labour's policy for today's pensioners has been to target state resources on those with the lowest incomes through more generous means-tested benefits, rather than to boost the level of the universal state pension. For future pensioners, Labour is keen to see a move away from reliance on the state. In 1998 their stated expectation was that the balance of pension provision would shift from 60 per cent public provision to 60 per cent private provision (DSS, 1998). In line with this, the government introduced stakeholder pensions to encourage those on modest incomes to make more private provision for their own retirement, and aims to help people make better decisions about pensions through the 'informed choice' agenda.

In this chapter we examine the extent to which the public are in tune with Labour's policies in two different ways. We start by looking at the impact of policy to date, exploring views about the level of the state pension, and the financial position of today's pensioners. The second part of the chapter focuses on the future and responds to a call from the Pensions Commission for public debate around the different ways in which pensions policy might develop.

How popular are Labour's policies on pensions so far?

In its first year of office, Labour committed itself to sticking to the previous government's spending policies. As a result, state pensions and means-tested benefits for pensioners rose only in line with price inflation in April 1998. Pensioner groups and others had long argued that state pensions should rise in line with earnings rather than prices, but over the next few years the basic state pension continued to be uprated only in line with prices. This policy turned out to be untenable: in April 2000, the low level of price inflation led to an increase of only 75 pence in the basic state pension for a single person. Such was the political fall-out that the next two years saw increases in the basic state pension which were not only greater than the rise in prices, but also greater than the increase in average earnings (Pension Provision Group, 2001). Labour then committed itself to increasing the state pension by either price inflation or 2.5 per cent – whichever is greater (HM Treasury, 2002).

Nevertheless, it is clear that the government's preference is for putting more emphasis on means-tested benefits aimed at the poorest pensioners. In 1999, the rates of means-tested benefits for pensioners were increased by more than prices and the main benefit – Income Support – was renamed the Minimum Income Guarantee (MIG). A restructuring of the MIG in 2001 resulted in above-earnings increases which were largest for younger pensioners, and a commitment in principle to earnings linking. In October 2003, the MIG was subsumed in a more generous 'Pension Credit' which gives help not just to those with incomes below the MIG level but also to those with incomes just above it, including those with modest savings *via* the Savings Credit element.

The *British Social Attitudes* series has asked a range of questions which allows us to examine what people think about policies for current pensioners. Do the public regard the state pension as adequate? And do they support means-testing as an approach to funding retirement? We also consider whether pensioners themselves feel they have enough to live on – and how this perception has changed over time.

Pensioners' views of the state pension

What do today's pensioners make of the level of the state pension? We asked pensioners the following question:

> *On the whole would you say the present* **state** *pension is on the low side, reasonable, or on the high side?*

If the answer was "on the low side" they were asked whether they thought it was "very low" or "a bit low". Figure 7.1 shows that, not surprisingly, a large majority of pensioners still feel the state pension is not adequate: over a third (35 per cent) feel it is "very low" and four in ten (41 per cent) say "a bit low". What is perhaps surprising is that as many as one in five pensioners (22 per cent) say that the state pension level is reasonable.

Figure 7.1 Change over time in pensioners' views about level of state pension

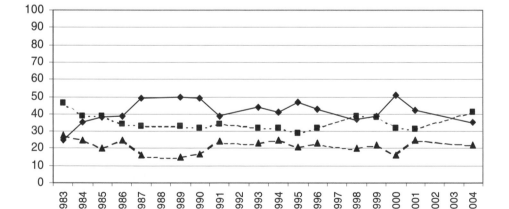

Most pensioners are also cautious about the future, as responses to the following question reveal:

> *Do you expect your state pension in a year's time to purchase **more** than it does now, **less**, or about the **same**?*

A majority feel that the level of their state pension will not change for the better. Nearly two-thirds (63 per cent) expect the state pension to be worth less in a year's time. A third (32 per cent) think it will stay the same, and only four per cent believe that it will increase.

We can discern differences in views among different groups of pensioners. In particular, the proportion of women who say the state pension is "reasonable" is 10 percentage points higher than men (27 per cent and 17 per cent respectively).[3] Perhaps this is because of men and women's different expectations, related to different experiences of income prior to retirement. Indeed, it may be the case that for some women, receiving the state pension is their first experience of having independent income, which may affect their views on its adequacy.

Figure 7.1 also shows how pensioners' views about the level of the state pension have varied over the last two decades. The 1980s were characterised by rising dissatisfaction, followed by a reversal of this trend and a rise in the proportion who were satisfied from 15 to 23 per cent between 1989 and 1993. Focusing on the period since Labour came into office it seems that pensioners were not impressed by the 75 pence pension increase in 2000. In that year the proportion who thought the state pension was "very low" was at an all time high (51 per cent) and the proportion thinking it was "reasonable" (16 per cent) was almost as low as it has ever been. Labour's subsequent efforts at damage limitation seem to have paid off to some extent. Now, the proportion of pensioners judging the state pension to be very low has fallen to a third (35 per cent) and the proportion saying it is reasonable has recovered to where it was in the 1990s. Respondents to our survey may not appreciate the fine details of Labour's policy reforms, but the views they express seem consistent with some knowledge of the policy developments.

The public's views of the state pension and related benefits

While views about the level of the basic state pension are important, it would be unfair to base any conclusions about support for Labour policies on this alone, as the government's aim has been to target additional benefits at the poorest pensioners. To assess whether the public are in tune with government policy, we need to look at views about the overall package of benefits for pensioners – the Pension Credit or the MIG as well as the state pension. We asked what respondents thought about the following scenario:

Think about a pensioner living alone. Her only income comes from the state pension and other benefits specially for pensioners. Would you say that she has more than enough to live on, has enough to live on, is hard up, or, is really poor?

We subsequently asked:

And thinking again about that pensioner living alone. After rent, her income is £105 a week. Would you say that she has more than enough to live on, has enough to live on, is hard up, or, is really poor?[4]

These questions were asked of all respondents, not just pensioners, and many people do not, of course, know very much about the level of benefits. They may imagine the state pension and associated benefits to be much lower than they really are. By asking the question in two stages, and looking at the differences in responses, we get a measure of this.

Looking first at the answers from 2004 in Table 7.1, we find that around three-quarters of respondents said that the pensioner is either "hard up" or "really poor" when no amount was mentioned. However, this fell to 60 per cent after being told the £105 figure, suggesting that people do underestimate the level of the benefits involved.[5]

Table 7.1 Views about a pensioner living solely on benefits, 2000 and 2004

	2000			2004		
	No amount	Amount (£82)	Change between Q1 & Q2	No amount	Amount (£105)	Change between Q1 & Q2
	%	%		%	%	
More than enough to live on	1	4	+3	1	2	+1
Enough to live on	19	48	+29	22	37	+15
Hard up	57	40	-17	59	50	-9
Really poor	20	8	-12	14	10	-4
Base	*3426*	*3426*		*3199*	*3199*	

The proportion saying that the pensioner was hard up or really poor in response to the first question, where no amount was mentioned, was similar in 2000 and 2004, around three-quarters in both years. But, in 2000, when the amount – which was then only £82 – was included, this fell to less than half (whereas in 2004 it fell to around three-fifths), suggesting that people were even more likely to underestimate the level of pensions in 2000. What is surprising is that, when the amount is mentioned, the proportion thinking the pensioner is hard up or really poor is higher now than in 2000 – after all, the increase from £82 to £105 is about 20 per cent greater than if Labour had simply continued with the price-only uprating over the period. This may reflect the heightened awareness of pensions and gives some measure of the uphill task that the government has in convincing the public that it really has tackled the problem of inadequate state pensions.

These findings beg the question of why public attitudes have not become more favourable in the face of a relatively large increase in benefit amounts. One explanation may lie in the relationship between people's characteristics and their views. If, for example, a person's age and income are related to views on pensions, and if the population as a whole is getting older and wealthier, then this goes some way to explaining why we do not see a shift in attitudes across the population as whole, even if pensions are objectively getting better.

In fact, a number of factors, including age, economic status, income, and party identification are all related to the view that state pensioners are hard up or really poor. For example, younger people are less likely to say the pensioner is hard up than older age groups (35 per cent of those aged 18–24 compared to 59 per cent of 55–59 year olds). Multivariate analysis found that all the factors shown in Figure 7.2 are related to views on the financial position of state pensioners, even when the other factors are taken into account. (Full details of this analysis are shown in the appendix to this chapter – see Model A.)

It is interesting to note the role of party identification. We might expect Labour supporters to be more likely to support the record of the Labour government. Instead it seems that people with traditionally left-wing, egalitarian political identities are more likely than average to have views which reveal concern about disadvantaged people (and this holds even when we take household income into account).

Figure 7.2 Characteristics related to saying a pensioner living on state benefits is "hard up" or "really poor"

More likely	Less likely

Older people
  (age groups 55–59, 60–64 & 65+)
Those in full-time education/training
Highest household income quartile
Labour and Liberal Democrat supporters
	Younger people
	  (age groups 18–24 & 25–34)
	Retired people
	Lowest household income quartile

Perceptions of what is adequate income in retirement

The fact that a majority of people still see state pensioners as hard up or really poor, even after a substantial increase in their income, suggests that public expectations of living standards for pensioners are rising, along possibly with greater awareness of the problems surrounding pensions. Moreover, the concept of financial adequacy may be interpreted in different ways – some people may be thinking of the bare minimum for essentials only, others may compare the state pension to their own income or earnings. To address these issues further, we asked pensioners to consider two more specific questions about their current financial circumstances.

First, we asked pensioners whether they felt that they had enough money to cover basic living costs:

> *Thinking about what you are living on in retirement, including any money from pensions, benefits, savings or investments, and any earnings. Do you have enough money to cover basic costs such as housing, heating and food?*

Responses to this question give a clearer indication of real financial need – shown in the 'All' column of Table 7.2. A sizeable minority of over a third of pensioners do not *always* have enough money to cover basic costs, although the proportion who say they "hardly ever or never" have enough is a tiny minority. While the majority say they always have enough for the basics, it is possible that this indicates only that pensioners are reluctant to admit to financial difficulties or have relatively low expectations, a common finding. For example, McKay (2004) found that older age groups are more likely than younger people to say that they do not *want* items which a majority of the population think of as necessities, rather than that they cannot *afford* them.

A second question asked pensioners to compare their current situation with the time when they were working:

> *Do you think you are now financially better off than you were before you retired from your main job, the same, or, worse off?*

The most common view, held by nearly six in ten pensioners (58 per cent) is that they are worse off in retirement than when working. Around a quarter (24 per cent) feel their finances are similar, while 15 per cent say they are better off in retirement. In this they are quite probably correct – the proportion of pensioners living in households with incomes below £10,000 is 33 per cent, compared with only four per cent of working respondents. Even bearing in mind that working people are likely to have more outgoings (such as mortgages and the bringing up of children), this is a substantial difference. Moreover, the figure rises to 38 per cent among pensioner-only households (where the respondent is either a pensioner living on their own or with a spouse who is also retired). Some 43 per cent of retired people are in the lowest income quartile.

Unsurprisingly, household income is strongly related to self-reported financial well-being: half of those pensioners in the lowest income quartile say they "always" have enough to cover basic costs, compared with three-quarters (76 per cent) of those in the second lowest quartile.

Due to the skewed income distribution for pensioners, we re-calculated quartiles based only on their household income – and it is these that are shown in Table 7.2. The proportion of pensioners in the highest pensioner income quartile who say they "always" have enough money to cover basic costs is almost double that of those in the lowest quartile. Age is also related, with older pensioners being less likely than their younger counterparts to say they are worse off in retirement than when they were working (41 per cent of those aged 80 plus compared with 68 per cent of 60–69 year olds).

Table 7.2 Pensioners' views on whether have enough for basic costs, by household income quartiles

	Household income quartiles for pensioners				All
	Lowest quartile	2nd lowest	2nd highest	Highest quartile	
	%	%	%	%	%
Always	42	59	73	82	63
Mostly	38	35	20	14	27
Sometimes	13	3	5	2	6
Hardly ever / never	7	2	2	1	3
Base	203	169	141	120	762

Base: all retired

Regression analysis confirms that the only characteristics significantly related to both of the questions on self-reported financial situation, once other factors are taken into account, are age and income. It also shows that gender is not a relevant factor here, despite the fact that women are, on average, worse off than men in retirement.

While these questions give an indication of how pensioners regard their financial status, it is hard to make sense of the findings without reference to other groups in society. All respondents were asked the following question about their feelings about their household's present income.

> Which of the phrases on this card would you say comes closest to your feelings about your household's income these days?
> Living comfortably on present income
> Coping on present income
> Finding it difficult on present income
> Finding it very difficult on present income

Comparing responses to this question by a person's economic activity reveals a more complex picture. Just one in ten of those who are retired are finding it difficult to cope on their present income, exactly the same proportion as is found among those in work. Considering that we know retired people generally have lower incomes than those in work, this is probably another illustration of older people being less willing to admit to financial difficulties, although some of it is likely to be accounted for by fewer outgoings and lower expectations among pensioners. On the other hand, a quarter of those in full-time education, three in ten of those doing 'other' activities (such as being sick or disabled or looking after the home and family), and more than four in ten (43 per cent) of unemployed people find it difficult to cope.[6] After all, pensioners are not the only group with limited resources.

Public attitudes to means-testing of pensions

The introduction of Pension Credit represents an increased role for means-testing in state pension policy. Entitlement to Pension Credit reaches higher up the income distribution than the MIG, and latest figures show that just over 2.7 million households are getting Pension Credit. This is 900,000 more than were receiving the MIG which it replaced (House of Commons Work and Pensions Committee, 2005). It has been estimated that the number of beneficiaries of Pension Credit will grow by 50 per cent in the next 10 years (Pensions Policy Institute, 2005). However, critics of means-testing say that it provides a disincentive to save – for example, the ABI estimate that there is a direct impact of a reduction in pensions saving of £3.7 billion.[7] In other words, they argue this policy is at odds with the government's own objective of encouraging more private pension saving. There is also an issue of low levels of take up of benefits and tax credits that are not universal; the latest official figures show take up of MIG as between 63 per cent and 74 per cent (DWP, 2005b).

Where do the public stand on means-testing? We asked two questions to tap attitudes on this subject. Sefton, in Chapter 1 of this Report, discusses these in detail (see Tables 1.2 and 1.3). The first question asked respondents how they thought government should spend a set amount of money on state pensions. Half the sample were asked whether all pensioners, or only those on low incomes, should get a state pension. The other half were asked whether pensioners on low incomes should get a higher state pension (even if they had to fill in forms to prove it), or if all pensioners should get the same amount.

The answer is mixed. On the one hand, there is a clear reluctance to move away from a universal state pension, with six in ten (59 per cent) feeling all pensioners should be entitled to it, rather than entitlement being limited to only those on low incomes. However, there is also support for targeting resources at the poorest pensioners. Virtually the same proportion (61 per cent) say those on low incomes should get more money, even though this would entail form-filling. These answers are not contradictory – they simply indicate that public support for the policy of targeting resources exists *within certain boundaries*; means-testing is seen as acceptable as a top-up but only over and above a basic state pension available to all. In effect, the public are supportive of the government's current policy – the state pension is available to all who have a sufficient contribution record, and there is also a means-testing element in the Pensions Credit.

However, it seems that the precise wording of the question makes a difference to responses. We asked a second question which referred to contributions through taxation rather than being in need – again, see the chapter by Sefton in this Report for a detailed discussion of this. This wording elicits lower levels of support for targeting resources at low *earners* than did the earlier question which asked about low *incomes*. In this context around three in ten support options which give lower earners more money (27 per cent say the low earner should get more, and a further four per cent say only the low earner should get a state pension). This is low in comparison to the six in ten who support higher levels of state pension for poorer pensioners in the earlier question. Sefton finds a similar pattern in the comparable questions about other types of benefits. Wide variations in attitudes depending on the wording of the question is often a sign that the issue is not well understood by the public.

Overall, the message for New Labour is mixed. The public are not positive about benefit amounts and the level of the state pension for today's pensioners: three-quarters of pensioners feel that the state pension is inadequate, and a majority of the public think that pensioners living on benefits are hard up or really poor. However, pensioner views are now a little more positive than they were in 2000–2001 when the diminutive increase in the state pension resulted in the most negative attitudes in a twenty year period. This suggests that the government's recent policy of increasing the basic state pension above inflation has had some impact. Of course, even pensioners themselves may not make a clear distinction between the basic state pension and the Pension Credit, so increases in this benefit may also have contributed to more positive views. When it comes to the specific measure of means-testing, the public are more supportive, particularly when it is seen as an approach to tackle poverty. However, a majority are also still in favour of retaining the basic state pension for all pensioners regardless of need.

Pensions policy: which way next?

The first section of this chapter focused on the financial circumstances of today's pensioners, current levels of benefits, and the degree of public support for Labour's policies so far. Policy for the longer term is less clear. In October 2004, the then Secretary of State for Work and Pensions, Alan Johnson, said "Pension Credit and means-testing should be there until we have solved the problem of abject pensioner poverty."[8] There has also been increased discussion recently around the idea of a universal citizens' pension which would break the link between pensions and contributions.

For future pensioners, the government wants to encourage greater private provision. Stakeholder pensions were introduced to encourage those on modest incomes to make more private provision for their retirement. But recent research suggests that the largest impact has been for those with low incomes rather than the middle earners who were the primary target group (Chung *et al.*, 2005).

In 2002, the government appointed the Pensions Commission to review the adequacy of private pension provision, and to advise on future policy – including a consideration of whether a move beyond a voluntary approach was necessary. The Commission's first descriptive report was published in 2004. In it the Pension Commission set out the stark choices for pensions policy in the face of striking demographic trends. Increasing life expectancy combined with low birth rates "will produce a near doubling in the percentage of the population aged 65 years and over between now and 2050" (Pensions Commission, 2004: 1). The number of working age people for each person over state pension age – the 'support ratio' – fell from 14 to 3.5 between 1900 and 2000 (Ginn, 2004), and is projected to fall to 2.3 by 2041 (computed from Government Actuary's Department, 2004).

In the light of its findings, the Pensions Commission concluded that the UK faced four options (or, most likely, some combination of the last three of these):

- pensioners to become poorer relative to the rest of the population;
- people to pay more in taxes and/or NI contributions to maintain the value of state pensions;
- people to provide for their retirement through greater private savings; and/or
- people to work longer and retire later.

The purpose of the Commission's report was to stimulate debate: the authors refer to the different choices that "society and individuals must choose between" in order to deal with the ageing population (Pensions Commission, 2004:1), and the Commissioners were well aware that there are no easy answers.[9] As part of that public debate, this chapter now considers to what extent the public are in tune with each of these choices, and whether their attitudes and behaviour lend support to any one choice – or a particular combination of them – over the others. Where we find support, we explore whether this is found across all groups in society, or if certain groups are most likely to be the source of this support. This in turn may help assess whether any public support we find is meaningful. By that we mean, for example, that if people of working age give their support to working longer and retiring later, that is more relevant than if we only find this view amongst the already-retired.

Would the public support pensioners becoming poorer?

We do not need to spend long discussing this option. Pensioners living on less money was not felt to be a realistic way forward in the Pensions Commission report; in essence, this option will be the end result if future policy fails to make adequate provision in one way or another. In fact, we have already considered public attitudes about the financial position of pensioners in the first section of this chapter, and have seen that there is little scope for reducing the level of the state pension or other benefits for pensioners. We found, for example, that around three-quarters of pensioners say the state pension is too low and a majority of people think that a pensioner living on benefits is either hard up or really poor (even after being told the exact amount they receive).

Are the public prepared to pay more taxes for the state pension?

To examine views about the Pension Commission's second option, we turn to attitudes towards taxation and public spending. The *British Social Attitudes* survey has a long-standing general question on this subject:

> *Suppose the government had to choose between the three options on this card. Which do you think it should choose?*
>
> - *Reduce taxes and spend less on health, education and social benefits*
> - *Keep taxes and spending on these services at the same level as now*
> - *Increase taxes and spend more on health, education and social benefits*

A number of chapters in this Report comment on trends in this question (see, for example, Figure 5.2 in the Chapter by Appleby and Alvarez-Rosete). Just under a half of all people (49 per cent) say they would like to increase levels of taxes and public spending. This is a comparatively *low* level of support for extra tax and spend. Throughout the 1990s and as late as 2002, around two-thirds of the public favoured more taxes. However, for the last two readings in 2003 and 2004, we have observed a sharp drop. In *The 20th Report*, Sefton speculated that support for increased tax and spend might fall after the explicit provision in the 2001 Budget to raise taxes in order to finance more spending on public services. While there was no evidence of this in 2002, he suggested there might be a lag in changes in attitudes (and indeed, that time was needed for the impact of policies to take effect) (Sefton, 2003). It appears that this is now happening and, if so, it will certainly undermine the scope for spending more public money on pensions.

But perhaps the public want existing levels of government expenditure to be switched to pensions, away from other areas. We can address this by considering answers to a more specific question. Respondents were asked whether they would like to see more or less government spending than now on a range of different benefits. As shown in Table 7.3, responses reveal clear support for more spending on pensions: nearly three-quarters say they want spending to increase and only two per cent want less spending on pensions. This has remained consistently so since this question was first asked in 1998 (when 71 per cent wanted government to spend more on pensions). Of course, it is easy to say that you want more spending when the question does not spell out the implications of that choice (such as an increase in taxation). The absolute levels of support for more spending on pensions are probably affected by this, but note that respondents do not give blanket support for extra spending on *all* benefits. In relative terms, spending on retirement comes out as one of the most popular social welfare benefits for extra spending – only spending on carers has a higher level of support.

Table 7.3 Views about spending on benefits

Views about spending on benefits for ...	% spend more	% spend less
Carers for the sick and disabled	81	1
Retired people	73	2
Disabled people who cannot work	63	3
Working parents on a low income	62	4
Single parents	35	18
Unemployed	15	44

Base: 3199

A time-series is available on a different question (last asked in 2003), which asked people to weigh up different benefits and to choose their first priority for extra spending. Retirement pensions have been the most popular answer in every year shown in Table 7.4, and was given by nearly six in ten in 2003. There has been a marked increase in the proportion giving pensions their first priority since 1983, which is particularly striking when we consider that this was already the top choice.

Table 7.4 First priority for extra spending on benefits, 1983 – 2003

First priority for extra spending	1983	1990	1996	2000	2003	Change '83–'03
	%	%	%	%	%	
Retirement pensions	41	42	50	52	59	+18
Benefits for disabled people	24	24	19	21	16	-8
Child benefits	8	17	12	14	15	+9
Benefits for single parents	8	7	6	7	5	-3
Benefits for the unemployment	18	8	11	4	3	-15
Base	*1761*	*2797*	*3620*	*3426*	*3272*	

So do responses to these questions suggest that there is room for increased spending on pensions without an overall increase in taxation by off-setting it against less spending on other areas? Well, not so far as the social benefits budget goes anyway. Table 7.3 showed that there is only one area – unemployment benefits – where there is more support for reducing spending than there is for increasing it, and one other area – benefits for single parents – where support for less spending even reaches double figures. Moreover, the government spends over ten times as much on pensions as it does on the unemployed and lone parents (Taylor-Gooby and Hastie, 2003), so even if these savings were politically acceptable, they would be unlikely to be large enough to pay for the favoured rise in spending on retired people.

Who supports paying more taxes for better state pensions?

If the government are to take forward tax increases to pay for better state pensions as a realistic option, it would be important that the people who would be paying the taxes (predominantly younger people and those in work) are those who support the measure. In fact, we find the opposite. The youngest people (aged 18–24) are the least likely to be in favour: 12 per cent say they want the government to spend much more on pensions – half the proportion among those aged 60 or above (24 per cent of 60–64 year olds and 25 per cent of those aged 65-plus). Moreover, those in their middle years are no more supportive of much more spending on pensions than the youngest group – despite the fact they are closer to retirement (14 per cent of 35–44 year olds and 13 per cent of 45–54 year olds). Those in work are also less likely than those in retirement to say this (14 per cent compared with 23 per cent). In other words, support for more spending is higher among the groups who are most likely to benefit than among those who would pay. Regression analysis confirms the importance of age and economic status, and also shows that those with no qualifications and those who say the government should increase tax and spend are more likely than average to support spending much more on retirement pensions.

Moreover, Sefton, examining responses to a separate series of questions, found that support for higher spending on pensions fell among 18–34 year olds between 1987 and 1996 but rose among other age groups (Sefton, 2003). The implications are not positive for a policy of raising taxes to spend more on pensions.

So, in summary, although there is clear support for more state spending on pensions, there is much less agreement about paying for it by raising taxes – the other part of the Pension Commission policy option. Amongst the 73 per cent of our respondents in favour of the government spending more on benefits for retired people, only around half (52 per cent) are in favour of tax increases. Indeed, a similar proportion want more pension spending *without* tax increases (39 per cent say keep tax and spend at the same level as now and six per cent say reduce tax and spend). And since there is little appetite for spending substantially less on other welfare benefits, it seems unlikely that the government can square this circle.

General attitudes towards saving for retirement

If public money cannot be found to improve pensions, perhaps private money can. Encouraging people to make provision for their own retirement by private saving – including personal and occupational pension plans – is an aim of the current government. However, if future policy relies on the public making their own pension provision this is likely to disadvantage people who have lower incomes, career breaks, and so on. Indeed, critics of this approach say that many people will simply never be able to save enough to provide a 'decent' pension.[10]

But how do the public feel about this? We look first at people's general attitudes towards saving for retirement to see if there is, at least, theoretical support for this option. We then consider how people's behaviour corresponds – are people saving for retirement at the moment and is saving linked to expectations about retirement income? We go on to assess whether people feel able to save, both in terms of having enough money to do so, and in terms of their confidence and level of understanding about pensions.

The *British Social Attitudes* survey contains some general questions which tap views about the importance of saving for retirement. As a starting point, we are interested in whether people support the principle of saving for retirement at all, bearing in mind the existence of a state pension. We asked respondents how much they agreed or disagreed that:

> *The government should encourage people to provide something for their own retirement instead of relying only on the state pension*

As shown in Table 7.5, there is overwhelming support for this: four-fifths of people agree – up six percentage points from an already high proportion in 2000.

It may be that responses to this question are, in part, driven by the suggestion that the government should *support* saving – people may have interpreted this as referring to specific measures of encouragement such as tax breaks. However, as also shown in Table 7.5, a similarly high proportion feel that saving for retirement should start at a relatively young age, even when government is not mentioned in the question:

> *Some people regularly put money aside into pensions or savings for their retirement. When do you think a person needs to start doing this in order to be sure of having a decent standard of living when they retire ...*
> *... in their 20s or earlier, their 30s, 40s, 50s, or 60s?*

The idea that saving should start when people are young is backed up by responses to the following question which asked people to weigh up two options – the second of which points out that saving may entail having to cut back on spending:

> *Young people should spend their money while they are young and worry about saving for retirement when they are older*
> *OR*
> *Young people should start saving for their retirement as soon as they can even if they have to cut back on other things*

Again, Table 7.5 shows overwhelming support for the saving option.[11] This level of support may seem surprisingly high given that today's society is often seen as being driven by consumerism and a "buy-now-pay-later" mentality.[12] It is hard to reconcile the two, though it may be that this is an issue where people are aware of the 'right' or 'sensible' thing to do – but their behaviour does not necessarily correspond![13]

Table 7.5 Views in favour of saving for retirement, by age

	18–24	65+	All
% agree government should encourage people to save for retirement	84	83	80
Base	*243*	*729*	*3199*
% say a person needs to start saving by 20s or earlier for decent standard of living in retirement	65	71	78
Base	*243*	*729*	*3199*
% say young people should save for retirement as soon as can even if they have to cut back on spending	48	84	72
Base	*181*	*595*	*2609*

Various characteristics including education are related to views on saving. For example, those with no qualifications are twice as likely as those with a higher education qualification to disagree that the government should encourage saving for retirement (14 *versus* seven per cent). Sex, class and political party affiliation are also associated with views on this statement (and regression analysis confirms that all remain significant when these and other factors are taken into account). But the relationship with age is particularly important – and curious. It is those in the middle of the age spectrum who are less keen that the government should encourage saving (76 per cent of 35–44 year olds agree with the statement compared to 84 per cent of 18–24 year olds and 83 per cent of those aged 65 or over). Perhaps the young think that 'other people' should be encouraged to save, and the old feel they have already done their saving (or wish they had). Those in their middle years know that this statement is aimed squarely at them.

Such an interpretation is supported by the fact that younger people (aged 18–24 years) are, not surprisingly, least likely to support the idea of saving from their 20s or earlier. Nevertheless, a majority still think this is a good idea.

We see the age difference again on the third question in Table 7.5. Those aged 18–24 are significantly more likely than any other age group to favour *spending* money rather than saving – 27 per cent do so, compared to 18 per cent or less of all other age groups – and just seven per cent of those aged 65 or more. Only around half of 18–24 year olds opt for saving rather than spending (compared to 84 per cent of those aged 65 or more). So while those in the youngest age group are in favour of saving *in general*, they are less keen when the question refers to saving from a young age. As any increase in personal savings for retirement will no doubt rely on this, it would appear that young people's attitudes will need to change in order for sufficient savings to happen. This conclusion is reinforced by the fact that, as we discuss later, the second two questions in Table 7.5 are significantly related to whether a person has private pension provision or not at the moment (see Model B3 in Figure 7.3).

Private pension provision

To what extent is this clear support for saving reflected in people's own behaviour? The *British Social Attitudes* survey does not ask about savings in general, but we did ask about two specific – and important – forms for saving for retirement: private pensions and property ownership. We asked all our respondents who were not yet retired whether they had any of the following types of pension arrangements:[14]

-   *A personal or private pension, or retirement annuity*[15]
-   *A company or occupational pension run by your employer*
-   *A stakeholder pension*

As shown in Table 7.6, almost half of respondents have a company or occupational pension, while just under a third have a personal or stakeholder pension. Just under two-fifths have made no provision for a pension beyond the state pension.

Table 7.6 Private pension provision among those who have not yet retired

	%
Company / occupational pension	46
Personal or private pension / retirement annuity	24
Stakeholder pension	5
None of these	39
Base	*2360*

Base: all not yet retired

This finding of a 'gap' in private pension provision ties in with evidence from other sources: the Pensions Commission estimated that around 9.6 million people either are not saving or are under-saving for their retirement. Meanwhile, membership of defined benefit schemes in the private sector has fallen markedly since the 1970s, with much of the recent decline due to schemes being closed to new members (Pension Commission, 2004).[16] But, although the 39 per cent of people who have no private pension arrangement are a matter for concern, we should not forget that by European standards Britain has relatively high private pension coverage. Two key issues are whether existing coverage rates can be maintained and whether those who are not contributing to a pension could afford to. The *British Social Attitudes* survey provides some insight into the second of these.

Table 7.7 No private pension provision by sex, age, household income, economic status, social class and educational achievement

% who have no pension provision		*Base*
All not yet retired	39	*2360*
Sex		
Male	32	*1061*
Female	45	*1299*
Age		
18–24	82	*238*
25–34	43	*516*
35–44	25	*634*
45–54	28	*534*
55–59	26	*240*
60–64*	38	*116*
65+*	66	*79*
Household income quartiles		
Lowest	75	*441*
Second lowest	41	*485*
Second highest	28	*567*
Highest	20	*616*
Economic status		
In work	27	*1767*
In education/training	87	*99*
Unemployed	76	*95*
Other	74	*399*
Social class		
Managerial/professional	18	*857*
Intermediate	30	*258*
Employers in small organisations	48	*202*
Lower supervisory & technical	40	*335*
Semi-routine and routine	61	*649*
Educational achievement		
Higher education	24	*735*
A level or equivalent	41	*433*
O level / CSE	42	*749*
No qualifications	58	*401*

Base: all not yet retired
*Only those who are not yet wholly retired from work are included here. Nevertheless, some of these respondents may already be drawing a pension

Table 7.7 shows how private pension provision varies between people with different characteristics.

The young, women, those with low incomes, those who are not in work, those in lower social classes and those with no qualifications are most likely to be without private pension provision. In other words, those who, in broad terms, tend to be socio-economically worse off and have lower incomes, are not saving for their retirement. However, income alone cannot explain a lack of pension provision, as regression analysis confirms the importance of all the characteristics in Table 7.7 even when income is taken into account. Figure 7.3, later in the chapter, shows a summary of this regression analysis (see Model B1, with full details in the chapter appendix). Moreover, when other factors such as expectations of retirement income and general attitudes to saving are included in the regression (Models B2 and B3 in Figure 7.3), all these characteristics, bar education, remain significant.

It is also worth noting the existence of certain groups who do not have a pension and yet appear to be in a position to be saving. The clearest example is that one in five of those in the highest household income quartile and three in ten of those in the second highest quartile do not have any pension provision (although some of these may be non-working spouses of high-earning partners).

On this evidence, while some people are saving into pension schemes, a sizeable minority have no form of private pension provision at present. It is, of course, possible that they are making other plans, like investments. But the people in this situation are generally those with lower incomes, who find it hardest to spare the money. For private savings to fill the pensions gap, the take up of such schemes by these groups would surely have to increase markedly. This suggests that a voluntary approach to private provision will not be sufficient. And for those who simply cannot afford to save, compulsion is not likely to be a popular option either.

Cashing in on the property ladder

Of course, pension schemes are not the only way to put money aside for retirement. Some people may decide that they prefer to save in alternative ways, for example, through investments. There is no general question about this on the *British Attitudes Survey* but we did ask about one specific type of investment: "how likely do you think it is that you will sell a house or flat to help fund your retirement?" Answers to this question could be interpreted in different ways. For example, some who say they are likely to sell a house may have made a deliberate investment plan to do so; others may have inadequate financial provisions so that they have no alternative but to think of selling up. We tackled this to some extent by asking what type of property they thought would be sold. As shown in Table 7.8, about a third of respondents thought it likely that they would sell a house or flat to help fund their retirement. Of these, almost three-quarters said this would be their own home, and only 19 per cent thought it would be an investment property. Those with no private pension provision are *less* likely than those with a pension arrangement to say they will sell a house

(35 per cent compared to 45 per cent). Interestingly, the reverse is true for selling an *investment* property: 24 per cent of those who have no private pension arrangement and who say they will sell a house to fund their retirement plan to sell an investment property, compared with 16 per cent of their counterparts who do have a pension. Among this small group, then, this may well be a deliberate plan to fill a pensions gap.

Table 7.8 Plans to sell property to fund retirement, by age

	% likely to sell property	Base*	% likely to sell own home	% likely to sell investment property	Base**
Age					
18–34	43	767	59	27	325
35–54	43	1194	77	17	505
55–64	30	489	88	7	135
65+	9	685	89	7	54
All	35	3141	73	19	1020

*Base for column 1: all who have not already sold a property
**Base for columns 2 and 3: All those who say it is likely they will sell a property to fund their retirement

There are also notable age differences in the type of property that people plan to sell: younger people who plan to sell a property are more likely than their older counterparts to say this will be an investment property – 27 per cent of 18–34 year olds compared with seven per cent of those aged 55-plus; the reverse is true for selling their own home (59 per cent of 18–34 year olds who plan to sell a property say this compared to 88 per cent of their 55–64 year old counterparts). Of course, the young are more likely to be answering hypothetically, while older age groups are more likely to be talking about properties that they actually own.

The ostrich approach to pensions?

Are there any signs that some people have a 'head in the sand' approach to pensions? In other words, do those who are not saving simply not realise the implications for their retirement? We can examine this by assessing whether saving behaviour is linked to expectations about future income. We asked all those not yet retired whether they thought that in retirement (or once retired from their main job) they would be:

- *financially better off than now*
- *the same*
- *or, worse off*

A majority (53 per cent) say that they will be worse off in retirement than now. The proportion who think they will have a comparable income or will be better off in retirement represent a sizeable group of over a third (35 per cent). This is actually not too dissimilar to the experience of our pensioners – as we saw earlier 58 per cent said they were worse off in retirement while 39 per cent thought they were better off or the same.

It is groups with higher incomes, and those in work, who are most likely to think they will be worse off – no doubt reflecting the fact that they have a higher income before retirement. So while 61 per cent of those in work think they will be worse off in retirement, this compares to just 16 per cent of those in education or training. This finding is reinforced by the fact that those who have some form of pension provision are actually more likely than those without such arrangements to say they will be worse off in retirement than now (63 and 38 per cent respectively). It seems that answers to this question tell us more about a person's current financial status rather than their financial plans for the future.

A further question brought the issue down to basics:

> *Thinking about what you will be living on in retirement, including any money from pensions, benefits, savings or investments, and any earnings. Do you think you will have enough money to cover basic costs such as housing, heating and food?*[17]

Three-quarters say they will "definitely" or "probably" be able to cover the basics while just 16 per cent are not so sure ("probably not") and only three per cent say "definitely not".

But the crucial question is whether these expectations are related to saving behaviour. The short answer is yes. Those who have no private pension provision are less likely to think they will definitely be able to cover the basics in retirement (16 per cent compared to 30 per cent of those with a pension). This finding certainly suggests that the lack of provision we have found is *not* due to a lack of awareness.[18]

We repeated the regression model for having no private pension provision (referred to earlier) including these two measures of expectations about retirement income. The results are summarised in Figure 7.3 (model B2) and are given in full in the chapter appendix (we will return to the final model B3 later). They show that both measures are significantly related to lack of pension provision, even when other characteristics such as age and income are accounted for. Thus, those who do not expect to have enough to cover the basics in retirement are more likely to be in the position of having no pension provision. In other words, people without pensions know they are facing a bleak retirement but are choosing not to or are not able to do anything about it. This implies either that the expectation of poverty in old age is not enough to make people save, or that they simply cannot afford it. Either way the conclusion is the same: it is not unrealistically high expectations of the state pension and benefits that are preventing people from saving.

Figure 7.3 Factors associated with private pension provision (groups more likely than average to have <u>no</u> provision)

	Model B1: socio-demographic characteristics	Model B2: as model B1 plus retirement income expectation	Model B3: as model B2 plus attitudes to saving and knowledge about pensions
Age	18–24, 25–34	18–24, 25–34	18–24
Sex	Women	Women	Women
Economic status	'Other': unemployed, looking after home, disabled	'Other': unemployed, looking after home, disabled	'Other': unemployed, looking after home, disabled
Household income	Lowest quartile	Lowest quartile	Lowest quartile
Social class	Employers in small organisations; routine/semi-routine	Employers in small organisations; routine/semi-routine	Employers in small organisations; routine/semi-routine
Education	No qualifications	n.s.	n.s.
Expectation of being able to cover basics in retirement		Probably not / definitely not	*
Expectation of retirement income		Same as now	n.s.
When a person needs to start saving for retirement			40s or later, never
Whether young person should spend or save			Spend
Whether can afford to save for retirement			Neither agree nor disagree
Own knowledge about pensions			Nothing at all

* While none of the categories were statistically related to being *more* likely to have no private pension, those saying "definitely" and "probably" were *less* likely to be in this position
n.s. = not statistically significant

Can't save, won't save

So is the problem that people cannot afford to save, or do they simply find the whole pensions jungle too confusing and intimidating? We asked people both whether they feel they have enough disposable income to save, and whether they feel adequately informed and confident about their pension choices. Respondents were asked to agree or disagree with the following statements:

I can't afford to put money aside for retirement at the moment

Sometimes pensions seem so complicated that a person like me cannot really understand the best thing to do

As shown in Table 7.9a, the answers are not at all reassuring for those who see private saving as the way forward. Half of all people who are not yet retired say that they cannot afford to save for retirement while four in ten (39 per cent) disagree. And two-fifths of those who agree feel this strongly (overall, 21 per cent "agree strongly" while 29 per cent "agree"). This is strongly correlated with whether they actually have a private pension. If we look at the group who have no such provision, they are more than twice as likely to say they cannot afford to save than those with some form of pension.

Meanwhile, when it comes to knowledge, nearly two-thirds (63 per cent) of the public say that pensions are so complicated that "a person like me cannot really understand the best thing to do"; only one in five (18 per cent) disagree with this statement. The proportion agreeing did not vary according to a person's private pension status, though those with a pension are twice as likely as those without to *disagree* that pensions are this complicated (22 *versus* 11 per cent).

Table 7.9a Ability to save for retirement, by own pension provision

	No pension provision	Some form of pension provision	All
% who agree that they can't afford to save for retirement at the moment	72	35	50
Base	*901*	*1456*	*2360*

Base: all those not yet retired

Table 7.9b Pensions knowledge, by own pension provision

	Of those not yet retired		All
	No pension provision	Some form of pension provision	
Knowledge about pensions (self-report)	%	%	%
Not very much	44	29	36
Nothing at all	23	5	11
Base	*901**	*1456**	*3199*

* Base: all those not yet retired

We also asked a different question which allowed people to say how much they knew about pensions:

How much do you feel you know about pensions and how they work ...
- *a great deal,*
- *quite a lot,*
- *a bit,*
- *not very much,*
- *or, nothing at all?*

Responses to this question (shown in Table 7.9b) also show that knowledge about pensions is woefully low. Only two per cent say that they knew "a great deal" with a further 14 per cent saying "quite a lot" – so around one in seven people feel they have a fairly good level of knowledge. Clearly this means that the vast majority say their knowledge level is lower than this. Indeed, nearly half say either "not very much" or "nothing at all". And these last two answers are twice as likely to be given by a person with no pension provision compared with someone with a private pension arrangement.

Not surprisingly, a person's educational achievement is related to their understanding and confidence about pensions: those with no qualifications are more likely than those with qualifications to agree that pensions are so complicated it is hard to know what to do (72 per cent for those with no qualifications compared to 57 per cent of those with an A level or Higher Education qualification). Knowledge and confidence is also related to age – younger people are more likely to say they do not know anything about pensions (a quarter of them say "nothing at all" compared to around one in ten of those aged 35 and older). In fact, the government is tackling this issue of knowledge and confidence, through the "informed choice" and simplification agendas – both of which aim to tackle the complexity of the pensions market and allow people to make sensible decisions about pension provision.

This all matters because ability to save and knowledge about pensions are both related to the likelihood of having no private pension provision (see Model B3 in Figure 7.3). This holds true even after income, education, expectations about retirement income and other factors are taken into account. Indeed, when it comes to explaining the factors associated with private pension provision, Model B3 shows quite how complex this is. The model includes socio-demographic characteristics, expectations of retirement income, knowledge and confidence about saving and general attitudes to saving – all of which are separately related to a person's private pension provision.

Our findings suggest that there is a long way to go before most people can make private provision for their own old age, not least because many feel they cannot afford to save for retirement at the moment. Indeed, it is evident that a complex mixture of socio-demographic and attitudinal factors are related to private pension provision, suggesting there is no simple way to encourage more people to save. Our findings also provide support for the Pension Commission's view that, if people do not understand pensions, they are likely to do nothing about making private pension provision (though arguably knowledge may come from having a pension rather than being a prerequisite to getting one).

Would people be prepared to work longer and retire later?

The government is already taking steps to encourage labour force activity among the over-65s – stating that "the concept of normal retirement age will vanish from tax legislation" and introducing measures such as the State Pension Deferral benefits to make paid work preferable to retirement (quoted in Mann, 2005: 106). The State Pension Age (SPA) is due to equalise for men and women by 2020, and yet DWP research shows that just 59 per cent of working age respondents are aware of the future increase, and only 43 per cent of women who will be affected by the increase knew their own SPA (Murphy, 2004). The Institute for Public Policy Research has recently argued that, at some point, policy makers will have to 'grasp the nettle' of an increase in the state pension age (Robinson *et al.*, 2005). But such a policy is likely to have to overcome opposition on the grounds that it would hit the poorest, who tend to have low life expectancies and a shorter period of retirement already (see, for example, Trades Union Congress, 2005)

In this section we try to assess whether a policy of encouraging people to work longer has any chance of success. First, we look at the age and reasons for retirement of pensioners. Then we go on to look at expectations among those currently working.

Retired respondents in the *British Social Attitudes* survey were asked the age they had retired from work. After comparing this to the SPA at the time of the survey (60 for women and 65 for men), it emerged that just over half (55 per cent) of retired respondents had retired early (i.e. before SPA). Around a quarter retired at SPA (24 per cent), and just 21 per cent retired later than this. So on this evidence alone, the government would effectively need to reverse this picture. But perhaps people do not have free choice over their retirement age. Is there evidence that some would have continued working if SPA was set at a higher age? One in seven (15 per cent) said they had to retire because of their employer's policy on retirement age. Although this is a small group, it is a group that might work longer if they had free choice. However, this was far less likely to be the reason for retirement given by those who retired early: just six per cent of this group retired due to their employer's policy, compared to 35 per cent of those who retired at SPA.

Retired people who did not have to retire due to their employer's policy were asked their reasons for retiring. As shown in Table 7.10, the most common answer was "I just wanted to", followed by two reasons that imply less choice: ill health and being made redundant. It is notable that those who retired early (the group that in the future will need to change their behaviour most if people are to work longer) are more likely than other groups to report reasons that were not a free choice. For example, just a quarter of this group retired because they wanted to, compared to around a half of those who retired at or after SPA. And ill health was mentioned by three in ten of those who retired early – double the proportion of those who retired later.

Table 7.10 Reasons for retiring from work, by retirement age

	Retired ...			All
	before SPA	at SPA	after SPA	
% who say they retired because of employer's policy on retirement age	6	35	17	15
*Base**	*385*	*184*	*172*	*741*
Reason given for retirement	%	%	%	%
... just wanted to	26	56	50	37
... ill health	30	16	16	25
... lost job/ made redundant/ firm closed	18	11	13	16
... to look after someone else	10	6	6	8
... attractive retirement package	12	2	3	8
... because partner retired	2	8	8	5
... other reason	8	8	9	8
*Base***	*364*	*120*	*141*	*625*

* Base for first half of table: all retired
**Base for second half of table: retired people who did not have to retire due to employer's policy

The figures from our retired respondents reflect the fact that the employment rates of people aged 50 and over declined between the late 1970s and the mid-1990s. Since then employment rates have gradually increased and between 1994 and 2004 the employment rate of people aged 50 and over rose from 31 per cent to 37 per cent (Whiting, 2005). This is still very low bearing in mind that SPA is at least 60.

  Moreover, this change does not seem to signal an end to the expectation among many current employees that they will retire early. We asked all current employees when they expected to retire from their main job: four in ten expect to retire at the current SPA, roughly the same proportion (37 per cent) expect to retire before SPA, and just 20 per cent think they will retire after this. Of those who expected to retire early, the vast majority (84 per cent) say that the reason for this is that they "just want to" (in contrast to being forced to through ill health or their employer). So for this group, it is apparent that a change in attitude will be needed if employees in the future are to work for longer and buck the trend for retiring early. Of those who expected to work past SPA, the main reason given was that they could not afford to stop earning (37 per cent), followed by the fact that they enjoyed working (27 per cent). While this is a small group, it may increase over time, if more employees realise that they do not have enough money to provide for their own retirement. Indeed, as Table 7.11 shows, expectations about retirement income are already related to early retirement plans, with those who think they will not have enough to cover the basics being more likely to plan to retire after SPA. Regression analysis confirms this, with those who say they will "definitely" have enough to cover basics being more likely than average to say they will retire before SPA, even after their current household income and other relevant factors are taken into account. (Age, sex, income and class are also related.)

Table 7.11 Retirement plans, by retirement income expectation

	Retirement income expectation		All
	Able to cover basics	Not able to cover basics	
	%	%	%
Plan to retire early	41	20	37
Plan to retire late	17	29	20
Base*	1213	256	1507

* Base: employees

Retiring from a 'main job' is one thing, but many people continue to do some form of paid work after that. We asked employees "do you think you are likely to do any further paid work after retiring from your main job?". Just over a half said "yes" (54 per cent). Those who expected to retire before SPA were more likely to say this than other employees (61 per cent compared to around 50 per cent). Perhaps, surprisingly, planning to work after retiring is not related to current income once other factors are taken into account – sex and educational qualifications are the only significant variables (men and those with qualifications being more likely than their counterparts to say they will do further work). When the regression analysis is repeated to include our two measures of expectation about retirement income, sex and educational qualifications remain significant, but added to this, a person's views on whether they will be able to cover the basics in retirement is also associated with expecting to work after retirement. Not surprisingly, those who expect to be able to cover the basics are less likely to expect to do further paid work after retiring.

The implications of these findings for whether people are becoming more willing to work for longer depends on whether expectations about retirement age are driven by whatever happens to be the current SPA. If so, we can expect a government-led increase in SPA to encourage more people to work for longer.

The alternative interpretation is that expectations are independent of SPA, in which case there is a lot more to do before most people of working age are prepared to work for longer. In any case, it is apparent that expecting an inadequate income in retirement provides some with an incentive to work until later in life.

Conclusions

In the first part of this chapter we found mixed messages about Labour's policies on pensions to date. There is support for targeting resources at the poorest pensioners, though a majority want the basic state pension to remain available to all. However, when asked about the actual amounts involved, views are less positive. Most pensioners feel that the state pension is inadequate, and a majority of the public think that pensioners living on benefits are hard up or really poor (though they also underestimate the amount of money pensioners receive in benefits). Taken together, these views effectively rule out public support for the suggestion that pensioners in the future should have to live on less money.

There is partial support for the suggestion that better state pensions should be funded through more taxation. Increased spending on pensions is certainly popular, and almost no one wants to see this spending decrease. There is a complication, however – even among those who want extra money to be spent on pensions, there is no great appetite for more taxes.

The suggestion that people should save more is also popular in principle, with most of the British public being in favour of people saving for their own retirement (and from a relatively early age). However, actual savings behaviour is not so clear-cut. We found that four in ten of those who are not yet retired have no private pension provision. Further analysis shows that while some of those in this position either have relatively high incomes or have plans to sell property to fund their retirement, most are in the least advantaged socio-economic groups. Many say they simply cannot afford to save at the moment. Added to that, there is widespread lack of knowledge and confusion around the complexities of pensions, suggesting that even an increase in disposable income might not be enough to encourage increased saving. It is not the case that people are simply ignoring the consequences of inadequate pension provision, as most seem to be aware of their likely financial position in later life. But the fact that knowing that they are facing a bleak retirement is not enough to encourage people to take out a private pension reinforces the finding that many of those without any such provision are just not in a position to save.

We have only found limited support for the suggestion that people should work longer and retire later. More than half of current pensioners retired early (before state pension age); most current employees expect to retire early or at the current state pension age, with just one in five saying they will retire later than this. However, around half thought they would do further paid work after retiring from their main job, which does suggest that people have some understanding that this may be necessary in order to have a reasonable retirement income. Indeed, expecting a low income in retirement is related to plans for working later in life. Those who think their expected retirement income will not be adequate are more likely than those who anticipate being able to cover the basics to say they will work beyond state pension age.

All in all, the way forward is unclear. There are various contradictions in people's views and behaviour which mean that we have not found clear support for any one of the four approaches suggested by the Pensions Commission. It is, however, likely that some combination of more taxation, more private savings and later retirement will be necessary. And we have found some support for this, particularly for increased government spending alongside more personal saving for retirement. Added to that, there are indications that working later in life may be the way that some plan to fill their own pensions gap. But support is very tentative, and we suspect that some respondents want 'other people' to pay more taxes and save more. It is clear that if any future pensions policy is to square this circle, substantial changes in the public's attitudes and behaviour will be required.

Notes

1. 'Pensions crisis: Will anyone fix it?', BBC News online, 1st April 2005, http://news.bbc.co.uk/go/pr/fr/-/1/hi/business/4119215.stm. Other examples include references to a "pensions 'timebomb'" in *The Guardian* (22nd June 2005), and the "retirement crisis" in *The Financial Times* (16th May 2005).
2. 'Government admits women's pensions a scandal', *The Times*, 21st October 2004.
3. In interpreting this finding, we need to bear in mind that men are more likely to have higher incomes than women and this could affect their views. In order to disentangle such relationships, we need to use multivariate analysis which can assess the importance of one factor while taking others into account (details of which are included in the appendix to this Report). Such analysis shows that once other characteristics (including age and household income) are controlled for, sex is the only one which remains significantly related to views, with men more likely to say the state pension is "very low" than women.
4. The amount of money quoted in the second of the two questions equates to the level of income guaranteed by Pension Credit (the equivalent of the MIG in earlier years) and in previous surveys was set at the then levels of the MIG or Income Support. The amounts therefore correspond to the minimum that single pensioners should have to live on after meeting their housing costs.
5. The questions were asked in a series which also included questions about other benefit recipients (namely a full-time carer and an unemployed single mother with a young child). The responses to the questions about the pensioner should therefore be seen in this context – in other words, respondents may have been answering with a comparison in mind. The benefits for the full-time carer and her husband were given

as £146 and the unemployed single mother as £130. In both cases, however, these benefits were meant to cover two people.

6. Although the bases are small for those in education and the unemployed, the differences are statistically significant.

7. *The Times*, 7th June 2005.

8. Hansard, 13 October 2004, col 309.

9. The Second Report of the Commission is due to be published in late 2005.

10. See, for example, Ros Altmann, 'Pensions cannot solve the retirement crisis', *The Financial Times*, 16th May 2005. There is a secondary debate around this option – whether there is a case for moving beyond the current voluntarist approach. Malcom Rifkind, the Conservative pensions spokesman is vehemently against compelling people to save – saying the objections are "powerful and overwhelming. It is wrong in principle for the state to tell people how they use their post-tax income" ('Blunkett hint on pension compulsion', *The Guardian*, 22nd June 2005). We cannot directly address compulsion to save here, though we will assess whether voluntary measures are sufficient.

11. It is possible that some people support the 'saving' option in this question because they do not agree with the assumption in the first option that spending means they should "worry" about retirement later. However, we have already found clear support for saving when the question is phrased differently (see earlier discussion).

12. See, for example, 'Girls learn to dodge debt timebomb', *The Observer*, 18th January 2004.

13. A similar question about older people was answered quite differently. In this case, the majority (67 per cent) think that an older person should "spend their money while they can and not worry about leaving an inheritance for their children" rather than trying to "pass on an inheritance to their children, even if they have to cut back on other things". However, this difference in view doesn't undermine support for saving for retirement: the question is about a different concept (inheritance rather than providing for retirement); and it is likely that people have different views about what a young person should do in comparison to an older person – arguably by the time a person is 'old' it is too late to save enough to make a difference.

14. The questions asked respondents to distinguish between schemes to which they (or their employer) are currently contributing, and schemes which they have, but to which contributions are not currently being made. For the purposes of this chapter, we have combined the two so that people are deemed to have a personal or occupational pension if they have either a scheme to which they are still contributing or a scheme to which they are no longer contributing.

15. In the question text, "private pension" was used to distinguish personal arrangements from employer-organised occupational pensions. In the chapter, the expression "private pension" is used in the more general sense to encompass both occupational and personal pensions, as distinct from the state pension.

16. This raises an important issue about whether employers should be compelled to contribute to a pension scheme for all employees; however, this issue is beyond the scope of the chapter.

17. Employees were asked "when you have retired from your main job" rather than "in retirement".

18. Though younger respondents were more likely than their older counterparts to answer "don't know" to these two questions about retirement income.

References

Chung W., Disney R., Emmerson, C. and Wakefield M. (2005), 'Public policy and saving for retirement: evidence from the introduction of stakeholder pensions in the UK', Paper presented to the Royal Economic Society Annual Conference, Nottingham, March

Department for Work and Pensions (2005a), *Households Below Average Income 1994/95 – 2003/04*, available at http://www.dwp.gov.uk/asd/hbai/hbai2004/

Department for Work and Pensions (2005b), *Income related benefits: estimates of take-up in 2002/2003*, available at http://www.dwp.gov.uk/asd/irb.asp

Ginn, J. (2004), 'UK Pension Policy: Denying and damaging solidarity', *Radical Statistics*, **86:** 83–99

Government Actuary's Department (2004), 2003-based Projections database, available at http://www.gad.gov.uk/Population/index.asp

HM Treasury (2002), *Budget 2002 Report*, available at http://www.hm-treasury.gov.uk/budget/bud_bud02/bud_bud02_index.cfm

House of Commons Work and Pensions Committee (2005), *Pension Credit and Delivery of Services to Ethnic Minority Clients: Government Responses to the Committee's 3rd and 4th Reports of Session 2005–06*, HC 397, London: The Stationery Office

Mann, K. (2005), 'Killing us softly with their words? Retirement pensions and New Labour', *Benefits*, **43(13/2)**: 104–108

McKay, S. (2004), 'Poverty or preference: what do "consensual deprivation indicators" really measure?' , *Fiscal Studies,* **25(2)**: 201–223

Murphy, C. (2004), *Public awareness of State Pension age equalisation*, DWP Research Report 221

Pensions Commission (2004), *Pensions: Challenges and Choices, The First Report of the Pensions Commission*, London: The Stationery Office

Pensions Policy Institute (2005), Memorandum submitted to the House of Commons Work and Pensions Committee's Pension Credit Inquiry in House of Commons Work and Pensions Committee, 2005, *Pension Credit: Third Report of Session 2004–05, volume II*, HC 43-II, London: The Stationery Office

Pension Provision Group (2001), *A Commentary on the Pension Credit Proposals*, available at http://www.pensionprovisiongroup.org.uk/

Robinson, P., Gosling, T. and Lewis, M (2005), *Working Later: Raising the Effective Age of Retirement*, London: Institute for Public Policy Research

Department for Social Security (1998), *A new contract for welfare: partnership in pensions,* Cm 4179, London: The Stationery Office

Sefton, T. (2003), 'What we want from the welfare state', in Park, A., Curtice, J., Thomson, K., Jarvis, L. and Bromley, C. (eds.), *British Social Attitudes: the 20th Report – Continuity and change over two decades*, London: Sage

Taylor-Gooby, P. and Hastie, C. (2003), 'Support for state spending: has New Labour got it right?', in Park, A., Curtice, J., Thomson, K., Jarvis, L. and Bromley, C. (eds.) *British Social Attitudes: the 20th Report – Continuity and change over two decades*, London: Sage

Trades Union Congress (2005), *TUC comment on IPPR retirement age report*, TUC press release, 22nd July

Whiting, E. (2005), 'The labour market participation of older people', Labour Market Trends, **113(07)**: 285–296

Acknowledgements

The *National Centre for Social Research* is grateful to the Department for Work and Pensions for their financial support which enabled us to ask the questions reported in this chapter. Responsibility for the analysis of these data lies solely with the authors.

Appendix

The multivariate analysis technique used is logistic regression (deviation contrast method) where categories of independent variables are compared to an average. Regressions referred to in Figure 7.2 and Figure 7.3 are given in full below. The other regression analyses referred to in the chapter are available from the authors. The statistic given is the parameter estimate (B).

Regression Model A: saying a pensioner living on state benefits is "hard up" or "really poor"

Age

18–24	-0.81**
25–34	-0.47**
35–44	-0.02
45–54	0.13
55–59	0.27*
60–64	0.33*
65+	0.57**

Economic status

Education / training	0.48*
Work	-0.14
Retired	-0.43**
Other (inc. unemployed, looking after home, disabled)	0.08

Household income quartiles

Lowest	-0.33**
2nd lowest	0.10
2nd highest	0.06
Highest	0.17*

Party identification

Conservative	-0.10
Labour	0.17*
Liberal Democrat	0.21*
Other	-0.12
None	-0.17

Sex	–
Education	–
Social class	–
Constant	0.54**
Base	*2529*

* = significant at 95% level
** = significant at 99% level
– = not significant in the final regression model

In the following table, results are shown for three different models, all with the dependent variable 'having no private pension provision'. The difference between the models is in terms of which independent variables were included as follows:

Model B1: socio-demographic characteristics only

Model B2: All variables included in model B1 plus two expectations of retirement income variables

Model B3: All variables included in model B2 plus variables about attitudes to saving and pensions knowledge

Regression Models B1-3: having no private pension provision

	Model B1	Model B2	Model B3
Age			
18–24	2.05**	1.90**	1.57**
25–34	0.36**	0.32*	0.31
35–44	-0.56**	-0.68**	-0.77**
45–54	-0.54**	-0.58**	-0.45*
55–59	-0.87**	-0.70**	-0.55*
60–64	-0.40	-0.22	0.26
65+	-0.04	-0.03	-0.36
Sex			
Male	-0.25**	-0.25**	-0.34**
Female	0.25**	0.25**	0.34**
Economic status			
Education / training	0.24	0.10	0.16
Work	-1.02**	-0.85**	-0.72**
Other (inc. unemployed, looking after home, disabled)	0.77**	0.75**	0.55**
Household income quartiles			
Lowest	0.66**	0.61**	0.55**
2nd lowest	0.04	0.11	-0.11
2nd highest	-0.30**	-0.31**	-0.38**
Highest	-0.40**	-0.41**	-0.06
Social class			
Managerial / professional	-0.79**	-0.79**	-0.69**
Intermediate	-0.54**	-0.60**	-0.77**
Small employers	0.88**	0.85**	0.91**
Lower supervisory / technical	0.01	0.02	0.16
Semi-routine / routine	0.43**	0.51**	0.39*
Education			
HE	-0.39**	–	–
A level	-0.07	–	–
O level / CSE	0.04	–	–
None	0.42**	–	–

continued on next page

	Model B1 (continued)	Model B2 (continued)	Model B3 (continued)
Cover basics in retirement			
Definitely	n.a.	-0.66**	-0.38*
Probably	n.a.	-0.51**	-0.43**
Probably not	n.a.	0.45**	0.25
Definitely not	n.a.	0.72**	0.57
Retirement income *vs* now			
Better off	n.a.	0.15	–
Same	n.a.	0.22*	–
Worse off	n.a.	-0.36**	–
When need to start saving			
20s or earlier	n.a.	n.a.	-0.67**
30s	n.a.	n.a.	0.06
40s–60s / never	n.a.	n.a.	0.60*
Young people should …			
Spend now, worry later	n.a.	n.a.	0.36**
Save now, cut back soon	n.a.	n.a.	-0.36**
Afford to save for retirement?			
Agree	n.a.	n.a.	0.18
Neither agree nor disagree	n.a.	n.a.	0.46**
Disagree	n.a.	n.a.	-0.64**
Knowledge about pensions			
A great deal / quite a lot	n.a.	n.a.	-0.61**
A bit	n.a.	n.a.	-0.47**
Not very much	n.a.	n.a.	0.07
Nothing at all	n.a.	n.a.	1.01**
Government should encourage people to save for retirement	n.a.	n.a.	–
Pensions are so complicated I don't know the best thing to do	n.a.	n.a.	–
Constant	0.28	0.52**	0.97**
Base	*2041*	*1813*	*1291*

 * = significant at 95% level
** = significant at 99% level
− = not significant in the final regression model
n.a. = not included in the analysis

8 Leaders or followers? Parties and public opinion on the European Union

Geoffrey Evans and Sarah Butt[*]

The failure of Britain to adopt the Euro or to ratify the new European Union (EU) constitution must ultimately be understood as a defeat for Tony Blair's New Labour project. Referendums on both had been planned for some time, particularly with regard to the Euro, but are now unlikely to take place in the foreseeable future: the odds of success for the government in the form of a 'yes' vote seem too long. So is this the limit of Britain's European venture? Will the British public through its long-standing enmity effectively frighten off the government from pursuing its European goals? The answer will in part depend on who shapes the public's views on the EU.

There are two possible scenarios with very different implications. The party-driven view emphasises Labour's powerful electoral mandate combined with the old and well-established vision of the voter with respect to matters relating to the European Union – a voter who is passive and unlikely to get in the way of the political elite's aspirations for integration. In contrast, the voter-driven view stresses that, since around the time of the Maastricht Treaty in 1991, the EU has become a more salient and contested issue (see previous chapters in this series: Evans (1995, 1998a, 2001, 2003), and for a more general consideration with respect to the EU as a whole, Van der Eijk and Franklin (1996), Marks and Steenbergen (2004)). According to this view, voters now have their own opinions and are less easily manipulated by elites.

From the perspective of the party-driven scenario, the period since 1997 should have been a good time to push the EU agenda because of Labour's powerful electoral mandate. Indeed, the Welsh referendum of 1997 saw a similar party-influenced result in the face of public opposition and apathy (Evans and Trystan, 1999). This assumes that a popular government can rely on a substantial proportion of the electorate following its lead and endorsing its

[*] Geoffrey Evans is Official Fellow in Politics, Nuffield College, and Professor of the Sociology of Politics and Director of the Centre for Research Methods in the Social Sciences, University of Oxford. Sarah Butt is a DPhil student in Politics, Nuffield College, University of Oxford.

position. Such a view has long been enshrined in Lindberg and Scheingold's (1970) notion of a 'permissive consensus' which sees the EU project as advancing more or less independently of the electorates of EU member states, who when asked (which is not very often), can usually be relied upon to come round to the 'progressive' position. Is this a true picture, however? Was it ever? This chapter sets out to examine this question for Britain. It also throws light on what the question of European integration has done, or might be doing, to the landscape of political divisions in this country – the pattern of issues and social groupings that most significantly divide the supporters of the main political parties.

The state of play: public opinion on the EU referendums

The adamant rejection in France and the Netherlands of the proposed new EU constitution must, ironically, have come as a great relief to the government's strategists. In Table 8.1 we can see what the British public's views were on this issue – even before the Dutch and French made their own views clear. The extent of the rejection is impressive – even greater than that expressed with regard to the government's other ailing EU project, the Euro.

Table 8.1 Likely vote in referendums on European issues

On the European constitution	%
To adopt	20
Not to adopt	56
Don't know	24
On joining the Euro	**%**
To join	27
Not to join	67
Don't know	6
Base	*3199*

Exactly one-fifth say they would vote 'yes' to the constitution, compared with just over a quarter who say the same with respect to a Euro referendum. The main difference between the two potential referendums lies in the high proportion of "don't knows" with respect to the constitution – the Euro has been around longer and the "don't knows" are now relatively few. There might therefore be 'room for manoeuvre' on the constitution given the sizeable minority of uncommitted citizens. But this again assumes that the public's attitudes and preferences can be changed by political parties. The possibility of straightforward across the board persuasion seems unlikely given the current divisions among even the political elite. Another route would be for the government to concentrate on persuading its own supporters. After all, there are more of them than there are Conservatives, and the Liberal Democrats are also pro-EU and might be able to do likewise with their supporters. If this happens, the hard core Conservative opponents of any future attempt at a constitutional or Euro referendum might simply be outnumbered. But can parties sway their supporters in this way: do parties lead or do they follow?

As we can see in Table 8.2, there are clear partisan divisions over the key European issues. Labour and Liberal Democrat partisans are rather similar to each other and twice as likely to say that they will vote 'yes' than are Conservatives and those who do not identify with a party. Don't knows – that is, the uncommitted – are spread across all party blocs. Note, however, that those who say they will vote 'no' heavily outnumber the 'yes' voters among the supporters of all parties.

Table 8.2 Likely vote in referendums on European issues, by party identification

	Conser-vative	Labour	LibDem	Other	None
On the European constitution	%	%	%	%	%
To adopt	13	28	28	17	12
Not to adopt	72	48	48	63	49
Don't know	16	24	23	20	37
On joining the Euro	%	%	%	%	%
To join	18	34	37	21	19
Not to join	79	60	59	76	67
Don't know	4	5	5	2	14
Base	*833*	*1011*	*414*	*164*	*516*

The key question, however, is whether these partisan differences derive from an acceptance by supporters of their parties' positions. After all, people might have a range of reasons for supporting the party and attitudes to the EU may not figure very largely in this decision. Having decided which party to support, people may be happy to take their cue on Europe from their party's policy. Or, is the contrary true – that people have their own independent positions on the EU and are attracted to particular parties who represent these?

A cross-sectional survey like *British Social Attitudes* (where any given respondent is interviewed only once) can show the *association* between voters' views and party identification, but it simply cannot prove which causes which. To obtain a better answer to this question we can examine change through time by both electorates and individuals. Fortunately, we can look at change over time in successive samples to the *British Social Attitudes* surveys. Moreover, the *British Election Panel Studies* re-interviewed the same individuals at several points in time: respondents to the 1987 *British Election Study* were re-interviewed in 1992, and similarly for the periods 1992–1997 and 1997–2001.[1] If we can use this evidence to untangle whether party identification drives attitudes to the EU or the other way round, then we should be able to make some predictions about what might happen in coming years to the EU and Britain's involvement with it.

Attitudes towards the EU over the long-term

First, we need to look at what has happened to attitudes towards Britain's involvement in the EU since the 1980s. Unfortunately, the same question has not been asked throughout on *British Social Attitudes*. The following question was asked on each survey from the start of the series in 1983 until 1991 and again in 1997:

> *Do you think Britain should continue to be a member of the European Union or should it withdraw?*[2]

The withdraw/continue question was replaced in 1993 by a question that gives people a fuller set of options on Britain's influence within the EU:

> *Do you think Britain's long-term policy should be ...*
> *... to leave the European Union,*
> *to stay in the EU and try to reduce the EU's powers,*
> *to leave things as they are,*
> *to stay in the EU and try to increase the EU's powers,*
> *or, to work for the formation of a single European government?*

In the analysis in this chapter, we have combined the categories "leave the European Union" and "stay in the EU and try to reduce the EU's powers" and call these "reduce influence". Similarly, we have combined the categories "to work for the formation of a single European government" and "stay in the EU and try to increase the EU's powers" and call these "increased influence".

The change in question causes a disruption in the time-series, but the trends can nevertheless be discerned. Figure 8.1 shows the development of attitudes to the EU over time. Moreover, both questions were asked on the *British General Election Study* in 1992. As observed before (for example, Evans, 2003), the

British Social Attitudes surveys show a decline in endorsement of EU membership after 1992. By 1992 support for staying in the EU, which rose during the 1980s, had begun to fall and there has since been a gradual increase in the desire to reduce the EU's influence. The start of the 1990s may therefore have been the high water mark of British public support for European integration. Of more interest for our purposes, however, is the way in which the partisan nature of attitudes towards the EU has evolved over this period. Despite changes in the question format, the *relative* positions of groups within the electorate can be compared over the full period with some confidence.

Figure 8.1 Trends in attitudes to the EU, 1983–2004

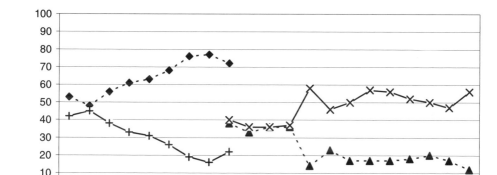

Figure 8.2 shows the gap between pro- and anti-EU attitudes for the supporters of each of the main parties on the withdraw/continue question. The nature of partisan differences has changed dramatically over the period. In the early to mid-1980s it was Conservative supporters who were more supportive of the EU. After 1987, though, party differences started to switch around: by 1992 they were fairly evenly balanced and by 1997 they were fully reversed. Labour (and Liberal Democrat) supporters were now more pro-EU than the Conservatives. Figure 8.3 picks up the story using the influence in the EU question. Here we see Conservative supporters slightly more negative in the early 1990s, but essentially the attitudes of the supporters of the three parties moving together. Since 1997, attitudes have diverged with Labour and Liberal Democrat supporters' views remaining fairly unchanged, while Conservative supporters have become much more Eurosceptic.

Figure 8.2 Balance of attitudes to the EU (continue/withdraw question), by party identification, 1983–1997

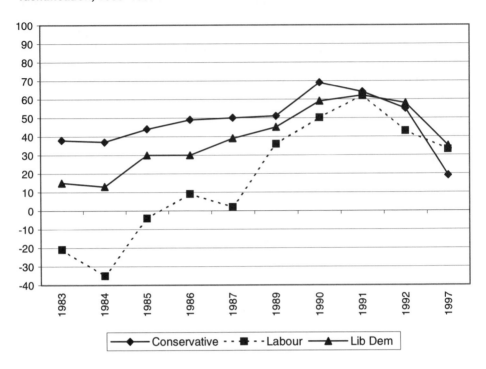

Figure 8.3 Balance of attitudes to the EU (British influence question), by party identification, 1992–2004

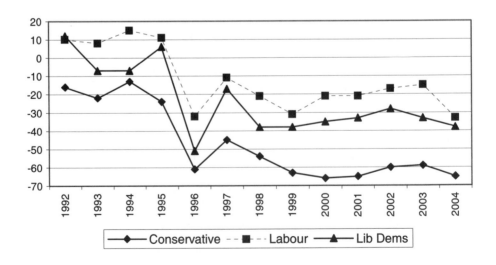

Moreover, this switch round in the partisan character of the European question has not been a minor shift: in 1987 no less than 40 per cent of Labour voters wanted to leave the European Union compared with only 23 per cent of Conservatives. By 1997 this figure had dropped to 25 per cent among Labour voters and jumped to 37 per cent among Conservatives. For Labour, this change took place very clearly between 1987 and 1992 – by which time only 24 per cent wanted to leave the EU, effectively the same as in 1997. For the Conservatives, however, the proportion wanting to leave the EU in 1992 (21 per cent) was still as low as in 1987. The change in attitudes occurred only after that election, when parts of the Conservative Party elite began to express their Euroscepticism with increasing fervour.

That the electorate picked up on this shift in elite opinion can be seen from answers to a question in the *British Election Panel Study* in 1992 and 1997 which asks respondents where they think parties stand on Europe. In 1992 only 36 per cent saw the Conservatives as being anti-integration. By 1997 this figure had risen to 53 per cent. In contrast, both Labour and the Liberal Democrats were perceived to have become more pro-integration over the same period. Despite the evident splits in the Conservative Party during this period, the general impression was of an increasingly anti-European party. From 1997 onwards, the pattern of partisan divisions in the EU appears to have consolidated.

So, how can we explain this evolution in the partisan nature of attitudes towards the EU? As we noted before, there are two main scenarios for explaining the changes: party-driven or voter-driven. We shall now examine the evidence for each of these in turn.

The party-driven scenario

When new issues arrive on the political scene they can change the structure of political divisions by providing a new source of support for, or rejection of, parties, thereby altering the ways in which parties compete for votes. However, a party-driven process of influence pre-empts this possibility: for the EU to have an impact on support for political parties it has to be an influence on voters' choices, rather than reflect the guiding hand of parties and leaders (see Flickinger, 1994). A party-driven model of EU opinion formation implies that when personal opinion is unformed or divergent from party position, party supporters should bring their opinions on Europe round to fit with that of their party. Little evidence of change should therefore be observed in the ideological composition of support for the main political parties, as long as those parties remain constant in their positions.

For example, the electoral basis of support for the Labour and Conservative Parties has traditionally been understood in ideological terms as reflecting voters' relative positions on a set of interrelated issues that can be characterised as a left–right dimension. This can be seen as being polarised between the adherents of more or less interventionist and redistributive policies *versus* laissez-faire, free market policy regimes (see Evans *et al.,* 1996; Heath *et al.,* 1994; Sanders, 1999). If parties lead and voters follow, the EU should have become increasingly integrated with this left–right division, as this is the one that links most closely to Labour *versus* Conservative support. Those on the right should become increasingly anti-EU; those on the left, pro-EU. This should result in a closer correlation between EU attitudes and left–right attitudes over time.

This picture is complicated, however, by the Labour Party's move from an anti-EU to a pro-EU stance during the 1980s, formally proclaiming its new position in the 1989 Policy Review (George and Rosamund, 1992). Labour's traditionally anti-European position fitted rather well with the 'old left' and Eurosceptic character of its working-class support base. The party's switch is likely to have produced an inconsistency between its support base, which as we have seen tended to be Eurosceptic prior to that time, and the official party position. The Conservative Party, in contrast, moved from being pro-European in the 1970s to becoming markedly less Europhile over time under Mrs Thatcher's leadership. The party was openly split over Europe in the early and mid-1990s (Sowemimo, 1996; Berrington and Hague, 1998) and was perceived to be so by the electorate (Evans, 1998b). Only after 1997 did these internal divisions and the electorate's perception of them subside as the party established itself as more clearly anti-EU (Evans, 2001). So, if parties shape their supporters' views we would expect that until this process of party realignment over the EU took hold, anti-EU opinion should have been correlated with being left-wing. During, and after this process those on the right should have become increasingly anti-EU and those on the left increasingly pro-EU. The party realignment will therefore have caused the voters to switch their own views accordingly, thus realigning the relationship between attitudes towards left–right issues and towards the EU.

The voter-driven scenario

If attitudes towards the EU derive from voters' preferences independently of party influence, then we should see vote switching, at least to the degree that there is incompatibility between voters' opinions and their parties' positions, and the issue is one that matters to voters. With vote switching comes a change in the sorts of people who vote for each party.

To form part of voters' decision calculus, new issues have to divide the public in fundamental ways and polarise parties. In other words, they should meet Butler and Stokes's (1974) classic specification of the requirements for issue voting, *viz.* an issue has to be salient, divisive and party polarised. To produce a decisive change in party support, moreover, these issues need also to produce ideological cleavages that cut across traditional bases of party support. The voter-driven view argues that the increasing personal relevance of the EU over the last 20 years has fundamentally affected the ways in which it is evaluated by the electorate – to the extent that these conditions now apply.

Traditionally, European integration was an issue with low political salience, only occasionally emerging as a topic that moved British public opinion (Janssen, 1991; Evans, 1995; Rasmussen, 1997).[3] Following the 1991 Maastricht Treaty, however, electorates all over Europe became increasingly sceptical about the integration agenda (Niedermayer, 1995; Franklin and Wlezien, 1997). The initial failure of the Danish electorate to endorse the ratification of the Maastricht Treaty and the extremely narrow pro-Maastricht result in the French referendum were two significant early examples of growing popular disquiet over European integration (Franklin *et al.*, 1994). Unsurprisingly, EU integration also affected British politics, with high profile splits within the Conservative administrations which formed the key axis of division in the party's leadership elections in 1990, 1995 and 1997. Meanwhile, the ERM crisis of September 1992 was the single event that most undermined their standing in the opinion polls. The emergence of the Referendum Party during the 1997 general election campaign served further to highlight the controversies surrounding integration (McAllister and Studlar, 2000).

It is reasonable to suppose, therefore, that the EU has become a more salient issue for the public since the early 1990s, with a consequent increase in its relevance to party political competition. These changes are consistent with evidence of the increasing public awareness of the issues posed by integration presented in Evans (1998a). This analysis of *British Social Attitudes* data found that the internal consistency of attitudes towards various aspects of integration increased substantially in the space of a few years as the public related their views on issues that had been seen as hitherto disparate – European Monetary Union and the increasingly centralised influence of various areas of policy-making – to their support for or opposition to integration in principle. These changes are what would be expected of an issue that has become increasingly salient and meaningful to the electorate. So, although earlier in the period the electorate might have been relatively disinterested in the EU issue and the influence process party-driven, as the electorate has become more informed/engaged and holds more independent views, the EU process has potentially become more voter-driven.

To summarize these complex changes and their interpretations, we can therefore discern three distinct periods:

(1)   a period of flux as the established alignment is revoked by the Labour Party Policy Review during the late 1980s (and Mrs Thatcher increasingly displayed her personal Euroscepticism);

(2)   an emerging realignment as both parties adjust to their new positions on the issue, which takes place during the early to mid-1990s; and

(3)   consolidation of this realignment following the 1997 general election.

We can also expect to see evidence of an increasingly meaningful public attitude to EU issues since the relatively quiet and disinterested days prior to Maastricht and the ERM crisis.

Changes in the ideological bases of attitudes towards Europe?

As we have seen in Figure 8.2, the partisan nature of attitudes towards the EU in the electorate appears to have switched after the parties changed their relative positions on integration. However, the explanation of this change is less obvious. As discussed, it could have occurred for two rather different reasons: either because their supporters switched their views to be consistent with the party, or because the parties attracted different sorts of voters as a result of their recently reversed positions on Europe. If the former is the case we would expect a change in the ideological bases of support for European integration: prior to the late 1980s voters on the left (i.e. traditional Labour supporters) should be anti-EU, while after that period they should be pro-EU.

To examine this we look at the pattern of correlations between attitudes towards the EU and left–right values, which provide the most significant basis of differences between the Conservative and Labour Parties. We look also at libertarian–authoritarian values, relating to social issues such as 'law and order', individual freedoms, censorship and the like, which differentiate less strongly between Labour and Conservative but are related to support for the Liberal Democrats (see Evans *et al.*, 1996). (The left–right and libertarian–authoritarian scales are described in more detail in the Appendix to this Report).

Table 8.4 looks at the 'withdraw/continue' question asked up to 1992. Table 8.5 picks up the story using the EU 'influence' question. The tables show the correlation coefficients which are a measure of the association between two variables. Positive correlation coefficients mean that the left-wing or libertarian attitudes are related to more pro-EU views, while negative correlations coefficients mean that they are related to more anti-EU views. The larger the coefficient, the stronger the association. Coefficients which are not statistically significantly different from zero – i.e., there is no evidence of an association – are shown in brackets.

Table 8.3 Correlations of attitudes towards the EU (withdraw/continue) with left–right and libertarian–authoritarian attitudes, 1986–1997

	1986	1987	1989	1990	1991	1992	1997
Left–right scale	-0.25	-0.24	-0.13	-0.15	-0.11	-0.07	0.04
Libertarian– authoritarian scale	0.14	0.15	0.15	0.11	(0.01)	0.15	0.22
Base	*1311*	*2462*	*2572*	*2410*	*1422*	*3284*	*1087*

Note: Scales coded so that higher values represent "left wing" or "libertarian" values
Figures in brackets are not statistically significant

Table 8.4 Correlations of attitudes towards EU influence with left–right and libertarian–authoritarian attitudes, 1992–2004

	1992	1994	1995	1996	1997	1998	1999	2000	2001	2002	2003	2004
Left–right	0.10	0.07	0.10	(0.05)	0.11	0.09	(0.04)	(0.03)	(0.03)	(0.04)	(0.01)	0.05
Libertarian– authoritarian scale	0.17	0.23	0.18	0.17	0.20	0.23	0.11	0.24	0.24	0.20	0.21	0.25
Base	*3284*	*964*	*1038*	*969*	*1087*	*830*	*788*	*1992*	*891*	*2821*	*1801*	*2544*

Note: Scales coded so that higher values represent "left wing" or "libertarian" values
EU influence coded on 5-point scale where higher values indicate a pro-EU attitude
Figures in brackets are not statistically significant

We can see that in the mid-1980s people on the left were indeed more opposed to the EU than were those on the right. After that period, this relationship declined – as the party-driven model of attitude formation would predict, given the changing alignment of the main parties. By the early 1990s, the EU and the left–right scale are effectively independent of each other. However, contrary to what the party-driven approach would lead us to expect, this relationship did not reverse in the 1990s as parties consolidated their realignment. There is little evidence that being left-wing now correlates with being pro-EU

The independence of EU attitudes from the left–right dimension allowed the EU question to be a separate and increasing *potential* influence on party preference from the mid-1990s onwards. This is more consistent with the voter-driven approach. If European integration has become important for voters' electoral choices, we would expect to see European issues providing a basis for major party support that cross-cuts and possibly weakens the traditional left–right divisions rather than being subsumed by them.

The more or less constant level of correlation between attitudes towards the EU and libertarian–authoritarianism over the period – being libertarian is associated with being pro-EU both before and after the parties' realignment on Europe – also fits with the voter-driven approach, which argues that voters' attitudes are not going to be changed just because parties have changed. Pro-EU attitudes would appear instead to have some basis in these libertarian values that in turn have their origins in higher education (Evans *et al.*, 1996; see also Evans, 1995, 2000). This would make pro-EU views unlikely to be dictated by parties. [4]

The key thing to take from Tables 8.3 and 8.4 is that after the party realignment of the late 1980s attitudes towards the EU became distinct from left–right issues, which means that the question of European integration cuts across more established bases of voting preferences rather than being integrated into them. To examine whether this change has been associated with an increase in the relevance of the EU for party support, we need to carry out multivariate analysis which allows us to take other factors into account. Attitudes towards the EU are clearly associated with partisanship, but so are the other core issues and it may be these issues that account for party preferences. Attitudes towards the EU might make no significant *extra* contribution to voting to that derived from other traditional 'bread and butter' issues of British politics. For this purpose we include in our analysis the scales shown above concerning the left–right conflicts over the relative 'slice-of-the-cake' received by different sections of society and the libertarian–authoritarian values concerning 'social issues'.

Figure 8.4 The effect of wanting to withdraw from the EU on the likelihood of voting Labour (rather than Conservative) (in log-odds ratios), once left–right and libertarian–authoritarian views are taken into account, 1986–1997

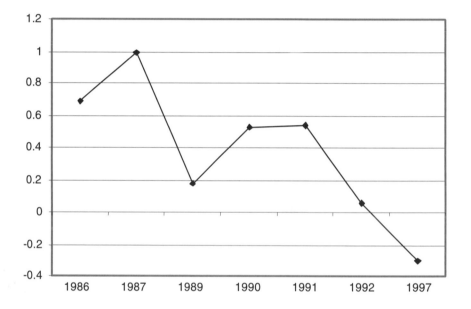

Figure 8.5 The effect of anti-EU views on the likelihood of voting Labour (rather than Conservative) (in log-odds ratios), once left–right and libertarian–authoritarian views are taken into account, 1992–2004

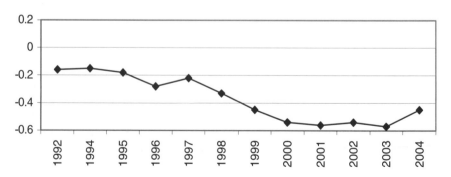

The full analysis is shown in the appendix to this chapter. The results are summarised in Figures 8.4 and 8.5 which show the effect of attitudes to the EU on the increased likelihood of voting Labour rather than Conservative (expressed in terms of log-odds ratios), once the effect of left–right and libertarian–authoritarian attitudes are taken into account.

The full details of the analysis in the appendix to this chapter show that throughout the period voting is predictably influenced by attitudes towards the redistribution of wealth, the so-called left–right division. As would be expected, given the convergence on the centre ground since the mid-1990s (Sanders, 1999; Bara and Budge, 2001), the strength of these effects has become more subdued. More importantly for this chapter, and illustrated in Figures 8.4 and 8.5, attitudes towards the European Union predict voting intention increasingly strongly over and above core aspects of British political values. Importantly, attitudes towards the European Union are also the only attitudes that change the direction of their effect. Until 1987 Euroscepticism was associated with Labour voting. By the early 1990s there was no effect on party choice of having an anti-EU attitude. At that time, only those who said "don't know" to the EU question were clearly more likely to be Labour voters – perhaps because the parties change of position on the EU was not yet fully consolidated in some voters' minds. But by the mid-1990s the reversal was complete and anti-EU views were negatively associated with voting Labour.

Examining change at the individual level

This aggregate pattern of association at least provides the possibility that the EU has an independent effect on political preferences. But cross-sectional data of this kind do not get to the heart of the question of the direction of influence between parties and voters. To examine this we shall look at change at the individual level over the electoral cycle using the *British Election Panel Studies* 1987–1992, 1992–1997 and 1997–2001. The difference here is that we can compare the views *of the same respondent* at the start and end of each panel.

Taking, for example, the period 1987 to 1992, we examine whether the influence of attitudes towards the Labour Party in 1987 had a stronger influence on attitudes towards the EU in 1992 than did attitudes towards the EU in 1987 on attitudes towards the Labour Party in 1992, or whether neither had any effect.[5] We then repeat these analyses for the other waves of the *British Election Panel Study* from 1992–1997 and from 1997–2001. The full analysis is shown in the appendix to this chapter, but Tables 8.5 and 8.6 summarise the key findings. As before, we have to do the analysis in two stages because of the change in question wording. Table 8.5 looks at the development of the effect of responses to the 'withdraw/continue' question over the period 1987–1997 and Table 8.6 uses the five-point EU influence question over the period 1992–2001. The figures to concentrate on are the ones in dotted boxes. These show the effect of party preference at time 1 on EU attitudes at time 2, and of EU attitudes at time 1 on party preference at time 2.

Table 8.5 Attitudes to withdrawal from the EU and to the Labour and Conservative Parties at time 2 by attitudes at time 1, 1987–1992, 1992–1997

	EU 1992	Labour 1992		EU 1992	Con 1992
EU 1987	2.06***	0.07	**EU 1987**	2.07***	-0.11*
Labour 1987	-0.08	0.72***	**Con 1987**	0.09	0.72***
Base: 1485			*Base: 1485*		
	EU 1997	Lab 1997		EU 1997	Con 1997
EU 1992	2.11***	-0.08	**EU 1992**	2.12***	0.08
Lab 1992	-0.22***	0.54***	**Con 1992**	0.26***	0.63***
Base: 1545			*Base: 1545*		

*** = significant at 0.1% level; ** = significant at 1% level; * = significant at 5% level
Source: *British Election Panel Studies*

Table 8.6 Attitudes to influence in the EU and to Labour and Conservative Parties at time 2 by attitudes at time 1, 1992–1997, 1997–2001

	EU 1997	Labour 1997		EU 1997	Con 1997
EU 1992	0.25***	-0.06**	**EU 1992**	0.24***	0.05*
Labour 1992	-0.14***	0.54***	**Con 1992**	0.15***	0.64***
Base: 1485			*Base: 1485*		
	EU 2001	Lab 2001		EU 2001	Con 2001
EU 1997	0.39***	-0.10***	**EU 1997**	0.39***	0.11***
Lab 1997	-0.10***	0.65***	**Con 1997**	0.06***	0.62***
Base: 1545			*Base: 1545*		

*** = significant at 0.1% level; ** = significant at 1% level; * = significant at 5% level

High score on EU variable signifies anti-EU sentiments
Source: *British Election Panel Studies*

From the period 1987–1992 the evidence is of flux. Which party the respondent supported in 1987 had no significant impact on their attitudes to the EU in 1992, which is hardly surprising given the changing nature of party stances on the EU over this period and the potential uncertainty this might have engendered in the minds of voters with respect to what the parties stood for. This could be consistent with both party-driven and voter-driven models as both would predict that without a clear signal from the parties, voters would be confused both about what attitude would be most consistent with the party line and about which party would be the closest to their own positions on the EU.

From 1992 onwards, however, as party positions stabilised, there is evidence of a party impact on EU attitudes – Labour partisans in 1992 are now more pro-EU in 1997, and Conservatives in 1992 are more anti-EU in 1997.

We see a hint of a voter-driven effect in Table 8.5: the weak effect of attitudes to the EU at time 1 on party support at time 2 reverses direction in 1992–1997 compared with 1987–1992. In other words, people who were anti-EU in 1987 were slightly more likely to be Labour and less likely to be Conservative in 1992, but people who were anti-EU in 1992 were less likely to be Labour and more likely to be Conservative in 1997. However, the effect is not strong enough to be statistically significant.

If we look at the more graduated EU influence question in Table 8.6, there is some evidence of EU attitudes influencing party choice in the 1992–1997 period: an anti-EU attitude in 1992 has a negative, and this time significant, effect on attitudes towards the Labour Party in 1997, and a positive effect on attitudes towards the Conservatives. None the less, it is again the party measures that drive change in attitudes towards the EU more strongly than *vice versa*.

Finally, from 1997 onwards we see stronger evidence of influence in both directions. Attitudes towards the EU in 1997 have a significant influence on attitudes towards the Conservative Party in 2001 (wanting less to do with the EU in 1997 being associated with positive feelings towards the Conservatives in 2001). Conversely, attitudes towards the Conservative Party in 1997 are significantly associated with attitudes to the EU in 2001 (being positive towards the Conservative Party in 1997 being associated with being more likely to be anti-EU in 2001). The picture is similar in reverse for Labour. With the consolidated realignment of the parties now in place, together with a relatively pro-EU Labour government and a relatively unified and anti-EU Conservative opposition, we see an interchange between attitudes to the EU and attitudes to the parties: signals from the parties are being read by voters who in turn send their own signals back to the parties.

The general change in direction and strengths of effects over these three rather different periods in the evolution of the EU issue is concisely summarised in Table 8.7 which summarises the party attitudes of voters by subtracting their support for the Conservatives from support for Labour. The table shows the standardised coefficients that allow us to compare the size of the effects on an equivalent metric even though we are looking at two different survey questions.[6] These show the relative size of the effects in each direction for each electoral cycle. Thus the effect of attitude to the EU at the previous election on party support was close to zero in 1992 and 1997. The effect of party at previous election on EU attitudes which had been close to zero in 1992, was, in 1997, -0.31 on the 'withdraw/continue' question and -0.24 on the EU influence question – the negative sign indicating that Labour support in 1992 was associated with being less likely to be anti-EU in 1997. None of these coefficients are particularly large – the EU is after all not the main issue which drives political change for most voters. But it is interesting to observe that over the period examined the relative size of the effect of EU attitudes on party support emerged to rival that of party support on EU attitudes in 2001. Thus, the effect of party in 1997 on EU attitudes in 2001 was -0.10 – only slightly stronger than the effect of -0.07 of EU attitude in 1997 on party choice in 2001.

Table 8.7 Standardized coefficients for Labour *versus* Conservative preference and attitudes to the EU, 1987–1992, 1992–1997, 1997–2001

Withdraw/ continue	EU 1992	Party 1992		EU 1997	Party 1997
EU 1987	0.48	-0.01	EU 1992	0.48	-0.03
Party 1987	-0.02	0.70	Party 1992	-0.31	0.61
EU influence	EU 1997	Party 1997		EU 2001	Party 2001
EU 1992	0.28	-0.04	EU 1997	0.38	-0.07
Party 1992	-0.24	0.60	Party 1997	-0.10	0.58

Source: *British Election Panel Studies*

We can also link the changes observed in individuals' attitudes over these three election cycles with the pattern of correlations through time which we observed earlier in the chapter. Contrary to the expectations of the party-driven approach, the increasing separation of EU attitudes and the main left–right dimension after 1987 signalled the possibility that EU attitudes were not reducible to an aspect of the left–right conflict and therefore had the potential to provide an alternative source of voter-driven influence on party support. It would seem that although the parties continue to influence the attitudes of their supporters, the EU has become a growing, independent influence on party support over the years and remains distinct from the established left–right cleavage in British politics.

Conclusions

European integration became a salient feature of the British political landscape in the 1990s. With the realignment in the positions of the Labour and Conservative Parties on the EU from the late 1980s onwards it also became an issue that had the potential to restructure partisan divisions in the British electorate. And this appears to have been exactly what happened: support for the EU was associated with Conservative voting during the 1980s, but in the 1990s this changed and Labour supporters became clearly more pro-EU than Conservatives. By the 1990s and early 21st century EU attitudes had become independent of the traditional left–right dimension of British electoral politics. The relationship between EU attitudes and party preference increased in magnitude over and above attitudes towards core political issues.

That EU attitudes now influence party support is indicated by our study of how individuals have changed their attitudes across three electoral cycles between

1987 and 2001. Initially, in 1987–1992, EU attitudes were neither influenced by nor influenced attitudes towards the parties. This changed first to a situation where attitudes to the parties strongly influenced attitudes towards the EU – voters were taking their cue on the EU from their parties. Finally, we arrive at a situation where voters' own attitudes towards the EU rival the party influence. We can think of this as a state of reciprocal influence. Increasingly, the influence of attitudes towards the EU on party support has become more substantial (though still not dramatic), reciprocating the influence of party policies on voter attitudes.

All this undermines the traditional view that on questions concerning the EU voters are acquiescent rather than directive with a prominent role being attributed to political parties as an influence on the public's attitudes. If this had been the case, Labour's Policy Review and the Tories' increasing Euroscepticism should have made little difference to the basis of party support – the party faithful would simply have shifted their views to coincide with their party's change of position. As we have seen, however, in recent decades, the signals sent to the party faithful on the merits of European integration have gone through a state of flux. The significance of cues from parties to voters declined as the parties themselves changed the messages sent to their supporters, which in turn has increased the possibility that voters themselves also send 'messages' to parties – through opinion polls and their electoral behaviour. When combined with evidence of greater awareness of the EU and greater relevance to party choice, this indicates clear grounds for believing that the EU has now become an issue where voters can lead and politicians follow. We should not overstate the case, however. Partisanship still influences EU attitudes, but this has been joined by an increasing EU-influence on support for parties. The pattern of reciprocal influences between elite preferences and public opinion is now more balanced.

If this is the case there are likely to be implications for the government's approach to further European integration. In particular, attempts to railroad through constitutional and Euro referendums by shaping and mobilizing pro-EU positions among their supporters are more than likely doomed to failure. These possibilities might once have existed, but with the increasing political salience of EU integration they are now far less likely. Such efforts are as likely to lose the government electoral support as they are to increase its mandate for further integration. As a consequence, Europe could also provide a route through which the hard-pressed Conservatives might win votes from Labour in future elections – as they did, though only in small numbers, in 2001 (Evans, 2001). On the EU, if not much else (apart from immigration, perhaps), the Conservatives are closer to the voters than Labour. Furthermore, a reduction in the relevance of the left–right dimension to vote choice in recent years provides the parties with room for manoeuvre on cross-cutting issues such as the EU.

If this were to be the case, it would in turn carry implications for the social bases of party support. It is generally considered that those Labour voters who are most anti-integration – i.e. their heartland of supporters in the working class – are those for whom left–right issues tend to be more politically important than 'social issues'. But, if there is no longer much perceived difference between the main parties on such economic and redistributive issues, these voters might find the Conservatives' Euroscepticism a distinctive and congenial option.[7]

Notes

1. The first round of the *British Election Panel Studies* was the *British General Election Study* in each of these years. For further details on this survey series, see Thomson (2001).
2. The wording of this question has altered over the years to fit common usage. The question referred to 'the EEC – the Common Market' until 1989; to 'the EC – the Common Market' in 1990; to 'the European Community' in 1991 and 1992; and to 'the European Union' in 1997. This chapter refers to 'the EU' throughout.
3. Rasmussen (1997) shows that even in the late 1980s when the Conservative government was giving voters clear messages – in the form of Mrs Thatcher's personal Euroscepticism – it appears to have had little impact on the electorate's attitudes.
4. This also fits with the argument that support for European integration has its basis, at least in part, in the emergence of what have been called 'postmaterial values' (Inglehart, 1977; Inglehart *et al.*, 1991).
5. The latter option reflecting the well-known tendency for people to find the holding of inconsistent political attitudes troublesome (Converse, 1964).
6. For logistic models, the standardised coefficient $= B*SD/sqrt(pi^2/3)$. See Hilbe (1996).
7. See Evans (2000). Elsewhere we have shown that, at least up to 1997, the emergence of the EU as a cross-cutting cleavage can account for the decline of differences between the professional middle classes and the working class in Labour *versus* Conservative voting (Evans, 1999).

References

Bara, J. and Budge, I. (2001), 'Party policy and ideology: still new Labour?', in Norris, P. (ed.), *Britain Votes 2001*, Oxford: Oxford University Press

Berrington, H. and Hague, R. (1998), 'Europe, Thatcherism and traditionalism: opinion, rebellion and the Maastricht treaty in the backbench Conservative Party, 1992–94.' in Berrington, H., (ed.), *Britain in the Nineties: The Politics of Paradox,* London: Frank Cass

Butler, D. and Stokes, D.E. (1974), *Political Change in Britain: the Evolution of Electoral Choice*, 2nd ed., London: Macmillan

Converse, P. (1964), 'The structure of belief systems in mass publics' in Apter, D. (ed.), *Ideology and Discontent*, New York: Free Press

Evans, G. (1995), 'The state of The Union: attitudes towards Europe', in Jowell, R., Curtice, J., Park, A. and Brook, L. (eds.), *British Social Attitudes: the 12th Report*, Aldershot: Dartmouth

Evans, G. (1998a), 'How Britain views the EU', in Jowell, R., Curtice, J., Park, A., Brook, L., Thomson, K. and Bryson, C., (eds.), *British – and European – Social Attitudes: the 15th Report,* Aldershot: Ashgate

Evans, G. (1998b), 'Euroscepticism and Conservative electoral support: how an asset became a liability', *British Journal of Political Science,* **28**: 573–90

Evans, G. (1999), 'Europe: A New Electoral Cleavage?' in Evans, G. and Norris, P. (eds.) *Critical Elections: British Parties and Voters in Long-term Perspective,* London: Sage

Evans, G. (2000), 'The Working Class and New Labour: A parting of the ways?', in Jowell, R., Curtice, J., Park, A., Thomson, K., Bromley, C., Jarvis, L., and Stratford, N. (eds.), *British Social Attitudes: the 17th Report – Focusing on diversity.* London: Sage

Evans, G. (2001), 'The Conservatives and Europe: waving or drowning?', in Jowell, R., Curtice, J., Park, A., Thomson, K., Bromley, C., Jarvis, L. and Stratford, N. (eds.), *British Social Attitudes: the 18th Report,* London: Sage

Evans, G. (2003), 'Will we ever vote for the Euro?' in Park, A., Curtice, J., Thomson, K., Jarvis, L. and Bromley, C. (eds.), *British Social Attitudes: the 20th Report – Continuity and change over two decades,* London: Sage

Evans, G., Heath, A.F. and Lalljee, M.G. (1996), 'Measuring left–right and libertarian–authoritarian values in the British electorate', *British Journal of Sociology,* **47**: 93–112

Evans, G and Trystan, D. (1999), 'Why was 1997 different? A comparative analysis of voting behaviour in the 1979 and 1997 Welsh referendums', in Taylor, B., and Thomson, K. (eds.), *Scotland and Wales, Nations Again?,* Cardiff: University of Wales Press

Flickinger, R. (1994), 'British political parties and public attitudes towards the European Community: leading, following or getting out of the way?', in Broughton, D., Farrell, D., Denver, D. and Rallings, C., (eds.), *British Elections and Parties Yearbook 1994,* London: Frank Cass

Franklin, M., Marsh M. and McLaren, L. (1994), 'Uncorking the bottle: popular opposition to European unification in the wake of Maastricht', *Journal of Common Market Studies,* **32**: 455–72

Franklin, M. and Wlezien, C. (1997), 'The responsive public: issue salience, policy change, and preferences for European unification' *Journal of Theoretical Politics,* **9**: 347–363

George, S. and Rosamund, B. (1992), 'The European Community', in Smith, M. and Spear, J. (eds.), *The Changing Labour Party,* London: Routledge

Heath, A., Evans, G., and Martin, J. (1994), 'The Measurement of Core beliefs and Values: The Development of Balanced Socialist/Laissez Faire and Libertarian/Authoritarian Scales', *British Journal of Political Science,* **24**: 115–132

Hilbe, J. (1996), 'Logistic Regression: Standardised Coefficients and Partial Correlation', Stata Technical Bulletin 35

Inglehart, R. (1977), *The Silent Revolution: Changing Values and Political Styles Among Western Publics,* Princeton, NJ: Princeton University Press

Inglehart, R., Rabier, J. and Reif, K. (1991), 'The Evolution of Public Attitudes Towards European Integration: 1970–86', in Reif, K. and Inglehart, R. (eds.), *Eurobarometer: The dynamics of European Public Opinion,* London: Macmillan

Janssen, J. (1991), 'Postmaterialism, Cognitive Mobilization and Public Support for European Integration' *British Journal of Political Science*, **21**: 443–468

Lindberg, L. and Scheingold, S. (1970), *Europe's Would-be Polity: Patterns of Change in the European Community*, Englewood Cliffs, NJ: Prentice-Hall

Marks, G. and Steenbergen, M. (eds.) (2004), *European Integration and Political Conflict: Citizens, Parties, Groups,* Cambridge: Cambridge University Press

McAllister, I. and Studlar, D.T. (2000), 'Conservative Euroscepticism and the Referendum Party in the 1997 British General Election' *Party Politics*, **6**: 359–72

Niedermayer, O. (1995), 'Trends and contrasts', in Niedermayer, O. and Sinnott, R. (eds.), *Public Opinion and Internationalized Governance*, Oxford: Oxford University Press

Rasmussen, J. (1997), 'What kind of vision is that? British public attitudes towards the European Community during the Thatcher era', *British Journal of Political Science*, **27**: 111–118

Sanders, D. (1999), 'The impact of left–right ideology', in Evans, G. and Norris, P. (eds.), *Critical Elections: British Parties and Voters in Long-term Perspective,* London: Sage

Sowemimo, M. (1996), 'The Conservative Party and European integration 1989–95', *Party Politics*, **2**: 77–97

Thomson, K. (2001), 'Appendix. The British Election Survey 1979–1997', in Heath, A.F., Jowell, R. and Curtice, J. *The Rise of New Labour: party policies and voter choices*, Oxford: Oxford University Press

Van der Eijk, C. and Franklin, M. N. (eds.) (1996), *Choosing Europe? The European Electorate and National Politics in the Face of Union*, Ann Arbor, Mich.: The University of Michigan Press

Appendix

Model 1: Attitudes towards EU by left–right and libertarian–authoritarian values

This analysis was conducted using logistic regression. The coefficients are the log-odds of voting for the Labour Party rather than the Conservative Party.

Effect of attitudes towards EU withdraw/continue on Labour *versus* Conservative Party preference 1986–1997

	1986	1987	1989	1990	1991	1992	1997
Left–right scale	2.08 (0.16)	2.13 (0.19)	2.08 (0.10)	1.85 (0.10)	1.74 (0.16)	2.97 (0.13)	2.46 (0.24)
Lib–auth scale	1.20 (0.15)	1.39 (0.21)	1.16 (0.11)	1.12 (0.11)	1.12 (0.18)	0.64 (0.11)	0.62 (0.21)
EU Withdraw	0.69 (0.20)	0.99 (0.23)	0.18^{ns} (0.15)	0.53 (0.16)	0.54 (0.23)	0.06^{ns} (0.14)	-0.30^{ns} (0.23)
Don't know	0.75^{ns} (0.41)	1.49 (0.51)	0.18^{ns} (0.29)	0.19^{ns} (0.39)	0.30^{ns} (0.50)	0.50 (0.24)	0.34^{ns} (0.29)
Model chi^2	449.7	445.4	869.9	781.0	337.7	1309.4	261.0
Base	916	838	1894	1779	863	2603	752

Effect of attitudes towards EU influence and Labour *versus* Conservative Party preference 1992–2004

	1992	1994	1995	1996	1997	1998
Left–right scale	2.97 (0.13)	1.99 (0.20)	1.53 (0.17)	2.66 (0.26)	2.46 (0.24)	1.11 (0.16)
Lib–auth scale	0.56 (0.11)	1.11 (0.19)	1.18 (0.20)	0.43 (0.21)	0.62 (0.21)	0.52 (0.17)
EU	-0.16 (0.05)	-0.15^{ns} (0.10)	-0.18^{ns} (0.10)	-0.28 (0.10)	-0.22 (0.10)	-0.33 (0.10)
Model chi^2	1320.5	258.9	234.4	283.1	236.4	100.8
Base	2617	649	718	703	753	598

	1999	2000	2001	2002	2003	2004
Left–right scale	1.50 (0.16)	1.08 (0.10)	1.12 (0.14)	1.13 (0.09)	0.96 (0.12)	1.12 (0.09)
Lib–auth scale	0.70 (0.19)	0.77 (0.14)	0.47 (0.17)	0.63 (0.11)	0.61 (0.14)	0.66 (0.12)
EU	-0.45 (0.14)	-0.54 (0.08)	-0.56 (0.11)	-0.54 (0.07)	-0.57 (0.08)	-0.45 (0.07)
Model chi^2	146.1	319.8	129.4	420.6	217.8	305.1
Base	513	1357	606	1767	1102	1413

Note: All coefficients significant at $p<0.05$ unless indicated (ns). The left–right scale is coded so that higher values indicate left–wing attitudes. The libertarian–authoritarian scale is coded so that higher values indicate libertarian values. EU influence is coded on a five-point scale: create single European state/increase power/stay same/reduce power/leave EU. Higher values indicate anti EU stance.

Cross-lagged panel analysis from the *British Election Panel Studies*

These are standard regression models. Party support is measured on a graduated five-point measure of attitude towards the two main parties rather than reported vote, as it is a more sensitive indicator of party evaluation and allows more variability over time to be observed. When analysing individual attitude change it is usually preferable to control for 'correlated measurement error' between attitudes expressed by the same individuals at different points in time. However, this error is more of a problem for interpreting the stability of attitudes than for examining their cross-lagged effects, so here we are able to keep the analysis relatively simple.

We conducted a range of models with different controls, such as left–right and libertarian–authoritarian values, as well as socio-demographic controls such as age and class. Findings were substantively the same for all of these model specifications, so we only report the most simple findings here.

Attitudes to EU (withdraw (1) *versus* continue (0))

1987–1992	Labour		Conservative	
	EU '92	Party '92	EU '92	Party '92
EU '87	2.06***	0.07	2.07***	-0.11*
	(0.05)	(0.16)	(0.05)	(0.16)
Party '87	-0.08	0.72***	0.09	0.72***
	(0.05)	(0.02)	(0.06)	(0.02)
R^2	0.14	0.55	0.15	0.57

Base: 1485

1992–1997	Labour		Conservative	
	EU '97	Party '97	EU '97	Party '97
EU '92	2.11***	-0.08	2.12***	0.08
	(0.06)	(0.15)	(0.06)	(0.15)
Party '92	-0.22***	0.54***	0.26***	0.63***
	(0.05)	(0.01)	(0.06)	(0.02)
R^2	0.14	0.46	0.15	0.48

Base: 1545

*** $p>0.001$ ** $p>0.01$ * $p>0.05$

Attitudes to EU influence (1= increase power/superstate, 4=withdraw)

1992–1997	Labour		Conservative	
	EU '97	Party '97	EU '97	Party '97
EU '92	0.25***	-0.06**	0.24***	0.05*
	(0.02)	(0.02)	(0.02)	(0.03)
Party '92	-0.14***	0.54***	0.15***	0.64***
	(0.02)	(0.02)	(0.02)	(0.02)
R^2	0.15	0.47	0.15	0.48

Base: 1549

1997–2001	Labour		Conservative	
	EU '01	Party '01	EU '01	Party '01
EU '97	0.39***	-0.10***	0.39***	0.11***
	(0.02)	(0.02)	(0.02)	(0.02)
Party '97	-0.10***	0.65***	0.06***	0.62***
	(0.02)	(0.02)	(0.02)	(0.02)
R^2	0.21	0.40	0.20	0.44

Base: 2315

9 Are trade unionists left-wing any more?

John Curtice and Ann Mair [*]

Members of trade unions have long been thought to be distinctive in their social attitudes and political behaviour. In much survey research conducted in the two or three decades after the end of the Second World War, trade unionists were regularly reported as being more left-wing in their attitudes than the rest of the population and more likely to support the Labour Party, an institution which after all had been founded by trade unionists (see, for example, Butler and Stokes, 1969; Franklin and Mughan, 1978; Heath and McDonald, 1987; Heath *et al.*, 1991; Rose, 1974; Särlvik and Crewe, 1983; Whiteley, 1983; though for a dissenting view see Dunleavy and Husbands, 1985). Moreover, this remained true even after other aspects of their background were taken into account, not least that they were more likely to be employed in working-class occupations. Doubtless, this was in part because those who favoured a more left-wing position were more inclined to join a trade union. However, prior to reforms introduced by the Conservative government in the 1980s, union membership was not necessarily voluntary but rather was sometimes a requirement of the job. Hence it seemed unlikely that selective recruitment was the whole explanation for the distinctive views of unionists. More probably, at least part of the explanation was that union membership exposed people to more left-wing arguments and thus socialised them into more left-wing views (Parkin, 1967).

However, the incidence and character of trade union membership is now very different from what it was when this picture was first painted (Fernie and Metcalf, 2005). Even in 1983, by which time the impact of the Conservative government's policy towards trade unions was beginning to be felt, the first *British Social Attitudes* survey found that trade unions could still count more than one in four (28 per cent) of all adults amongst their number. Now, they

[*] John Curtice is Research Consultant at the *Scottish Centre for Social Research*, part of NatCen, Deputy Director of CREST, and Professor of Politics at Strathclyde University. Ann Mair is a Computing Officer in the Social Statistics Laboratory at Strathclyde University.

represent and organise less than one in five (18 per cent). In 1983, for every two women who were members of a trade union there were at least three men; now women are just as likely to belong to a trade union as men. Meanwhile, whereas in 1983 nearly half of trade unionists were or had been in a 'working-class' occupation, now little more than a quarter are.

Such changes would appear to have the potential to result in important changes in the distinctiveness of the attitudes of trade unionists. However, two different scenarios are possible. On the one hand, the decline in the proportion of the population that belongs to a trade union, together with the fact that all trade union membership nowadays is voluntary, could mean that trade unionists are now even more distinctive in their attitudes than they once were. Perhaps it is the case that those who join trade unions today are those who are already committed to the labour movement and who already hold left-wing attitudes. On the other hand, the changed character of trade union members, and in particular the fact that they are both absolutely and relatively less likely to be employed in a working-class occupation, could have had the very opposite effect. If trade unions are no longer distinctively working-class institutions, then there seems little reason why they should foster the more left-wing views that are typically associated with membership of that class. And if trade unions are now predominantly middle-class institutions then perhaps interaction with fellow members and even trade union leaders, may no longer be particularly likely to result in exposure to and socialisation in more left-wing views.

This chapter considers which of these two possibilities is correct. We examine whether the social and political attitudes of trade unionists have become more or less different from those of non-members since the *British Social Attitudes* survey was first conducted in 1983. While their membership may be diminished in size, perhaps trade unions actually represent a more coherent and distinctive section of British society than they once did. Or is it instead the case that trade unions have lost not only members but also the distinctively left-wing culture that they once had?

The changing character of trade unionists

Just how much the social character of those who belong to a trade union has changed is illustrated in Table 9.1. This shows, for selected years between 1983 and 2004, the proportion of trade unionists who are male, working class and in full-time employment. In 1983, almost two-thirds of trade unionists were men. In contrast, women comprised a majority of members for the first time in the 2004 survey. Meanwhile the proportion of trade unionists whose current or last occupation was a working-class one (as defined by the Goldthorpe class schema about which further details can be found in the appendix to this book), has fallen from just under half in 1986 to just over a quarter.[1] Trade unionists are now also less likely to be currently engaged in full-time employment, partly because rather more of them are, in fact, retired from work.

Table 9.1 The changing characteristics of trade unionists, 1983–2004

	% who are male	% who are working class	% in full time employment	Bases
1983	64	n.a.	76	474/n.a.
1986	64	46	76	749/732
1990	58	41	68	589/586
1995	56	37	63	651/650
2000	55	29	61	598/598
2004	47	27	67	546/436

n.a. = not available
The first figure under bases is the base for per cent male and per cent in full-time employment; the second that for per cent working class.

In part these changes in the character of trade unionists are a reflection of changes in Britain's population as a whole. For example, rather more people nowadays are retired or only work part-time. Similarly, the proportion of the population employed in working-class occupations has declined. But the changes that have occurred in the characteristics of trade unionists since 1983 have outpaced the changes that have occurred in society as a whole over the same period. For example, as more women are engaged nowadays in full-time employment, the proportion of full-time employees who are men has fallen from 67 per cent in 1983 to 59 per cent now. However, this means that whereas in 1983 the predominance of men amongst the membership of trade unions was more or less a faithful reflection of their predominance amongst the nation's full-time workforce as a whole, the proportion of trade unionists who are men is now notably lower than the equivalent proportion amongst full-time employees.

Perhaps even more remarkable is that the decline in the proportion of trade unionists who are (or had been) in working-class occupations has so outstripped the decline in the size of the working class amongst the population in general that trade unions are no longer distinctively working-class institutions. In 1986 when 46 per cent of trade unionists were working class, only 37 per cent of the adult population as a whole fell into that category. Those who were (or had been) in working-class occupations were clearly more likely to belong to a trade union. Now, the proportion of trade unionists who are working class (27 per cent) is much the same as the size of the working class in the population as a whole (28 per cent).[2] A trade union member is now no longer more likely to be working class than is any other member of the adult population.[3]

Not all of the distinctive characteristics of trade unionists have disappeared. In particular, they continue to be far more likely to be employed in the public sector. Just over half (55 per cent) were in public sector occupations in 1984 and this remains true now (56 per cent). In contrast only around 30 per cent of the adult population as a whole are (or were) engaged in the public sector. Nevertheless, the feminisation of the trade union movement, together with the loss of its distinctively working-class character, means that not only has its absolute character changed, but so also has its character relative to that of society as a whole.

The loss of the movement's working-class character, in particular, raises doubts about the degree to which trade unions are still institutions that foster left-wing views. If it were the relative preponderance of working-class members that gave them their distinctively left-wing culture, then we may begin to doubt whether this culture still exists today. On the other hand, perhaps trade unions have simply been particularly successful in recruiting that section of the middle class that is more likely to be left wing – in particular, those employed in the public sector. To establish which of these possibilities is the more plausible account, we need to examine whether, over time, the attitudes of trade unionists have become more or less similar to those of the rest of the population.

In so doing, however, we should distinguish between two different ways in which the attitudes of trade unionists may have become less distinctive. The first possibility is that any change in the distinctiveness of their attitudes is simply the result of changes in the distinctiveness of their social character. For example, trade unionists may be less distinctively left-wing than they once were, but this might be wholly accounted for by the fact that they are no longer particularly working class. Once we take this into account, the degree to which someone is more likely to uphold a left-wing viewpoint may be much the same as ever. In that event we might wish to argue that, despite their changed social character, trade unions continue to be institutions that foster left-wing viewpoints amongst their members.[4] On the other hand, if we are able to demonstrate that the attitudes of trade unionists have become less distinctive even after we have taken into account the changes that have occurred in their (relative) social character, then we might conclude that in fact trade unions are no longer as effective as they once were in socialising their members.[5]

Trends in left–right attitudes

In order to investigate whether or not the attitudes of trade union members have become more or less distinctive over time, we need access to responses to questions that have been asked on a regular basis since 1983. Fortunately, a number of such key time-series exist about issues that form the heart of what it is to hold a left-wing or right-wing opinion in Britain. One of these series comprises five items that constitute a left–right scale and which have been administered on every *British Social Attitudes* survey, bar one, since 1986 (see the appendix to this book for further details).[6] In Table 9.2 we summarise the long-term trends in the responses that both trade unionists and non-unionists have given to these questions over the years.

In order to simplify matters, in the table we have pooled the surveys into three groups:

- those surveys conducted up to and including 1990, the year that Mrs Thatcher resigned as Prime Minister:

- those conducted during the years that her successor as Prime Minister, John Major, was in charge of the country; and
- those surveys conducted from 1997 onwards, that is, the era of Tony Blair's New Labour administration.

As well as showing the percentage of trade union members and non-members that agreed (or, in one case, strongly agreed) with each of the statements that comprise the scale, we also show on the right-hand side of the table the 'gap' between the two groups. As each of the statements is worded in a left-wing direction, a positive figure for this 'gap' means that trade unionists are more left-wing than non-members. It is the trend in this difference between the views of trade union members and non-members in which we are primarily interested.

Table 9.2 Trends in attitudes of trade unionists and non-unionists to items on the left–right scale, 1986–2004[7]

% who agree:	Trade unionists	Non-unionists	Gap
Government should redistribute income from the better off to the less well off			
1986–1990	54	46	8
1991–1996	54	46	8
1998–2004	42	37	5
Big business benefits owners at the expense of workers			
1986–1990	63	49	14
1991–1996	66	56	10
1998–2004	62	52	10
Ordinary working people do not get their fair share of the nation's wealth			
1986–1990	74	62	12
1991–1996	73	64	9
1998–2004	67	59	8
Management will always try to get the better of employees if it gets the chance			
1985–1990	67	55	12
1991–1996	71	60	11
1998–2004	64	56	8
% who agree strongly that there is one law for the rich and one for the poor			
1986–1990	32	26	6
1991–1996	30	24	6
1997–2004	22	19	3

Each of these five items tells a similar story. Those who belong to a trade union are more likely than the rest of the population to support a left-wing position. The gap is not large, but it is consistent across all the questions. However, in each case this gap has been somewhat narrower in the period since 1997, and especially as compared with the position in the 1980s. This narrowing of the gap has occurred despite the fact that, for the most part, non-unionists have become less likely to uphold a left-wing viewpoint. Opinion amongst trade unionists has simply switched to the right even more rapidly than it has amongst non-unionists.[8] It appears, then, that trade unionists have in recent years become both absolutely and relatively more right-wing, clearly raising questions about the degree to which they continue to foster more left-wing views amongst their members.

However, while it is statistically significant, the decline in the size of the various gaps between members and non-members is for the most part relatively small.[9] Perhaps it simply reflects the change in the social character of trade union members and, in particular, the fact that they are no longer particularly working class. One reasonably straightforward way in which we can take account of this possibility is to look separately at the trends in the gap amongst those in the working class and those in professional and managerial occupations, the 'salariat'. In Table 9.3 we show, by way of example, what this analysis produces for one of the items in the previous table that might be thought to be of particular concern to trade unionists, that is, whether "management will always try to get the better of employees if it gets the chance".

Table 9.3 Trends in attitudes towards management of trade unionists and non-unionists, by class, 1985–2004[10]

% who agree	Trade unionists	Non-unionists	Gap
Management will always try to get the better of employees if it gets the chance			
Salariat			
1985–1990	52	40	12
1991–1996	58	47	11
1998–2004	53	44	9
Working Class			
1985–1990	81	71	10
1991–1996	84	73	11
1998–2004	79	71	8

One important point clearly emerges from this example. The relatively left-wing views of trade unionists are not simply a reflection of their class position. Even within each class, those who belong to a trade union have always been more likely to support a left-wing viewpoint. This is what we would expect to find if it is indeed the case that trade unions help foster left-wing views amongst their members. At the same time, however, we can see that the gap has narrowed somewhat within each class. It would seem that the decline in the relative propensity of trade union members to adopt a left-wing view is not simply a result of trade unions no longer being distinctively working-class institutions.

We do, however, need to exercise some caution before coming to this conclusion. As we saw in Table 9.2, across the population as a whole, the gap between trade unionists and others in their attitudes towards management was four points lower from 1997 onwards than it had been between 1985 and 1990. In Table 9.3 the decline is just two to three points. Moreover, we can see that working-class trade unionists have always been more likely to take a left-wing position on this subject than trade unionists in the salariat. Thus the loss of trade unions' distinctively working-class character could be part of the reason why trade unionists' views overall have become less distinctive. More importantly, if we analyse the data for all of the items on Table 9.2 using statistical modelling which allows us to take into account not just whether someone is a trade union member or not but also their class position and their gender, we find that the decline in the gap between trade unionists and others is not statistically significant – that is, we cannot safely reject the possibility that it is simply the product of chance.[11] In short, the decline in the gap between trade union members and non-members may be no more than a reflection of the change in the social character of trade unionists.

So far, then, we have established that trade unionists have become less distinctively left-wing in their views. It is possible, however, that this may simply be the result of the fact that trade union members are no longer distinctively working class, rather than because trade unions are less successful in fostering and maintaining left-wing views amongst their members. There are, however, other time-series in the *British Social Attitudes* data that we can analyse. We turn next to items that tap attitudes towards various aspects of the welfare state.

Trends in attitudes towards the welfare state

In Table 9.4 we show, in much the same way as we did in Table 9.2, the responses given by trade unionists and non-unionists, together with the gap between them, to four questions that tap attitudes towards a wide range of aspects of the welfare state. The first two questions are about benefits. The first asks respondents whether they think benefits for unemployed people are "too high and discourage them from findings jobs", or whether they are "too low and cause hardship"; we show the proportion agreeing with the latter statement. This question is of particular interest because we have demonstrated in previous research that it discriminates well between Labour and Conservative supporters (Curtice, 1986; Curtice and Fisher, 2003). The second question asks respondents whether they agree or disagree that

> *Large numbers of people who are eligible for benefits these days fail to claim them*

and we show the proportion who give a response other than that they "strongly disagree".

Table 9.4 Trends in attitudes of trade unionists and non-unionists towards the welfare state, 1983–2004[12]

% who agree	Trade unionists	Non-unionists	Gap
Benefits for the unemployed are too low and cause hardship			
1983–1990	57	46	11
1991–1996	59	50	9
1997–2004	36	32	4
% who do <u>not</u> disagree strongly			
Large number of people who are eligible for benefits these days fail to claim them			
1983–1990	55	48	7
1994, 1998–2004	54	55	-1
% who agree			
It is the responsibility of government to reduce the differences in income between people with high incomes and those with low incomes			
1985–1990	65	54	11
1993, 1996	64	50	14
1999, 2000, 2004	56	51	5
% who say			
Increase taxes and spend more on health, education and social benefits			
1983–1990	54	46	8
1991–1996	69	59	10
1997–2004	63	56	7

On the two items in Table 9.4 we can see that the gap between trade unionists and the remainder of the population has narrowed considerably. Trade unionists are now only a little more likely to say that benefits for unemployed people are too low, whereas in the late 1980s they were as much as 12 percentage points more likely to do so. As in the case of the items shown in Table 9.2, this narrowing has occurred despite the fact that there has been a sharp drop in the proportion of non-unionists who think that benefits for unemployed people are too low. Meanwhile trade unionists are no longer more likely, as they once were, to feel that many people fail to claim the benefits to which they are entitled. Moreover, in both cases the decline in the gap is much sharper than it was in any of the instances in Table 9.2.

Indeed, further analysis reveals that the relationship between union membership and attitudes towards these two questions has been weaker in recent years than it was previously, even when we take into account the change in the class composition of trade union membership, together with the growing proportion who are women.[13] This is illustrated in Table 9.5, which shows separately for members of the salariat and for the working class the attitudes of trade unionists and non-unionists towards benefits for unemployed people. Within the salariat, the gap between trade unionists and non-unionists has more than halved in recent years. Indeed, given that trade unionists in the salariat have always been just as likely as those in the working class to believe that benefits for the unemployed are too low, there is in fact little reason why the decline in the proportion of trade unionists who are working class should have resulted in trade unionists' views on this subject becoming less distinctive.

Table 9.5 Trends in attitudes towards unemployment benefit of trade unionists and non-unionists, by class, 1983–2004[14]

% who agree	Trade unionists	Non-unionists	Gap
Benefits for the unemployed are too low and cause hardship			
Salariat			
1983–1990	57	41	16
1991–1996	62	46	16
1997–2004	37	30	7
Working Class			
1983–1990	59	54	5
1991–1996	60	57	3
1997–2004	38	35	3

Much the same can be said about the third item in Table 9.4 which looks at people's attitudes towards what might be considered one of the policy objectives of the welfare state, that is, to reduce the differences in incomes between the rich and the poor. The degree to which trade unionists are more likely to support such a policy has been rather less marked since 1997 than previously. On this occasion, however, further analysis indicates that, once we have taken into account both respondents' class and gender, this decline is not quite statistically significant. Nevertheless, taken together, these three items provide considerable evidence that the decline in the distinctiveness of the attitudes of trade unionists cannot simply be accounted for by changes in the social composition of trade unions. Whatever ability trade unions might have previously had to foster and maintain support for more left-wing positions does appear, on some issues at least, to have declined.

At the same time, however, we should also acknowledge that on some subjects the views of trade unionists continue to be just as different from the rest of the population as they ever were. One such example is the final item in Table 9.4, which shows the proportion of people who favour an increase in welfare state spending even if it means an increase in taxes (as opposed to either keeping the two as they are now or even cutting both taxes and spending). In the late 1980s, trade unionists were eight percentage points more likely than non-unionists to favour more state spending; they remain seven points more likely to do so now. It should perhaps be noted that, in contrast to the previous items in Table 9.4, the answer to this question might be thought to have implications for the level of public sector employment. Perhaps the fact that trade unionists continue to be disproportionately employed in the public sector may have helped to ensure that their views on this subject remain distinctive.

Trade unionists and the Labour Party

Trade unions have historically had a close relationship with the Labour Party. The Labour Party was founded in 1900 by the trade union movement in order to promote working-class representation in parliament, trade unions are represented directly in the key formal decision-making mechanisms of the party outside parliament, and trade unions have long given financial and other support to the party. While some trade unions are not formally affiliated with the Labour Party, most trade unions indicate in various ways to their members their belief that they would prefer to see the election of a Labour rather than a Conservative government.

But does this preference continue to be reflected amongst trade union members themselves? In Table 9.6 we show the proportion of trade unionists and non-unionists who in each of our three time periods indicated that they identified with the Labour Party. Trade unionists are markedly more likely to identify with Labour than are other respondents. Indeed they are more distinctive in this respect than they are in terms of any of the attitudes shown in Tables 9.2 or 9.4. Nevertheless, we can see that the gap has been somewhat narrower since 1997.

Table 9.6 Trends amongst trade unionists and non-unionists in identification with the Labour Party, 1983–2004[15]

% who identify with Labour	Trade unionists	Non-unionists	Gap
1983–1990	47	30	17
1991–1996	54	37	17
1997–2004	51	38	13

Even so, the decline of four percentage points in the gap does not appear to be a large one. Given that working-class voters are more likely to support Labour perhaps it could reflect no more than the change in the social composition of trade unionists. Further statistical analysis, details of which are given in the appendix to this chapter, indicates, however, that this is not the case. Indeed, as we can see in Table 9.7, there has been a clear decline in the gap between trade unionists and non-unionists both within the salariat and within the working class. Trade unionists are now distinctively less pro-Labour, and thus are apparently less likely to help foster and maintain Labour loyalties than they once were.

Table 9.7 Trends amongst trade unionists and non-unionists in identification with Labour, by class, 1983–2004[16]

% who identify with Labour	Trade Unionists	Non-unionists	Gap
Salariat			
1983–1990	37	17	20
1991–1996	48	26	22
1997–2004	48	32	16
Working Class			
1983–1990	57	43	14
1991–1996	63	52	11
1997–2004	55	46	9

However, in interpreting these results we should bear in mind that not only have trade unions changed but so also has the Labour Party. Under the leadership of Tony Blair the party has sought to widen its appeal beyond its traditional sources of support – such as trade unionists – not least by refusing to repeal much of the industrial relations legislation introduced by the last Conservative government. The decline in the gap between trade unionists and others may then be not simply an indication of a declining ability of trade unions to foster support for Labour but also a reflection of the relative success of the Labour Party in broadening the basis of its electoral appeal in recent years (Heath *et al.*, 2001). But, in so far as that success has been founded on distancing Labour from the trade union movement, it may also have simply compounded whatever increased difficulty that trade unions are already facing in promoting pro-Labour sympathies amongst their members.

Conclusions

Trade union members have historically been distinctive in social character and political outlook. Socially, they were predominantly male and disproportionately both working class and concentrated in the public sector. Politically, they were rather more left-wing than their fellow citizens and more inclined to support the Labour Party. Now, however, much of that distinctiveness has been eroded. While trade unionists are still concentrated in the public sector, they are no longer either disproportionately male or working class. Meanwhile, many of their political views are now less distinctively left-wing, and while they are still more inclined to identify with Labour than is the rest of the population, even that gap has narrowed somewhat.

In part the decline in the political distinctiveness of trade unionists may simply be a reflection of their changed social character – in particular, the loss of their working-class profile. But, in some instances at least, including sympathy for the Labour Party, the decline appears to have been greater than can be accounted for by that change. It may be that this is because of a change in the kind of person who becomes a trade unionist in the first place; despite the fact that the last Conservative government outlawed the practice of making trade union membership a condition of employment, holding left-wing views may no longer influence whether or not someone joins a trade union to the degree that it once did. But if this is the case it may be a sign that trade unions are now less likely to be regarded by their potential members as organisations that promote a left-wing agenda. At the same time, however, it may well be true that, as the social and political character of their membership has changed, so trade unions have actually lost some of their ability to promote and foster left-wing views and pro-Labour sympathies amongst their members. Either way, the continued role of trade unions as part of the 'left' in Britain appears to be in some doubt.

Notes

1. From 2001 onwards, respondent's Goldthorpe class has been derived by matching the 2000 Standard Occupational Code and employment status to the nearest 1990

equivalent. However, in 14 per cent of cases this process results in an impermissible combination of 1990 Standard Occupational Code and employment status, making it impossible to derive respondent's Goldthorpe class. These cases, together with the much smaller proportion of respondents who have never had a job are excluded from Table 9.1. Together these two features of the post-2000 Goldthorpe class data mean that some caution should be exercised in interpreting them.

2. Indeed, if we use the National Statistics Socio-Economic Classification to measure social class (see the appendix to this report for further details) the proportion of trade unionists in semi-routine or routine occupations (23 per cent) is actually lower than the proportion in the population as a whole (29 per cent).

3. We might also note that the age profile of trade union members has become markedly older. Whereas in 1983, 30 per cent of trade unionists were aged under 35, now only 20 per cent are. Over the same period the proportion of those in work or unemployed who were aged less than 35 fell from only 37 per cent to 33 per cent.

4. Though, of course, it might simply be the case that the relative chances of someone who already has a relatively left-wing viewpoint joining a trade union has not changed.

5. Though equally it may be the case that nowadays those joining trade unions are more heterogeneous in their views at the time of joining.

6. One of the items, 'management will always try to get the better of employees if it gets the chance' was first asked in 1985. Note that the *British Social Attitudes* survey was not conducted in 1988 or 1992.

7. The bases for Table 9.2 are as follows:

	Trade unionists	Non-unionists
1986–1990	*2065*	*6771*
1991–1996	*2631*	*10415*
1998–2004	*3605*	*15829*
Except:		
Ordinary working people do not get their fair share of the nation's wealth (1991–1996)	*2002*	*8119*
Management will always try to get the better of employees if it gets the chance (1985–1990)	*2438*	*7925*
There is one law for the rich and one for the poor (1997–2004)	*3807*	*16677*

8. For an analysis of the drift of public opinion in general to the right see Curtice and Fisher (2003).

9. We fitted a series of logistic regressions to the pooled data in Table 9.2 in which we included terms for whether a person was a union member, the year of the study (in order to control for year-to-year variation in the overall level of support for each item) and an interaction term that distinguished union members from 1997 onwards. In each case the interaction term was statistically significant and indicated that trade union members were less distinctive in their attitudes from 1997 onwards. Our

ability to detect this interaction effect is of course much enhanced by the large sample size made available to us by pooling the data across surveys.

10. The bases for Table 9.3 are as follows:

	Trade unionists	Non-unionists
Salariat		
1985–1990	*581*	*1593*
1991–1996	*944*	*2818*
1998–2004	*1153*	*3924*
Working class		
1985–1990	*867*	*2117*
1991–1996	*964*	*2996*
1998–2004	*880*	*3813*

11. We extended the analysis described in note 9 by including terms for a person's class and their gender, thereby modelling the data in the same way as identification with the Labour Party is modelled in the appendix to this chapter. While in each case the interaction effect was still correctly signed, it was no longer significant at the five per cent level.

12. The bases for Table 9.4 are as follows:

	Trade unionists	Non-unionists
Benefits for the unemployed are too low and cause hardship		
1983–1990	*4044*	*12843*
1991–1996	*2758*	*11262*
1997–2004	*4224*	*19362*
Large number of people who are eligible for benefits these days fail to claim them		
1983–1990	*4044*	*12843*
1994, 1998–2004	*4714*	*21021*
It is the responsibility of government to reduce the differences in income between people with high incomes and those with low incomes		
1985–1990	*1241*	*4011*
1993, 1996	*642*	*2587*
1999, 2000, 2004	*597*	*2841*
Increase taxes and spend more on health, education and social benefits		
1983–1990	*4044*	*12843*
1991–1996	*3186*	*13230*
1997–2004	*3820*	*17635*

13. In contrast to the position in note 11, the interaction effect in our models remained significant even after we included both a person's class and their gender.
14. The bases for Table 9.5 are as follows:

	Trade unionists	Non-unionists
Salariat		
1983–1990	737	2023
1991–1996	966	2877
1997–2004	1330	4685
Working class		
1983–1990	1177	2893
1991–1996	1036	3369
1997–2004	1085	4940

15. The bases for Table 9.6 are as follows:

	Trade unionists	Non-unionists
1983–1990	4044	12843
1991–1996	3186	13230
1997–2004	4436	20267

16. The bases for Table 9.7 are as follows:

	Trade unionists	Non-unionists
Salariat		
1983–1990	737	2023
1991–1996	1109	3425
1997–2004	1395	4923
Working class		
1983–1990	1177	2893
1991–1996	1184	3893
1997–2004	1132	5181

References

Butler, D. and Stokes, D. (1969), *Political Change in Britain*, 1st ed, London: Macmillan

Curtice, J. (1986), 'Political partisanship', in Jowell, R., Witherspoon, S. and Brook, L. (eds.), *British Social Attitudes: the 1986 Report*, Aldershot: Gower

Curtice, J. and Fisher, S. (2003), 'The power to persuade: a tale of two Prime Ministers', in Park, A., Curtice, J., Thomson, K., Jarvis, L. and Bromley, C. (eds.), *British Social Attitudes: the 20th report – Continuity and change over two decades*, London: Sage

Dunleavy, P. and Husbands, C. (1985), *British Democracy at the Crossroads: Voting and party competition in the 1980s*, London: George Allen and Unwin

Fernie, S. and Metcalf, D. (2005), *Trade Unions*, London: Routledge

Franklin, M. and Mughan, A. (1978), 'The decline of class voting in Britain: problems of analysis and interpretation', *American Political Science Review*, **72**: 523–534

Heath, A., Jowell, R. and Curtice, J. (2001), *The Rise of New Labour*, Oxford: Oxford University Press

Heath, A., Jowell, R., Curtice, J., Evans, G., Field, J. and Witherspoon, S. (1991), *Understanding Political Change: The British Voter 1964–87*, Oxford: Pergamon

Heath, A. and McDonald, S.K. (1987), 'Social change and the future of the left', *Political Quarterly,* **58**: 364–377

Parkin, F. (1967), 'Working class Conservatives: a theory of political deviance', *British Journal of Sociology*, **18**: 278–290

Rose, R. (1974), 'Britain: simple abstractions and complex realities', in Rose, R. (ed.), *Electoral Behavior; A Comparative Handbook*, New York: Free Press

Särlvik, B. and Crewe, I. (1983), *Decade of Dealignment*, Cambridge: Cambridge University Press

Whiteley, P. (1983), *The Labour Party in Crisis*, London: Methuen

Appendix

In Table A.1 we display the results of a logistic regression analysis in which the dependent variable is identifying with Labour *versus* not doing so. Variation from year to year in the overall level of Labour identification is captured by a variable that identifies each year's survey. In addition there are terms for whether someone is a member of a trade union or not, gender and Goldthorpe social class. Respondents who did not have a Goldthorpe social class are excluded as are those for whom party identification is missing; as Goldthorpe social class is only available for 1986 onwards, data from the 1983–1985 surveys are excluded from the model. In addition we include an interaction term that separately identifies those people who identified themselves as a trade union member in any year between 1997 and 2004. It will be noted that this variable is negatively signed and statistically significant, indicating that the relationship between being a union member and identifying with Labour was weaker from 1997 onwards than beforehand.

Table A.1 Logistic regression model of Labour Party identification

---

Dependent variable: identify with Labour versus not doing so

	Coefficient	Standard error
Year of Survey		
1986	-0.13	0.06*
1987	-0.40	0.06*
1989	-0.12	0.06*
1990	0.16	0.06*
1991	-0.01	0.06
1993	0.11	0.06
1994	0.26	0.06*
1995	0.45	0.06*
1996	0.39	0.06*
1997	0.41	0.07*
1998	0.52	0.06*
1999	0.42	0.06*
2000	0.35	0.06*
2001	0.46	0.06*
2002	0.36	0.06*
2003	0.19	0.06*
Gender		
Female	-0.02	0.02
(Male)		
Goldthorpe Class		
Salariat	-0.89	0.03*
Routine non-manual	-0.69	0.03*
Petty bourgeoisie	-0.98	0.04*
Foremen and supervisors	-0.28	0.04*
(Working class)		
Trade union		
Member	0.52	0.04*
(Not a member)		
Interaction term		
Union member 1997–2004	-0.18	0.05*
(Union member before 1997)		
Constant	-0.05	0.04

---

* = significant at the five per cent level.

Appendix I
Technical details of the survey

In 2004, the sample for the *British Social Attitudes* survey was split into three sections: versions A, B and C each made up a third of the sample. Depending on the number of versions in which it was included, each 'module' of questions was thus asked either of the full sample (3,199 respondents) or of a random two-thirds or one-third of the sample.

The structure of the questionnaire is shown at the beginning of Appendix III.

Sample design

The *British Social Attitudes* survey is designed to yield a representative sample of adults aged 18 or over. Since 1993, the sampling frame for the survey has been the Postcode Address File (PAF), a list of addresses (or postal delivery points) compiled by the Post Office.[1]

For practical reasons, the sample is confined to those living in private households. People living in institutions (though not in private households at such institutions) are excluded, as are households whose addresses were not on the PAF.

The sampling method involved a multi-stage design, with three separate stages of selection.

Selection of sectors

At the first stage, postcode sectors were selected systematically from a list of all postal sectors in Great Britain. Before selection, any sectors with fewer than 500 addresses were identified and grouped together with an adjacent sector; in Scotland all sectors north of the Caledonian Canal were excluded (because of the prohibitive costs of interviewing there). Sectors were then stratified on the basis of:

- 37 sub-regions
- population density with variable banding used, in order to create three equal-sized strata per sub-region
- ranking by percentage of homes that were owner-occupied in England and Wales and percentage of homes where the head of household was non-manual in Scotland.

Two hundred postcode sectors were selected, with probability proportional to the number of addresses in each sector.

Selection of addresses

Thirty-one addresses were selected in each of the 200 sectors. The issued sample was therefore 200 x 31 = 6,200 addresses, selected by starting from a random point on the list of addresses for each sector, and choosing each address at a fixed interval. The fixed interval was calculated for each sector in order to generate the correct number of addresses.

The Multiple-Output Indicator (MOI) available through PAF was used when selecting addresses in Scotland. The MOI shows the number of accommodation spaces sharing one address. Thus, if the MOI indicates more than one accommodation space at a given address, the chances of the given address being selected from the list of addresses would increase so that it matched the total number of accommodation spaces. The MOI is largely irrelevant in England and Wales as separate dwelling units generally appear as separate entries on PAF. In Scotland, tenements with many flats tend to appear as one entry on PAF. However, even in Scotland, the vast majority of MOIs had a value of one. The remainder, which ranged between three and 13, were incorporated into the weighting procedures (described below).

Selection of individuals

Interviewers called at each address selected from PAF and listed all those eligible for inclusion in the *British Social Attitudes* sample – that is, all persons currently aged 18 or over and resident at the selected address. The interviewer then selected one respondent using a computer-generated random selection procedure. Where there were two or more households or 'dwelling units' at the selected address, interviewers first had to select one household or dwelling unit using the same random procedure. They then followed the same procedure to select a person for interview.

Weighting

Data were weighted to take account of the fact that not all the units covered in the survey had the same probability of selection. The weighting reflects the relative selection probabilities of the individual at the three main stages of selection: address, household and individual. First, because addresses in Scotland were selected using the MOI, weights had to be applied to compensate for the greater probability of an address with an MOI of more than one being selected, compared to an address with an MOI of one. (This stage was omitted for the English and Welsh data.) Secondly, data were weighted to compensate for the fact that dwelling units at an address which contained a large number of dwelling units were less likely to be selected for inclusion in the survey than ones which did not share an address. (We use this procedure because in most cases where the MOI is greater than one, the two stages will cancel each other out, resulting in more efficient weights.) Thirdly, data were weighted to compensate for the lower selection probabilities of adults living in large households compared with those in small households. The weights were capped at 6.00 (causing two cases to have their weights reduced). The resulting weight is called 'WtFactor' and the distribution of weights is shown in Table A.1.

Table A.1 Distribution of unscaled and scaled weights

Unscaled weight	Number	%	Scaled weight
0.0769	1	0.0	0.0425
0.0833	1	0.0	0.0461
0.0909	1	0.0	0.0503
0.1000	1	0.0	0.0553
0.1111	1	0.0	0.0614
0.1667	2	0.1	0.0922
0.2500	2	0.1	0.1382
0.2857	1	0.0	0.1580
0.3333	1	0.0	0.1843
0.3750	1	0.0	0.2074
0.5000	1	0.0	0.2765
0.7500	2	0.1	0.4147
1.0000	1142	35.7	0.5530
2.0000	1653	51.7	1.1059
3.0000	254	7.9	1.6589
4.0000	111	3.5	1.2118
5.0000	17	0.5	2.7648
6.0000	7	0.2	3.3177

Base: 3199

The mean weight was 1.81. The weights were then scaled down to make the number of weighted productive cases exactly equal to the number of unweighted productive cases (n =3,199).

All the percentages presented in this Report are based on weighted data.

Questionnaire versions

Each address in each sector (sampling point) was allocated to either the A, B or C portion of the sample. If one serial number was version A, the next was version B and the third version C. Thus, each interviewer was allocated 10 or 11 cases from each of versions A, B and C. There were 2,067 issued addresses for versions A and B and 2,066 for version C.

Fieldwork

Interviewing was mainly carried out between June and September 2004, with a small number of interviews taking place in October and November.

Table A.2 Response rate on *British Social Attitudes*, 2004

	Number	%
Addresses issued	6,200	
Vacant, derelict and other out of scope	540	
In scope	5,660	100.0
Interview achieved	3,199	56.5
Interview not achieved	2,461	43.5
Refused[1]	1,881	33.2
Non-contacted[2]	305	5.4
Other non-response	275	4.9

1 'Refused' comprises refusals before selection of an individual at the address, refusals to the office, refusal by the selected person, 'proxy' refusals (on behalf of the selected respondent) and broken appointments after which the selected person could not be recontacted

2 'Non-contacted' comprises households where no one was contacted and those where the selected person could not be contacted

Fieldwork was conducted by interviewers drawn from the *National Centre for Social Research*'s regular panel and conducted using face-to-face computer-assisted interviewing.[2] Interviewers attended a one-day briefing conference to familiarise them with the selection procedures and questionnaires.

The mean interview length was 68 minutes for versions A and B of the questionnaire, and 63 minutes for version C.[3] Interviewers achieved an overall response rate of 57 per cent. Details are shown in Table A.2.

As in earlier rounds of the series, the respondent was asked to fill in a self-completion questionnaire which, whenever possible, was collected by the interviewer. Otherwise, the respondent was asked to post it to the *National Centre for Social Research*. If necessary, up to three postal reminders were sent to obtain the self-completion supplement.

A total of 590 respondents (18 per cent of those interviewed) did not return their self-completion questionnaire. Version A of the self-completion questionnaire was returned by 80 per cent of respondents to the face-to-face interview, version B by 82 per cent and version C by 83 per cent. As in previous rounds, we judged that it was not necessary to apply additional weights to correct for non-response.

Advance letter

Interviewers were supplied with letters describing the purpose of the survey and the coverage of the questionnaire, which they posted to sampled addresses before making any calls.[4]

Analysis variables

A number of standard analyses have been used in the tables that appear in this Report. The analysis groups requiring further definition are set out below. For further details see Exley and Thomson (2005).

Region

The dataset is classified by the 12 Government Office Regions.

Standard Occupational Classification

Respondents are classified according to their own occupation, not that of the 'head of household'. Each respondent was asked about their current or last job, so that all respondents except those who had never worked were coded. Additionally, if the respondent was not working but their spouse or partner *was* working, their spouse or partner is similarly classified. (On Version A, all job details were collected for all spouses and partners in work.)

With the 2001 survey, we began coding occupation to the new Standard Occupational Classification 2000 (SOC 2000) instead of the Standard Occupational Classification 1990 (SOC 90). The main socio-economic grouping based on SOC 2000 is the National Statistics Socio-Economic Classification (NS-SEC). However, to maintain time-series, some analysis has continued to use the older schemes based on SOC 90 – Registrar General's Social Class, Socio-Economic Group and the Goldthorpe schema.

National Statistics Socio-Economic Classification (NS-SEC)

The combination of SOC 2000 and employment status for current or last job generates the following NS-SEC analytic classes:

- Employers in large organisations, higher managerial and professional
- Lower professional and managerial; higher technical and supervisory
- Intermediate occupations
- Small employers and own account workers
- Lower supervisory and technical occupations
- Semi-routine occupations
- Routine occupations

The remaining respondents are grouped as "never had a job" or "not classifiable". For some analyses, it may be more appropriate to classify respondents according to their current socio-economic status, which takes into account only their present economic position. In this case, in addition to the seven classes listed above, the remaining respondents not currently in paid work fall into one of the following categories: "not classifiable", "retired", "looking after the home", "unemployed" or "others not in paid occupations".

Registrar General's Social Class

As with NS-SEC, each respondent's Social Class is based on his or her current or last occupation. The combination of SOC 90 with employment status for current or last job generates the following six Social Classes:

I	Professional etc. occupations	
II	Managerial and technical occupations	'Non-manual'
III (Non-manual)	Skilled occupations	
III (Manual)	Skilled occupations	
IV	Partly skilled occupations	'Manual'
V	Unskilled occupations	

They are usually collapsed into four groups: I & II, III Non-manual, III Manual, and IV & V.

Socio-Economic Group

As with NS-SEC, each respondent's Socio-Economic Group (SEG) is based on his or her current or last occupation. SEG aims to bring together people with jobs of similar social and economic status, and is derived from a combination of employment status and occupation. The full SEG classification identifies 18 categories, but these are usually condensed into six groups:

- Professionals, employers and managers
- Intermediate non-manual workers
- Junior non-manual workers
- Skilled manual workers
- Semi-skilled manual workers
- Unskilled manual workers

As with NS-SEC, the remaining respondents are grouped as "never had a job" or "not classifiable".

Goldthorpe schema

The Goldthorpe schema classifies occupations by their 'general comparability', considering such factors as sources and levels of income, economic security, promotion prospects, and level of job autonomy and authority. The Goldthorpe schema was derived from the SOC 90 codes combined with employment status. Two versions of the schema are coded: the full schema has 11 categories; the 'compressed schema' combines these into the five classes shown below.

- Salariat (professional and managerial)
- Routine non-manual workers (office and sales)
- Petty bourgeoisie (the self-employed, including farmers, with and without employees)
- Manual foremen and supervisors
- Working class (skilled, semi-skilled and unskilled manual workers, personal service and agricultural workers)

There is a residual category comprising those who have never had a job or who gave insufficient information for classification purposes.

Industry

All respondents whose occupation could be coded were allocated a Standard Industrial Classification 1992 (SIC 92). Two-digit class codes are used. As with Social Class, SIC may be generated on the basis of the respondent's current occupation only, or on his or her most recently classifiable occupation.

Party identification

Respondents can be classified as identifying with a particular political party on one of three counts: if they consider themselves supporters of that party, as closer to it than to others, or as more likely to support it in the event of a general election (responses are derived from Qs.203–205). The three groups are generally described respectively as *partisans, sympathisers* and *residual identifiers*. In combination, the three groups are referred to as 'identifiers'.

Attitude scales

Since 1986, the *British Social Attitudes* surveys have included two attitude scales which aim to measure where respondents stand on certain underlying value dimensions – left–right and libertarian–authoritarian.[5] Since 1987 (except 1990), a similar scale on 'welfarism' has been asked. Some of the items in the welfarism scale were changed in 2000–2001. The current version of the scale is listed below.

A useful way of summarising the information from a number of questions of this sort is to construct an additive index (DeVellis, 1991; Spector, 1992). This approach rests on the assumption that there is an underlying – 'latent' – attitudinal dimension which characterises the answers to all the questions within each scale. If so, scores on the index are likely to be a more reliable indication of the underlying attitude than the answers to any one question.

Each of these scales consists of a number of statements to which the respondent is invited to "agree strongly", "agree", "neither agree nor disagree", "disagree" or "disagree strongly".

The items are:

Left–right scale

Government should redistribute income from the better off to those who are less well off. *[Redistrb]*

Big business benefits owners at the expense of workers. *[BigBusnN]*

Ordinary working people do not get their fair share of the nation's wealth. *[Wealth]*[6]

There is one law for the rich and one for the poor. *[RichLaw]*

Management will always try to get the better of employees if it gets the chance. *[Indust4]*

Libertarian–authoritarian scale

Young people today don't have enough respect for traditional British values. *[TradVals]*

People who break the law should be given stiffer sentences. *[StifSent]*

For some crimes, the death penalty is the most appropriate sentence. *[DeathApp]*

Schools should teach children to obey authority. *[Obey]*

The law should always be obeyed, even if a particular law is wrong. *[WrongLaw]*

Censorship of films and magazines is necessary to uphold moral standards. *[Censor]*

Welfarism scale

The welfare state encourages people to stop helping each other. *[WelfHelp]*

The government should spend more money on welfare benefits for the poor, even if it leads to higher taxes. *[MoreWelf]*

Around here, most unemployed people could find a job if they really wanted one. *[UnempJob]*

Many people who get social security don't really deserve any help. *[SocHelp]*

Most people on the dole are fiddling in one way or another. *[DoleFidl]*

If welfare benefits weren't so generous, people would learn to stand on their own two feet. *[WelfFeet]*

Cutting welfare benefits would damage too many people's lives. *[DamLives]*

The creation of the welfare state is one of Britain's proudest achievements. *[ProudWlf]*

The indices for the three scales are formed by scoring the leftmost, most libertarian or most pro-welfare position as 1 and the rightmost, most authoritarian or most anti-welfarist position as 5. The "neither agree nor disagree" option is scored as 3. The scores to all the questions in each scale are added and then divided by the number of items in the scale, giving indices ranging from 1 (leftmost, most libertarian, most pro-welfare) to 5 (rightmost, most authoritarian, most anti-welfare). The scores on the three indices have been placed on the dataset.[7]

The scales have been tested for reliability (as measured by Cronbach's alpha). The Cronbach's alpha (unstandardised items) for the scales in 2004 are 0.83 for the left–right scale, 0.81 for the 'welfarism' scale and 0.72 for the libertarian–authoritarian scale. This level of reliability can be considered "very good" for the left–right and welfarism scales and "respectable" for the libertarian–authoritarian scale (DeVellis, 1991: 85).

Other analysis variables

These are taken directly from the questionnaire and to that extent are self-explanatory. The principal ones are:

Sex (Q.39)
Age (Q.40)
Household income (Q.972)
Economic position (Q.580)
Religion (Q.703)
Highest educational qualification obtained (Qs.829–830)
Marital status (Q.133)
Benefits received (Qs.927–965)

Sampling errors

No sample precisely reflects the characteristics of the population it represents, because of both sampling and non-sampling errors. If a sample were designed as a random sample (if every adult had an equal and independent chance of inclusion in the sample) then we could calculate the sampling error of any percentage, p, using the formula:

$$s.e.\ (p) = \sqrt{\frac{p(100 - p)}{n}}$$

where n is the number of respondents on which the percentage is based. Once the sampling error had been calculated, it would be a straightforward exercise to calculate a confidence interval for the true population percentage. For example, a 95 per cent confidence interval would be given by the formula:

$$p \pm 1.96 \times s.e.\ (p)$$

Clearly, for a simple random sample (srs), the sampling error depends only on the values of p and n. However, simple random sampling is almost never used in practice because of its inefficiency in terms of time and cost.

As noted above, the *British Social Attitudes* sample, like that drawn for most large-scale surveys, was clustered according to a stratified multi-stage design into 200 postcode sectors (or combinations of sectors). With a complex design like this, the sampling error of a percentage giving a particular response is not simply a function of the number of respondents in the sample and the size of the percentage; it also depends on how that percentage response is spread within and between sample points.

The complex design may be assessed relative to simple random sampling by calculating a range of design factors (DEFTs) associated with it, where:

$$\text{DEFT} = \sqrt{\frac{\text{Variance of estimator with complex design, sample size n}}{\text{Variance of estimator with srs design, sample size n}}}$$

and represents the multiplying factor to be applied to the simple random sampling error to produce its complex equivalent. A design factor of one means that the complex sample has achieved the same precision as a simple random sample of the same size. A design factor greater than one means the complex sample is less precise than its simple random sample equivalent. If the DEFT for a particular characteristic is known, a 95 per cent confidence interval for a percentage may be calculated using the formula:

$$p \pm 1.96 \text{ x complex sampling error } (p)$$

$$= p \pm 1.96 \text{ x DEFT x } \sqrt{\frac{p(100 - p)}{n}}$$

Calculations of sampling errors and design effects were made using the statistical analysis package STATA.

Table A.3 gives examples of the confidence intervals and DEFTs calculated for a range of different questions. Most background variables were fielded on the whole sample, whereas many attitudinal variables were asked only of two-thirds or a third of the sample; some were asked on the interview questionnaire and some on the self-completion supplement. The table shows that most of the questions asked of all sample members have a confidence interval of around plus or minus two to three per cent of the survey proportion. This means that we can be 95 per cent certain that the true population proportion is within two to three per cent (in either direction) of the proportion we report.

Variables with much larger variation are, as might be expected, those closely related to the geographic location of the respondent (for example, whether they live in a big city, a small town or a village). Here the variation may be as large as six or seven per cent either way around the percentage found on the survey. Consequently the design effects calculated for these variables in a clustered sample will be greater than the design effects calculated for variables less strongly associated with area. Also, sampling errors for proportions based only on respondents to just one of the versions of the questionnaire, or on subgroups within the sample, are larger than they would have been had the questions been asked of everyone.

Table A.3 Complex standard errors and confidence intervals of selected variables

	% (p)	Complex standard error of p	95% confidence interval	DEFT	Base
Classification variables					
Q205 **Party identification (full sample)**					
Conservative	26.1	1.2	23.7 – 28.6	1.55	
Labour	31.6	1.3	29.1 – 34.2	1.57	
Liberal Democrat	12.9	0.8	11.4 – 14.6	1.34	
Q633 **Housing tenure (full sample)**					
Owns	75.4	1.0	73.3 – 77.4	1.36	
Rents from local authority	9.0	0.8	7.5 – 10.7	1.55	
Rents privately/HA	14.4	0.9	12.7 – 16.2	1.40	
Q703 **Religion (full sample)**					
No religion	43.4	1.2	41.1 – 45.8	1.35	
Church of England	29.0	1.3	26.5 – 31.6	1.61	
Roman Catholic	8.9	0.7	7.5 – 10.4	1.41	
Q766 **Age of completing continuous full-time education (full sample)**					
16 or under	55.7	1.5	52.8 – 58.7	1.69	
17 or 18	18.2	0.8	16.7 – 19.8	1.12	
19 or over	25.6	1.3	23.0 – 28.1	1.67	
Q831 **Home internet access (full sample)**					
Yes	60.2	1.3	57.6 – 62.7	1.47	
No	39.7	1.3	37.2 – 42.2	1.47	
Q697 **Urban or rural residence (full sample)**					
A big city	34.0	3.3	27.8 – 40.1	3.95	
A small city/town	43.3	3.0	37.6 – 49.2	3.37	
Village/countryside	22.1	2.7	17.1 – 28.0	3.74	
Attitudinal variables (face-to-face interview)					
Q227 **Benefits for the unemployed are ... (full sample)**					
... too low	23.4	1.0	21.5 – 25.3	1.29	
... too high	54.0	1.4	51.2 – 56.8	1.58	
Q409 **NHS should be available to those with lower incomes (full sample)**					
Support a lot	7.8	0.6	6.7 – 9.0	1.19	
Support a little	14.7	0.8	13.1 – 16.5	1.34	
Oppose a little	17.4	0.8	15.8 – 19.2	1.26	
Oppose a lot	58.2	1.2	55.8 – 60.5	1.38	
Q230 **Government should ... (2/3 sample)**					
Reduce tax & spend less on health, education etc.	5.6	0.7	4.4 – 7.1	1.35	
Keep taxes & spending as is on health, education etc.	41.7	1.1	39.4 – 44.0	1.07	
Increase taxes & spend more on health, education etc.	49.1	1.1	46.9 – 51.2	1.01	

	% (p)	Complex standard error of p	95% confidence interval	DEFT *Base*
Q627 Prejudiced against people of other races (1/3 sample)				
Very / a little	27.6	1.6	24.6 – 30.8	1.14
Not at all	69.9	1.7	66.5 – 73.1	1.19
Attitudinal variables (self-completion)				
A64a B45a C45a Government should redistribute income from the better off to those who are less well off (full sample)				
Agree strongly	6.7	0.5	5.8 – 7.8	1.04
Agree	24.8	1.1	22.8 – 27.0	1.24
Neither agree nor disagree	28.0	0.9	26.3 – 29.8	1.02
Disagree	29.5	1.0	27.6 – 31.4	1.09
Disagree strongly	8.8	0.7	7.5 – 10.3	1.27
B34b C35b Not good if man stays at home with children and woman goes out to work (2/3 of sample)				
Agree strongly	3.4	0.5	2.6 – 4.5	1.05
Agree	10.5	0.8	8.9 – 12.3	1.15
Neither agree nor disagree	30.4	1.2	28.1 – 32.8	1.09
Disagree	38.3	1.3	35.7 – 40.9	1.14
Disagree strongly	13.3	1.1	11.3 – 15.5	1.30
C12a How important to cut down on number of cars (1/3 of sample)				
Very important	26.2	1.6	23.1 – 29.6	1.09
Fairly important	46.0	1.7	42.3 – 49.4	1.01
Not very / Not at all important	21.4	1.7	18.2 – 25.0	1.23

Analysis techniques

Regression

Regression analysis aims to summarise the relationship between a 'dependent' variable and one or more 'independent' variables. It shows how well we can estimate a respondent's score on the dependent variable from knowledge of their scores on the independent variables. It is often undertaken to support a claim that the phenomena measured by the independent variables *cause* the phenomenon measured by the dependent variable. However, the causal ordering, if any, between the variables cannot be verified or falsified by the technique. Causality can only be inferred through special experimental designs or through assumptions made by the analyst.

All regression analysis assumes that the relationship between the dependent and each of the independent variables takes a particular form. In *linear regression*, it is assumed that the relationship can be adequately summarised by a straight line. This means that a one percentage point increase in the value of an independent variable is assumed to have the same impact on the value of the dependent variable on average irrespective of the previous values of those variables.

Strictly speaking the technique assumes that both the dependent and the independent variables are measured on an interval level scale, although it may sometimes still be applied even where this is not the case. For example, one can use an ordinal variable (e.g. a Likert scale) as a *dependent* variable if one is willing to assume that there is an underlying interval level scale and the difference between the observed ordinal scale and the underlying interval scale is due to random measurement error. Often the answers to a number of Likert-type questions are averaged to give a dependent variable that is more like a continuous variable. Categorical or nominal data can be used as *independent* variables by converting them into dummy or binary variables; these are variables where the only valid scores are 0 and 1, with 1 signifying membership of a particular category and 0 otherwise.

The assumptions of linear regression cause particular difficulties where the *dependent* variable is binary. The assumption that the relationship between the dependent and the independent variables is a straight line means that it can produce estimated values for the dependent variable of less than 0 or greater than 1. In this case it may be more appropriate to assume that the relationship between the dependent and the independent variables takes the form of an S-curve, where the impact on the dependent variable of a one-point increase in an independent variable becomes progressively less the closer the value of the dependent variable approaches 0 or 1. *Logistic regression* is an alternative form of regression which fits such an S-curve rather than a straight line. The technique can also be adapted to analyse multinomial non-interval level dependent variables, that is, variables which classify respondents into more than two categories.

The two statistical scores most commonly reported from the results of regression analyses are:

A measure of variance explained: This summarises how well all the independent variables combined can account for the variation in respondent's scores in the dependent variable. The higher the measure, the more accurately we are able in general to estimate the correct value of each respondent's score on the dependent variable from knowledge of their scores on the independent variables.

A parameter estimate: This shows how much the dependent variable will change on average, given a one unit change in the independent variable (while holding all other independent variables in the model constant). The parameter estimate has a positive sign if an increase in the value of the independent variable results in an increase in the value of the dependent variable. It has a negative sign if an increase in the value of the independent variable results in a decrease in the value of the dependent variable. If the parameter estimates are standardised, it is possible to compare the relative impact of different independent variables; those variables with the largest standardised estimates can be said to have the biggest impact on the value of the dependent variable.

Regression also tests for the statistical significance of parameter estimates. A parameter estimate is said to be significant at the five per cent level if the range of the values encompassed by its 95 per cent confidence interval (see also section on sampling errors) are either all positive or all negative. This means that there is less than a five per cent chance that the association we have found between the dependent variable and the independent variable is simply the result of sampling error and does not reflect a relationship that actually exists in the general population.

Factor analysis

Factor analysis is a statistical technique which aims to identify whether there are one or more apparent sources of commonality to the answers given by respondents to a set of questions. It ascertains the smallest number of *factors* (or dimensions) which can most economically summarise all of the variation found in the set of questions being analysed. Factors are established where respondents who give a particular answer to one question in the set, tend to give the same answer as each other to one or more of the other questions in the set. The technique is most useful when a relatively small number of factors are able to account for a relatively large proportion of the variance in all of the questions in the set.

The technique produces a *factor loading* for each question (or variable) on each factor. Where questions have a high loading on the same factor then it will be the case that respondents who give a particular answer to one of these questions tend to give a similar answer to the other questions. The technique is most commonly used in attitudinal research to try to identify the underlying ideological dimensions which apparently structure attitudes towards the subject in question.

International Social Survey Programme

The *International Social Survey Programme (ISSP)* is run by a group of research organisations, each of which undertakes to field annually an agreed module of questions on a chosen topic area. Since 1985, an *International Social Survey Programme* module has been included in one of the *British Social Attitudes* self-completion questionnaires. Each module is chosen for repetition at intervals to allow comparisons both between countries (membership is currently standing at almost 40) and over time. In 2004, the chosen subject was Citizenship, and the module was carried on the A version of the self-completion questionnaire (Qs.1–26).

Notes

1. Until 1991 all *British Social Attitudes* samples were drawn from the Electoral Register (ER). However, following concern that this sampling frame might be deficient in its coverage of certain population subgroups, a 'splicing' experiment was conducted in 1991. We are grateful to the Market Research Development Fund for contributing towards the costs of this experiment. Its purpose was to investigate whether a switch to PAF would disrupt the time-series – for instance, by lowering response rates or affecting the distribution of responses to particular questions. In the event, it was concluded that the change from ER to PAF was unlikely to affect time trends in any noticeable ways, and that no adjustment factors were necessary. Since significant differences in efficiency exist between PAF and ER, and because we considered it untenable to continue to use a frame that is known to be biased, we decided to adopt PAF as the sampling frame for future *British Social Attitudes* surveys. For details of the PAF/ER 'splicing' experiment, see Lynn and Taylor (1995).

2. In 1993 it was decided to mount a split-sample experiment designed to test the applicability of Computer-Assisted Personal Interviewing (CAPI) to the *British Social Attitudes* survey series. CAPI has been used increasingly over the past decade as an alternative to traditional interviewing techniques. As the name implies, CAPI involves the use of lap-top computers during the interview, with interviewers entering responses directly into the computer. One of the advantages of CAPI is that it significantly reduces both the amount of time spent on data processing and the number of coding and editing errors. There was, however, concern that a different interviewing technique might alter the distribution of responses and so affect the year-on-year consistency of *British Social Attitudes* data.

   Following the experiment, it was decided to change over to CAPI completely in 1994 (the self-completion questionnaire still being administered in the conventional way). The results of the experiment are discussed in *The 11th Report* (Lynn and Purdon, 1994).

3. Interview times recorded as less than 20 minutes were excluded as these timings were likely to be errors.

4. An experiment was conducted on the 1991 *British Social Attitudes* survey (Jowell *et al.*, 1992), which showed that sending advance letters to sampled addresses before fieldwork begins has very little impact on response rates. However, interviewers do find that an advance letter helps them to introduce the survey on the doorstep, and a majority of respondents have said that they preferred some advance notice. For these reasons, advance letters have been used on the *British Social Attitudes* surveys since 1991.

5. Because of methodological experiments on scale development, the exact items detailed in this section have not been asked on all versions of the questionnaire each year.

6. In 1994 only, this item was replaced by: Ordinary people get their fair share of the nation's wealth. *[Wealth1]*

7. In constructing the scale, a decision had to be taken on how to treat missing values ('Don't knows,' 'Refused' and 'Not answered'). Respondents who had more than two missing values on the left–right scale and more than three missing values on the

libertarian–authoritarian and welfarism scale were excluded from that scale. For respondents with just a few missing values, 'Don't knows' were recoded to the midpoint of the scale and 'Refused' or 'Not answered' were recoded to the scale mean for that respondent on their valid items.

References

DeVellis, R.F. (1991), 'Scale development: theory and applications', *Applied Social Research Methods Series*, **26**, Newbury Park: Sage

Exley, S. and Thomson, K. (2005), *British Social Attitudes 2001 and 2002 surveys: Technical Report*, London: *National Centre for Social Research*

Jowell, R., Brook, L., Prior, G. and Taylor, B. (1992), *British Social Attitudes: the 9th Report*, Aldershot: Dartmouth

Lynn, P. and Purdon, S. (1994), 'Time-series and lap-tops: the change to computer-assisted interviewing', in Jowell, R., Curtice, J., Brook, L. and Ahrendt, D. (eds.), *British Social Attitudes: the 11th Report*, Aldershot: Dartmouth

Lynn, P. and Taylor, B. (1995), 'On the bias and variance of samples of individuals: a comparison of the Electoral Registers and Postcode Address File as sampling frames', *The Statistician*, **44**: 173–194

Spector, P.E. (1992), 'Summated rating scale construction: an introduction', *Quantitative Applications in the Social Sciences*, **82**, Newbury Park: Sage

Appendix II
Notes on the tabulations in chapters

1. Figures in the tables are from the 2004 *British Social Attitudes* survey unless otherwise indicated.
2. Tables are percentaged as indicated by the percentage signs.
3. In tables, '*' indicates less than 0.5 per cent but greater than zero, and '–' indicates zero.
4. When findings based on the responses of fewer than 100 respondents are reported in the text, reference is made to the small base size.
5. Percentages equal to or greater than 0.5 have been rounded up (e.g. 0.5 per cent = one per cent; 36.5 per cent = 37 per cent).
6. In many tables the proportions of respondents answering "Don't know" or not giving an answer are not shown. This, together with the effects of rounding and weighting, means that percentages will not always add to 100 per cent.
7. The self-completion questionnaire was not completed by all respondents to the main questionnaire (see Appendix I). Percentage responses to the self-completion questionnaire are based on all those who completed it.
8. The bases shown in the tables (the number of respondents who answered the question) are printed in small italics. The bases are unweighted, unless otherwise stated.

Appendix III
The questionnaires

As explained in Appendix I, three different versions of the questionnaire (A, B and C) were administered, each with its own self-completion supplement. The diagram that follows shows the structure of the questionnaires and the topics covered (not all of which are reported on in this volume).

The three interview questionnaires reproduced on the following pages are derived from the Blaise computer program in which they were written. For ease of reference, each item has been allocated a question number. Gaps in the numbering system indicate items that are essential components of the Blaise program but which are not themselves questions, and so have been omitted. In addition, we have removed the keying codes and inserted instead the percentage distribution of answers to each question. We have also included the SPSS variable name, in square brackets, at each question. Above the questions we have included filter instructions. A filter instruction should be considered as staying in force until the next filter instruction. Percentages for the core questions are based on the total weighted sample, while those for questions in versions A, B or C are based on the appropriate weighted sub-samples.

The three versions of the self-completion questionnaire follow. We begin by reproducing version A of the interview questionnaire in full; then those parts of version B and version C that differ.

The percentage distributions do not necessarily add up to 100 because of weighting and rounding, or for one or more of the following reasons:

(i)   Some sub-questions are filtered – that is, they are asked of only a proportion of respondents. In these cases the percentages add up (approximately) to the proportions who were asked them. Where, however, a series of questions is filtered, we have indicated the reduced weighted base (for example, all employees), and have derived percentages from that base.

(ii)   At a few questions, respondents were invited to give more than one answer and so percentages may add to well over 100 per cent. These are clearly marked by interviewer instructions on the questionnaires.

As reported in Appendix I, the 2004 *British Social Attitudes* self-completion questionnaire was not completed by 18 per cent of respondents who were successfully interviewed. The answers in the supplement have been percentaged on the base of those respondents who returned it. This means that the distribution of responses to questions asked in earlier years are comparable with those given in Appendix III of all earlier reports in this series except in *The 1984 Report*, where the percentages for the self-completion questionnaire need to be recalculated if comparisons are to be made.

BRITISH SOCIAL ATTITUDES: 2004 SURVEY

Version A **(one third of sample)**	**Version B** **(one third of sample)**	**Version C** **(one third sample)**

Face-to-face questionnaires

Household grid, newspaper readership and party identification		
Public spending and social security		
Equality and inequality		Transport
Education		
Health		
Job details and employment relations		
—	Flexible working	
Political and moral attitudes		
Housing		
Classification		

Self-completion questionnaires

ISSP (Citizenship)	—	—
Public spending and social security		
Equality and inequality		Transport
Education		
Health		
Employment relations		
—	Flexible working	
Housing		
Standard scales		

Contents

BRITISH SOCIAL ATTITUDES 2004

FACE-TO-FACE QUESTIONNAIRE

Introduction

Q1 ASK ALL
[Serial] **(NOT ON SCREEN)**
Serial Number
N=3199

Q17 [GOR2] **(NOT ON SCREEN)**
% Government office region 2003 version
4.8 North East
11.7 North West
8.8 Yorkshire and Humberside
9.5 East Midlands
9.1 West Midlands
8.5 SW
9.8 Eastern
3.8 Inner London
6.4 Outer London
12.9 South East
5.4 Wales
9.3 Scotland
N=3199

Q27 [ABCVer] **(NOT ON SCREEN)**
% A, B or C?
32.3 A
34.2 B
33.4 C
N=3199

Q28 [Country] **(NOT ON SCREEN)**
England, Scotland or Wales?
% England
85.0 England
9.3 Scotland
5.7 Wales
N=3199

Household grid

Q37 **ASK ALL**
[Household]
(You have just been telling me about the adults that live in this household. Thinking now of **everyone** living in the household, **including children:**)
Including yourself, how many people live here regularly as members of this household?
CHECK INTERVIEWER MANUAL FOR DEFINITION OF HOUSEHOLD IF NECESSARY.
IF YOU DISCOVER THAT YOU WERE GIVEN THE WRONG INFORMATION FOR THE RESPONDENT SELECTION ON THE ARF:
***DO NOT** REDO THE ARF SELECTION PRODECURE
***DO** ENTER THE CORRECT INFORMATION HERE
***DO** USE <CTRL + M> TO MAKE A NOTE OF WHAT HAPPENED.
% **Median: 2 people**
- (Don't know)
- (Refusal/Not answered)
N=3199

FOR EACH PERSON AT [Household]

Q38 [Name] **(NOT ON DATAFILE)**
FOR RESPONDENT: (Can I just check, what is your first name?)
PLEASE TYPE IN THE FIRST NAME (OR INITIALS) OF RESPONDENT
FOR OTHER HOUSEHOLD MEMBERS: PLEASE TYPE IN THE FIRST NAME (OR INITIALS) OF PERSON NUMBER (number)
N=3199

Q39 [RSex] (figures refer to respondent)
% PLEASE CODE SEX OF (name)
45.8 Male
54.2 Female
- (Don't know)
- (Refusal/Not answered)

Q40 [RAge] (figures refer to the respondent) N=3199
FOR RESPONDENT IF ONLY ONE PERSON IN HOUSEHOLD: I would
now like to ask you a few details about yourself.
What was your **age** last birthday?
FOR RESPONDENT IF SEVERAL PERSONS IN HOUSEHOLD: I would
like to ask you a few details about each person in your
household. Starting with yourself, what was your **age**
last birthday?
FOR OTHER PERSONS IN HOUSEHOLD: What was (name)'s age
last birthday?
FOR 97+, CODE 97.

% **Median: 46 years**
- (Don't know)
- (Refusal/Not answered)

FOR PEOPLE IN THE HOUSEHOLD OTHER THAN RESPONDENT

Q47 [P2Rel3] (figures refer to second person in household)
N=3199
% PLEASE ENTER RELATIONSHIP OF (name) TO RESPONDENT
61.6 Partner/ spouse/ cohabitee
8.2 Son/ daughter (inc step/adopted)
0.1 Grandson/ daughter (inc step/adopted)
7.5 Parent/ parent-in-law
0.1 Grand-parent
2.1 Brother/ sister (inc. in-law)
0.4 Other relative
1.8 Other non-relative
- (Don't know)
- (Refusal/Not answered)

ASK ALL
Q133 [MarSta2b]
CARD A1
Can I just check, which of these applies to you at
present?
Please choose the first on the list that applies
N=3199
%
54.8 Married
10.2 Living with a partner
2.4 Separated (after being married)
6.5 Divorced
7.3 Widowed
18.8 Single (never married)
- (Don't know)
0.1 (Refusal/Not answered)

Q148- Can I just check which, if any, of these types of N=3199
Q155   relatives do you yourself have alive at the moment.
Please include adoptive and step relatives.
PROBE: Which others?
DO NOT INCLUDE FOSTER RELATIVES
CODE ALL THAT APPLY
Multicoded (Maximum of 8 codes)
%
46.4 Father   [RelFath]
58.1 Mother   [RelMoth]
60.1 Brother   [RelBroth]
62.4 Sister   [RelSist]
52.7 Son   [RelSon]
50.7 Daughter   [RelDaug]
21.0 Grandchild (daughter's child)   [RelGrChD]
17.7 Grandchild (son's child)   [RelGrChS]
1.5   None of these   [RelNone3]

Q539
ASK ALL
[REconAct]
CARD A3   N=3199
Which of these descriptions applied to what you were
doing last week, that is the seven days ending last
Sunday?
PROBE: Which others? CODE ALL THAT APPLY
Multicoded (Maximum of 11 codes)
(ANSWERS REFER TO FIRST ANSWER ON THE LIST)
%
4.0   In full-time education (not paid for by employer,
including on vacation)
0.4   On government training/employment programme
59.0   In paid work (or away temporarily) for at least 10
hours in week
0.5   Waiting to take up paid work already accepted
1.4   Unemployed and registered at a benefit office
0.9   Unemployed, **not** registered, but actively looking for a
job (of at least 10 hrs a week)
0.7   Unemployed, wanting a job (of at least 10 hrs per week)
but not actively looking for a job
4.6   Permanently sick or disabled
19.9   Wholly retired from work
8.1   Looking after the home
0.6   (Doing something else) (WRITE IN)
-   (Don't know)
-   (Refusal/Not answered)

Q540
ASK ALL NOT WORKING OR WAITING TO TAKE UP WORK
[RLastJob]   N=1297
How long ago did you last have a paid job of at least
10 hours a week?
GOVERNMENT PROGRAMS/SCHEMES DO NOT COUNT AS `PAID
JOBS'.
%
17.4   Within past 12 months
21.5   Over 1, up to 5 years ago
17.7   Over 5, up to 10 years ago
24.4   Over 10, up to 20 years ago
13.1   Over 20 years ago
5.9   Never had a paid job of 10+ hours a week
0.0   (Don't know)
-   (Refusal/Not answered)

Q858
ASK ALL WHO ARE MARRIED OR LIVING WITH A PARTNER
[SEconAct]   N=2083
Which of these descriptions applied to what your
(husband/wife/partner) was doing last week, that is
the seven days ending last Sunday?
PROBE: Which others? CODE ALL THAT APPLY
Multicoded (Maximum of 11 codes)
%
1.4   In full-time education (not paid for by employer,
including on vacation)
0.0   On government training/employment programme
65.8   In paid work (or away temporarily) for at least 10
hours in week
0.2   Waiting to take up paid work already accepted
0.8   Unemployed and registered at a benefit office
0.9   Unemployed, not registered, but actively looking for
a job (of at least 10 hrs a week)
0.5   Unemployed, wanting a job (of at least 10 hrs per
week) but not actively looking for a job
3.1   Permanently sick or disabled
16.9   Wholly retired from work
9.6   Looking after the home
0.6   (Doing something else) (WRITE IN)
-   (Don't know)
0.2   (Refusal/Not answered)

Q859
**ASK ALL WHO ARE MARRIED OR LIVING WITH A PARTNER
AND WHOSE SPOUSE/PARTNER IS NOT WORKING OR WAITING
TO TAKE UP WORK**
[SLastJob]   N=706
How long ago did (he/she) last have a paid job of at
least 10 hours a week?
GOVERNMENT PROGRAMS/SCHEMES DO NOT COUNT AS `PAID
JOBS'.
%
14.5   Within past 12 months
21.6   Over 1, up to 5 years ago
20.7   Over 5, up to 10 years ago
24.7   Over 10, up to 20 years ago
12.7   Over 20 years ago
4.4   Never had a paid job of 10+ hours a week
0.8   (Don't know)
0.6   (Refusal/Not answered)

VERSIONS B AND C: IF IN PAID WORK OR WAITING TO TAKE UP WORK

Q925 [S2PartF1]   N=444
     Is the job ... READ OUT ...
%
79.6 ... full-time - that is, 30 or more hours per week,
19.7 or, part-time?
0.5 (Don't know)
0.2 (Refusal/Not answered)

Newspaper readership

ASK ALL

Q197 [Readpap]   N=3199
     Do you normally read any daily **morning** newspaper at
     least 3 times a week?
%
49.8 Yes
50.2 No
  - (Don't know)
  - (Refusal/Not answered)

IF 'yes' AT [ReadPap]

Q198 [WhPaper]   N=3199
     Which one do you normally read?
     IF MORE THAN ONE: Which one do you read **most**
     frequently?
%
2.9   (Scottish) Daily Express
10.8 (Scottish) Daily Mail
5.5   Daily Mirror (/Scottish Mirror)
1.6   Daily Star
11.7 The Sun
1.8   Daily Record
3.7   Daily Telegraph
0.3   Financial Times
2.2   The Guardian
1.1   The Independent
3.5   The Times
0.1   Morning Star
4.4   Other Irish/Northern Irish/Scottish/Welsh, regional
      or local **daily morning** paper (WRITE IN)
0.2   Other (WRITE IN)
0.1   MORE THAN ONE PAPER READ WITH EQUAL FREQUENCY
  -   (Don't know)
  -   (Refusal/Not answered)

Party identification

Q203 **ASK ALL**
[SupParty] N=3199
Generally speaking, do you think of yourself as a supporter of any one political party?
%
34.0 Yes
66.0 No
0.1 (Don't know)
- (Refusal/Not answered)

Q204 **IF 'no' or DON'T KNOW AT [SupParty]**
[ClosePty] N=3199
Do you think of yourself as a little closer to one political party than to the others?
25.4 Yes
40.5 No
0.1 (Don't know)
- (Refusal/Not answered)

Q206 **IF 'yes' at [SupParty] or 'yes'/'no'/DON'T KNOW AT [ClosePty]**
[PartyID1] N=3199
IF 'yes' AT [SupParty] OR AT [ClosePty]: Which one?
IF 'no'/DON'T KNOW AT [ClosePty]: If there were a general election tomorrow, which political party do you think you would be most likely to support?
DO NOT PROMPT
%
26.1 Conservative
31.6 Labour
12.9 Liberal Democrat
1.3 Scottish National Party
0.6 Plaid Cymru
0.8 Other party
0.8 Other answer
16.1 None
1.5 UKIP
0.8 BNP/NF
0.5 Scot Socialist / Respect / Socialist
1.7 Green Party
3.9 (Don't know)
1.8 (Refusal/Not answered)

Q213 **IF PARTY GIVEN AT [PartyID1]**
[Idstrng] N=3199
Would you call yourself very strong (party), fairly strong, or not very strong?
%
5.2 Very strong (party)
25.8 Fairly strong
46.1 Not very strong
0.1 (Don't know)
6.7 (Refusal/Not answered)

Q214 **ASK ALL**
[Politics] N=3199
How much interest do you generally have in what is going on in politics...READ OUT ...
%
9.2 a great deal
21.3 quite a lot
33.6 some
24.1 not very much
11.8 none at all
0.0 (Don't know)
- (Refusal/Not answered)

Q215 [DfWnEur] N=3199
CARD A4
Some people say that it makes no difference which party wins in elections, things go on much the same. Using this card, please say how much of a difference you think it makes who wins in elections to the **European Parliament?**
%
10.1 A great deal
24.4 Quite a lot
24.0 Some
28.0 Not very much
10.2 None at all
3.4 (Don't know)
- (Refusal/Not answered)

Public spending and social welfare

Q217 **ASK ALL**
[Spend1]
CARD B1
Here are some items of government spending.
Which of them, if any, would be your highest priority
for **extra** spending?
Please read through the whole list before deciding.
ENTER ONE CODE ONLY FOR HIGHEST PRIORITY
N=3199

Q218 **IF NOT 'none', DON'T KNOW, REFUSAL AT [Spend1]**
[Spend2]
CARD B1 AGAIN
And which next?
ENTER ONE CODE ONLY FOR NEXT HIGHEST
N=3199

	[Spend1]	[Spend2]
	%	%
Education	25.9	36.3
Defence	1.7	3.1
Health	52.1	25.8
Housing	3.9	8.1
Public transport	3.9	6.8
Roads	1.7	4.2
Police and prisons	5.1	7.5
Social security benefits	1.8	3.3
Help for industry	2.0	2.7
Overseas aid	1.0	1.0
(None of these)	0.7	0.4
(Don't know)	0.1	0.1
(Refusal/Not answered)	-	0.8

Q219 **ASK ALL**
[SocSpnd1]
CARD B2
Some people think that there should be more
government spending on social security, while other
people disagree. For each of the groups I read out
please say whether you would like to see **more** or
less government spending on them than now. Bear in
mind that if you want more spending, this would
probably mean that you would have to pay more taxes.
If you want less spending, this would probably mean
paying less taxes.
Firstly, ...READ OUT... benefits for unemployed
people: would you like to see more or less
government spending than now?
N=3199

Q220 [SocSpnd2]
CARD B2 AGAIN
(Would you like to see more or less government
spending than now on ...)
... benefits for disabled people who cannot work?
N=3199

Q221 [SocSpnd3]
CARD B2 AGAIN
(Would you like to see more or less government
spending than now on ...)
... benefits for parents who work on very low
incomes?
N=3199

Q222 [SocSpnd4]
CARD B2 AGAIN
(Would you like to see more or less government
spending than now on ...)
... benefits for single parents?
N=3199

Q223 [SocSpnd5]
CARD B2 AGAIN
(Would you like to see more or less government
spending than now on ...)
.. benefits for retired people?
N=3199

Q224   [SocSpnd6]
CARD B2 AGAIN
(Would you like to see more or less government spending than now on ...) ... benefits for people who care for those who are sick or disabled?

N=3199

	[SocSpnd1]	[SocSpnd2]	[SocSpnd3]
	%	%	%
Spend much more	2.2	8.5	6.4
Spend more	12.8	54.5	56.1
Spend the same as now	38.7	30.7	30.7
Spend less	35.7	2.4	3.9
Spend much less	8	0.3	0.5
(Don't know)	2.6	3.5	2.4
(Refusal/Not answered)	-	-	-

	[SocSpnd4]	[SocSpnd5]	[SocSpnd6]
	%	%	%
Spend much more	4.5	16.7	18.0
Spend more	30.2	55.9	62.5
Spend the same as now	42.9	23.3	16.4
Spend less	15.1	2.0	0.6
Spend much less	3.2	0.1	0.1
(Don't know)	4.0	2.0	2.3
(Refusal/Not answered)	-	-	-

Q225   [FalseClm]   N=3199
I will read two statements. For each one please say whether you agree or disagree. Firstly...
Large numbers of people these days **falsely** claim benefits.
IF AGREE OR DISAGREE: Strongly or slightly?

Q226   [FailClm]   N=3199
(And do you agree or disagree that...)
Large numbers of people who are eligible for benefits these days **fail** to claim them.
IF AGREE OR DISAGREE: Strongly or slightly?

	[FalseClm]	[FailClm]
	%	%
Agree strongly	57.0	37.8
Agree slightly	26.7	42.3
Disagree slightly	7.4	11.5
Disagree strongly	4.3	2.6
(Don't know)	4.5	5.8
(Refusal/Not answered)	-	-

Q227   [Dole]   N=3199
Opinions differ about the level of benefits for unemployed people.
Which of these two statements comes closest to your own view ...READ OUT...

%	
23.4	..benefits for unemployed people are **too low** and cause hardship,
54.0	or, benefits for unemployed people are **too high** and discourage them from finding jobs?
15.8	(Neither)
0.0	**EDIT ONLY:** BOTH: UNEMPLOYMENT BENEFIT CAUSES HARDSHIP BUT CAN'T BE HIGHER OR THERE WOULD BE NO INCENTIVE TO WORK
0.3	**EDIT ONLY:** BOTH: UNEMPLOYMENT BENEFIT CAUSES HARDSHIP TO SOME, WHILE OTHERS DO WELL OUT OF IT
0.6	**EDIT ONLY:** ABOUT RIGHT/IN BETWEEN
0.6	Other answer (WRITE IN)
2.8	(Don't know)
3.1	(Refusal/Not answered)
-	

VERSIONS A AND B: ASK ALL

Q230   [TaxSpend]
CARD B3
Suppose the government had to choose between the three options on this card. Which do you think it should choose?

N=2130

%
5.6   Reduce taxes and spend **less** on health, education and social benefits
41.7   Keep taxes and spending on these services at the **same** level as now
49.1   Increase taxes and spend **more** on health, education and social benefits
2.7   (None)
1.0   (Don't know)
-    (Refusal/Not answered)

Q231   [IncomGap]
Thinking of income levels generally in Britain today, would you say that the **gap** between those with high incomes and those with low incomes is ..READ OUT...

N=2130

%
72.9   ... too large,
21.5   about right,
2.2   or, too small?
3.4   (Don't know)
0.1   (Refusal/Not answered)

Q232   [SRInc]
%
Among which group would you place yourself ...READ OUT...

N=2130

5.0   ... high income,
56.6   middle income,
38.0   or, low income?
0.4   (Don't know)
0.1   (Refusal/Not answered)

Q233   [HIncDiff]
CARD B4
Which of the phrases on this card would you say comes closest to your feelings about your household's income these days?

N=2130

%
39.7   Living comfortably on present income
45.6   Coping on present income
11.2   Finding it difficult on present income
3.2   Finding it very difficult on present income
0.3   (Other answer (WRITE IN))
0.1   (Don't know)
0.1   (Refusal/Not answered)

ASK ALL

Q236   [MumPoor]
Think of an unemployed single mother with a young child. Their only income comes from state benefits. Would you say that they ... **READ OUT**...

N=3199

%
3.3   ... have more than enough to live on,
36.4   have enough to live on,
44.2   are hard up,
6.9   or, are really poor?
9.1   (Don't know)
-    (Refusal/Not answered)

Q237   [PenlPoor]
Now think about a pensioner living alone. Her only income comes from the state pension and other benefits specially for pensioners. Would you say that she ... **READ OUT**...

N=3199

%
0.8   ... has more than enough to live on,
21.9   has enough to live on,
59.3   is hard up,
14.2   or, is really poor?
3.9   (Don't know)
-    (Refusal/Not answered)

Q238 [CarPoor] *N=3199*
And what about a woman who can't work because she has to look after her husband or partner who has a long-term illness. Their only income comes from state benefits.
Would you say that they ... **READ OUT** ..
%
0.4 ... have more than enough to live on,
16.6 have enough to live on,
63.4 are hard up,
12.5 or, are really poor?
7.1 (Don't know)
- (Refusal/Not answered)

Q239 [MumOn130] *N=3199*
Now thinking again about that unemployed single mother with a young child. After rent, their income is £130 a week. Would you say that they
... **READ OUT** ...
%
7.7 ... have more than enough to live on,
48.2 have enough to live on,
37.7 are hard up,
4.8 or, are really poor?
1.6 (Don't know)
- (Refusal/Not answered)

Q240 [PenOn105] *N=3199*
And thinking again about that pensioner living alone. After rent, her income is £105 a week. Would you say that she ... **READ OUT** ...
%
2.2 ... has more than enough to live on,
36.8 has enough to live on,
50.3 is hard up,
9.6 or, is really poor?
1.1 (Don't know)
- (Refusal/Not answered)

Q241 [CarOn146] *N=3199*
And thinking again about that woman who can't work because she has to look after her husband or partner who has a long-term illness. After rent, their income is £146 a week. Would you say they ... **READ OUT** ...
%
1.9 ... have more than enough to live on,
27.5 have enough to live on,
59.0 are hard up,
9.8 or, are really poor?
1.9 (Don't know)
- (Refusal/Not answered)

Q242 [PenKnow] *N=3199*
How much do you feel you know about pensions and how they work ...READ OUT...
%
2.5 ...a great deal,
14.5 quite a lot,
35.7 a bit,
36.1 not very much,
11.2 or, nothing at all?
- (Don't know)
- (Refusal/Not answered)

ASK ALL RETIRED
Q243 [SoldHome] *N=636*
Have you sold a house or flat to help fund your retirement?
IF ASKED: 'House or flat' is the building but not the contents.
%
7.9 Yes
91.9 No
- (Don't know)
0.2 (Refusal/Not answered)

ASK ALL NOT RETIRED AND RETIRED PEOPLE WHO HAVE NOT SOLD HOME

N=3149

Q244 [SellHom2]
CARD (B3/B5)
How likely do you think it is that you will sell a house or flat to help fund your retirement?
IF ASKED: 'House or flat' is the building but not the contents.

%
14.9 Very likely
19.9 Fairly likely
31.2 Not very likely
31.0 Not at all likely
3.0 (Don't know)
0.1 (Refusal/Not answered)

ASK ALL WHO HAVE SOLD HOME OR ARE LIKELY TO DO

Q245- CARD (B4/B6)
Q248   N=1241
Which of the options on this card best describes this house or flat that you (have sold/will sell)?
INTERVIEWER: IF MORE THAN ONE HOUSE OR FLAT CODE ALL THAT APPLY
Multicoded (Maximum of 4 codes)

%
67.8 Own home   [SellOwnH]
16.8 House or flat bought as an investment   [SellInv]
6.3 Inherited house or flat that is not main home   [SellInh]
2.5 Other house or flat   [SellOth]
1.0 (Don't know)
7.7 (Refusal/Not answered)

ASK ALL NOT RETIRED

Q249-   N=2492
Q251 CARD (B5/B7)
Are you (or your employer) currently paying contributions to any of the pension arrangements on this card?
PROBE: Which others?
CODE ALL THAT APPLY
INTERVIEWER: DO NOT INCLUDE 'FROZEN' PENSIONS NOT BEING CONTRIBUTED TO
Multicoded (Maximum of 3 codes)

%
15.2 A personal or private pension, or retirement annuity,   [PenCPriv]
35.6 A company or occupational pension run by your employer   [PenCOcc]
      A stakeholder pension   [PenCStak]
3.6 None of these   [PenCNone]
50.9
0.0 (Don't know)
0.0 (Refusal/Not answered)

Q252-   N=2492
Q254 CARD (B6/B8)
(Apart from these) do you have any of the pension arrangements on this card - I mean pensions that you (or an employer) are **not** currently contributing to?
PROBE: Which others?
CODE ALL THAT APPLY
Multicoded (Maximum of 3 codes)

%
11.3 A personal or private pension, or retirement annuity,   [PenNPriv]
18.6 A company or occupational pension run by a current or past employer   [PenNOcc]
1.9 A stakeholder pension   [PenNStak]
70.7 None of these   [PenNNone]
0.2 (Don't know)
0.0 (Refusal/Not answered)

Q255 [RetFin]
(When you have retired from you main job/ In retirement), do you think you will be ...READ OUT..

%
13.2 ...financially better off than now,
21.9 the same,
53.1 or, worse off?
7.8 (No main job)
4.0 (Don't know)
- (Refusal/Not answered)

N=2492

Q256 [RetMon]
CARD (B7/B9)   N=2492
Thinking about what you will be living on (when you have retired from you main job/in retirement), including any money from pensions, benefits, savings or investments, and any earnings. Do you think you will have enough money to cover basic costs such as housing, heating and food?

%
24.3 Definitely
50.8 Probably
15.9 Probably not
2.8 Definitely not
3.5 (No main job)
2.8 (Don't know)
-    (Refusal/Not answered)

ASK ALL RETIRED
Q257- CARD (B8/B10)   N=636
Q229 Which, if any, of these are you **yourself** currently receiving money from (Do not include any pensions your spouse/partner receives)?
PROBE: Which others?
CODE ALL THAT APPLY
Multicoded (Maximum of 3 codes)

%
21.2 A personal or private pension, or retirement annuity   [PenRPriv]
52.0 A company or occupational pension run by a past employer   [PenROcc]
0.8 A stakeholder pension   [PenRStak]
32.2 None of these   [PenRNone]
0.3 (Don't know)
0.6 (Refusal/Not answered)

ASK ALL RETIRED WHO ARE MARRIED OR LIVING WITH A PARTNER WHO IS ALSO RETIRED
N=266
Q260- CARD (B8/B10) AGAIN
Q262 And which, if any, of these is your spouse/partner currently receiving money from?
PROBE: Which others?
CODE ALL THAT APPLY
Multicoded (Maximum of 3 codes)

%
15.2 A personal or private pension, or retirement annuity   [PenPPriv]
51.4 A company or occupational pension run by a past employer   [PenPOcc]
1.7 A stakeholder pension   [PenPStak]
35.3 None of these   [PenPNone]
0.8 (Don't know)
0.8 (Refusal/Not answered)

ASK ALL RETIRED
Q263 [RetdFin]   N=636
Do you think you are now ...READ OUT.. ..financially better off than you were before you retired from your main job,
the same,
or, worse off?
(No main job)
(Don't know)
(Refusal/Not answered)

%
14.6
24.2
57.6
2.6
0.5
0.3

Q264 [RetdMon]
CARD (B9/B11)   N=636
Thinking about what you are living on in retirement, including any money from pensions, benefits, savings or investments, and any earnings. Do you have enough money to cover basic costs such as housing, heating and food?

%
63.4 Always
27.0 Mostly
6.4 Sometimes
2.8 Hardly ever / never
0.2 (Don't know)
0.3 (Refusal/Not answered)

ASK ALL RETIRED ABOVE STATE PENSION AGE   N=548
Q265 [RPension]
      On the whole would you say the present **state** pension is
      on the low side, reasonable, or on the high side?
      IF 'ON THE LOW SIDE': Very low or a bit low?
      %
35.5 Very low
40.5 A bit low
22.4 Reasonable
0.2   On the high side
1.1   (Don't know)
0.3   (Refusal/Not answered)

Q266 [RPenInYr]   N=548
      Do you expect your state pension in a year's time to
      purchase **more** than it does now, **less**, or about the **same**?
      %
3.7   More
62.6 Less
32.0 About the same
1.4   (Don't know)
0.3   (Refusal/Not answered)

ASK ALL RETIRED
Q267 [RetirAg2]   N=636
      At what age did you retire from work?
      NEVER WORKED, CODE: 00
      Median: 60 years

IF ANSWER GIVEN AT [RetirAg2]
Q268 [RRetPlcy]   N=636
      Did you have to retire because of your employer's
      policy on retirement age?
      %
14.7 Yes
81.2 No
2.1   Left work before retirement
-     (Don't know)
0.2   (Refusal/Not answered)

IF 'no' AT [RRetPlcy]
Q269- CARD (B10/B12)   N=636
Q275 Why did you retire?
      Please choose a phrase from this card.
      CODE AS MANY AS APPLY.
      Multicoded (Maximum of 7 codes)
      %
20.4 I left because of ill health   [RRetIll]
6.7   I left to look after someone else   [RRetCare]
3.7   I left because my husband/wife/partner retired [RRetPrtn]
6.7   It was made attractive to me to retire early [RRetPack]
13.2 I lost my job/I was made redundant/
30.4 My firm closed down   [RRetLJob]
7.0   I just wanted to retire   [RRetWant]
-     Other answer (WRITE IN)   [RRetOth]
      (Don't know)
0.2   (Refusal/Not answered)

ASK ALL
      [WhenSave]
Q278 Some people regularly put money aside into pensions   N=3199
      or savings for their retirement. When do you think a
      person needs to start doing this in order to be sure
      of having a decent standard of living when they
      retire...READ OUT...
      %
77.7 ...in their 20s or earlier,
14.6 their 30s,
3.3   40s,
0.7   50s,
0.2   or 60s?
2.1   (Not necessary to do this/Never)
1.5   (Don't know)
0.0   (Refusal/Not answered)

Q279 [SavFrRet]
CARD (B11/B13)   N=3199
Please tell me, from this card, how much you agree or
disagree with the following statement.
The government should encourage people to provide
something for their own retirement instead of relying
only on the state pension.

%
33.4   Agree strongly
46.6   Agree
9.1   Neither agree nor disagree
7.8   Disagree
2.6   Disagree strongly
0.6   (Don't know)
-      (Refusal/Not answered)

ASK ALL NOT RETIRED
Q280 [AffSvRet]
CARD (B11/B13) AGAIN   N=2492
(And how much do you agree or disagree with this
statement...)
...I can't afford to put money aside for retirement at
the moment.

%
20.8   Agree strongly
29.0   Agree
10.3   Neither agree nor disagree
31.5   Disagree
7.9   Disagree strongly
0.5   (Don't know)
0.0   (Refusal/Not answered)

ASK ALL
[InfoRet1]   N=3199
Q281 CARD (B12/B14)
Which of these would be your first choice for
information and advice on pensions and money in
retirement?
CODE ONE ONLY

%
33.3   Financial adviser
12.3   Bank/Building society
6.0   Employer
4.7   Accountant
12.3   Friends/ family/ colleagues
3.3   The Government/ DSS/ DWP
0.8   Insurance company
6.8   Pension provider
0.9   Trade union
6.8   Citizens Advice Bureau
2.8   Help the Aged, Age Concern or a similar organisation
3.0   The media (newspapers, TV, radio)
2.3   Internet generally
0.4   Other (SPECIFY)
2.7   (None of these)
1.7   (Don't know)
-      (Refusal/Not answered)

Q284 **IF NOT 'none of these' OR DON'T KNOW AT [InfoRet1]**
[InfoRet2]
CARD (B12/B14) AGAIN
And which would be your second choice?
CODE ONE ONLY

N=3199

%
15.7 Financial adviser
13.8 Bank/Building society
6.3 Employer
7.3 Accountant
10.7 Friends/ family/ colleagues
3.7 The Government/ DSS/ DWP
3.3 Insurance company
11.2 Pension provider
1.9 Trade union
5.9 Citizens Advice Bureau
4.2 Help the Aged, Age Concern or a similar organisation
3.5 The media (newspapers, TV, radio)
4.1 Internet generally
0.2 Other (SPECIFY)
2.6 (None of these)
1.1 (Don't know)
1.8 (Refusal/Not answered)

Equality and inequality (versions A and B)

Q288 **VERSIONS A AND B: ASK ALL**
[WhyNeed]
CARD C1

N=2130

Why do you think there are people who live in need?
Of the four views on this card, which **one** comes
closest to your own?
CODE ONE ONLY

%
15.8 Because they have been unlucky
21.0 Because of laziness or lack of willpower
16.1 Because of injustice in our society
38.3 It's an inevitable part of modern life
6.2 (None of these)
2.6 (Don't know)
- (Refusal/Not answered)

Q289 [GovPri1]
CARD C2

N=2130

Some people think that government is best at running
important services like health and education. Others
think that private companies would do a better job.
Please say, for each of the following, who you think
would be best at ...:
...making sure services go to the people who need
them most?

Q290 [GovPri2]
CARD C2 AGAIN

N=2130

(Who do you think would be best at ...)
...running services cost-effectively?

Q291 [GovPri3]
CARD C2 AGAIN

N=2130

(Who do you think would be best at ...)
...providing a good quality service?

	[GovPri1]	[GovPri2]	[GovPri3]
	%	%	%
Definitely government	30.2	13.3	12.3
Probably government	42.8	25.2	28.4
Probably private companies	17.4	43.7	41.2
Definitely private companies	3.6	11.2	9.8
(Neither / other answer)	2.1	2.4	3.5
(Same / no difference)	1.6	1.8	2.1
(Don't know)	2.3	2.4	2.7
(Refusal/Not answered)	-	-	-

N=2130

Q292   [PriPay]
Imagine that people paid privately for things like schools and health insurance, and taxes were lower as a result. In the long run, would a system like this mean you and your household were financially better off, or would you be worse off?
INTERVIEWER PROMPT: Is that a **lot** or a **little** (better/worse) off?

%
8.5   A lot better off
24.2   A little better off
25.7   A little worse off
25.8   A lot worse off
10.1   (No difference)
5.7   (Don't know)
-   (Refusal/Not answered)

VERSIONS A AND B: ASK ALL WITH ODD SERIAL NUMBERS
N=1053

Q293   [MeanCBa]
Suppose the government has a set amount of money to spend on child benefits. Which of these do you think is the best way to spend that money ...READ OUT ...
INTERVIEWER: IF ASKED, YOU CAN CONFIRM THIS IS ABOUT MEANS TESTING

%
73.5   ...families on low incomes should get higher child benefits, even if that means they have to fill in forms to prove it,
23.9   or, every family should get the same amount of child benefits even if that means money goes to families who don't really need it?
1.5   (Other answer - please specify)
0.7   (Don't know)
0.3   (Refusal/Not answered)

Q296   [MeanSPa]
N=1053
Now, suppose the government has a set amount of money to spend on state pensions. Which of these do you think is the best way to spend that money ...READ OUT ...
INTERVIEWER: IF ASKED, YOU CAN CONFIRM THIS IS ABOUT MEANS TESTING

%
61.2   ...pensioners on low incomes should get a higher state pension, even if that means they have to fill in forms to prove it,
37.1   or, every pensioner should get the same state pension even if that means money goes to pensioners who don't really need it?
0.8   (Other answer - please specify)
0.7   (Don't know)
0.2   (Refusal/Not answered)

Q299   [MeanDBa]
N=1053
Now, suppose the government has a set amount of money to spend on disability benefits. Which of these do you think is the best way to spend that money ...READ OUT ...
INTERVIEWER: IF ASKED, YOU CAN CONFIRM THIS IS ABOUT MEANS TESTING

%
68.2   ...disabled people on low incomes should get higher disability benefits, even if that means they have to fill in forms to prove it,
28.4   or, every disabled person should get the same amount of disability benefits even if that means money goes to disabled people who don't really need it?
2.1   (Other answer - please specify)
1.1   (Don't know)
0.2   (Refusal/Not answered)

VERSIONS A AND B: ASK ALL WITH EVEN SERIAL NUMBERS

N=1076

Q302 [MeanCBb]
Suppose the government has a set amount of money to
spend on child benefits. Which of these do you think is
the best way to spend that money ...READ OUT...
INTERVIEWER: IF ASKED, YOU CAN CONFIRM THIS IS ABOUT
MEANS TESTING

%
68.3   ..only families on low incomes should get child
       benefits, even if that means they have to fill in forms
       to prove it,
29.0   or, every family should get child benefits even if that
       means money goes to families who don't really need it?
1.6   (Other answer - please specify)
0.9   (Don't know)
0.2   (Refusal/Not answered)

Q305 [MeanSPb]   N=1076
Now, suppose the government has a set amount of money
to spend on state pensions. Which of these do you think
is the best way to spend that money ...READ OUT...
INTERVIEWER: IF ASKED, YOU CAN CONFIRM THIS IS ABOUT
MEANS TESTING

%
37.6   ..only pensioners on low incomes should get a state
       pension, even if that means they have to fill in forms
       to prove it,
59.4   or, every pensioner should get a state pension even if
       that means money goes to pensioners who don't really
       need it?
1.6   (Other answer - please specify)
1.2   (Don't know)
0.2   (Refusal/Not answered)

Q308 [MeanDBb]   N=1076
Now, suppose the government has a set amount of
money to spend on disability benefits. Which of
these do you think is the best way to spend that
money ...READ OUT...
INTERVIEWER: IF ASKED, YOU CAN CONFIRM THIS IS ABOUT
MEANS TESTING

%
45.7   ..only disabled people on low incomes should get
       disability benefits, even if that means they have to
       fill in forms to prove it,
50.9   or, every disabled person should get disability
       benefits even if that means money goes to disabled
       people who don't really need it?
1.9   (Other answer - please specify)
1.3   (Don't know)
0.2   (Refusal/Not answered)

VERSIONS A AND B: ASK ALL

N=2130

Q311 [TaxRaise]
CARD C3
Suppose the government had to raise extra money from
taxes to pay for spending on education, health, and
social benefits. This card shows three different
ways they could do this, and what this would mean
for two different people, one earning £15,000
before tax and the other earning £30,000 before tax.
Which option do you think the government should
choose?

%
7.0   Each person should pay the **same amount** of money in
       tax (say, £200 a year extra)
42.9   Each person should pay the **same share** of their
       earnings in tax
       (so the person earning £15,000 might pay £150 and
       the person earning £30,000 might pay £300)
47.3   The person earning less should pay a **smaller share**
       of their earnings in tax, and the person earning
       more pay a **larger share**
       (so the person earning £15,000 might pay £100 and
       the person earning £30,000 might pay £400)
0.9   (None of these)
1.9   (Don't know)
0.0   (Refusal/Not answered)

Q312 [TaxPayD2]
CARD C4   N=2130

Do you think that people with high incomes pay a **larger** share of their income in various taxes than those with low incomes, the **same share**, or a **smaller share**?

%
16.7 Much larger share
48.1 Larger share
19.3 The same share
10.7 Smaller share
1.2 Much smaller share
4.0 (Don't know)
0.0 (Refusal/Not answered)

Q313 [HiLow1]
CARD C5   N=2130

Imagine two people who had to stop work due to a disability. One had been a high earner and the other had been a low earner. Which of the options on this card comes closest to your view about their entitlement to disability benefits?

%
10.4 The high earner should get more than the low earner because they have paid more in taxes
55.4 The high and low earner should get the same amount
29.8 The low earner should get more than the high earner because they are more likely to be in need
2.2 The high earner should not get anything because they can afford to provide for themselves
0.7 (Other answer (PLEASE SPECIFY))
1.5 (Don't know)
0.0 (Refusal/Not answered)

Q316 [HiLow2]
CARD C5 AGAIN   N=2130

Now suppose two people in a firm retired. Which of the options on this card comes closest to your view about their entitlement to a state pension?

%
11.7 The high earner should get more than the low earner because they have paid more in taxes
55.6 The high and low earner should get the same amount
26.8 The low earner should get more than the high earner because they are more likely to be in need
3.7 The high earner should not get anything because they can afford to provide for themselves
0.5 (Other answer (PLEASE SPECIFY))
1.5 (Don't know)
0.0 (Refusal/Not answered)

Q319 [HiLow3]
CARD C5 AGAIN   N=2130

Now what about child benefits. Which of the options on this card comes closest to your view?

%
3.8 The high earner should get more than the low earner because they have paid more in taxes
41.8 The high and low earner should get the same amount
44.3 The low earner should get more than the high earner because they are more likely to be in need
7.7 The high earner should not get anything because they can afford to provide for themselves
0.8 (Other answer (PLEASE SPECIFY))
1.5 (Don't know)
0.0 (Refusal/Not answered)

Q322   [TaxREduc]   N=2130
        Now think of people who choose not to use the state
        education system for their children, and instead pay
        for private education. Which of these views comes
        closest to yours ...READ OUT...
   %
77.1   ...it's their choice to go private and they should pay
        the same taxes as everyone else,
20.5   or, their taxes should be reduced because it's not fair
        that they are paying twice?
 1.7   (Neither/It depends)
 0.7   (Don't know)
 0.0   (Refusal/Not answered)

Q323   [TaxRNHS]   N=2130
        Now think of people who choose not to use the National
        Health Service for certain treatments, and instead pay
        for these privately. Which of these views comes closest
        to yours ...READ OUT...
   %
76.8   ...it's their choice to go private and they should pay
        the same taxes as everyone else,
20.6   or, their taxes should be reduced because it's not fair
        that they are paying twice?
 2.2   (Neither/It depends)
 0.4   (Don't know)
 0.0   (Refusal/Not answered)

Q324   [TaxRpen]   N=2130
        Now think of people who give up the right to part of
        their state pension and instead make contributions to a
        private pension scheme. Which of these views comes
        closest to yours ...READ OUT...
   %
65.7   ...it's their choice to go private and they should pay
        the same taxes as everyone else,
29.8   or, their taxes should be reduced because it's not fair
        that they are paying twice?
 2.6   (Neither/It depends)
 1.8   (Don't know)
 0.0   (Refusal/Not answered)

Q325   [HhBetOff]   N=2130
        In Britain, some households are financially better
        off than others. Of every 100 households in this
        country how many would you say were financially
        better off than yours?
        INTERVIEWER ENTER NUMBER OF HOUSEHOLDS
        Range: 0 ... 100
   %
13.0   Median: 50 out of 100
 0.1   (Don't know)
        (Refusal/Not answered)

Q326   [WhatIncH]
        A lot of people talk about incomes being high or
        low. Thinking about a person living on their own,
        how large would their income have to be before you
        would say they had a high income?
        INTERVIEWER: ENTER WHOLE POUNDS. TIME PERIOD AT NEXT
        QUESTION
   %
        Median: £30,000 per year
 8.3   (Don't know)
 0.1   (Refusal/Not answered)

        IF ANSWER GIVEN AT [WhatIncH]
Q327   [IncHPd]
        INTERVIEWER CODE OR ASK IF NECESSARY: What time
        period does that cover?
   %
15.8   per week
 1.8   per month
74.1   per year
 -      other time period (specify)
 -      (Don't know)
 8.3   (Refusal/Not answered)

        VERSIONS A AND B: ASK ALL
Q330   [WhatIncL]
        And again, thinking about a person living on their
        own, how small would their income have to be before
        you would say they had a low income?
        INTERVIEWER: IF ASKED, INCOME INCLUDES BENEFITS
        INTERVIEWER: ENTER WHOLE POUNDS. TIME PERIOD AT NEXT
        QUESTION
   %
        Median: £10,000 per Year
 -      (Don't know)
 6.3   (Refusal/Not answered)

Q331 [IncLPd]
IF ANSWER GIVEN AT [WhatIncL]
INTERVIEWER CODE OR ASK IF NECESSARY: What time period does that cover?
N=2130
%
20.0 per week
1.8 per month
71.8 per year
0.1 other time period (specify)
- (Don't know)
6.3 (Refusal/Not answered)

Q334 [BenGovSp]
VERSIONS A AND B: ASK ALL
N=2130
CARD C6
Thinking of people on low incomes, how much do you think they benefit from overall government spending on health and education, compared to people on high incomes?
%
10.0 Benefit a lot less
13.8 Benefit a little less
41.4 Benefit about the same
20.7 Benefit a little more
9.8 Benefit a lot more
1.5 (It depends)
2.7 (Don't know)
0.0 (Refusal/Not answered)

Transport (version C)

Q335 **VERSION C: ASK ALL**
[FourWay] **(NOT ON SCREEN)**
DIVIDES THE SAMPLE IN FOUR RANDOM QUARTERS
Range: 1 ... 4
N=1069

Q336 [TransCar]
(May I just check...) ... do you, or does anyone in your household, own or have the regular use of a car or a van?
IF 'YES': Is this yourself, someone else in the household or both?
N=1069
%
27.4 Yes, respondent only
17.6 Yes, other(s) only
37.9 Yes, both
17.0 No
- (Don't know)
- (Refusal/Not answered)

Q337 [TrfPb6U]
CARD C1
Now thinking about traffic and transport problems, how serious a problem **for you** is congestion on motorways?
N=1069

Q338 [TrfPb9U]
CARD C1 AGAIN
(And how serious a problem **for you** is ...) traffic congestion in towns and cities?
N=1069

Q339 [TrfPb10U]
CARD C1 AGAIN
(And how serious a problem **for you** are ...) exhaust fumes from traffic in towns and cities?
N=1069

Q340 [TrfPb11U]
CARD C1 AGAIN
(And how serious a problem **for you** is ...) noise from traffic in towns and cities?
N=1069

VERSION C: RANDOM VERSION 1: IF RESPONDENT HAS ACCESS TO CAR VAN (AT [TransCar]) OR RANDOM VERSION 4: IF RESPONDENT DRIVES (AT [Drive])   N=526

Q342 [GetAbB1]
CARD C2
I am going to read out some of the things that might get people to **cut down** on the number of car journeys they take. For each one, please tell me what effect, if any, this might have on how much **you yourself** use the car to get about.
...gradually doubling the cost of petrol over the next ten years.

Q343 [GetAbB12]   N=526
CARD C2 AGAIN
(What effect, if any, might this have on how much **you yourself** use the car:)
...charging all motorists around £2 each time they enter or drive through a city or town centre outside London at peak times?

Q344 [GetAbB5]   N=526
CARD C2 AGAIN
(What effect, if any, might this have on how much **you yourself** use the car:)
...charging £1 for every 50 miles motorists travel on motorways?

Q345 [GetAbB6]   N=526
CARD C2 AGAIN
(What effect, if any, might this have on how much **you yourself** use the car)
...making parking penalties and restrictions much more severe?

	[GetAbB1]	[GetAbB12]
	%	%
Might use car even more	0.6	0.1
Might use car a little less	22.4	22.5
Might use car quite a bit less	15.9	13.9
Might give up using car	4.6	4.1
It would make no difference	25.7	28.1
(Don't know)	0.1	0.6
(Refusal/Not answered)	-	-

	[Trfpb6U]	[Trfpb9U]
	%	%
A very serious problem	9.4	17.5
A serious problem	19.7	35.9
Not a very serious problem	34.2	29.5
Not a problem at all	36.4	17.0
(Don't know)	0.3	0.1
(Refusal/Not answered)	-	-

	[Trfpb10U]	[Trfpb11U]
	%	%
A very serious problem	20.2	8.2
A serious problem	37.5	25.0
Not a very serious problem	26.7	43.5
Not a problem at all	15.1	23.2
(Don't know)	0.4	0.2
(Refusal/Not answered)	-	-

Q341 [Drive]
May I just check, do you yourself drive a car at all these days?   N=1069

%	
69.9	Yes
30.1	No
-	(Don't know)
-	(Refusal/Not answered)

VERSION C: RANDOM VERSION 3: IF RESPONDENT HAS ACCESS TO CAR VAN (AT [TransCar]) OR RANDOM VERSION 2: IF RESPONDENT DRIVES (AT [Drive])

Q349   [GetAbB1X]   N=544
CARD C6
I am going to read out some of the things that might get people to **cut down** on the number of car journeys they take. For each one, please tell me what effect, if any, this might have on how much **you yourself** use the car to get about.
...gradually doubling the cost of petrol over the next ten years.

Q350   [GetAB12X]   N=544
CARD C6 AGAIN
(What effect, if any, might this have on how much **you yourself** use the car:)
...charging all motorists around £2 each time they enter or drive through a city or town centre outside London at peak times?

Q351   [GetAbB5X]   N=544
CARD C6 AGAIN
(What effect, if any, might this have on how much **you yourself** use the car:)
...charging £1 for every 50 miles motorists travel on motorways?

Q352   [GetAbB6X]   N=544
CARD C6 AGAIN
(What effect, if any, might this have on how much **you yourself** use the car)
...making parking penalties and restrictions much more severe?

	[GetAbB5]	[GetAbB6]
	%	%
Might use car even more	0.2	0.5
Might use car a little less	16.7	15.6
Might use car quite a bit less	7.9	8.5
Might give up using car	2.8	2.9
It would make no difference	41.3	41.0
(Don't know)	0.4	0.7
(Refusal/Not answered)	-	-

Q346   [GetBoth3]   N=526
CARD C3
Now suppose that the two things on this card were done **at the same time**. What effect, if any, might this have on how much you yourself use the car?
Charging motorists £2 for entering town centres outside London at peak times **but at the same time** greatly improving the **reliability** of local public transport?

Q347   [GetBoth4]   N=526
CARD C4
And what about charging motorists £2 for entering town centres outside London at peak times **but at the same time** greatly improving the **frequency** of local public transport?

Q348   [GetBoth5]   N=526
CARD C5
And what about charging motorists £2 for entering town centres outside London at peak times **but at the same time halving the fares** for local public transport?

	[GetBoth3]	[GetBoth4]	[GetBoth5]
	%	%	%
Might use car even more	0.7	-	0.4
Might use car a little less	22.4	22.7	14.3
Might use car quite a bit less	21.0	21.3	24.0
Might give up using car	5.2	6.0	7.9
It would make no difference	20.1	19.4	22.4
(Don't know)	-	-	0.3
(Refusal/Not answered)	-	-	-

	[GetAB1X]	[GetAB12X]
	%	%
Might use car even more	0.8	0.6
Might use car a little less	19.4	19.3
Might use car quite a bit less	15.2	15.7
Might give up having a car altogether	6.0	2.1
It would make no difference	25.3	28.7
(Don't know)	-	0.3
(Refusal/Not answered)	-	-

	[GetAbB5X]	[GetAbB6X]
	%	%
Might use car even more	1.0	0.4
Might use car a little less	13.0	14.4
Might use car quite a bit less	10.0	11.4
Might give up having a car altogether	2.2	2.7
It would make no difference	40.1	37.5
(Don't know)	0.4	0.3
(Refusal/Not answered)	-	-

Q353 [GetBot3X]
CARD C7　　　　　　　　　　　N=544
Now suppose that the two things on this card were done **at the same time**. What effect, if any, might this have on how much you yourself use the car?
Charging motorists £2 for entering town centres outside London at peak times greatly improving the **reliability** of local public transport?

Q354 [GetBot4X]
CARD C8　　　　　　　　　　　N=544
And what about charging motorists £2 for entering town centres outside London at peak times **but at the same time** greatly improving the **frequency** of local public transport?

Q355 [GetBot5X]
CARD C9　　　　　　　　　　　N=544
And what about charging motorists £2 for entering town centres outside London at peak times **but at the same time halving the fares** for local public transport?

	[GetBot3X]	[GetBot4X]	[GetBot5X]
	%	%	%
Might use car even more	0.3	0.2	0.7
Might use car a little less	19.5	18.4	14.5
Might use car quite a bit less	21.0	21.6	21.9
Might give up having a car altogether	4.5	3.8	7.0
It would make no difference	21.2	22.3	22.2
(Don't know)	0.2	0.4	0.4
(Refusal/Not answered)	-	-	-

N=1069

VERSION C: IF 'yes' AT [Drive]

Q356 [Travel1]
CARD C10
How often nowadays do you **usually** travel ...by car as a driver?

N=1069

VERSION C: ASK ALL

Q357 [Travel2]
CARD C10 AGAIN
(How often nowadays do you **usually**) ...travel by car as a passenger?

N=1069

Q358 [Travel3]
CARD C10 AGAIN
(How often nowadays do you **usually**) ...travel by local bus?

N=1069

Q359 [Travel4]
CARD C10 AGAIN
(How often nowadays do you **usually**) ...travel by train?

	[Travel1]	[Travel2]
	%	%
Every day or nearly every day	45.1	9.9
2-5 days a week	18.7	25.9
Once a week	3.6	22.3
Less often but at least once a month	1.1	15.8
Less often than that	0.9	11.7
Never nowadays	0.6	14.4
(Don't know)	-	-
(Refusal/Not answered)	-	-

Education

ASK FIRST HALF OF SAMPLE (ODD SERIAL NUMBER)   N=1591
Q362   [EdSpend1]
       CARD D1
       Now some questions about education.
       Which of the groups on this card, if any, would be
       your highest priority for extra government spending
       on education?

       IF ANSWER AT [EdSpend1]   N=1591
Q363   [EdSpend2]
       CARD D1 AGAIN
       And which is your next highest priority?

	[EdSpend1]	[EdSpend2]
	%	%
Nursery or pre-school children	10.9	12.8
Primary school children	20.2	22.7
Secondary school children	29.9	23.1
Children with special educational needs	23.2	23.1
Students at colleges or universities	13.7	15.4
(None of these)	0.9	0.4
(Don't know)	1.0	0.6
(Refusal/Not answered)	0.1	2.1

ASK SECOND HALF OF SAMPLE (EVEN SERIAL NUMBER)   N=1608
Q364   [EdSpnd1c]
       CARD D2
       Now some questions about education.
       Which of the groups on this card, if any, would be
       your highest priority for extra government spending
       on education?

       IF ANSWER AT [EdSpnd1c]   N=1608
Q365   [EdSpnd2c]
       CARD D2 AGAIN
       And which is your next highest priority?

	[Travel3]	[Travel4]
	%	%
Every day or nearly every day	9.3	1.2
2-5 days a week	9.1	2.0
Once a week	8.0	2.4
Less often but at least once a month	8.5	12.6
Less often than that	15.3	35.6
Never nowadays	49.8	46.3
(Don't know)	0.1	-
(Refusal/Not answered)	-	-

Q360   [AirTrvl]   N=1069
       And how many trips did you make by plane during the
       last 12 months? Please count the outward and return
       flight and any transfers as one trip.
       INTERVIEWER WRITE IN ANSWER
       ACCEPT BEST ESTIMATE IF NECESSARY
       CODE 'NONE' AS 0
       Median : 1 trip

	[EdSpnd1c]	[EdSpnd2c]
	%	%
Nursery or pre-school children	10.1	9.9
Primary school children	19.2	24.5
Secondary school children	31.9	22.3
Children with special educational needs	23.7	19.2
Students at universities	9.5	12.3
Students in further education	3.7	9.2
(None of these)	1.0	0.5
(Don't know)	0.8	0.3
(Refusal/Not answered)	0.1	1.9

ASK ALL

Q366 [PrimImp1]
CARD D3
Here are a number of things that some people think
would improve education in our schools.
Which do you think would be the **most** useful one for
improving the education of children in **primary** schools
- aged (5-11/5-12) years? Please look at the whole list
before deciding.

N=3199

%	
1.8	More information available about individual schools
8.0	More links between parents and schools
12.9	More resources for buildings, books and equipment
16.3	Better quality teachers
39.4	Smaller class sizes
1.0	More emphasis on exams and tests
15.2	More emphasis on developing the child's skills and interests
2.4	Better leadership within individual schools
1.7	Other (WRITE IN)
1.3	(Don't know)
0.0	(Refusal/Not answered)

Q369 **IF ANSWER GIVEN AT [PrimImp1]**
[PrimImp2]
CARD D3 AGAIN
And which do you think would be the **next** most useful
one for children in **primary** schools?

N=3199

%	
1.4	More information available about individual schools
10.3	More links between parents and schools
21.6	More resources for buildings, books and equipment
15.8	Better quality teachers
18.9	Smaller class sizes
1.9	More emphasis on exams and tests
22.7	More emphasis on developing the child's skills and interests
4.5	Better leadership within individual schools
1.2	Other (WRITE IN)
0.3	(Don't know)
1.3	(Refusal/Not answered)

ASK ALL

Q372 [SecImp1]
CARD D4
And which do you think would be the **most** useful
thing for improving the education of children in
secondary schools aged (11-18/12-18) years?

%	
1.2	More information available about individual schools
5.1	More links between parents and schools
12.1	More resources for buildings, books and equipment
19.7	Better quality teachers
25.4	Smaller class sizes
3.5	More emphasis on exams and tests
14.1	More emphasis on developing the child's skills and interests
13.8	More training and preparation for jobs
1.7	Better leadership within
1.9	Other (WRITE IN)
1.5	(Don't know)
0.1	(Refusal/Not answered)

Q375 N=3199

IF ANSWER GIVEN AT [SecImp1]
[SecImp2]
CARD D4 AGAIN
And which do you think would be the **next** most useful one for children in **secondary** schools?

%
- 0.9 More information available about individual schools
- 6.2 More links between parents and schools
- 14.6 More resources for buildings, books and equipment
- 14.2 Better quality teachers
- 14.8 Smaller class sizes
- 4.3 More emphasis on exams and tests
- 16.9 More emphasis on developing the child's skills and interests
- 21.4 More training and preparation for jobs
- 3.6 Better leadership within individual schools
- 1.2 Other (WRITE IN)
- 0.3 (Don't know)
- 1.6 (Refusal/Not answered)

Q378 N=3199

ASK ALL
[SchSelec]
CARD D5
Which of the following statements comes closest to your views about what kind of secondary school children should go to?

%
- 47.8 Children should go to a different kind of secondary school, according to how well they do at primary school
- 49.7 All children should go to the same kind of secondary school, no matter how well or badly they do at primary school
- 2.4 (Don't know)
- 0.1 (Refusal/Not answered)

Q379 N=3199

[Advise16]
Suppose you were advising a 16 year old about their future. Would you say they should... READ OUT ...

%
- 42.2 ... stay on in full-time education to get their (A-levels (or A2-levels)/Highers (or Higher Stills))
- 13.5 or, study full-time to get vocational, rather than academic qualifications,
- 11.7 or, leave school and get training through a job?
- 32.2 (Varies/depends on the person)
- 0.3 (Don't know)
- 0.1 (Refusal/Not answered)

Q380 N=3199

IF 'stay on in full time education' OR 'varies' AT [Advise16]
[AdFail16]
Suppose this 16 year old had failed their school exams. If you were advising them on their future, would you say they should ... READ OUT ...

%
- 24.9 ... stay in full-time education and retake their exams,
- 16.6 or, study full-time to get vocational, rather than academic, qualifications,
- 12.6 or, leave school and get training through a job?
- 20.2 (Varies/depends on the person)
- 0.1 (Don't know)
- 0.4 (Refusal/Not answered)

Q381 N=3199

ASK ALL
[VocVAcad]
In the long-run, which do you think gives people more opportunities and choice in life ... READ OUT ...

%
- 46.9 ...having good practical skills and training,
- 22.5 or, having good academic results?
- 30.2 (Mixture/depends)
- 0.4 (Don't know)
- 0.1 (Refusal/Not answered)

Q382   [NursImpl]   N=3199
        Card D6
        This card shows a number of things that some people
        think would improve the nursery education and childcare
        outside the family, available for children aged under
        5. From what you know or have heard, which, if any,
        would be the **most important** improvement? Please look
        at the whole list before deciding.

%
20.9   Increasing the number of available nursery education
        and childcare places
13.5   More choice for parents in the sorts of nursery
        education and childcare available
25.0   Cheaper nursery education and childcare
10.4   More flexible opening hours or term times
5.8   More places for very young children
13.0   Better quality nursery and childcare staff
4.1   More information about the nursery education and
        childcare available locally
1.9   Other (please say what)
1.5   (None of these)
4.0   (Don't know)
0.1   (Refusal/Not answered)

**IF ANSWER GIVEN AT [NursImpl] (I.E. NOT
DK/REFUSAL/NONE)**
Q385   [NursImp2]   N=3199
        CARD D6
        And which, if any, would be the **next most** important
        improvement?
%
16.7   Increasing the number of available nursery education
        and childcare places
14.6   More choice for parents in the sorts of nursery
        education and childcare available
17.0   Cheaper nursery education and childcare
14.9   More flexible opening hours or term times
9.2   More places for very young children
13.8   Better quality nursery and childcare staff
5.9   More information about the nursery education and
        childcare available locally
0.8   Other (please say what)
1.1   (None of these)
0.5   (Don't know)
5.5   (Refusal/Not answered)

ASK ALL
Q388   [NurPayHi]   N=3199
        CARD D7
        I'd now like you to think about a couple with a
        relatively high income. Their child goes to a
        nursery while they both work. Who do you think
        should **mainly** be responsible for paying for the cost
        of this childcare?

Q389   [NurPayAv]   N=3199
        CARD D7 AGAIN
        Now think of a couple whose income is **about average**
        and whose child goes to a nursery while they both
        work. Who do you think should **mainly** be responsible
        for paying for the cost of this childcare?

Q390   [NurPayLo]   N=3199
        CARD D7
        And now think of a couple whose income is relatively
        low and whose child goes to a nursery while they
        both work. Who do you think should **mainly** be
        responsible for paying for the cost of this
        childcare?

	[NurPayHi]	[NurPayAv]	[NurPayLo]
	%	%	%
Mainly the government, through taxation,	9.8	30.3	65.4
Mainly their employers,	5.4	14.6	11.0
Mainly the couple themselves,	81.3	45.6	16.3
(Two or more groups equally)	2.9	8.5	6.5
(Don't know)	0.6	1.0	0.8
(Refusal/Not answered)	0.1	0.1	0.1

Q391 [HEdOpp]
CARD D8   N=3199
Do you feel that opportunities for young people in Britain to go on to **higher education** – to a university or college – should be increased or reduced, or are they at about the right level now?
IF INCREASED OR REDUCED: a lot or a little?

%
14.4 Increased a lot
20.3 Increased a little
47.3 About right
12.4 Reduced a little
3.5 Reduced a lot
2.2 (Don't know)
0.1 (Refusal/Not answered)

ASK ALL RESPONDENTS WHO HAVE OWN CHILD AGED 5-16 IN HOUSEHOLD

Q392 [ChLikUn2]
CARD D9   N=657
Taking your answers from this card, how likely do you think it is that any of your children who are still at school will go to university?

%
32.2 Very likely
42.7 Fairly likely
17.7 Not very likely
5.4   Not at all likely
0.2   (None or one child(ren) at school)
1.7   (Don't know)
0.2   (Refusal/Not answered)

Q393 **ASK ALL**
[HEFee]
CARD D10   N=3199
I'm now going to ask you what you think about university or college students or their families paying towards the costs of their tuition, either while they are studying or after they have finished. Which of the views on this card comes closest to what you think about that?

%
10.5 **All** students or their families should pay towards the costs of their tuition
65.9 **Some** students or their families should pay towards the costs of their tuition, depending on their circumstances
22.7 **No** students or their families should pay towards the costs of their tuition
0.7   (Don't know)
0.1   (Refusal/Not answered)

Q394 **IF 'all students' OR 'some students' AT [HEFee]**
[HEFeeWhn]   N=3199
And when should students or their families start paying towards the costs of their tuition...READ OUT...

%
30.7 ...while they are studying,
36.7 or, after they have finished studying and have got a job?
8.8   (Depends)
0.3   (Don't know)
0.8   (Refusal/Not answered)

Q395 **ASK ALL**
[FeesUni]   N=3199
Which of the following statements comes closest to your own view ..READ OUT...

%
64.5 ..tuition fees for **all universities and colleges** should be the same,
32.5 or, tuition fees should be different depending on the university or college students go to?
2.9   (Don't know)
0.1   (Refusal/Not answered)

Q396 [FeesSub]
And which of these two statements comes closest to your
own view ...READ OUT...:

  %

54.4   ..tuition fees for **all subjects studied** should be the
same,

42.8   or, tuition fees should be different depending on
subject students study at university or college?

2.7   (Don't know)

0.1   (Refusal/Not answered)

                              N=3199

Q397 [GoHE100]
Of every 100 young people leaving school in Britain
today, about how many do you think **will** go to
university?

Median: 40

  %

5.1   (Don't know)

0.1   (Refusal/Not answered)

                              N=3199

Q398 [ShdHE100]
And of every 100 young people leaving school in Britain
today, about how many do you think **should** go to
university?
Range: 0 ... 100

Median: 50

  %

8.1   (Don't know)

0.1   (Refusal/Not answered)

                              N=3199

Health

ASK ALL

Q400 [NHSSat]
CARD E1
All in all, how satisfied or dissatisfied would you
say you are with the way in which the National
Health Service runs nowadays?
Choose a phrase from this card.

                              N=3199

Q401 [GPSat]
CARD E1 AGAIN
From your own experience, or from what you have
heard, please say how satisfied or dissatisfied you
are with the way in which each of these parts of the
National Health Service runs nowadays:
First, local doctors or GPs?

                              N=3199

Q402 [DentSat]
CARD E1 AGAIN
(And how satisfied or dissatisfied are you with the
NHS as regards...)
... National Health Service dentists?

	[NHSSat]	[GPSat]	[DentSat]
	%	%	%
Very satisfied	7.4	23.9	11.6
Quite satisfied	36.1	47.6	30.5
Neither satisfied nor dissatisfied	19.6	10.9	15.7
Quite dissatisfied	23.0	11.7	17.9
Very dissatisfied	13.6	5.4	20.1
(Don't know)	0.3	0.4	4.1
(Refusal/Not answered)	0.0	0.0	0.0

Q403 [InpatSat] N=3199
CARD E1 AGAIN
(And how satisfied or dissatisfied are you with the NHS
as regards...)
... being in hospital as an **in**-patient?

Q404 [OutpaSat] N=3199
CARD E1 AGAIN
(And how satisfied or dissatisfied are you with the NHS
as regards...)
... attending hospital as an **out**-patient?

Q405 [AESat] N=3199
CARD E1 AGAIN
(And how satisfied or dissatisfied are you with the NHS
as regards...)
... Accident and Emergency departments?

	[InpatSat]	[OutpaSat]	[AESat]
	%	%	%
Very satisfied	13.1	11.7	13.4
Quite satisfied	35.0	42.7	33.1
Neither satisfied nor dissatisfied	20.2	19.1	16.9
Quite dissatisfied	16.6	16.1	18.3
Very dissatisfied	7.5	6.4	12.6
(Don't know)	7.5	4.0	5.8
(Refusal/Not answered)	0.0	0.0	0.0

Q406 **ASK ALL IN ENGLAND AND WALES**
[NDirSat] N=2902
CARD E1 AGAIN
(And how satisfied or dissatisfied are you with the NHS
as regards...)
... NHS Direct, the telephone or internet advice
service?
%
8.8 Very satisfied
19.3 Quite satisfied
32.3 Neither satisfied nor dissatisfied
4.7 Quite dissatisfied
3.8 Very dissatisfied
31.1 (Don't know)
0.0 (Refusal/Not answered)

Q407 **VERSIONS A & B: ASK ALL** N=2130
[PrivMed]
Are **you yourself** covered by a private health
insurance scheme, that is an insurance scheme that
allows you to get private medical **treatment**?
ADD IF NECESSARY: 'For example, BUPA or PPP'.
IF INSURANCE COVERS DENTISTRY **ONLY**, CODE 'No'
%
20.7 Yes
78.8 No
0.4 (Don't know)
- (Refusal/Not answered)

Q408 **IF 'yes' AT [PrivMed]** N=2130
[PrivPaid]
Does your employer (or your partner's employer) pay
the majority of the cost of membership of this
scheme?
%
10.9 Yes
9.6 No
0.2 (Don't know)
0.5 (Refusal/Not answered)

Q409 **ASK ALL** N=3199
[NHSLimit]
It has been suggested that the National Health
Service should be available **only to those with lower
incomes**. This would mean that contributions and
taxes could be lower and most people would then take
out medical insurance or pay for health care.
Do you support or oppose this idea?
IF 'SUPPORT' OR 'OPPOSE': A lot or little?
%
7.8 Support a lot
14.7 Support a little
17.4 Oppose a little
58.2 Oppose a lot
1.8 (Don't know)
0.1 (Refusal/Not answered)

Q410 [OutPat1]
CARD E2
Now suppose you had a back problem and your GP referred you to a hospital out-patients' department. From what you know or have heard, please say whether you think...
...you would get an appointment within three months?
N=3199

Q411 [OutPat2]
CARD E2 AGAIN
(And please say whether you think ...)
...when you arrived, the doctor would see you within half an hour of your appointment time?
N=3199

Q412 [OutPat3]
CARD E2 AGAIN
(And please say whether you think ...)
...if you wanted to complain about the treatment you received, you would be able to without any fuss or bother?
N=3199

	[OutPat1]	[OutPat2]	[OutPat3]
	%	%	%
Definitely would	10.0	7.0	12.8
Probably would	36.3	34.2	42.9
Probably would not	34.7	39.9	28.4
Definitely would not	16.7	17.1	9.3
(Don't know)	2.3	1.8	6.6
(Refusal/Not answered)	0.1	0.1	0.1

Q413 [HosSaySh]
CARD E3
How much say do you think NHS patients **should have** over which hospital to go to if they need treatment?
N=3199

Q414 [HosSayDs]
CARD E3 AGAIN
And how much say do you think NHS patients **actually have** over which hospital to go to if they need treatment?
N=3199

Q415 [TimSaySh]
CARD E3 AGAIN
How much say **should** NHS hospital out-patients have over the time of their appointments?
N=3199

	[HosSaySh]	[HosSayDs]	[TimSaySh]
	%	%	%
A great deal	21.4	1.1	11.3
Quite a lot	41.6	7.7	42.0
A little	27.5	43.9	36.5
None at all	8.6	44.3	9.4
(Don't know)	0.9	2.9	0.8
(Refusal/Not answered)	0.1	0.1	0.1

Q416 [TimSayDs]
CARD E3 AGAIN
And how much say do you think NHS hospital out-patients **actually have** over the time of their appointments?
N=3199

Q417 [TreSaySh]
CARD E3 AGAIN
How much say **should** NHS patients have over the kind of treatment they receive?
N=3199

Q418 [TreSayDs]
CARD E3 AGAIN
And how much say do you think NHS patients **actually have** over the kind of treatment they receive?
N=3199

	[TimSayDs]	[TreSaySh]	[TreSayDs]
	%	%	%
A great deal	1.9	22.2	2.0
Quite a lot	12.0	42.9	14.6
A little	43.7	25.3	52.9
None at all	40.3	7.4	27.4
(Don't know)	2.1	2.1	3.0
(Refusal/Not answered)	0.1	0.1	0.1

Q419 [GPAptR]   N=3199
Suppose you wanted to see a GP about a back problem
that had been bothering you for a while but was **not**
stopping you from doing the things you normally do.
How long do you think it would be reasonable to have to
wait for an appointment to see a GP about this?
Please give me your answer in hours, days or weeks.
INTERVIEWER: FIRST CODE WHETHER THE ANSWER IS GIVEN IN
HOURS, DAYS, OR WEEKS. THEN CODE AMOUNT OF TIME AT NEXT
QUESTION.
CODE 30 MINUTES AS 0.5 HOURS, 90 MINUTES AS 1.5 HOURS
ETC
IF RESPONDENT SAYS 'Should be seen straight away' CODE
0 HOURS

	%
hours	8.0
days	48.5
weeks	43.0
(Don't know)	0.5
(Refusal/Not answered)	0.1

Median : 5 days

Q423 [GPAptU]   N=3199
Now suppose you wanted to see a GP about a bad chest
infection that **was** stopping you from doing the things
you normally do.
How long do you think it would be **reasonable** to have to
wait for an appointment to see a GP about this?
Please give me your answer in hours, days or weeks.
INTERVIEWER: FIRST CODE WHETHER THE ANSWER IS GIVEN IN
HOURS, DAYS, OR WEEKS. THEN CODE AMOUNT OF TIME AT NEXT
QUESTION.
CODE 30 MINUTES AS 0.5 HOURS, 90 MINUTES AS 1.5 HOURS
IF RESPONDENT SAYS 'Should be seen straight away' CODE
0 HOURS

	%
hours	45.9
days	50.1
weeks	3.5
(Don't know)	0.3
(Refusal/Not answered)	0.1

Median : 1 day

Q427 [OPAptR]   N=3199
Now suppose your GP referred you to a hospital out-
patients' department about a back problem that had
been bothering you for a while but was **not** stopping
you from doing the things you normally do.
How long do you think it would be reasonable to have
to wait for an appointment at a hospital
outpatients' department about a problem like this?
Please give me your answer in days, weeks, or
months.
INTERVIEWER: FIRST CODE WHETHER THE ANSWER IS GIVEN
IN DAYS, WEEKS OR MONTHS. THEN CODE AMOUNT OF TIME
AT NEXT QUESTION.
IF RESPONDENT SAYS 'Should be seen straight away'
CODE 0 DAYS

	%
days	10.2
weeks	49.8
months	38.7
(Don't know)	1.2
(Refusal/Not answered)	0.1

Median : 28 days

Q431 **[OpAptU]** *N=3199*
Now suppose your GP referred you to a hospital out-
patients' department about a more serious back problem
that **was** stopping you from doing the things you
normally do.
How long do you think it would be **reasonable** to have to
wait for an appointment at a hospital outpatients'
department about a problem like this?
Please give me your answer in days, weeks, or months.
INTERVIEWER: FIRST CODE WHETHER THE ANSWER IS GIVEN IN
DAYS, WEEKS OR MONTHS. THEN CODE AMOUNT OF TIME AT NEXT
QUESTION.
IF RESPONDENT SAYS 'Should be seen straight away' CODE
0 DAYS

%
40.4 days
51.0 weeks
7.6 months
0.9 (Don't know)
0.1 (Refusal/Not answered)
Median : 7 days

Q435 **[AEApt]** *N=3199*
Now suppose you had an accident and were worried that
you might have broken your wrist and went to an
accident and emergency department for treatment.
How long do you think it would be **reasonable** to have to
wait to be seen by a **doctor** about a problem like this?
Please give me your answer in hours.
IF RESPONDENT SAYS 'Should be seen straight away' CODE
0 HOURS
CODE 30 MINUTES AS 0.5 HOURS, 90 MINUTES AS 1.5 HOURS
ETC
ROUND **UP** TO THE NEAREST **HALF** HOUR
INTERVIEWER: ENTER THE NUMBER OF **HOURS**
Median : 1 hour

Q436 **[NHSWorkS]** *N=3199*
Do you currently work for the National Health
Service in any way?
INTERVIEWER: INCLUDE MEDICAL AND NON-MEDICAL STAFF
%
6.6 Yes
93.3 No / Not currently working
- (Don't know)
0.1 (Refusal/Not answered)

Q437 **IF ANSWER 'no', DON'T KNOW OR REFUSAL AT [NHSWorkS]**
[NHSWorkO] *N=3199*
Leaving aside any visits to a doctor or nurse about
your own health, do you ever **talk** to anyone who
currently works for the National Health Service in
any way? Please include friends, relatives,
neighbours and anyone else you might know.
INTERVIEWER: INCLUDE MEDICAL AND NON-MEDICAL STAFF
%
34.9 Yes
58.5 No
- (Don't know)
0.1 (Refusal/Not answered)

ASK ALL
Q439 **[SRHealth]**
How is your health in general for someone of your
age?
Would you say that it is ... READ OUT ...
%
38.6 ... very good,
40.5 fairly good,
14.3 fair,
5.0 bad,
1.5 or, very bad?
0.0 (Don't know)
0.1 (Refusal/Not answered)

Employment

Job details

Q541   **ASK ALL WHO HAVE EVER HAD A JOB**   N=3122
[Title] **(NOT ON DATAFILE)**
Now I want to ask you about your *(present/last/future)* job.
What *(is/was/will)* your job *(be)*?
PROBE IF NECESSARY: What *(is/was)* the name or title of the job?

Q542   [Typewk] **(NOT ON DATAFILE)**   N=3122
What kind of work *(do/did/will)* you do most of the time?
IF RELEVANT: What materials/machinery *(do/did/will)* you use?

Q543   [Train] **(NOT ON DATAFILE)**   N=3122
What training or qualifications *(are/were)* needed for that job?

Q544   [Remplyee]   N=3122
%   In your (main) job *(are/were/will)* you *(be)* ... READ OUT
87.7   ... an employee,
12.1   or self-employed?
0.1   (Don't know)
0.1   (Refusal/Not answered)

Q548   [RSuperv]   N=3122
In your job, *(did/do/will)* you have any formal responsibility for supervising the work of other *(employees/people)*?
DO NOT INCLUDE PEOPLE WHO ONLY SUPERVISE:
- CHILDREN, E.G. TEACHERS, NANNIES, CHILDMINDERS
- ANIMALS
- SECURITY OR BUILDINGS, E.G. CARETAKERS, SECURITY GUARDS
%
37.2   Yes
62.6   No
0.1   (Don't know)
0.1   (Refusal/Not answered)

Q551   IF 'yes' AT [RSuperv]   N=3122
[RMany]
How many?
Median: 6 (of those supervising any)
0.3   (Don't know)
0.1   (Refusal/Not answered)

Q553   **ASK ALL EMPLOYEES IN CURRENT/LAST JOB**   N=2745
[ROcSect2]
Card (F1/H5)
Which of the types of organisation on this card *(do you work/did you work/will you be working)* for?
%
65.4   PRIVATE SECTOR FIRM OR COMPANY Including, for example, limited companies and PLCs
3.3   NATIONALISED INDUSTRY OR PUBLIC CORPORATION Including, for example, the Post Office and the BBC
27.2   OTHER PUBLIC SECTOR EMPLOYER
Incl eg:
- Central govt/ Civil Service/ Govt Agency
- Local authority/ Local Educ Auth (INCL 'OPTED OUT' SCHOOLS)
- Universities
- Health Authority / NHS hospitals / NHS Trusts/ GP surgeries
- Police / Armed forces
2.9   CHARITY/ VOLUNTARY SECTOR Including, for example, charitable companies, churches, trade unions
0.8   Other answer (WRITE IN)
0.0   (Don't know)
0.4   (Refusal/Not answered)

Q558   **ASK ALL WHO HAVE EVER HAD A JOB**   N=3122
[EmpMake] **(NOT ON DATAFILE)**
IF EMPLOYEE: What *(does/did)* your employer make or do at the place where you *(will)* usually work(ed) from?
IF SELF-EMPLOYED: What *(do/did/will)* you make or do at the place where you *(will)* usually work(ed) from?
Open Question (Maximum of 80 characters)

Q560 **ASK ALL SELF-EMPLOYED IN CURRENT/LAST JOB** N=381
[SEmpNum]
In your work or business, (do/did/will) you have any employees, or not?
IF YES: How many?
IF `NO EMPLOYEES', CODE 0.
FOR 500+ EMPLOYEES, CODE 500.
NOTE: FAMILY MEMBERS MAY BE EMPLOYEES ONLY IF THEY RECEIVE A REGULAR WAGE OR SALARY.
Median : 0 employees
%
0.5 (Don't know)
2.3 (Refusal/Not answered)

Q568 **ASK ALL IN PAID WORK** N=1886
[WkJbTim]
In your present job, are you working ... READ OUT ...
RESPONDENT'S OWN DEFINITION
%
76.3 ... full-time,
23.7 or, part-time?
- (Don't know)
0.0 (Refusal/Not answered)

Q571 [WkJbHrsI] N=1886
How many hours do you normally work a week in your main job - **including** any paid or unpaid overtime?
ROUND TO NEAREST HOUR.
IF RESPONDENT CANNOT ANSWER, ASK ABOUT LAST WEEK.
IF RESPONDENT DOES NOT KNOW EXACTLY, ACCEPT AN ESTIMATE.
FOR 95+ HOURS, CODE 95.
FOR `VARIES TOO MUCH TO SAY', CODE 96.
Median: 40 hours
%
0.7 (Varies too much to say)
0.2 (Don't know)
0.0 (Refusal/Not answered)

Q572 **ASK ALL CURRENT EMPLOYEES** N=1621
[EJbHrsX]
What are your **basic or contractual hours** each week in your main job - **excluding** any paid and unpaid overtime?
ROUND TO NEAREST HOUR.
IF RESPONDENT CANNOT ANSWER, ASK ABOUT LAST WEEK.
IF RESPONDENT DOES NOT KNOW EXACTLY, ACCEPT AN ESTIMATE.
FOR 95+ HOURS, CODE 95.
FOR `VARIES TOO MUCH TO SAY', CODE 96.
Median: 37 hours
%
2.3 (Varies too much to say)
1.4 (Don't know)
0.0 (Refusal/Not answered)

Q573 **ASK ALL WHO HAVE EVER WORKED BUT ARE NOT CURRENTLY WORKING** N=1220
[ExPrtFul]
(Is/was/will) the job (be) ... READ OUT ...
%
70.9 ... full-time - that is, 30 or more hours per week,
28.6 or, part-time?
0.2 (Don't know)
0.2 (Refusal/Not answered)

Employment relations

Q604 **ASK ALL** N=3199
[UnionSA]
(May I just check) are you **now** a member of a trade union or staff association?
CODE FIRST TO APPLY
%
17.8 Yes, trade union
2.9 Yes, staff association
76.7 No
0.1 (Don't know)
0.0 (Refusal/Not answered)

Q605 **IF 'no'/DK AT [UnionSA]**
[TUSAEver]
Have you **ever** been a member of a trade union or staff association?
CODE FIRST TO APPLY
N=3199

%
25.4 Yes, trade union
2.4 Yes, staff association
48.7 No
0.1 (Don't know)
0.2 (Refusal/Not answered)

ASK ALL NOT WORKING
Q441 [NPWork10]
In the seven days ending last Sunday, did you have any paid work of less than 10 hours a week?
N=1313

%
4.2 Yes
95.7 No
0.1 (Don't know)
- (Refusal/Not answered)

ASK ALL CURRENT EMPLOYEES
Q442 [WpUnion3]
At your place of work are there any unions or staff associations?
IF ASKED: A union or staff association is any independent organisation that represents the interests of people at work.
IF YES, PROBE FOR UNION OR STAFF ASSOCIATION. CODE FIRST TO APPLY.
N=1621

%
48.3 Yes : trade union(s)
4.8 Yes : staff association
43.0 No, none
3.8 (Don't know)
0.1 (Refusal/Not answered)

IF 'yes, trade unions' OR 'yes, staff association' AT [WpUnion3]
Q443 [UnionRec]
Does management recognise these unions or staff associations for the purposes of negotiating pay and conditions of employment?
N=1621

%
47.7 Yes
4.0 No
1.4 (Don't know)
3.9 (Refusal/Not answered)

Q444 [WpUnioW3]
On the whole, do you think (these unions do their/this staff association does its) job well or not?
N=1621

%
30.3 Yes
17.4 No
5.5 (Don't know)
3.9 (Refusal/Not answered)

Q445 [TUElig]
Are people doing your job eligible to join a union or staff association at your workplace?
IF ASKED: A union or staff association is any independent organisation that represents the interests of people at work.
IF YES, PROBE FOR UNION OR STAFF ASSOCIATION. CODE FIRST TO APPLY.
N=1621

%
45.4 Yes : trade union(s)
4.5 Yes : staff association
2.5 No
0.7 (Don't know)
3.9 (Refusal/Not answered)

ASK ALL

Q446   [TUMstImp]
CARD F2   N=3199
Listed on this card are a number of things that trade unions or staff associations can do. Which, if any, do you think should be the **most important** thing they should try to do?

	%
Reduce pay differences in the workplace	5.2
Promote equality for women or for ethnic and other minority groups	7.9
Represent individual employees in dealing with their employer about problems at work	29.2
Protect existing employees' jobs	12.1
Improve working conditions across the workplace	27.1
Improve pay for all employees	11.0
Have an input into the running the business	2.5
(None of these)	1.7
(Don't know)	3.3
(Refusal/Not answered)	0.1

ASK ALL CURRENT EMPLOYEES

Q447   [IndRel]   N=1621
In general how would you describe relations between management and other employees at your workplace ...
READ OUT ...

	%
... very good,	36.5
quite good,	47.0
not very good,	10.6
or, not at all good?	4.6
(Don't know)	1.2
(Refusal/Not answered)	0.1

Q448   [SayJob]   N=1621
Suppose there was going to be some decision made at your place of work that changed the way you do your job. Do you think that **you personally** would have any say in the decision about the change, or not?
IF 'DEPENDS': Code as 'Don't know' <CTRL+K+Enter>

	%
Yes	56.8
No	40.6
(Don't know)	2.4
(Refusal/Not answered)	0.1

Q449   **IF 'yes' at [SayJob]**
[MuchSay]   N=1621
How much say or chance to influence the decision do you think you would have ... READ OUT ...

	%
...a great deal,	15.8
quite a lot,	22.5
or, just a little?	18.4
(Don't know)	0.1
(Refusal/Not answered)	2.5

Q450   **ASK ALL CURRENT EMPLOYEES**
[WorkOld]
Does your employer currently allow people to carry on working past State Pension Age if they want to.
At the moment State Pension Age is 60 for women and 65 for men?
INTERVIEWER: IF RESPONDENT REFERS TO A CHANGE IN STATE PENSION AGE, ASK THEM TO ANSWER FOR CURRENT STATE PENSION AGE

	%
Yes	46.5
No	30.6
(Don't know)	22.8
(Refusal/Not answered)	0.1

Q451   [PrefHr2]   N=1621
Thinking about the number of hours you work including regular overtime, would you prefer a job where you worked ... READ OUT ...

	%
...more hours per week,	5.0
fewer hours per week,	31.7
or, are you happy with the number of hours you work at present?	63.0
(Don't know)	0.2
(Refusal/Not answered)	0.1

Q452 **IF 'fewer hours per week' AT [PrefHr2]**
[EarnHr2]
Would you still prefer to work fewer hours, if it meant earning less money as a result?

N=1621

	%
Yes	8.1
No	21.5
It depends	2.1
(Don't know)	0.1
(Refusal/Not answered)	0.3

Career preferences

ASK ALL
Q453 [FrstJb1c]
CARD F3

N=3199

Suppose you were advising a young person who was looking for his or her first job. Which **one** of these would you say is **most** important?

Q454 **IF ANSWER GIVEN AT [FrstJb1c]**
[FrstJb2c]
CARD F3 AGAIN

N=3199

(Still supposing you were advising a young person looking for his or her first job.)
And which **next**?

	[FrstJb1c]	[FrstJb2c]
	%	%
Good starting pay	5.1	10.9
A secure job for the future	33.1	18.8
Opportunities for promotion	11.6	22.6
Interesting work	31.8	22.8
A good work-life balance	16.7	20.9
A chance to help other people	1.3	3.3
(Don't know)	0.5	0.1
(Refusal/Not answered)	0.1	0.6

ASK ALL
Q455 [JobBSec1]
CARD F4

N=3199

Suppose this young person had the ability to go into any of **these** careers. From what you know or have heard, which **one** of these careers would offer him or her the **most job security**?

Q456 **IF ANSWER GIVEN AT [JobBSec1]**
[JobBSec2]
CARD F4 AGAIN
And which would offer him or her the **next best** job security?

N=3199

	[JobBSec1]	[JobBSec2]
	%	%
Nurse	8.2	14.1
Computer engineer	13.4	7.3
School teacher	7.1	10.7
Lawyer	21.1	18.4
Police officer	15.9	18.4
Journalist	0.7	1.2
Doctor	30.7	27.0
(None of these)	1.1	0.4
(Don't know)	1.6	0.8
(Refusal/Not answered)	0.1	1.7

ASK ALL
Q457 [JobBPrm1]
CARD F4 AGAIN

N=3199

Again, from what you know or have heard, which **one** of these careers would offer him or her the **best opportunities for promotion**?

Q458 **IF ANSWER GIVEN AT [JobBPrm1]**
[JobBPrm2]
CARD F4 AGAIN
And which would offer him or her the **next best** opportunities for promotion?

	[JobBPrm1]	[JobBPrm2]
	%	%
Nurse	9.4	18.4
Computer engineer	16.7	12.3
School teacher	5.2	11.9
Lawyer	12.9	12.3
Police officer	38.5	19.8
Journalist	2.3	4.9
Doctor	9.4	12.7
(None of these)	0.6	0.7
(Don't know)	5.0	1.9
(Refusal/Not answered)	0.1	5.1

ASK ALL

Q459 [Career1]

CARD F5

Now suppose you were thinking about a person's career in general and the choices that they have to make. Which **one** of these would you say is the **most** important for them to think about?

N=3199

Q460 **IF ANSWER GIVEN AT [Career1]**

[Career2]

CARD F5 AGAIN

And which next?

N=3199

	[Career1]	[Career2]
	%	%
Good pay	9.5	17.1
A secure job	35.4	19.5
Opportunities for promotion	7.7	18.5
Interesting work	24.4	20.8
A good work-life balance	20.9	20.0
A chance to help other people	0.9	2.6
(Don't know)	1.2	0.1
(Refusal/Not answered)	0.1	1.3

Flexible working (versions B and C)

Q461 **VERSIONS B OR C: ASK ALL CURRENT EMPLOYEES**

[TimeOff]

CARD F6

And now some more questions about your job. I'd like you to think about the person at work you go to if you have to take time off - this may be your supervisor, your line manager or someone else. How understanding would this person be if you had to take time off for family or personal reasons?

N=1099

	%
Very understanding	58.3
Fairly understanding	30.3
Not very understanding	4.5
Not at all understanding	2.4
Varies too much to say	2.3
(Doesn't have to ask anyone if takes time off)	1.7
(Don't know)	0.3
(Refusal/Not answered)	0.2

Q462 **IF NOT 'Doesn't have to ask anyone if takes time off' AT [TimeOff]**

[ManWoman]

Is this person a man or a woman?

N=1099

	%
Man	56.5
Woman	41.1
(Don't know)	0.6
(Refusal/Not answered)	0.2

Q463 **VERSIONS B OR C: ASK ALL CURRENT EMPLOYEES**

[EwrkarA2]

CARD F7

Please use this card to say whether any of the following arrangements are available to you, at your workplace ...

Part-time working, allowing you to work less than the full working day?

N=1099

Q464 [EwrkarB2]

CARD F7 AGAIN

(Is this available to you at your workplace?)

... flexible hours, so that you can adjust your own daily working hours?

N=1099

Q465 [EwrkarC2]
CARD F7 AGAIN
(Is this available to you at your workplace?)
... job-sharing schemes, where part-timers share one full-time job?

N=1099

	[EwrkarA2]	[EwrkarB2]	[EwrkarC2]
	%	%	%
Not available - and I **would not** use it if it were	23.4	17.7	43.1
Not available - but I **would** use it if it were	10.4	31.9	15.3
Available - but I **have not** used it and am not likely to do so in the next year	34.0	16.4	29.0
Available - and I **have** used it or am likely to do so in the next year	30.2	3.1	9.0
(Don't know)	1.9	0.8	3.5
(Refusal/Not answered)	0.2	0.2	0.2

Q466 [EwrkarD2]
CARD F7 AGAIN
(Is this available to you at your workplace?)
... working from home at least some of the time?

N=1099

Q467 [EwrkarE2]
CARD F7 AGAIN
(Is this available to you at your workplace?)
... term-time contracts, allowing parents special time off during school holidays?

N=1099

VERSIONS B OR C: ASK ALL MALE CURRENT EMPLOYEES

Q468 [EwrkArP]
CARD F7 AGAIN
(Is this available to you at your workplace?)
... extended paternity leave, allowing fathers more than two weeks extra leave, when their children are born?

N=523

	[EwrkarD2]	[EwrkarE2]	[EwrkarP]
	%	%	%
Not available - and I **would not** use it if it were	49.6	44.8	27.1
Not available - but I **would** use it if it were	25.6	24.6	18.8
Available - but I **have not** used it and am not likely to do so in the next year	7.5	15.0	36.2
Available - and I **have** used it or am likely to do so in the next year	16.4	8.7	3.2
(Don't know)	0.8	6.8	14.4
(Refusal/Not answered)	0.2	0.2	0.3

VERSIONS B OR C: ASK ALL FEMALE CURRENT EMPLOYEES

N=576

Q469 [EwrkArPW]
Is this available at your workplace?
... extended paternity leave, allowing fathers more than two weeks extra leave, when their children are born?

	%
Not available	31.6
Available	34.0
(Don't know)	34.5
(Refusal/Not answered)	-

VERSIONS B OR C: ASK ALL CURRENT EMPLOYEES

Q470 [EwrkarL2]
CARD F7 AGAIN
(Is this available to you at your workplace?)
... time off, either paid or unpaid, to care for sick children?

N=1099

Q471 [EwrkArM2]
CARD F7 AGAIN
(Is this available to you at your workplace?)
... time off, either paid or unpaid, to care for children for reasons other than their sickness?

N=1099

Q472 [EwrkArN2]
CARD F7 AGAIN
(Is this available to you at your workplace?)
... time off, either paid or unpaid, to care for people other than children?

N=1099

	[EwrkArL2]	[EWrkArM2]	[EWrkArN2]
	%	%	%
Not available - and I **would** **not** use it if it were	9.8	18.8	14.7
Not available - but I **would** use it if it were	11.1	13.1	15.8
Available - but I **have not** used it and am not likely to do so in the next year	51.0	41.9	44.1
Available - and I **have** used it or am likely to do so in the next year	16.6	10.7	10.4
(Don't know)	11.3	15.4	14.8
(Refusal/Not answered)	0.2	0.2	0.2

VERSIONS B OR C: ASK ALL MALE CURRENT EMPLOYEES   N=523

Q473 [EwrkArQM]
Is this available at your workplace?
... extended maternity leave for longer than six months?

%	
39.6	Not available
29.3	Available
30.8	(Don't know)
0.3	(Refusal/Not answered)

VERSIONS B OR C: ASK ALL FEMALE CURRENT EMPLOYEES   N=576

Q474 [EwrkArQ]
CARD F7
Is this available at your workplace?
... extended maternity leave for longer than six months?

%	
17.8	**Not** available - and I **would not** use it if it were
8.8	**Not** available - but I **would** use it if it were
42.5	Available - but I **have not** used it and am not likely to do so in the next year
7.4	Available - and I **have** used it or am likely to do so in the next year
23.4	(Don't know)
-	(Refusal/Not answered)

IF 'not available and would not use' OR 'available but have not used and am not likely to do so in the next year' AT [EWrkArA2]

Q475 [YNPartT]   N=1099
CARD F8
You said that (you would not work part-time even if this was available at your workplace/part-time working is available at your workplace but you have not used this and are not likely to in the next year)
What is the **main** reason for this?

IF 'not available and would not use' OR 'available but have not used and am not likely to do so in the next year' AT [EWrkArB2]

Q478 [YNFlex]   N=1099
CARD F8 AGAIN
You said that (would not work flexible hours even if this was available at your workplace/flexible hours are available at your workplace but you have not used this and are not likely to in the next year).
What is the **main** reason for this?

IF 'not available and would not use' OR 'available but have not used and am not likely to do so in the next year' AT [EWrkArC2]

Q481 [YNJobSh]   N=1099
CARD F8 AGAIN
You said that (you would not do a job share even if this was available at your workplace/job shares are available at your workplace but you have not used this and are not likely to in the next year)
What is the **main** reason for this?

	[YNPartT] %	[YNFlex] %	[YNJobSh] %
I have no need for it/ I don't want it	30.6	21.6	42.3
Not available or not possible for my job/grade	5.2	6.7	11.6
Too much work to do/ I'm too busy	2.5	1.3	0.9
Concerned about the extra workload for my colleagues	0.2	0.6	0.2
Concerned about my career progression	0.6	-	0.2
Concerned about my job security	0.4	0.3	1.3
Do not feel confident to ask my employer	-	0.1	-
Could not afford the reduction in my income	16.9	2.9	14.3
Other (WRITE IN)	0.9	0.4	1.2
(Don't know)	0.3	0.4	0.3
(Refusal/Not answered)	2.0	0.9	3.5

Q484 **IF 'not available and would not use' OR 'available but have not used and am not likely to do so in the next year' AT [EWrkArD2]**
[YNWHome]   N=1099
CARD F8 AGAIN
You said that (you would not work from home some of the time even if this was available at your workplace/working from home some of the time is available at your workplace but you have not done this and are not likely to in the next year)
What is the main reason for this?

Q487 **IF 'not available and would not use' OR 'available but have not used and am not likely to do so in the next year' AT [EWrkArB2]**
[YNTerm]   N=1099
CARD F8 AGAIN
You said that (you would not work term-time only even if this was available at your workplace/ term-time only working is available at your workplace but you have not used this and are not likely to in the next year)
What is the main reason for this?

Q490 **MEN ONLY: IF 'not available and would not use' OR 'available but have not used and am not likely to do so in the next year' AT [EWrkArP]**
[YNPater]   N=523
CARD F8 AGAIN
You said that (you would not take extended paternity leave even if this was available at your workplace/ extended paternity leave is available at your workplace but you have not used this and are not likely to in the next year)
What is the main reason for this?

	[YNWHome] %	[YNTerm] %	[YNPater] %
I have no need for it/ I don't want it	24.1	44.0	53.1
Not available or not possible for my job/grade	29.4	8.1	3.4
Too much work to do/ I'm too busy	0.8	1.7	1.2
Concerned about the extra workload for my colleagues	0.2	0.2	-
Concerned about my career progression	0.1	0.1	-
Concerned about my job security	0.3	0.1	0.5
Do not feel confident to ask my employer	-	0.1	-
Could not afford the reduction in my income	1.2	4.9	3.9
Other (WRITE IN)	1.2	0.5	0.6
(Don't know)	0.2	0.3	0.5
(Refusal/Not answered)	0.8	6.9	14.7

Q493 **IF 'not available and would not use' OR 'available but have not used and am not likely to do so in the next year' AT [EWrkArL2]**
[YNSickCh]   N=1099
CARD F8 AGAIN
You said that (you would not take time off to care for sick children even if this was available at your workplace/time off to care for sick children is available at your workplace but you have not used this and are not likely to in the next year)
What is the main reason for this?

IF 'not available and would not use' OR 'available but have not used and am not likely to do so in the next year' AT [EWrkArM2]   N=1099

Q496   [YNOthCh]
CARD F8 AGAIN
You said that (you would not take time off to care for children other than when they are sick even if this was available at your workplace/ time off to care for children other than when they are sick is available at your workplace but you have not used this and are not likely to in the next year)
What is the main reason for this?

	[YNSickCh] %	[YNOthCh] %
I have no need for it/ I don't want it	54.9	54.5
Not available or not possible for my job/grade	1.9	2.7
Too much work to do/ I'm too busy	0.3	0.6
Concerned about the extra workload for my colleagues	0.1	0.2
Concerned about my career progression	0.1	-
Concerned about my job security	0.6	0.3
Do not feel confident to ask my employer	0.1	0.2
Could not afford the reduction in my income	1.9	1.6
Other (WRITE IN)	0.4	-
(Don't know)	0.7	0.6
(Refusal/Not answered)	11.5	15.5

IF 'not available and would not use' OR 'available but have not used and am not likely to do so in the next year' AT [EWrkArN2]   N=1099

Q499   [YNCare]
CARD F8 AGAIN
You said that (you would not take time off to care for people other than children even if this was available at your workplace/time off to care for people other than children is available at your workplace but you have not used this and are not likely to in the next year)
What is the main reason for this?

WOMEN ONLY: IF 'not available and would not use' OR 'available but have not used and am not likely to do so in the next year' AT [EWrkArQ]   N=135

Q502   [YNExMat]
CARD F8 AGAIN
You said that (you would not use extended maternity leave even if this was available at your workplace/extended maternity leave is available at your workplace but you have not used this and are not likely to in the next year)
What is the main reason for this?

	[YNCare] %	[YNExMat] %
I have no need for it/ I don't want it	53.1	55.0
Not available or not possible for my job/grade	2.2	1.5
Too much work to do/ I'm too busy	0.5	0.2
Concerned about the extra workload for my colleagues	0.2	-
Concerned about my career progression	-	0.2
Concerned about my job security	0.2	-
Do not feel confident to ask my employer	0.2	-
Could not afford the reduction in my income	1.6	2.8
Other (WRITE IN)	0.3	0.4
(Don't know)	0.7	0.3
(Refusal/Not answered)	14.9	23.4

Pensions and retirement

ASK ALL CURRENT EMPLOYEES

Q505 [RetExp]
At the moment when do you expect to retire from your main job? In your ...READ OUT...
N=1621

%	
2.2	...40s,
21.7	50s,
66.7	60s,
4.0	70s,
0.5	80s,
1.2	or, at some other time?
2.3	(Not planning to retire)
0.2	(No main job)
1.0	(Don't know)
0.0	(Refusal/Not answered)

IF '60s' OR 'at some other time' AT [RetExp]

Q506 [RetExp2]
And specifically, at what age do you expect to retire from your main job?
N=1621

ASK ALL CURRENT EMPLOYEES

Q507 [DVRetSPA] (NOT ON SCREEN)
Computed variable - whether expects to retire before, at, or after SPA
N=1621

%	
36.6	before SPA
39.6	at SPA
19.6	after SPA including not planning to retire
4.1	other - no main job/DK when will retire
-	(Don't know)
0.0	(Refusal/Not answered)

IF NOT 'Not planning to retire'/'No main job' AT [RetExp]

Q508 [FutrWrk]
Do you think you are likely to do any further paid work after retiring from your main job?
N=1621

%	
52.4	Yes
39.5	No
5.5	(Don't know)
0.0	(Refusal/Not answered)

ASK ALL PLANNING TO RETIRE EARLY

Q509 [WhyRtBf]
At the moment State Pension Age is 60 for women and 65 for men. You have told us that you expect to retire from your main job before this. Is this mainly ...READ OUT...
CODE ONE ONLY
N=601

%	
84.4	...because you want to,
6.4	because your employer will not allow you to continue working,
2.1	due to ill health,
4.3	or, for some other reason?
-	(Don't know)
2.8	(Refusal/Not answered)

ASK ALL PLANNING TO RETIRE LATE OR NOT AT ALL

Q512 [WhyRtAft]
CARD (F6/F9)
At the moment State Pension Age is 60 for women and 65 for men. You have told us that you expect to retire from your main job after this (if at all). Which of the options on the card is the main reason for this?
CODE ONE ONLY
N=318

%	
27.0	Because you enjoy working
37.4	Because you can't afford to stop earning money
3.0	Because you are not sure what else to do
20.7	Because in the future that's when I think people will generally retire
7.8	Because my employer has (or will have) extended retirement age past 60/65
2.8	Some other reason (WRITE IN)
1.2	(Don't know)
0.2	(Refusal/Not answered)

Political and moral attitudes

VERSION A: ASK ALL

Q607 [NIreland] N=1034
Do you think the long-term policy for Northern Ireland should be for it ... READ OUT ...

%
32.3 ...to remain part of the United Kingdom
44.7 or, to unify with the rest of Ireland?
0.5 **NORTHERN IRELAND SHOULD BE AN INDEPENDENT STATE**
- **NORTHERN IRELAND SHOULD BE SPLIT UP INTO TWO**
4.6 **IT SHOULD BE UP TO THE IRISH TO DECIDE**
2.3 Other answer (WRITE IN)
15.4 (Don't know)
0.2 (Refusal/Not answered)

ASK ALL

Q610 [EngParl2] N=3199
CARD (F7/F10)
With all the changes going on in the way the different parts of Great Britain are run, which of the following do you think would be best for England ..READ OUT...

%
51.8 ...for England to be governed as it is now, with laws made by the UK parliament,
20.6 for each region of England to have its own elected assembly that makes decisions about the region's economy, planning and housing,
20.8 or, for England as a whole to have its own new parliament with law-making powers?
1.7 (None of these)
5.1 (Don't know)
0.0 (Refusal/Not answered)

Q611 [VotedEU] N=3199
A lot of people did not vote in the European election. How about you? Did you vote in the elections on the 10th of June or didn't you manage to?

%
44.7 Yes: voted
55.0 No
0.1 (Refused to say)
0.1 (Don't know)

Q612 **IF 'yes' AT [VotedEU]**
[VoteEU] N=3199
Which party did you vote for in the European election?

%
   DO NOT PROMPT
10.8 Conservative
11.4 Labour
7.5 Liberal Democrat
0.7 Scottish National Party (SNP)
0.4 Plaid Cymru
1.9 Green Party
6.0 UK Independence Party
0.8 British National Party (BNP)
0.5 (Scottish Socialist Alliance/RESPECT)
0.7 Other (WRITE IN)
2.6 Refused to disclose voting
1.2 (Don't know)
0.3 (Not answered)

ASK ALL

Q615 [ECPolicy] N=3199
CARD (F8/F11)
Do you think Britain's long-term policy should be... READ OUT ...

%
18.1 ... to leave the European Union,
38.2 to stay in the EU and try to **reduce** the EU's powers,
22.9 to leave things as they are,
7.4 to stay in the EU and try to **increase** the EU's powers,
5.1 or, to work for the formation of a single European government?
8.1 (Don't know)
0.1 (Refusal/Not answered)

Q616 [EUConRef] N=3199
How do you think you would vote in a referendum on the proposed new **European constitution**? Would you vote in favour of Britain adopting the new constitution or against?
IF 'would not vote', PROBE: If you did vote, how would you vote?
IF RESPONDENT INSISTS THEY WOULD NOT VOTE, CODE DON'T KNOW
%
20.0 To adopt the constitution
55.7 Not to adopt the constitution
24.1 (Don't know)
0.1 (Refusal/Not answered)

Q617 [EuroRef] N=3199
And if there were a referendum on whether Britain should **join the single European currency, the Euro**, how do you think you would vote? Would you vote to join the Euro, or not to join the Euro?
IF 'would not vote', PROBE: If you did vote, how would you vote?
IF RESPONDENT INSISTS THEY WOULD NOT VOTE, CODE DON'T KNOW
%
26.6 To join the Euro
67.3 Not to join the Euro
6.0 (Don't know)
0.1 (Refusal/Not answered)

Q618 [EuroLkly] N=3199
And how likely do you think it is that Britain **will** join the single European currency in the next ten years
...READ OUT...
33.0 ...very likely,
42.7 fairly likely,
17.0 not very likely,
3.5 or, not at all likely?
3.8 (Don't know)
0.0 (Refusal/Not answered)

VERSION B: ASK ALL
Q619 [CharOft]
CARD F12
Generally speaking, how often, on average, do you give **money** to charity - please do **not** include money spent in charity shops or buying lottery or raffle tickets?
Please just tell me a letter from this card.
IF ASKED: DO NOT INCLUDE MONEY TO BEGGARS OR BUYING THE BIG ISSUE
%
8.5 A: Never
11.7 B: Occasionally but less often than once a year
22.4 C: Once or twice a year
24.3 D: Once every few months
23.8 E: Once or twice a month
8.9 F: Once a week or more
0.4 (Don't know)
- (Refusal/Not answered)

IF ANSWER GIVEN AT [CharOft]
Q620 [CharAmt] N=1096
CARD F13
And how much, on average, do you give to charity each year?
Again, please just tell me a letter from this card.
%
11.1 A: Less than £5
23.1 B: £5.00 - £12
27.1 C: £12.01 - £50
15.1 D: £50.01 - £120
10.0 E: £120.01 - £500
2.3 F: More than £500
1.3 (Don't know)
1.5 (Refusal/Not answered)

VERSION A: ASK ALL

Q621 [PrejNow]   N=1034
Do you think there is generally more racial prejudice in Britain now than there was 5 years ago, less, or about the same amount?

```
  %
50.5   More now
16.5   Less now
30.4   About the same
 0.6   Other (WRITE IN)
 1.9   (Don't know)
 0.1   (Refusal/Not answered)
```

Q624 [PrejFut]   N=1034
Do you think there will be more, less, or about the same amount of racial prejudice in Britain in 5 years time compared with now?

```
  %
50.6   More in 5 years
18.3   Less
27.2   About the same
 0.5   Other (WRITE IN)
 3.3   (Don't know)
 0.1   (Refusal/Not answered)
```

Q627 [SRPrej]   N=1034
How would you describe yourself ... READ OUT ...

```
  %
 2.2   ... as very prejudiced against people of other races,
25.4   a little prejudiced,
69.9   or, not prejudiced at all?
 2.1   Other (WRITE IN)
 0.3   (Don't know)
 0.2   (Refusal/Not answered)
```

Housing

Q631 ASK ALL [HomeLong]   N=3199
How long have you lived in this home?
ENTER YEARS. ROUND TO NEAREST YEAR.
PROBE FOR BEST ESTIMATE.
IF LESS THAN ONE YEAR, CODE 0.
Median = 8 years

Q632 [NghBrHd]   N=3199
Can I just check, how long have you lived in your present neighbourhood?
ENTER YEARS. ROUND TO NEAREST YEAR.
PROBE FOR BEST ESTIMATE.
IF LESS THAN ONE YEAR, CODE 0.
Median = 18 years

Q633 [Tenure6]   N=3199
Does your household own or rent this accommodation?
PROBE IF NECESSARY
IF OWNS: Outright or on a mortgage? IF RENTS: From whom?

```
  %
30.6   Owns outright
44.8   Buying on mortgage
 9.0   Rents: local authority
 0.1   Rents: New Town Development Corporation
 4.8   Rents: Housing Association
 0.9   Rents: property company
 0.6   Rents: employer
 0.6   Rents: other organisation
 0.4   Rents: relative
 6.4   Rents: other individual
 0.2   Rents: Housing Trust
 0.4   Rent free, squatting
 0.3   Shared ownership (e.g. part rent, part buy)
 0.5   Other (WRITE IN)
 0.3   (Don't know)
 0.2   (Refusal/Not answered)
```

Q637
ASK ALL WHO OWN OUTRIGHT OR ARE BUYING ON A MORTGAGE   N=2425
[BuyFLAHA]
Did you, or the person responsible for the mortgage, buy your home from the local authority or Housing Association as a tenant?
If yes, was that from the Local Authority or Housing Association?

%
9.2 Yes - from Local Authority
0.9 Yes - from Housing Association
88.8 No
0.5 (Don't know)
0.6 (Refusal/Not answered)

Q638
ASK ALL WHO OWN OUTRIGHT, ARE BUYING ON A MORTGAGE, ARE IN RENT-FREE ACCOMMODATION OR HAVE SHARED OWNERSHIP   N=2445
[Rentpr2b]
CARD G1
If you were to rent your accommodation, from which sort of landlord would you prefer to rent? Please choose an answer from this card.

%
28.5 Housing Association, co-operative or Trust
28.8 Local Authority or Council
32.8 Private landlord
1.7 Some other landlord
7.5 (Don't know)
0.7 (Refusal/Not answered)

Q639
ASK ALL WHO RENT   N=752
[Rentpr1b]
CARD G1
From which sort of landlord would you prefer to rent? Please choose an answer from this card.

%
23.4 Housing Association, co-operative or Trust
43.6 Local Authority or Council
24.5 Private landlord
2.1 Some other landlord
3.9 (Don't know)
2.6 (Refusal/Not answered)

Q640
ASK ALL   N=3199
[Tenurep]
When you were a child, did your parents own their own home, rent it from a local authority or Housing Association, or rent it from someone else?
IF DIFFERENT TYPES OF TENURE PROBE FOR ONE RESPONDENT LIVED IN LONGEST

%
51.9 Owned it
30.1 Rented from Local Authority
1.6 Rented from Housing Association
12.8 Rented from someone else
2.8 Other (WRITE IN)
0.7 (Don't know)
0.1 (Refusal/Not answered)

Q644
ASK ALL   N=3199
[TenPref]
CARD G2
Leaving aside any plans you might have for the future, which of these, if any, is the type of housing you would most want to live in?

%
3.5 Rent from housing association
6.7 Rent from council/local authority
2.0 Rent from a private landlord
81.6 Owner occupier/buying
0.8 Shared ownership/do-it-yourself shared ownership (i.e. part rent, part buy)
1.7 Live with friends/relatives (not sure what type of housing)
2.4 Sheltered accommodation
0.4 Other (WRITE IN)
0.8 (Don't know)
0.1 (Refusal/Not answered)

Q647 [OwnAdvt]   N=3199
CARD G2B
If you had to choose just **one** of the things on this
card, which one would you say is the main advantage of
owning a home?

%	
21.2	Gives you the freedom to do what you want with it
12.9	Works out less expensive than paying rent
22.5	Is more secure in the long-term than renting
9.1	Is something to leave to your family
32.5	Is a good investment
0.8	Something else (WRITE IN)
1.0	(Don't know)
0.1	(Refusal/Not answered)

Q650 [RentAdvt]   N=3199
CARD G2C
And if you had to choose just **one** of the things on this
card, which one would you say is the main advantage of
renting a home?

%	
23.6	Gives you flexibility if you need to move at short notice
9.2	Gives you greater choice over where to live
30.7	Means someone else is responsible for repairs and maintenance
6.3	Is less risky than owning a home
12.6	Is less responsibility than owning a home
13.1	Means you don't have to worry about taking on a mortgage
1.6	Something else (WRITE IN)
2.9	(Don't know)
0.1	(Refusal/Not answered)

Q653 [MoveLike]   N=3199
Would you **like** to move home in the next two years?

%	
33.9	Yes
65.1	No
0.9	(Don't know)
0.1	(Refusal/Not answered)

Q654 [MovePlan]   N=3199
CARD G3
Are you **planning** to move home in the next two years?
Please choose an answer from this card.

%	
13.3	Definitely planning to move
12.2	Probably planning to move
15.1	Probably not planning to move
58.7	Definitely not planning to move
0.6	(Don't know)
0.1	(Refusal/Not answered)

ASK ALL DEFINITELY OR PROBABLY PLANNING TO MOVE

Q656 [TenMove]   N=835
CARD G4
Which of these, if any, is the type of housing you
are planning to move to?

%	
5.2	Rent from housing association
6.8	Rent from council/local authority
13.7	Rent from a private landlord
61.6	Owner occupier/buying
1.6	Shared ownership/do-it-yourself shared ownership (i.e. part rent, part buy)
4.2	Live with friends/relatives (not sure what type of housing)
0.9	Sheltered accommodation
2.8	Other (WRITE IN)
0.7	(Don't know)
2.6	(Refusal/Not answered)

ASK ALL WHO WOULD LIKE TO MOVE OR ARE PLANNING TO MOVE

Q659-Q677   CARD G5   N=1164

Why (would you like / are you planning) to move home?
Please select all the answers that apply from this card.

PROBE FOR ALL REASONS
IF CODING 'Other' TRY TO FIND OUT WHETHER REASON IS TO DO WITH HOUSING/ AREA/ PERSONAL/ FINANCIAL.
Multicoded (Maximum of 19 codes)

HOUSING:

%		
38.7	Want larger / smaller house	[MoveSize]
3.6	Home is in poor condition	[MovePCon]
1.7	Lease is up / accommodation will be not available for other reason	[MoveLeas]
2.5	Problems with landlord / other tenants	[MoveProb]
1.9	On the waiting list for a house and one has come up	[MoveWait]
26.1	Simply to move to a house that I / we prefer	[MovePref]

AREA:

28.7	To move to a better area	[MoveArea]
6.9	To be close to work	[MoveWork]
11.6	To be nearer family or friends	[MoveFamF]

PERSONAL:

1.9	Divorce or separation	[MoveDivo]
4.0	Marriage or cohabitation	[MoveMarr]
13.5	Moving out of parents' home	[MoveLeft]

FINANCIAL:

12.1	Want to buy	[MoveBuy]
2.5	Can't afford current mortgage or rent	[MoveCost]
2.6	OTHER REASONS TO DO WITH **HOUSING**	[MoveOAcc]
1.9	OTHER REASONS TO DO WITH **AREA**	[MoveOAre]
2.5	OTHER **FINANCIAL** REASONS	[MoveOFin]
3.8	OTHER **PERSONAL** REASONS	[MoveOPer]
3.5	OTHER REASON (WRITE IN)	[MoveOth]
0.6	(Don't know)	
0.3	(Refusal/Not answered)	

ASK ALL

Q681   [HAView]
CARD G6   N=3199

Who do you think Housing Association homes should **mainly** be for?

%	
25.8	People on very low incomes
39.4	People on very low incomes **and** people like nurses or teachers if local property is very expensive
28.4	Anyone, regardless of their income
1.5	(None of these)
4.8	(Don't know)
0.1	(Refusal/Not answered)

IF NOT 'Rents: Housing Association' AT [Tenure6]

Q682   [LikeHA]
CARD G7   N=3199

Please use this card to tell me how much you agree or disagree with the following statement:
I would like to live in a Housing Association property if I could get it.

Q683   [HANotFM]
CARD G7 AGAIN   N=3199

(And how much you agree or disagree with the following statement:)
Housing Associations do not provide housing for people like me.

	[LikeHA]	[HANotFM]
	%	%
Agree strongly	4.2	10.9
Agree	11.7	27.8
Neither agree nor disagree	20.2	20.6
Disagree	30.3	22.4
Disagree strongly	24.0	3.6
(Don't know)	4.6	9.8
(Refusal/Not answered)	0.1	0.1

ASK ALL

Q684- CARD G8   N=3199
Q686 From what you know or have heard, what do you think are the three main **good points** about being a housing association tenant?
PROBE: What else?
CODE UP TO THREE
Multicoded (Maximum of 3 codes)

%		
2.4	(None of these)	[HAGdNone]
10.6	Being able to choose where to live	[HAGdWLiv]
41.0	Fair rent	[HAGdRent]
10.1	Better than being a council tenant	[HAGdBCou]
26.3	Cheaper than buying	[HAGdChea]
4.3	Friendly neighbours	[HAGdNeig]
13.5	Good landlords	[HAGdLand]
5.3	Access to tenant's associations	[HAGdTenA]
5.3	More choice over what happens to the property	[HAGdChoi]
7.0	Access to other housing association services	[HAGdHASe]
29.9	Good repairs and maintenance service	[HAGdGRep]
5.2	Access to support services	[HAGdSupp]
17.2	Good quality housing	[HAGdQual]
18.3	Homes are kept in a good state of repair	[HAGdGSta]
14.0	Housing Associations provide decent homes	[HAGdDecH]
5.4	Housing Associations provide modern homes	[HAGdModH]
0.9	Other (WRITE IN)	[HAGdOth]
19.2	(Don't know)	
0.1	(Refusal/Not answered)	

ASK ALL

Q689- CARD G9   N=3199
Q691 And what do you think are the three main **bad points**?
PROBE: What else?
CODE UP TO THREE
Multicoded (Maximum of 3 codes)

%		
3.5	(None of these)	[HABdNone]
17.1	The location of their homes	[HABdLoca]
10.7	Rents are too high	[HABdRent]
30.7	Antisocial neighbours	[HABdNeig]
5.7	Bad landlords	[HABdLand]
4.6	Having to deal with tenants' associations	[HABdTenA]
25.3	Little choice over what happens to the property	[HABdChoi]
7.5	Poor repairs and maintenance service	[HABdRep]
18.1	Little choice over the type of house tenants can live in	[HABdTypH]
4.2	Poor quality housing	[HABdQual]
3.4	Homes are kept in a poor state of repair	[HABdPSta]
2.6	Homes are of a poor standard	[HABdStan]
26.2	Can't invest in the housing market	[HABdNBuy]
33.7	Don't own the property	[HABdNOwn]
0.8	Other (WRITE IN)	[HABdOth]
23.3	(Don't know)	
0.1	(Refusal/Not answered)	

Q694 [HAQuiz1]
CARD G10   N=3199
For each of the following please use this card to tell me whether you think it is true or false. If you don't know, just say so and we'll skip to the next one.
Most Housing Association tenants have a job.
FOR DON'T KNOW, USE CTRL+K

Q695 [HAQuiz2]
CARD G10 AGAIN   N=3199
(Is it true or false that)
Most Housing Association tenants are dependent on state benefits.
FOR DON'T KNOW, USE CTRL+K

Q696   [HAQuiz3]
        CARD G10 AGAIN
        (Is it true or false that)
        Most Housing Association tenants have school age
        children living with them.
        FOR DON'T KNOW, USE CTRL+K

                                                                        N=3199

	[HAQuiz1]	[HAQuiz2]	[HAQuiz3]
	%	%	%
Definitely true	2.6	4.3	7.4
Probably true	33.4	32.2	44.8
Probably false	17.5	21.2	8.9
Definitely false	3.5	2.7	1.1
(Don't know)	42.9	39.5	37.7
(Refusal/Not answered)	0.1	0.1	0.1

Classification

Housing

        ASK ALL
Q697   [ResPres]
        Can I just check, would you describe the place where
        you live as ... READ OUT ...

        N=3199

        %
7.7   ...a big city,
26.3   the suburbs or outskirts of a big city,
43.3   a small city or town,
18.5   a **country** village,
3.6   or, a farm or home in the country?
0.4   (Other answer (WRITE IN))
0.1   (Don't know)
0.1   (Refusal/Not answered)

Family when growing up

        VERSION B: ASK ALL
Q700   [Sibs]

        N=1096

        Now a few questions about your family as you were
        growing up.
        Were you an only child, or did you have any brothers
        or sisters?
        IF RESPONDENT QUERIES WHETHER TO INCLUDE STEP,
        ADOPTED AND FOSTER SIBLINGS: Please include any that
        you think of as brothers and sisters.
        %
9.1   Only child
90.6   Had brother(s)/sister(s)
0.2   (Don't know)
0.1   (Refusal/Not answered)

        IF 'had brother(s)/sister(s)' AT [Sibs]
Q701   [SibOld]

        N=1096

        Were you ... READ OUT ....
        %
31.2   ... the oldest,
29.9   the youngest,
29.3   or, somewhere in the middle?
0.1   (Don't know)
0.4   (Refusal/Not answered)
        VERSION B: ASK ALL

Q702   [LiveWPar]   N=1096
        And, while you were growing up, did you always live
        with both of your parents?
%
86.6   Yes, always lived with both parents
13.1   No, didn't always live with both parents
0.2   (Don't know)
0.1   (Refusal/Not answered)

Religion and ethnicity

        ASK ALL   N=3199
Q710   [Religion]
        Do you regard yourself as belonging to any particular
        religion?
        IF YES: Which?
        CODE ONE ONLY - DO NOT PROMPT
%
43.4   No religion
7.4   Christian - no denomination
8.8   Roman Catholic
29.0   Church of England/Anglican
0.7   Baptist
1.7   Methodist
2.7   Presbyterian/Church of Scotland
0.1   Other Christian
0.8   Hindu
0.3   Jewish
1.5   Islam/Muslim
0.1   Sikh
0.3   Buddhist
0.3   Other non-Christian
0.1   Free Presbyterian
0.0   Brethren
0.5   United Reform Church (URC)/Congregational
1.7   Other Protestant
0.1   (Don't know)
0.0   (Refusal/Not answered)

Q713   [FamRelig]   N=3199
        In what religion, if any, were you bought up?
        PROBE IF NECESSARY: What was your family's religion?
        CODE ONE ONLY - DO NOT PROMPT
%
16.2   No religion
8.5   Christian - no denomination
13.6   Roman Catholic
45.6   Church of England/Anglican
1.3   Baptist
3.6   Methodist
4.8   Presbyterian/Church of Scotland
0.1   Other Christian
1.1   Hindu
0.4   Jewish
1.5   Islam/Muslim
0.2   Sikh
0.1   Buddhist
0.1   Other non-Christian
0.2   Free Presbyterian
0.0   Brethren
0.7   United Reform Church (URC)/Congregational
1.1   Other Protestant
0.1   (Don't know)
0.1   (Refusal/Not answered)

        IF RELIGION GIVEN AT [Religion] OR AT [FamRelig]
Q721   [ChAttend]   N=3199
        Apart from such special occasions as weddings,
        funerals and baptisms, how often nowadays do you
        attend services or meetings connected with your
        religion?
        PROBE AS NECESSARY.
%
10.0   Once a week or more
2.4   Less often but at least once in two weeks
5.6   Less often but at least once a month
9.3   Less often but at least twice a year
5.6   Less often but at least once a year
4.9   Less often than once a year
46.2   Never or practically never
0.7   Varies too much to say
0.0   (Don't know)
0.1   (Refusal/Not answered)

ASK ALL
CARD H1   N=3199
Please say which, if any, of the words on this card
describes the way you think of yourself. Please choose
as many or as few as apply.
PROBE: Any other?
Multicoded (Maximum of 8 codes)

Q722-
Q729

%		
66.3	British	[NatBrit]
48.2	English	[NatEng]
11.1	European	[NatEuro]
2.1	Irish	[NatIrish]
0.4	Northern Irish	[NatNI]
10.0	Scottish	[NatScot]
0.2	Ulster	[NatUlst]
5.4	Welsh	[NatWelsh]
3.0	Other answer (WRITE IN)	[NatOth]
0.3	(None of these)	[NatNone]
1.5	OTHER - ASIAN MENTIONED	[NatAsia]
1.0	OTHER - AFRICAN /CARIBBEAN MENTIONED	[NatAfric]
0.1	(Don't know)	
0.1	(Refusal/Not answered)	

IF MORE THAN ONE ANSWER AT [NationU]
[BNationU]
CARD H1 AGAIN   N=3199
And if you had to choose, which one best describes the
way you think of yourself?

Q744

ASK ALL
[RaceOri2]
CARD H2
To which of these groups do you consider you belong?

Q748

%	
0.8	BLACK: of African origin
0.7	BLACK: of Caribbean origin
0.2	BLACK: of other origin (WRITE IN)
1.5	ASIAN: of Indian origin
0.6	ASIAN: of Pakistani origin
0.1	ASIAN: of Bangladeshi origin
0.3	ASIAN: of Chinese origin
0.5	ASIAN: of other origin (WRITE IN)
93.1	WHITE: of any European origin
1.0	WHITE: of other origin (WRITE IN)
0.7	MIXED ORIGIN (WRITE IN)
0.5	OTHER (WRITE IN)
0.1	(Don't know)
0.1	(Refusal/Not answered)

N=3199

Education

VERSION A & B: ASK ALL

Q759 [RPrivEd]   N=2130
Have you ever attended a fee-paying, private primary or secondary school in the United Kingdom?
'PRIVATE' PRIMARY OR SECONDARY SCHOOLS INCLUDE:
* INDEPENDENT SCHOOLS
* SCHOLARSHIPS AND ASSISTED PLACES AT FEE-PAYING SCHOOLS
THEY EXCLUDE:
* DIRECT GRANT SCHOOLS (UNLESS FEE-PAYING)
* VOLUNTARY-AIDED SCHOOLS
* GRANT-MAINTAINED ('OPTED OUT') SCHOOLS
* NURSERY SCHOOLS

       %
12.2   Yes
87.6   No
0.1   (Don't know)
0.1   (Refusal/Not answered)

IF NO OWN CHILDREN IN THE HOUSEHOLD AGED 5 OR OVER (AS GIVEN IN THE HOUSEHOLD GRID)

Q760 [OthChld3]   N=2130
Have you ever been responsible for bringing up any children of school age, including stepchildren?

34.2   Yes
34.1   No
0.1   (Don't know)
0.1   (Refusal/Not answered)

VERSIONS A AND B: IF CHILDREN IN THE HOUSEHOLD (AS GIVEN IN THE HOUSEHOLD GRID) OR 'yes' AT [OthChld3]

Q761 [CHPrivEd]   N=2130
And (have any of your children / has your child) ever attend a fee-paying, private primary or secondary school in the United Kingdom?
'PRIVATE' PRIMARY OR SECONDARY SCHOOLS INCLUDE:
* INDEPENDENT SCHOOLS
* SCHOLARSHIPS AND ASSISTED PLACES AT FEE-PAYING SCHOOLS
THEY EXCLUDE:
* DIRECT GRANT SCHOOLS (UNLESS FEE-PAYING)
* VOLUNTARY-AIDED SCHOOLS
* GRANT-MAINTAINED ('OPTED OUT') SCHOOLS
* NURSERY SCHOOLS

       %
8.8   Yes
56.9   No
0.0   (Don't know)
0.2   (Refusal/Not answered)

ASK ALL

Q763 [Tea]   N=3199
How old were you when you completed your continuous full-time education?
PROBE IF NECESSARY
'STILL AT SCHOOL' - CODE 95
'STILL AT COLLEGE OR UNIVERSITY' - CODE 96
'OTHER ANSWER' - CODE 97 AND WRITE IN

       %
28.5   15 or under
27.2   16
8.2   17
10.0   18
21.7   19 or over
0.8   Still at school
3.0   Still at college or university
0.2   Other answer (WRITE IN)
0.3   (Don't know)
0.1   (Refusal/Not answered)

Q767 [SchQual]
CARD H3
Have you passed any of the examinations on this card?

N=3199

%
68.1 Yes
31.7 No
0.1 (Don't know)
0.1 (Refusal/Not answered)

IF 'yes' AT [SchQual]
Q768- CARD H3 AGAIN Please tell me which sections of the
Q771 card they are in?
PROBE : Any other sections?
CODE ALL THAT APPLY
Multicoded (Maximum of 4 codes)

N=3199

%
27.9 Section 1: [Edqual1]
GCSE Grades D-G/Short course GCSE/Vocational GCSE
CSE Grades 2-5
O-level Grades D-E or 7-9
Scottish (SCE) Ordinary Bands D-E
Scottish Standard Grades 4-7
SCOTVEC/SQA National Certificate modules
School leaving certificate (no grade)

47.5 Section 2: [Edqual2]
GCSE Grades A*-C
CSE Grade 1
O-level Grades A-C or 1-6
School Certif/Matriculation
Scottish SCE Ord. Bands A-C or pass
Scottish Standard Grades 1-3 or Pass
Scottish School Leaving Certificate Lower Grade
SUPE Ordinary
N Ireland Junior Certificate

26.6 Section 3: [Edqual3]
A-level, S-level, A2-level, AS-level
International Baccalaureate
Vocational A-level (AVCE)
Scottish Higher/ Higher-Still Grades
Scottish SCE/SLC/SUPE at Higher Grade
Scot. Higher School Certif
Certif Sixth Year Studies/ Advanced Higher Grades

2.9 Section 4: [Edqual4]
Overseas school leaving exam or certificate
0.2 (Refusal/Not answered)

Q772 **ASK ALL**
[PschQual]
CARD H4
And have you passed any of the exams or got any of
the qualifications on this card?

%
54.9 Yes
44.9 No
0.1 (Don't know)
0.1 (Refusal/Not answered)

IF 'yes' AT [PschQual]
Q773- CARD H4 AGAIN Which ones? PROBE: Which others?   N=3199
Q797   PROBE FOR CORRECT LEVEL

%		
16.8	Multicoded (Maximum of 25 codes)	
4.0	Univ/CNAA first degree/diploma	[EdQual135]
4.8	Postgraduate degree	[EdQual136]
2.9	Teacher training qualification	[EdQual112]
1.6	Nursing qualification	[EdQual113]
2.7	Foundation/advanced modern apprenticeship	[EdQual126]
2.6	Other recognised trade apprenticeship	[EdQual127]
1.8	OCR/RSA - (Vocational) Certificate	[EdQual128]
1.2	OCR/RSA - (First) Diploma	[EdQual129]
0.4	OCR/RSA - Advanced Diploma	[EdQual130]
1.5	OCR/RSA - Higher Diploma	[EdQual131]
6.3	Other clerical, commercial qualification	[EdQual132]
5.7	City&Guilds - Level 1/ Part I	[EdQual122]
	City&Guilds - Level 2/ Craft/ Intermediate/	
	Ordinary/ Part II	
3.4	City&Guilds - Level 3/Advanced/ Final/ Part III	[EdQual123]
2.0	City&Guilds - Level 4/Full Technological/	[EdQual124]
	Part IV	
1.1	Edexcel/BTEC First Certificate	[EdQual125]
0.9	Edexcel/BTEC First/General Diploma	[EdQual133]
3.7	Edexcel/BTEC/BEC/TEC (General/Ordinary) National	[EdQual134]
	Certif or Diploma (ONC/OND)	
5.2	Edexcel/BTEC/BEC/TEC Higher National Certif (HNC)	[EdQual110]
	or Diploma (HND)	
2.9	NVQ/SVQ Lev 1/GNVQ/GSVQ Foundation lev	[EdQual111]
5.4	NVQ/SVQ Lev 2/GNVQ/GSVQ Intermediate lev	[EdQual117]
4.3	NVQ/SVQ Lev 3/GNVQ/GSVQ Advanced lev	[EdQual118]
0.7	NVQ/SVQ Lev 4	[EdQual119]
0.3	NVQ/SVQ Lev 5	[EdQual120]
7.5	Other recogn academic or vocational qual	[EdQual121]
	(WRITE IN)	
0.2	(Don't know)	[EdQual137]
0.2	(Refusal/Not answered)	

Internet use

ASK ALL
Q831   [Internet]
Does anyone have access to the Internet or World
Wide Web
from this address?   N=3199

%	
60.2	Yes
39.7	No
0.1	(Don't know)
0.1	(Refusal/Not answered)

Q832   [WWWUse]
Do you yourself ever use the Internet or World Wide
Web for any reason (other than your work)?   N=3199

%	
59.6	Yes
40.3	No
0.1	(Don't know)
0.1	(Refusal/Not answered)

IF 'yes' AT [WWWUse]
Q833   [WWWHrsWk]
How many hours a week on average do you spend using
the Internet or World Wide Web (other than for your
work)?   N=3199
INTERVIEWER: ROUND UP TO NEAREST HOUR

%	**Median = 2 hours**
0.1	Don't know
0.2	Not answered

Recall vote

ASK ALL

Q834 [Voted01]
Thinking back to the last general election - that is N=3199
the one in 2001 - we have found that a lot of people
didn't manage to vote. How about you - did you manage
to vote in that election?
IF NECESSARY, SAY: The one where Tony Blair won against
William Hague.
IF NOT ELIGIBLE / TOO YOUNG TO VOTE: CODE 'NO'.
IF 'CAN'T REMEMBER', CODE 'DON'T KNOW' (Ctrl + K)
%
67.8 Yes, voted
31.0 No
1.0 (Don't know)
0.2 (Refusal/Not answered)

Partner/spouse's job details

VERSION A: ASK ALL WITH SPOUSE OR PARTNER WHO IS
WORKING OR WAITING TO TAKE UP WORK N=444

Q860 [Title] **NOT ON DATAFILE**
Now I want to ask you about
(husband's/wife's/partner's) (present/future) job.
What (is his/her job/ will that job be)?
PROBE IF NECESSARY: What ^iswas the name or title of
the job?

Q861 [Typewk] **NOT ON DATAFILE** N=444
What kind of work (do/will) (he/she) do most of the
time?
IF RELEVANT: What materials/machinery (do/will)
(he/she) use?

Q862 [Train] **NOT ON DATAFILE** N=444
What training or qualifications ^arewere needed for
that job?

Q865 [S2Employ] N=444
Q866 In your (husband's/wife's/partner's) (main) job
% (is/will) (he/she) (be) ... READ OUT ...
82.3 ... an employee,
16.1 or self-employed?
1.1 (Don't know)
0.5 (Refusal/Not answered)

Q868 [S2Superv] N=444
Q869 In (his/her) job, (does/will) (he/she) have any
formal responsibility for supervising the work of
other (employees/people)?
DO NOT INCLUDE PEOPLE WHO ONLY SUPERVISE:
- CHILDREN, E.G. TEACHERS, NANNIES, CHILDMINDERS
- ANIMALS
- SECURITY OR BUILDINGS, E.G. CARETAKERS, SECURITY
  GUARDS
%
40.2 Yes
58.4 No
0.9 (Don't know)
0.5 (Refusal/Not answered)

VERSION A: ASK ALL WITH SPOUSE OR PARTNER WHO IS WORKING OR WAITING TO TAKE UP WORK AS EMPLOYEE

Q875 [S2OcSec2]
Q876 CARD H5   N=373
Which of the types of organisation on this card (does he/she work/will he/she be working) for?

%

63.8   PRIVATE SECTOR FIRM OR COMPANY Including, for example, limited companies and PLCs

3.7   NATIONALISED INDUSTRY OR PUBLIC CORPORATION Including, for example, the Post Office and the BBC

27.4   OTHER PUBLIC SECTOR EMPLOYER
Incl eg:
- Central govt/ Civil Service/ Govt Agency
- Local authority/ Local Educ Auth (INCL 'OPTED OUT' SCHOOLS)
- Universities
- Health Authority / NHS hospitals / NHS Trusts/ GP surgeries
- Police / Armed forces

2.8   CHARITY/ VOLUNTARY SECTOR Including, for example, charitable companies, churches, trade unions

0.6   Other answer (WRITE IN)
1.0   (Don't know)
0.6   (Refusal/Not answered)

VERSION A: ASK ALL WITH SPOUSE OR PARTNER WHO IS WORKING OR WAITING TO TAKE UP WORK

Q884 [S2EmpWr2]   N=444
IF EMPLOYEE: Including (himself/herself), how many people are employed at the place where (he/she) usually works from?
IF SELF-EMPLOYED: (Does/Will) (he/she) have any employees?
IF YES: PROBE FOR CORRECT PRECODE.

%

11.7   Self employed: No employees
16.1   Under 10
11.1   10-24
8.2   25-49
7.8   50-99
10.5   100-199
10.1   200-499
16.9   500+
6.0   (Don't know)
1.6   (Refusal/Not answered)

Q925 [S2PartF1]   N=444
Is the job ... READ OUT ...
... full-time - that is, 30 or more hours per week,
or, part-time?
(Don't know)
(Refusal/Not answered)

%

79.6
19.7
0.5
0.2

Income and benefits

VERSION A AND B: ASK ALL

Q927 [AnyBN3]
CARD H6   N=2130
Do you (or your husband/wife/partner) receive any of the state benefits or tax credits on this card at present?

%
58.6 Yes
41.1 No
0.2 (Don't know)
0.2 (Refusal/Not answered)

IF 'yes' AT [AnyBN3]

Q928- CARD H6 AGAIN Which ones? PROBE: Which others?
Q945 Multicoded (Maximum of 18 codes)   N=2130

%
21.7 State retirement pension (National Insurance)   [BenefOAP]
0.6 War Pension (War Disablement Pension or War Widows Pension)   [BenefWar]
0.8 Bereavement Allowance/ Widow's Pension/ Widowed Parent's Allowance   [BenefWid]
1.7 Jobseeker's Allowance   [BenefUB]
4.6 Income Support (not for pensioners)   [BenefIS2]
3.2 Pension Credit / Minimum Income Guarantee / Income Support for pensioners   [BenefPC]
26.3 Child Benefit (formerly Family Allowance)   [BenefCB]
14.6 Child Tax Credit   [BenefCTC]
6.9 Working Tax Credit   [BenefFC]
6.0 Housing Benefit (Rent Rebate/ Rent Allowance)   [BenefHB]
7.2 Council Tax Benefit (or Rebate)   [BenefCT]
4.8 Incapacity Benefit / Sickness Benefit / Invalidity Benefit   [BenefInc]
4.7 Disability Living Allowance (for people under 65)   [BenefDLA]
1.8 Attendance Allowance (for people aged 65+)   [BenefAtA]
0.4 Severe Disablement Allowance   [BenefSev]
0.8 Invalid Care Allowance   [BenefICA]
0.6 Industrial Injuries Disablement Benefit   [BenefInd]
0.4 Other state benefit (WRITE IN)   [BenefOth]

ASK ALL

Q967 [MainInc3]
CARD (H6/H7)   N=3199
Which of these is the main source of income for you (and your husband/wife/partner) at present?

%
65.5 Earnings from employment (own or spouse / partner's)
8.6 Occupational pension(s) - from previous employer(s)
1.4 Private pension(s)
11.7 State retirement or widow's pension(s)
1.7 Jobseeker's Allowance/ Unemployment benefit
1.0 Pension Credit/ Minimum Income Guarantee/ Income Support for pensioners
3.4 Invalidity, sickness or disabled pension or benefit(s)
2.1 Other state benefit or tax credit (WRITE IN)
0.7 Interest from savings or investments
1.7 Student grant, bursary or loans
1.1 Dependent on parents/other relatives
0.5 Other main source (WRITE IN)
0.2 (Don't know)
0.3 (Refusal/Not answered)

Q972 [HHincome]
CARD (H7/H8)   N=3199
Which of the letters on this card represents the total income of your household from all sources before tax?
Please just tell me the letter.
NOTE: INCLUDES INCOME FROM BENEFITS, SAVINGS, ETC.

Administration

Q976 [SCXplain]
ASK ALL N=3199
INTERVIEWER: THANK RESPONDENT FOR (HIS/HER) HELP AND
EXPLAIN ABOUT THE SELF-COMPLETION QUESTIONNAIRE.
PLEASE MAKE SURE YOU GIVE THE RESPONDENT THE VERSION
(A/B/C) (orange/yellow/green) QUESTIONNAIRE
ENTER THE SERIAL NUMBER : (serial number)
...POINT NUMBER : (sample point)
...INTERVIEWER NUMBER : (interviewer number)
ON THE FRONT PAGE OF THE SELF COMPLETION.
THEN TELL US WHETHER IT IS TO BE ...

%	
22.9	... filled in immediately after interview in your presence,
70.5	or, left behind to be filled in later,
6.4	or, if the respondent refused.
0.2	(Don't know)
0.1	(Refusal/Not answered)

Q978 [PhoneX] N=3199

%	Do you have a telephone?
96.7	Yes
3.0	No
0.2	(Don't know)
0.2	(Refusal/Not answered)

IF 'yes' AT [PhoneX]
Q979 [PhoneBc2] N=3199
A few interviews on any survey are checked by my
office to make sure that people are satisfied with
the way the interview was carried out. In case my
office needs to contact you, it would be helpful if
we could have your telephone number.
ADD IF NECESSARY: Your 'phone number will not be
passed to anyone outside the National Centre without
your consent.
IF NUMBER GIVEN, WRITE ON THE ARF
IF MORE THAN ONE NUMBER, ASK WHICH WOULD BE MOST
CONVENIENT FOR RECONTACT

%	
92.7	Number given
3.9	Number refused
0.0	(Don't know)
0.3	(Refusal/Not answered)

Q973 [REarn] ASK ALL IN PAID WORK (AT [REconAct]) N=1886
CARD (H7/H8) AGAIN
Which of the letters on this card represents your own
gross or total earnings, before deduction of income tax
and national insurance?

	[HhIncome]	[REarn]
	%	%
Less than 3,999	1.9	3.0
4,000 to 5,999	4.7	5.5
6,000 to 6,999	4.6	5.8
8,000 to 8,999	5.0	5.3
10,000 to 11,999	4.5	7.6
12,000 to 14,999	6.0	9.4
15,000 to 17,999	4.8	9.6
18,000 to 19,999	4.3	5.8
20,000 to 22,999	5.2	7.6
23,000 to 25,999	5.5	6.3
26,000 to 28,999	4.8	5.4
29,000 to 31,999	4.8	4.0
32,000 to 37,999	6.4	6.2
38,000 to 43,999	5.4	3.1
44,000 to 49,999	4.8	2.7
50,000 to 55,999	3.2	1.3
56,000 or more	10.1	4.5
Refused information	7.6	5.8
Don't know	6.6	0.9

Q974 [CarOwn2] VERSION A AND B: ASK ALL N=2130
Do you, or does anyone else in your household, have a
car or van?
INTERVIEWER: IF ASKED, INCLUDE LEASED AND COMPANY CARS

%	
82.4	Yes
17.4	No
0.1	(Don't know)
0.1	(Refusal/Not answered)

Q980   **ASK ALL**
            [ComeBac3]
            From time to time we do follow-up studies and may wish   N=3199
            to contact you again. Would this be all right?

     %
  80.7   Yes
  18.8   No
   0.4   (Don't know)
   0.1   (Refusal/Not answered)

Q981   **IF 'yes' AT [ComeBac3]**
            [Stable]   N=3199
            Could you give us the address and phone number of
            someone who knows you well, just in case have
            difficulty in getting in touch with you.
            IF NECESSARY, PROMPT: Perhaps a relative or friend who
            is unlikely to move?
            WRITE DETAILS ON THE BACK PAGE OF THE ARF.
     %
  35.7   INFORMATION GIVEN
  44.9   INFORMATION NOT GIVEN
   0.0   Don't know
   0.6   Not answered

N=833

1. There are different opinions as to what it takes to be a good citizen. As far as you are concerned personally, on a scale of 1 to 7, where 1 is not at all important and 7 is very important, how important is it...?

PLEASE TICK *ONE* BOX ON EACH LINE

	Not at all Important 1	2	3	4	5	6	Very Important 7	Can't choose	Not answered
[citduty1] a. ...always to vote in elections	7.9	2.7	6.8	13.6	11.8	14.7	38.8	3.1	0.7
[citduty2] b. ...never to try to evade taxes	2.1	1.1	2.1	3.3	7.6	15.9	64.4	1.4	2.1
[citduty3] c. ...always to obey laws and regulations	0.9	0.1	1.2	2.7	7.9	17.4	67.3	0.7	1.7
[citduty4] d. ...to keep watch on the actions of government	4.6	2.8	5.8	17.2	20.1	16.8	27.9	2.7	2.3
[citduty5] e. ...to be active in social or political associations	19.4	10.9	17.3	21.5	16.5	6.0	3.3	3.1	2.1
[citduty6] f. ...to try to understand the reasoning of people with other opinions	2.1	1.5	3.5	12.6	18.7	24.4	34.7	1.2	1.3
[citduty7] g. ...to choose products for political, ethical or environmental reasons, even if they cost a bit more	10.2	6.7	10.9	21.3	20.1	14.1	11.4	3.2	2.1
[citduty8] h. ...to help people in Britain who are worse off than yourself	1.7	1.9	9.4	16.7	20.8	24.3	23.0	1.1	1.2
[citduty9] i. ...to help people in the rest of the world who are worse off than yourself	4.5	7.9	12.1	17.9	21.9	16.1	16.3	1.7	1.7
[citduty10] j. ...to be willing to serve in the military at a time of need	12.3	6.0	8.8	13.7	14.3	14.8	19.4	8.0	2.7

BRITISH SOCIAL ATTITUDES SELF-COMPLETION QUESTIONNAIRE VERSION A

[relmeet]
2. There are a number of groups in society. Should religious extremists be allowed to hold public meetings?

PLEASE TICK ONE BOX ONLY

N=833

	%
Should definitely be allowed	7.1
Should probably be allowed	25.5
Should probably not be allowed	26.2
Should definitely not be allowed	34.0
Can't choose	6.8
Not answered	0.4

[relmeet3]
3. Should people who want to overthrow the government by force be allowed to hold public meetings?

PLEASE TICK ONE BOX ONLY

N=833

	%
Should definitely be allowed	4.0
Should probably be allowed	12.1
Should probably not be allowed	23.0
Should definitely not be allowed	55.3
Can't choose	5.1
Not answered	0.4

[racmeet2]
4. Should people prejudiced against any racial or ethnic group be allowed to hold public meetings?

PLEASE TICK ONE BOX ONLY

N=833

	%
Should definitely be allowed	5.6
Should probably be allowed	18.7
Should probably not be allowed	24.4
Should definitely not be allowed	46.4
Can't choose	3.8
Not answered	1.1

5. Here are some different forms of political and social action that people can take. Please indicate, for each one, whether: you have done any of these things in the past year; you have done it in the more distant past; you have not done it but might do it; or have not done it and would never, under any circumstances, do it.

N=833

PLEASE TICK ONE BOX ON EACH LINE		Have done it in the past year	Have done it in the more distant past	Have not done it but might do it	Have not done it and would never do it	Can't choose	Not answered
[socact1] a. Signed a petition	%	33.5	39.6	17.4	6.4	1.4	1.7
[socact2] b. Boycotted, or deliberately bought, certain products for political, ethical or environmental reasons	%	21.8	16.6	30.1	26.8	2.4	2.3
[socact3] c. Took part in a demonstration	%	2.3	11.3	41.5	42.1	1.1	1.9
[socact4] d. Attended a political meeting or rally	%	2.7	11.7	35.9	46.1	1.3	2.5
[socact5] e. Contacted, or attempted to contact, a politician or a civil servant to express your views	%	9.1	14.3	47.6	25.3	2.2	1.5
[socact6] f. Donated money or raised funds for a social or political activity	%	14.1	16.3	24.4	41.5	1.6	2.1
[socact7] g. Contacted or appeared in the media to express your views	%	3.3	6.7	38.6	47.1	2.3	1.9
[socact8] h. Joined an Internet political forum or discussion group	%	2.1	1.3	22.8	69.1	3.1	1.7

6. People sometimes belong to different kinds of groups or associations. For each type of group, please indicate whether you: belong and actively participate; belong but don't actively participate; used to belong but do not any more; or have never belonged to it.

PLEASE TICK ONE BOX ON EACH LINE

N=833

		Belong, actively participate	Belong, don't participate	Used to belong	Never belonged	Can't choose	Not answered
[grpmemb1]							
a.	A political party	% 1.5	8.7	6.4	81.0	0.7	1.8
[grpmemb2]							
b.	A trade union, business, or professional association	% 4.9	16.7	30.6	45.9	0.4	1.5
[grpmemb3]							
c.	A church or other religious organisation	% 16.0	17.9	23.0	40.9	0.9	1.3
[grpmemb4]							
d.	A sports, leisure or cultural group	% 22.8	6.1	32.5	35.9	0.8	2.0
[grpmemb5]							
e.	Another voluntary association	% 11.6	4.6	20.7	57.6	2.5	2.9

7. There are different opinions about people's rights in a democracy. On a scale of 1 to 7, where 1 is not at all important and 7 is very important, how important is it:

PLEASE TICK ONE BOX ON EACH LINE

N=833

		Not at all Important 1	2	3	4	5	6	Very Important 7	Can't choose	Not answered
[demrigh1]										
a.	...that all citizens have an adequate standard of living	% 0.5	0.2	2.2	6.4	11.5	14.3	62.8	1.3	0.8
[demrigh2]										
b.	...that government authorities respect and protect the rights of minorities	% 1.3	0.3	5.2	12.6	16.7	17.2	42.4	3.1	1.2
[demrigh3]										
c.	...that government authorities treat everybody equally regardless of their position in society	% 1.1	0.5	2.8	6.5	10.2	15.6	60.1	2.0	1.1
[demrigh4]										
d.	...that politicians take into account the views of citizens before making decisions	% 0.4	0.7	0.8	4.1	8.6	17.3	65.5	1.6	1.1
[demrigh5]										
e.	...that people be given more opportunities to participate in public decision-making	% 0.3	0.5	2.2	10.1	18.3	19.2	45.2	3.0	0.9
[demrigh6]										
f.	...that citizens may engage in acts of civil disobedience when they oppose government actions	% 17.6	10.2	11.1	17.4	10.2	7.6	12.8	11.7	1.3

8. To what extent do you agree or disagree with the following statements?

PLEASE TICK ONE BOX ON EACH LINE

N=833

		Agree strongly	Agree	Neither agree nor disagree	Disagree	Disagree strongly	Can't choose	Not answered
[govnosa2]								
a.	People like me don't have any say about what the government does	% 20.0	31.7	19.0	22.5	2.9	1.7	2.2
[govnocar]								
b.	I don't think the government cares much what people like me think	% 20.1	37.3	16.7	19.4	3.1	1.5	1.9
[polundst]								
c.	I feel I have a pretty good understanding of the important political issues facing Britain	% 8.8	40.9	24.9	16.6	3.2	3.5	2.1
[infpoli2]								
d.	I think most people in Britain are better informed about politics and government than I am	% 1.7	13.1	31.7	40.7	6.8	3.8	2.1

9. Suppose a law were being considered by parliament that you considered to be unjust or harmful.

N=833

[protgrp]
a. If such a case arose, how likely is it that you, acting alone or together with others, would be able to try to do something about it?

PLEASE TICK ONE BOX ONLY

	%
Very likely	11.9
Fairly likely	25.4
Not very likely	41.9
Not at all likely	14.6
Can't choose	4.8
Not answered	1.4

[protattn]
b. If you made such an effort, how likely is it that parliament would give serious attention to your demands?

PLEASE TICK ONE BOX ONLY

	%
Very likely	1.6
Fairly likely	15.3
Not very likely	53.2
Not at all likely	23.8
Can't choose	4.8
Not answered	1.3

[politsc]
10. How interested would you say you personally are in politics?

N=833

*PLEASE TICK **ONE** BOX ONLY*

	%
Very interested	9.1
Fairly interested	40.2
Not very interested	35.0
Not at all interested	13.8
Can't choose	0.7
Not answered	1.1

11. To what extent do you agree or disagree with the following statements?

N=833

*PLEASE TICK **ONE** BOX ON EACH LINE*

	Agree strongly	Agree	Neither agree nor disagree	Disagree	Disagree strongly	Can't choose	Not answered
[govright] a. Most of the time we can trust people in government to do what is right %	1.1	26.4	31.8	28.5	9.0	1.5	1.8
[govself] b. Most politicians are in politics only for what they can get out of it personally %	10.5	30.8	31.3	22.1	1.7	1.9	1.7

[peopadvt]
12. How often do you think that people would try to take advantage of you if they got the chance, and how often would they try to be fair?

N=833

*PLEASE TICK **ONE** BOX ONLY*

	%
Try to take advantage almost all of the time	3.7
Try to take advantage most of the time	31.2
Try to be fair most of the time	49.2
Try to be fair almost all of the time	5.5
Can't choose	8.8
Not answered	1.6

[peoptrst]
13. Generally speaking, would you say that people can be trusted or that you can't be too careful in dealing with people?

N=833

*PLEASE TICK **ONE** BOX ONLY*

	%
People can almost always be trusted	0.9
People can usually be trusted	44.7
You usually can't be too careful in dealing with people	45.4
You almost always can't be too careful in dealing with people	5.1
Can't choose	2.7
Not answered	1.2

[poltalk]
14. When you get together with your friends, relatives or fellow workers how often do you discuss politics?

N=833

*PLEASE TICK **ONE** BOX ONLY*

	%
Often	8.5
Sometimes	36.4
Rarely	35.9
Never	18.9
Can't choose	0.2
Not answered	0.2

[polinfl]
15. When you hold a strong opinion about politics, how often do you try to persuade your friends, relatives or fellow workers to share your views?

N=833

*PLEASE TICK **ONE** BOX ONLY*

	%
Often	3.8
Sometimes	25.8
Rarely	33.8
Never	34.5
Can't choose	1.6
Not answered	0.5

[untnats]
16. Now we would like to ask your opinion about international issues.
Thinking about the United Nations, which comes closest to your view?

N=833

PLEASE TICK ONE BOX ONLY

	%
The United Nations has too much power	8.2
The United Nations has about the right amount of power	37.3
The United Nations has too little power	30.0
I don't know what the United Nations is	5.6
Can't choose	18.4
Not answered	0.5

[intorg]
17. Which of these two statements comes closer to your view?

N=833

PLEASE TICK ONE BOX ONLY

	%
In international organisations, decisions should be left to national government representatives	29.7
OR	
In international organisations, citizens' organisations should be involved directly in the decision-making process	39.8
Can't choose	30.0
Not answered	0.5

[inthumrt]
18. Which of these two statements comes closer to your view?

N=833

PLEASE TICK ONE BOX ONLY

	%
If a country seriously violates human rights, the United Nations should intervene	75.6
OR	
Even if human rights are seriously violated, the country's sovereignty must be respected, and the United Nations should not intervene	8.0
I don't know what the United Nations is	4.5
Can't choose	11.5
Not answered	0.5

[untnats]
19. Thinking now about politics in Britain, to what extent do you agree or disagree with the following statements?

N=833

PLEASE TICK ONE BOX ON EACH LINE

		Agree strongly	Agree	Neither agree nor disagree	Disagree	Disagree strongly	Can't choose	Not answered
[polpar1] a. Political parties encourage people to become active in politics	%	1.7	23.4	35.1	27.3	3.2	5.8	3.5
[polpar2] b. Political parties do not give voters real policy choices	%	6.6	40.8	26.5	15.5	1.4	6.0	3.6
[polpar3] c. Referendums are a good way to decide important political questions	%	16.9	44.3	20.9	6.7	1.8	7.6	1.8

[honelec]
20. Thinking of the last national election in Britain, how honest was it regarding the counting and reporting of the votes?

N=833

PLEASE TICK ONE BOX ONLY

	%
Very honest	31.6
Somewhat honest	24.9
Neither honest or dishonest	14.8
Somewhat dishonest	6.5
Very dishonest	0.7
Can't choose	20.7
Not answered	0.7

[fairelec]
21. Thinking of the last national election in Britain, how fair was it regarding the opportunities of the candidates and parties to campaign?

N=833

PLEASE TICK ONE BOX ONLY

	%
Very fair	25.1
Somewhat fair	27.9
Neither fair or unfair	18.7
Somewhat unfair	4.2
Very unfair	1.6
Can't choose	21.9
Not answered	0.6

[civser1]
22. Thinking of the civil service in Britain, how committed is it to serving the people?

PLEASE TICK ONE BOX ONLY

N=833

	%
Very committed	7.2
Fairly committed	54.8
Not very committed	23.4
Not at all committed	3.7
Can't choose	9.7
Not answered	1.2

[civser2]
23. When the civil service makes serious mistakes in Britain how likely is it they will be corrected?

PLEASE TICK ONE BOX ONLY

N=833

	%
Very likely	6.9
Somewhat likely	36.8
Not very likely	40.3
Not at all likely	6.8
Can't choose	8.2
Not answered	1.1

[civser3]
24. How widespread do you think corruption is in the civil service in Britain?

PLEASE TICK ONE BOX ONLY

N=833

	%
Hardly anyone is involved	6.5
A small number of people are involved	42.3
A moderate number of people are involved	23.9
A lot of people are involved	7.2
Almost everyone is involved	1.1
Can't choose	17.9
Not answered	1.1

25. On the whole, on a scale of 0 to 10, where 0 is very poorly and 10 is very well...

N=833

[demonow]
a. ...how well does democracy work in Britain today?

PLEASE TICK ONE BOX ONLY

Very poorly 0	1	2	3	4	5	6	7	8	9	Very well 10	Can't choose	Not answered
% 1.6	0.6	2.5	4.8	7.8	17.8	13.1	15.9	15.6	6.5	3.6	8.7	1.3

[demo10yr]
b. And what about 10 years ago? How well did democracy work in Britain then?

PLEASE TICK ONE BOX ONLY

Very poorly 0	1	2	3	4	5	6	7	8	9	Very well 10	Can't choose	Not answered
% 1.5	0.9	1.8	4.8	7.1	15.0	12.4	14.0	13.8	8.2	4.4	14.7	1.3

[demofut]
c. And how about 10 years from now? How well do you think democracy will work in Britain then?

PLEASE TICK ONE BOX ONLY

Very poorly 0	1	2	3	4	5	6	7	8	9	Very well 10	Can't choose	Not answered
% 3.6	3.1	4.0	6.2	5.7	14.0	10.0	11.0	12.3	6.0	3.6	18.8	1.6

[restdemo]
26. Here are some views regarding Britain's political system. Which of these statements is closer to your view?

PLEASE TICK ONE BOX ONLY

N=833

	%
Under no circumstances should democratic rights be restricted by government	59.3
OR	
When the government thinks it is necessary it should restrict democratic rights	17.1
Can't choose	22.0
Not answered	1.5

[singmum1]
27. Thinking about a single mother with a child under school age. Which one of these statements comes closest to your view?

PLEASE TICK ONE BOX ONLY

N=2610

	%
She has a special duty to go out to work to support her child	17.5
She has a special duty to stay at home to look after her child	25.4
She should do as she chooses, like everyone else	51.2
Can't choose	5.4
Not answered	0.5

[singmmc2]
28. Suppose this single mother did go out to work. How much do you agree or disagree that the government should provide money to help with child care?

PLEASE TICK ONE BOX ONLY

N=2610

	%
Agree strongly	21.7
Agree	49.7
Neither agree nor disagree	14.8
Disagree	9.6
Disagree strongly	1.8
Can't choose	2.0
Not answered	0.4

[smumsch1]
29. And what about when the child reaches school age? Which one of these statements comes closest to your view about what the single mother should do?

PLEASE TICK ONE BOX ONLY

N=2610

	%
She has a special duty to go out to work to support her child	46.6
She has a special duty to stay at home to look after her child	5.0
She should do as she chooses, like everyone else	44.6
Can't choose	3.5
Not answered	0.4

[smumsch2]
30. Suppose this single mother did go out to work. How much do you agree or disagree that the government should provide money to help with child care outside school?

PLEASE TICK ONE BOX ONLY

N=2610

	%
Agree strongly	15.1
Agree	43.4
Neither agree nor disagree	20.9
Disagree	15.3
Disagree strongly	1.9
Can't choose	3.1
Not answered	0.4

[coupmum1]
31. And finally thinking about a married mother with a child under school age. Which one of these statements comes closest to your own view?

PLEASE TICK ONE BOX ONLY

N=2610

	%
She has a special duty to go out to work to support her child	8.2
She has a special duty to stay at home to look after her child	30.7
She should do as she chooses, like everyone else	57.3
Can't choose	3.2
Not answered	0.6

[coupmum2]
32. Suppose this married mother did go out to work. How much do you agree or disagree that the government should provide money to help with child care?

N=2610

PLEASE TICK ONE BOX ONLY

	%
Agree strongly	9.9
Agree	34.5
Neither agree nor disagree	25.8
Disagree	22.2
Disagree strongly	3.6
Can't choose	3.2
Not answered	0.8

33. Please tick one box on each line to show how much you agree or disagree with each of these statements.

N=2610

PLEASE TICK ONE BOX ON EACH LINE

	Agree strongly	Agree	Neither agree nor disagree	Disagree	Disagree strongly	Can't choose	Not answered
[pencomp] a. Sometimes pensions seem so complicated that a person like me cannot really understand the best thing to do. %	18.1	45.4	13.7	15.0	3.3	2.9	1.6
[enjlife] b. It's better to enjoy life now rather than worrying about making plans for the future. %	4.7	14.3	16.2	41.0	16.9	2.0	4.9

[inherit]
34. Which of these two statements comes closest to your view?

N=2610

PLEASE TICK ONE BOX ONLY

	%
Older people should try to pass on an inheritance to their children, even if they have to cut back on other things	14.5
OR	
Older people should spend their money while they can and not worry about leaving an inheritance for their children	67.5
Can't choose	17.1
Not answered	0.9

[moneyret]
35. And which of these two statements comes closest to your own view?

N=2610

PLEASE TICK ONE BOX ONLY

	%
Young people should spend their money while they are young and worry about saving for retirement when they are older	14.7
OR	
Young people should start saving for their retirement as soon as they can even if they have to cut back on other things	72.5
Can't choose	12.5
Not answered	0.4

36. The government raises money through taxation to pay for benefits and services like education and health. How much do you agree or disagree with each of these statements?

N=1721

PLEASE TICK ONE BOX ON EACH LINE

	Agree strongly	Agree	Neither agree nor disagree	Disagree	Disagree strongly	Can't choose	Not answered
[majtax] a. It's only right that taxes paid by the majority help support those in need %	14.2	54.8	14.4	9.4	1.4	2.2	3.6
[soctax] b. If we want to live in a healthy, well-educated society we have to be willing to pay the taxes to fund it %	18.8	65.0	8.5	3.2	0.4	1.7	2.3
[nousesec] c. It's not fair that some people pay a lot of money in tax and hardly use the services their taxes pay for %	8.1	24.2	23.5	33.5	5.2	2.4	3.2
[bestrtax] d. The best reason for paying taxes now is that you never know when you might need benefits and services yourself %	14.1	60.0	14.1	6.8	1.1	2.0	2.0
[benfrsec] e. It's not right that people benefit from services that they haven't helped to pay for %	16.5	31.1	20.9	22.9	3.1	2.3	3.1

37. Do you agree or disagree with each of these statements?

N=1721

PLEASE TICK ONE BOX
ON EACH LINE

		Agree strongly	Agree	Neither agree nor disagree	Disagree	Disagree strongly	Can't choose	Not answered
[ineqrich] a. Inequality continues to exist because it benefits the rich and powerful	%	11.6	36.1	24.4	17.2	2.4	5.8	2.5
[paystudy] b. No one would study for years to become a lawyer or doctor unless they expected to earn a lot more than ordinary workers	%	12.8	51.7	13.4	16.7	1.5	2.2	1.8
[diffsnec] c. Large differences in income are necessary for Britain's prosperity	%	2.7	20.4	30.3	34.1	5.4	4.5	2.5

38. Is it right or wrong that people with higher incomes can …

N=1721

PLEASE TICK ONE BOX
ON EACH LINE

		Definitely right	Somewhat right	Neither right nor wrong.	Somewhat wrong	Very wrong	Can't choose	Not answered
[buyhlth] a. Buy better health care than people with lower incomes	%	17.0	29.6	27.0	13.7	9.4	1.9	1.3
[buyeducn] b. Buy better education for their children than people with lower incomes	%	17.5	30.9	24.9	13.2	9.8	1.7	2.1

39. Please show how much you agree or disagree with each of these statements.

N=1721

PLEASE TICK ONE BOX
ON EACH LINE

		Agree strongly	Agree	Neither agree nor disagree	Disagree	Disagree strongly	Can't choose	Not answered
[incdiffs] a. Differences in income in Britain are too large.	%	17.0	45.6	21.5	11.2	1.0	2.1	1.7
[incdiff] b. It is the responsibility of the government to reduce the differences in income between people with high incomes and those with low incomes	%	10.2	32.7	22.1	23.0	6.8	3.2	2.0

N=1721

40. Think of a person who can't find a job at the moment. Do you think there are any circumstances where it would be right to limit this person's access to unemployment benefits? Please read through all the options before choosing.

YES, it would be right to limit someone's access to unemployment benefits if:

PLEASE TICK ALL THAT APPLY

%

[acunsave] They had enough savings or private insurance to look after themselves	30.9
[acunwshy] They were not actively looking for work	77.6
[acuntbbr] They were not born in Britain but settled here more than 2 years ago	22.4
[acunbrec] They had recently come to Britain hoping to find work here	59.3
[acunrefu] They had recently come to Britain because they were in danger at home	21.5
[acunchil] They had lived in Britain all their life but not paid much in taxes because they were bringing up children	9.2
[acunpoor] They had lived in Britain all their life but not paid much in taxes because they were unemployed for a long time	25.1
[acunoth] Some other reason (*PLEASE WRITE IN*)	2.1
[acunnone] **NO, it would <u>never</u> be right to limit access to unemployment benefits**	4.1
Can't choose	4.1
Not answered	1.4

41. Now think of a person with an on-going illness who needs medical treatment. Do you think there are any circumstances where it would be right to limit would be right to limit this person's access to free NHS treatment? Please read through all the options before choosing.

N=1721

YES, it would be right to limit someone's access to free NHS treatment if:

PLEASE TICK ALL THAT APPLY

		%
[acnhaff]	They could afford to pay for private treatment	16.7
[acnhsmok]	Their illness was due to a heavy smoking or drinking habit	23.9
[acnhbbr]	They were not born in Britain but settled here more than 2 years ago	15.8
[acnhbrec]	They had recently come to Britain hoping to find work here	41.4
[acnhrefu]	They had recently come to Britain because they were in danger at home	16.8
[acnhvisi]	They had come to Britain as visitors	42.9
[acnhchil]	They had lived in Britain all their life but not paid much in taxes because they were bringing up children	4.2
[acnhpoor]	They had lived in Britain all their life but not paid much in taxes because they were unemployed for a long time	8.9
[acnhpoor]	Some other reason (PLEASE WRITE IN)	2.2
[acnhnone]	**NO, it would never be right to limit access to free NHS treatment**	25.6
	Can't choose	4.7
	Not answered	1.7

42. Think of a 65 year-old man who is not working. Do you think there are any circumstances where it would be right to limit this person's rights to a state pension? Please read through all the options before choosing.

N=1721

YES, it would be right to limit someone's access to a state pension if:

PLEASE TICK ALL THAT APPLY

		%
[acpesave]	They had enough savings and private or occupational pension to look after themselves	18.0
[acpenbbr]	They were not born in Britain but settled here more than 2 years ago	29.3
[acpebrec]	They had recently come to Britain hoping to find work here	56.9
[acperefu]	They had recently come to Britain because they were in danger at home	25.9
[acpechil]	They had lived in Britain all their life but not paid much in taxes because they were bringing up children	6.1
[acpepoor]	They had lived in Britain all their life but not paid much in taxes because they were unemployed for a long time	16.4
[acpeoth]	Some other reason (PLEASE WRITE IN)	1.3
[acpenone]	**NO, it would never be right to limit access to a state pension**	21.4
	Can't choose	6.7
	Not answered	2.1

43. How important do you think it is for parents with a computer at home to encourage their children to use this to...

N=2610

PLEASE TICK ONE BOX ON EACH LINE

		Very important	Fairly important	Not very important	Not at all important	Can't choose	Not answered
[comphwrk1] a.	... complete their homework?	% 32.1	43.3	14.2	5.1	3.5	1.9
[comphwrk2] b.	... contact teachers at their school about work or other problems?	% 20.2	33.0	25.7	13.1	4.7	3.2
[comphwrk3] c.	... look at their school's website?	% 19.5	38.0	25.9	8.6	4.7	3.3

44. From what you know or have heard, please tick one box on each line to show how well you think state secondary schools nowadays ...

PLEASE TICK ONE BOX ON EACH LINE		Very well	Quite well	Not very well	Not at all well	(Don't know)	Not answered
[statsec1] a. ... prepare young people for work?	%	6.0	43.0	43.6	4.8	0.2	2.6
[statsec2] b. ... teach young people basic skills such as reading, writing and maths?	%	16.4	55.2	22.4	3.1	0.2	2.8
[statsec3] c. ... bring out young people's natural abilities?	%	7.7	42.3	40.1	6.7	0.2	3.0

N=2610

45. From what you know or have heard, please tick one box for each statement about state secondary schools now compared with 10 years ago.

PLEASE TICK ONE BOX ON EACH LINE		Much better now than 10 years go	A little better	About the same	A little worse	Much worse now than 10 years ago	(Don't know)	Not answered
[schlleav] a. On the whole, do you think school-leavers are better qualified or worse qualified nowadays than they were 10 years ago?	%	13.8	32.5	26.6	18.1	6.5	0.2	2.4
[teachpay] b. Do you think teachers are better paid or worse paid nowadays than they were 10 years ago?	%	19.9	38.6	25.9	10.1	2.1	0.3	3.1
[classbeh] c. And do you think classroom behaviour is better or worse nowadays than it was 10 years ago?	%	1.3	3.5	12.3	34.1	46.5	0.2	2.3
[teachbet] d. And do you think the standard of teaching is better or worse nowadays than it was 10 years ago?	%	5.6	19.0	42.7	21.9	8.0	0.3	2.5

N=2610

46. From what you know or have heard, please tick a box for each of the items below to show whether you think the National Health Service in your area is, on the whole, satisfactory or in need of improvement.

PLEASE TICK ONE BOX ON EACH LINE		In need of a lot of improvement	In need of some improvement	Satisfactory	Very good	(Don't know)	Not answered
[hsarea1] a. GPs' appointment systems	%	16.0	32.9	36.7	12.9	-	1.5
[hsarea2] b. Amount of time GP gives to each patient	%	10.5	23.7	53.2	11.0	-	1.5
[hsarea5] c. Hospital waiting lists for non-emergency operations	%	28.9	46.9	20.1	1.6	-	2.5
[hsarea6] d. Waiting time before getting appointments with hospital consultants	%	39.0	42.4	14.9	1.8	0.1	1.9
[hsarea7] e. General condition of hospital buildings	%	23.9	37.9	30.3	5.8	-	2.1
[hsarea13] f. Waiting areas in accident and emergency departments in hospitals	%	19.1	35.8	37.9	4.0	-	3.1
[hsarea14] g. Waiting areas for out-patients in hospitals	%	11.8	35.1	45.7	4.5	-	2.9
[hsarea15] h. Waiting areas at GPs' surgeries	%	4.6	15.9	62.8	14.0	-	2.6
[hsarea16] i. Time spent waiting in out-patient Departments	%	21.9	46.7	26.4	1.8	0.2	3.1
[hsarea17] j. Time spent waiting in accident and emergency departments before being seen by a doctor	%	34.9	40.6	19.5	1.9	0.3	2.8
[hsarea18] k. Time spent waiting for an ambulance after a 999 call	%	11.0	31.3	42.2	9.3	0.4	5.9

47. In the last twelve months, have you or a close family member or close friend...

N=2610

PLEASE TICK ONE BOX ON EACH LINE

	Yes, just me	Yes, not me but close family member or friend	Yes, both me and close family member or friend	No, neither	(Don't know)	Not answered
[rhsdoc2] a. ... visited an NHS GP? %	22.6	16.4	54.6	4.4	0.1	1.9
[rhsoutp2] b. ... been an out-patient in an NHS hospital? %	21.7	30.7	18.3	25.5	0.1	3.7
[rhsinp2] c. ... been an in-patient in an NHS hospital? %	10.0	27.2	6.1	50.7	0.1	5.9
[nhsvis2] d. ... visited a patient in an NHS hospital? %	15.6	16.3	26.9	37.2	-	4.0
[privpat2] e. ... had any medical treatment as a private patient? %	6.9	9.7	2.9	76.6	0.1	3.9

[pdjocsc]
48. Are you currently in paid work for at least 10 hours a week?

N=2610

PLEASE TICK ONE BOX ONLY

%

Yes 59.5 → PLEASE ANSWER QUESTION 49

No 39.0 → PLEASE GO TO QUESTION 54 ON PAGE 19

(Don't know) 0.4
Not answered 1.1

PLEASE ANSWER IF YOU ARE CURRENTLY IN PAID WORK FOR AT LEAST 10 HOURS A WEEK

N=2610

[employsc]
49. Are you an employee or self-employed? (If you have several jobs, please answer about your main job.)

PLEASE TICK ONE BOX ONLY

%

Employee 51.3 → PLEASE ANSWER QUESTION 50

Self-employed 7.9 → PLEASE GO TO QUESTION 54 ON PAGE 19

(Don't know) 0.1
Not answered 1.5

PLEASE ANSWER IF YOU ARE AN EMPLOYEE

N=1385

50. Do you agree, or disagree, with the following statements about working at your present workplace?

PLEASE TICK ONE BOX ON EACH LINE

	Agree strongly	Agree	Neither agree nor disagree	Disagree	Disagree strongly	Can't choose	Not answered
[safejob] a. I feel there will be a job for me where I work now for as long as I want it %	19.0	40.1	15.0	14.8	6.1	1.7	3.4
[wellinf] b. People at my workplace usually feel well-informed about what is happening there %	7.5	43.2	15.4	23.1	6.1	1.1	3.6
[proudjb] c. I am proud to tell people which organisation I work for %	16.3	42.6	26.0	7.9	3.0	0.9	3.4
[loggem] d. At my workplace, management and employees are always at loggerheads %	3.2	11.2	23.6	41.6	15.2	1.4	3.9
[lookdjob] e. I'm always on the look-out for a job that is better than mine %	7.1	17.3	20.2	35.3	15.2	1.0	3.8
[shareval] f. I share many of the values of my organisation %	6.9	39.4	31.4	12.3	3.8	2.6	3.6
[loyalorg] g. I feel loyal to my organisation %	13.0	48.0	21.3	9.4	3.5	1.4	3.4

51. Thinking now about the management at your workplace. To what extent do you agree or disagree with the following?

N=1385

PLEASE TICK ONE BOX ON EACH LINE

Management at my workplace ...

	Agree strongly	Agree	Neither agree nor disagree	Disagree	Disagree strongly	Can't choose	Not answered
[manrelkp] a. ... can be relied upon to keep their promises %	8.0	37.0	24.4	18.1	7.1	1.4	4.0
[manrelun] b. ... are sincere in attempting to understand employees' views %	9.9	43.1	20.1	15.5	6.5	1.0	4.0
[manrelho] c. ... deal with employees honestly %	10.7	43.1	20.4	14.0	6.5	1.5	3.8

N=1385

52. How good do you think your employer is at keeping you informed about ...

PLEASE TICK ONE BOX ON EACH LINE

	Very good	Fairly good	Not very good	Not at all good	Can't choose	Not answered
[inffemp] a. Plans for future employment in your organisation %	14.0	49.1	18.7	10.2	4.0	4.0
[inffper] b. The financial performance of the organisation %	19.4	43.3	17.3	10.1	6.0	4.0
[inftran] c. Training opportunities for you to advance your career %	18.2	43.7	18.3	11.8	4.0	4.0
[inflegal] d. Your legal rights at work %	14.0	45.5	20.5	11.7	4.3	4.0

N=1385

53. How good do you think your employer is at taking into account your views about ...

PLEASE TICK ONE BOX ON EACH LINE

	Very good	Fairly good	Not very good	Not at all good	Can't choose	Not answered
[acvfemp] a. Plans for future employment in your organisation %	10.8	44.0	23.9	10.5	6.8	3.9
[acviper] b. Improving business performance of the organisation %	17.2	43.4	17.5	9.5	8.4	4.0
[acvtrain] c. Training opportunities for you to advance your career %	16.8	41.8	21.3	9.6	6.7	3.9

EVERYONE PLEASE ANSWER

54. We are interested in views about different types of landlords.

Firstly, thinking of councils. From what you know or have heard, how good or bad do you think they are at ...

N=2610

PLEASE TICK ONE BOX ON EACH LINE

	Nearly always good	Often good	Sometimes good and sometimes bad	Often bad	Nearly always bad	Can't choose	Not answered
[counrep] a. ...providing a good standard of repairs and maintenance in their homes? %	6.8	20.3	45.2	8.8	2.6	14.0	2.3
[counrep] b. ...charging reasonable rents? %	7.8	34.1	30.0	7.3	1.2	17.0	2.4
[counstay] c. ...allowing tenants to stay in their homes as long as they want to? %	14.1	36.2	23.2	3.4	0.6	19.9	2.5
[counneig] d. ...providing housing in good neighbourhoods? %	3.9	14.9	38.8	19.3	4.1	16.8	2.3

N=2610

55. Thinking now about housing associations. Again from what you know or have heard, how good or bad do you think they are at ....

PLEASE TICK ONE BOX ON EACH LINE

	Nearly always good	Often good	Sometimes good and sometimes bad	Often bad	Nearly always bad	Can't choose	Not answered
[harep] a. ...providing a good standard of repairs and maintenance in their homes? %	8.1	29.2	31.7	4.3	0.9	23.6	2.2
[harren] b. ...charging reasonable rents? %	5.6	32.6	27.5	6.1	1.0	24.6	2.6
[hastay] c. ...allowing tenants to stay in their homes as long as they want to? %	8.3	30.6	26.3	2.8	0.6	29.0	2.6
[haneig] d. ...providing housing in good neighbourhoods? %	5.1	21.7	36.2	8.4	1.8	24.5	2.4

N=2610

56. Thinking finally about private landlords. From what you know or have heard, how good or bad do you think they are at ...

PLEASE TICK ONE BOX ON EACH LINE

	Nearly always good	Often good	Sometimes good and sometimes bad	Often bad	Nearly always bad	Can't choose	Not answered
[privrep] a. ...providing a good standard of repairs and maintenance in their homes? %	3.3	12.7	41.0	21.1	3.5	15.8	2.6
[privren] b. ...charging reasonable rents? %	1.8	7.8	37.8	27.8	5.7	16.4	2.7
[privstay] c. ...allowing tenants to stay in their homes as long as they want to? %	2.4	10.2	39.3	20.8	5.0	19.6	2.8
[privneig] d. ...providing housing in good neighbourhoods? %	4.2	18.6	42.1	10.9	2.3	19.4	2.7

N=2610

[rentbuy]

57. Suppose a newly-married young couple, both with steady jobs, asked your advice about whether to buy or rent a home. If they had the choice, what would you advise them to do?

PLEASE TICK ONE BOX ONLY

	%
To buy a home as soon as possible	71.0
To wait a bit, then try to buy a home	23.6
Not to plan to buy a home at all	1.1
Can't choose	3.3
Not answered	1.1

[moveeasy]
58. All things considered, how easy or difficult do you think it would be for you to move home if you wanted to do so now?

PLEASE TICK *ONE BOX ONLY*

N=2610

	%
Very easy	12.7
Quite easy	27.5
Neither easy nor difficult	18.5
Quite difficult	22.6
Very difficult	14.8
Can't choose	2.8
Not answered	1.1

59. Please tick one box for each statement below to show how much you agree or disagree with it.

PLEASE TICK *ONE BOX ON EACH LINE*

N=2610

		Agree strongly	Agree	Neither agree nor disagree	Disagree	Disagree strongly	Can't choose	Not answered
[imparea1] a. It is just too difficult for someone like me to do much about improving my local area	%	6.6	29.9	30.0	24.8	2.8	4.2	1.6
[imparea2] b. There is no point in doing my bit to improve my local area unless others do the same	%	7.4	37.0	18.7	27.3	4.1	3.6	1.8

[areahelp]
60. In some areas people do things together to try and help each other, while in other areas people mostly go their own way. In general would you say you live in an area where...

PLEASE TICK *ONE BOX ONLY*

N=2610

	%
... people help each other,	26.9
or, people go their own way?	23.6
Mixture	44.9
Can't choose	3.7
Not answered	1.0

61. Please tick one box for each statement below to show how much you agree or disagree with it.

PLEASE TICK *ONE BOX ON EACH LINE*

N=833

		Agree strongly	Agree	Neither agree nor disagree	Disagree	Disagree strongly	Not answered
[ponsolc] a. The police should be allowed to question suspects for up to a week without letting them see a solicitor	%	3.9	13.4	16.3	46.3	18.5	1.6
[refugees] b. Refugees who are in danger because of their political beliefs should always be welcome in Britain	%	3.4	17.5	31.0	33.8	12.9	1.5
[pccompln] c. Serious complaints against the police should be investigated by an independent body, not by the police themselves	%	33.3	55.2	6.8	2.7	0.9	1.2
[idcards] d. Every adult in Britain should have to carry an identity card	%	25.9	39.2	20.8	8.0	4.8	1.3

[voteduty]
62. Which of these statements comes closest to your view about general elections?

PLEASE TICK *ONE BOX ONLY*

In a general election ...

N=2610

	%
It's not really worth voting	11.8
People should vote only if they care who wins	27.0
It's everyone's duty to vote	59.7
Not answered	1.5

63. Please tick one box for each statement to show how much you agree or disagree with it.

N=2610

PLEASE TICK ONE BOX ON EACH LINE	Agree strongly	Agree	Neither agree nor disagree	Disagree	Disagree strongly	Not answered
[welfhelp] a. The welfare state encourages people to stop helping each other %	3.0	20.8	39.3	30.9	3.0	2.9
[morewelf] b. The government should spend more money on welfare benefits for the poor, even if it leads to higher taxes %	4.4	31.6	29.6	28.1	3.6	2.6
[unempjob] c. Around here, most unemployed people could find a job if they really wanted one %	16.5	52.3	18.9	9.1	0.7	2.5
[sochelp] d. Many people who get social security don't really deserve any help %	8.0	30.9	33.2	22.6	2.6	2.6
[dolefid] e. Most people on the dole are fiddling in one way or another %	9.7	31.1	33.1	21.1	2.3	2.6
[welffeet] f. If welfare benefits weren't so generous, people would learn to stand on their own two feet %	11.4	35.4	27.3	20.1	3.5	2.4
[damlives] g. Cutting welfare benefits would damage too many people's lives %	6.6	41.3	31.5	16.0	2.2	2.5
[proudwlf] h. The creation of the welfare state is one of Britain's proudest achievement %	14.9	36.4	33.3	10.7	2.3	2.4

64. Please tick one box for each statement below to show how much you agree or disagree with it.

N=2610

PLEASE TICK ONE BOX ON EACH LINE	Agree strongly	Agree	Neither agree nor disagree	Disagree	Disagree strongly	Not answered
[redistrb] a. Government should redistribute income from the better-off to those who are less well off %	6.7	24.8	28.0	29.5	8.8	2.2
[bigbusnn] b. Big business benefits owners at the expense of workers %	10.7	37.1	31.0	16.3	2.3	2.6
[wealth] c. Ordinary working people do not get their fair share of the nation's wealth %	10.9	42.5	27.9	15.1	1.5	2.1
[richlaw] d. There is one law for the rich and one for the poor %	15.2	36.6	25.0	18.2	2.9	2.2
[indust4] e. Management will always try to get the better of employees if it gets the chance %	13.6	37.1	27.3	16.9	3.0	2.1

[redist2]
65. Do you think government does too much or too little to redistribute income from the better off to those who are less well off, or have they got it about right?

PLEASE TICK ONE BOX ONLY

N=1721

	%
Far too much	3.4
A bit too much	9.4
About right	27.8
A bit too little	24.3
Far too little	13.5
Can't choose	19.6
Not answered	2.0

N=2610

66. Please tick one box for each statement below to show how much you agree or disagree with it.

PLEASE TICK ONE BOX ON EACH LINE

	Agree strongly	Agree	Neither agree nor disagree	Disagree	Disagree strongly	Not answered
[tradvals] a. Young people today don't have enough respect for traditional British values %	21.6	49.4	19.6	6.4	0.8	2.2
[stiffsent] b. People who break the law should be given stiffer sentences %	32.7	45.9	15.3	3.8	0.4	1.9
[deathapp] c. For some crimes, the death penalty is the most appropriate sentence %	26.7	27.0	14.3	17.0	17.0	2.0
[obey] d. Schools should teach children to obey authority %	32.1	52.9	9.5	3.0	0.6	2.0
[wronglaw] e. The law should always be obeyed, even if a particular law is wrong %	7.1	32.9	32.2	22.8	2.8	2.2
[censor] f. Censorship of films and magazines is necessary to uphold moral standards %	19.3	44.2	19.2	11.6	3.7	2.1

[qtimea]
67a. To help us plan better in future, please tell us about how long it took you to complete this questionnaire.

N=833

PLEASE TICK ONE BOX ONLY

	%
Less than 15 minutes	5.3
Between 15 and 20 minutes	26.6
Between 21 and 30 minutes	28.1
Between 31 and 45 minutes	22.6
Between 46 and 60 minutes	10.0
Over one hour	5.7
Not answered	1.7

b. And on what date did you fill in the questionnaire?

PLEASE WRITE IN:

DATE   MONTH   2004

BRITISH SOCIAL ATTITUDES 2004 SELF-COMPLETION QUESTIONNAIRE VERSION B

Note: Questions 1-27 on Version B are the same as Questions 27-53 on Version A.

PLEASE ANSWER IF YOU ARE AN EMPLOYEE

28. Please tick <u>one</u> box for <u>each</u> statement below to show how much you agree or disagree with it.

N=937

PLEASE TICK *ONE* BOX ON EACH LINE		Agree strongly	Agree	Neither agree nor disagree	Disagree	Disagree strongly	Can't choose	Not answered
[tosnpro2] a. If you take time off work at short notice, it makes things difficult for the people you work with	%	16.5	42.4	14.5	20.2	2.4	0.4	3.7
[longhrs2] b. People in my kind of job are expected to work longer hours these days than they used to	%	13.5	31.5	20.6	27.2	2.3	1.1	3.8
[more48hr] c. People in my kind of job are expected to work more than 48 hours a week	%	9.1	15.4	17.3	42.0	11.6	0.7	3.9

29. Please tick one box for each statement below to show how much you agree or disagree with it.

N=937

PLEASE TICK *ONE* BOX ON EACH LINE		Agree strongly	Agree	Neither agree nor disagree	Disagree	Disagree strongly	Can't choose	Not answered
[timegn1b] a. There are so many things to do at home, I often run out of time before I get them all done	%	25.1	40.9	12.8	15.4	1.7	0.4	3.7
[nostrs1b] b. My life at home is rarely stressful	%	6.3	30.7	20.9	31.8	5.7	0.5	4.1
[timegn2b] c. There are so many things to do at work, I often run out of time before I get them all done	%	14.6	37.0	18.3	23.1	2.1	0.7	4.2
[nostrs1b] d. My job is rarely stressful	%	2.7	16.4	18.1	41.5	16.4	0.5	4.4

30. How often has each of the following happened to you during the past three months?

PLEASE TICK ONE BOX ON EACH LINE

N=937

		Several times a week	Several times a month	Once or twice	Never	Not answered
[hometrd2] a. I have come home from work too tired to do the chores which need to be done	%	25.3	28.6	34.1	8.0	4.0
[homehrd2] b. It has been difficult for me to fulfil my family responsibilities because of the amount of time I spent on my job	%	9.9	16.8	32.4	36.5	4.5
[worktrd2] c. I have arrived at work too tired to function well because of the household work I had done	%	2.5	7.1	26.9	59.3	4.2
[workdif2] d. I have found it difficult to concentrate at work because of my family responsibilities	%	2.3	9.2	39.3	44.9	4.2

[jobsat2]
31. All things considered, how satisfied are you with your (main) job?

N=937

PLEASE TICK ONE BOX ONLY

	%
Completely satisfied	12.3
Very satisfied	23.5
Fairly satisfied	39.7
Neither satisfied nor dissatisfied	8.5
Fairly dissatisfied	7.9
Very dissatisfied	3.3
Completely dissatisfied	1.1
Can't choose	0.1
Not answered	3.5

[famsat2]
32. All things considered, how satisfied are you with your family life?

N=937

PLEASE TICK ONE BOX ONLY

	%
Completely satisfied	25.2
Very satisfied	36.4
Fairly satisfied	26.4
Neither satisfied nor dissatisfied	3.6
Fairly dissatisfied	3.5
Very dissatisfied	0.7
Completely dissatisfied	0.5
Can't choose	0.4
Not answered	3.4

EVERYONE PLEASE ANSWER

[famwork]
33. How much, if at all, do you think your family responsibilities have got in the way of your progress at work or your job prospects?

N=1777

PLEASE TICK ONE BOX ONLY

	%
A great deal	6.2
Quite a lot	11.0
A bit	14.0
Not very much	20.8
Not at all	38.8
Can't say	6.3
Not answered	3.0

34. How much do you agree or disagree with the following statements?

PLEASE TICK ONE BOX ON EACH LINE

N=1777

		Agree strongly	Agree	Neither agree nor disagree	Disagree	Disagree strongly	Not answered
[ladderwf] a	It is important to move up the ladder at work, even if this gets in the way of family life	% 1.8	9.3	21.9	50.0	12.8	4.2
[househus] b	It is not good if the man stays at home and cares for the children and the woman goes out to work	% 3.4	10.5	30.4	38.3	13.3	4.2
[fathcare] c	Fathers are just as capable as mothers of caring for their children	% 20.7	48.7	14.8	10.6	1.2	3.9

Note: Questions 35-41 on Version B are the same as Questions 54-60 on Version A.

42. Here are a number of circumstances in which a woman might consider an abortion. Please say whether or not you think the law should allow an abortion in each case.

N=888

PLEASE TICK ONE BOX ON EACH LINE

		Should abortion be allowed by law?		
		Yes	No	Not answered
[abort1] a.	The woman decides on her own she does not wish to have the child	% 56.0	33.5	10.5
[abort2] b.	The couple agree they do not wish to have the child	% 64.3	25.4	10.3
[abort3] c.	The woman is not married and does not wish to marry the man	% 51.6	35.4	13.0
[abort4] d.	The couple cannot afford any more children	% 52.9	34.0	13.0
[abort5] e.	There is a strong chance of a defect in the baby	% 80.5	11.6	7.9
[abort6] f.	The woman's health is seriously endangered by the pregnancy	% 90.9	3.9	5.2
[abort7] g.	The woman became pregnant as a result of rape	% 89.2	5.5	5.3

Note: Questions 43-47 on Version B are the same as Questions 62-66 on Version A.

N=888

[qtimeb]

48a. To help us plan better in future, please tell us about how long it took you to complete this questionnaire.

PLEASE TICK ONE BOX ONLY

	%
Less than 15 minutes	16.6
Between 15 and 20 minutes	33.6
Between 21 and 30 minutes	27.8
Between 31 and 45 minutes	14.5
Between 46 and 60 minutes	3.4
Over one hour	2.8
Not answered	1.4

Note: Question 48b on Version B is the same as Question 67b on Version A.

BRITISH SOCIAL ATTITUDES 2004 SELF-COMPLETION QUESTIONNAIRE VERSION C

Note: Questions 1-9 on Version C are the same as Questions 27-35 on Version A.

10. Please tick one box for each of these statements to show how much you agree or disagree.

N=889

PLEASE TICK ONE BOX ON EACH LINE		Agree strongly	Agree	Neither agree nor disagree	Disagree	Disagree strongly	I never travel by car	Can't choose	Not answered
[carwalk] a. Many of the short journeys I now make by car I could just as easily walk	%	8.0	26.9	9.2	30.3	13.7	8.4	2.2	1.2
[carbus] b. Many of the short journeys I now make by car I could just as easily go by bus	%	5.8	22.8	7.2	35.0	18.0	7.4	2.5	1.3
[carbike] c. Many of the short journeys I now make by car I could just as easily cycle, if I had a bike	%	7.8	29.8	9.6	24.2	16.1	7.1	3.2	2.1

11. Please tick one box for each of these statements to show how much you agree or disagree.

N=889

PLEASE TICK ONE BOX ON EACH LINE		Agree strongly	Agree	Neither agree nor disagree	Disagree	Disagree strongly	Can't choose	Not answered
[busnooth] a. I would only travel somewhere by bus if I had no other way of getting there	%	15.5	45.4	7.4	22.0	7.0	1.4	1.1
[cartaxhi] b. For the sake of the environment, car users should pay higher taxes	%	1.9	10.0	15.3	45.6	23.9	1.9	1.5
[motorway] c. The government should build more motorways to reduce traffic congestion	%	6.4	26.0	25.0	27.7	9.9	3.8	1.3
[buildtra] d. Building more roads just encourages more traffic	%	8.5	32.3	20.7	29.4	4.9	2.2	2.0
[carallow] e. People should be allowed to use their cars as much as they like, even if it causes damage to the environment	%	1.7	14.7	29.1	35.4	13.9	3.9	1.4

[cutcars]
12a. How important do you think it is to cut down the number of cars on Britain's roads?

PLEASE TICK ONE BOX ONLY

	%
Very important	26.2
Fairly important	46.0
Not very important	18.0
Not at all important	3.4
Can't choose	5.7
Not answered	0.7

[ptimprim]
b. And how important is it to improve public transport in Britain?

PLEASE TICK ONE BOX ONLY

	%
Very important	77.4
Fairly important	18.3
Not very important	1.7
Not at all important	0.1
Can't choose	1.7
Not answered	0.7

13. Here are some things that might be done to reduce congestion. Please tick one box for each to show how much you would be in favour of or against it.

N=889

PLEASE TICK ONE BOX ON EACH LINE

	Strongly in favour	In favour	Neither in favour nor against	Against	Strongly against	Can't choose	Not answered
[cutcpetr] a. Gradually doubling the cost of petrol over the next ten years	% 1.6	3.9	11.2	40.1	39.2	3.0	1.0
[cutctch2] b. Charging all motorists £2 each time they enter or drive through a city or town centre outside London at peak times	% 4.7	23.4	17.4	28.3	21.5	3.0	1.7
[cutcmoch] c. Charging £1 for every 50 miles motorists travel on motorways	% 2.7	20.0	16.1	31.6	25.5	2.4	1.6
[cutcpark] d. Increasing parking costs in town and city centres	% 2.4	13.3	15.1	39.1	25.1	3.1	2.0
[cutctaxe] e. Taxing employers for each car parking space they provide for their employees	% 3.4	14.5	18.4	31.7	26.6	4.1	1.3

14. Please tick one box for each of these statements to show how much you agree or disagree.

N=889

PLEASE TICK ONE BOX ON EACH LINE

	Agree strongly	Agree	Neither agree nor disagree	Disagree	Disagree strongly	Can't choose	Not answered
[busprior] a. Buses should be given more priority in towns and cities, even if this makes things more difficult for car drivers	% 13.9	44.5	18.0	18.8	2.6	1.7	0.5
[cycpedpr] b. Cyclists and pedestrians should be given more priority in towns and cities even if this makes things more difficult for other road users	% 17.7	41.8	19.5	16.4	2.4	1.4	0.9

15. Here are some things that could be done about traffic in residential streets that are not main roads. Please tick one box for each to show whether you would be in favour or not in favour.

N=889

PLEASE TICK ONE BOX ON EACH LINE

	Strongly in favour	In favour	Neither in favour nor against	Against	Strongly against	Can't choose	Not answered
[resclose] a. Closing residential streets to through traffic	% 9.8	39.5	20.4	23.5	3.7	1.7	1.5
[res20mph] b. Having speed limits of 20 miles per hour in residential streets	% 21.1	52.9	10.8	10.3	2.6	1.2	1.2
[rescross] c. Making cars stop for people to cross residential streets even if they are not at a pedestrian crossing	% 8.5	19.8	23.8	36.7	8.2	1.9	1.1
[resbumps] d. Having speed bumps to slow down traffic in residential streets	% 11.7	34.6	14.2	24.1	12.8	1.6	1.0

16. Please tick one box for each of these statements to show how much you agree or disagree.

N=889

PLEASE TICK ONE BOX ON EACH LINE

		Agree strongly	Agree	Neither agree nor disagree	Disagree	Disagree strongly	Can't choose	Not answered
[specams]								
a. Speed cameras save lives	%	13.1	33.9	19.8	21.3	9.1	1.7	1.1
[specammo]								
b. Speed cameras are mostly there to make money	%	27.0	31.0	16.4	18.1	3.7	2.0	1.8

17. Now some questions about air travel. Please tick one box for each statement to show how much you agree or disagree.

N=889

PLEASE TICK ONE BOX ON EACH LINE

		Agree strongly	Agree	Neither agree nor disagree	Disagree	Disagree strongly	Can't choose	Not answered
[plnallow]								
a. People should be able to travel by plane as much as they like	%	17.8	59.5	13.7	3.9	1.4	2.7	1.0
[plnterm]								
b. People should be able to travel by plane as much as they like, even if new terminals or runways are needed to meet the demand	%	7.7	35.1	28.2	19.9	2.9	4.4	1.8
[plnenvt]								
c. People should be able to travel by plane as much as they like, even if this harms the environment	%	2.1	12.6	33.6	38.3	8.0	3.7	1.6
[plnuppri]								
d. The price of a plane ticket should reflect the environmental damage that flying causes, even if this makes air travel much more expensive	%	5.9	30.1	25.2	27.5	6.0	3.7	1.6

Note: Questions 18-28 on Version C are the same as Questions 43-53 on Version A

Note: Questions 29-35 on Version C are the same as Questions 28-34 on Version B

Note: Questions 36-42 on Version C are the same as Questions 54-60 on Version A

Note: Questions 43-45 on Version C are the same as Questions 62-64 on Version A

Note: Question 46 on Version C is the same as Question 66 on Version A

[qtimec]

47a. To help us plan better in future, please tell us about how long it took you to complete this questionnaire.

PLEASE TICK ONE BOX ONLY

N=889

	%
Less than 15 minutes	20.1
Between 15 and 20 minutes	37.7
Between 21 and 30 minutes	24.9
Between 31 and 45 minutes	10.4
Between 46 and 60 minutes	2.9
Over one hour	2.7
Not answered	1.2

Note: Question 47b on Version C is the same as Question 67b on Version A

Subject index